Social Problems:

Definition, Impact, and Solution

Social Problems:

Definition, Impact, and Solution

John Stimson
William Paterson College

Ardyth Stimson
Kean College

Vincent N. Parrillo
William Paterson College

JOHN WILEY & SONS

New York   Chichester   Brisbane   Toronto   Singapore

Cover Painting:

Caprogrossi, Surface Superficies, 335.
Modern Art Gallery, Rome; Scala/Art Resource.

Library of Congress Cataloging in Publication Data:

Stimson, John.
  Social problems.

  Includes bibliographies.
  1. United States—Social conditions—1980–   —
Addresses, essays, lectures.   2. United States—Moral
conditions—Addresses, essays, lectures.   3. Social
problems—Addresses, essays, lectures.   I. Stimson,
Ardyth.   II. Parrillo, Vincent.   III. Title.

HN59.2.S75 1985   361.1   84-25599
ISBN 0-471-86980-5 (pbk.)

Printed in the United States of America

10 9 8 7 6 5 4 3 2 1

Preface

Social structures and the social issues that are created when their elements are unequal or disorganized are proper subject matter for a social problems course. All too often, however, the analysis becomes too historical or too abstract, or lost in the conflicts between rival theoretical camps. The individual society member is lost somewhere in the discussion. Our selections are carefully chosen to be sociological, but they also emphasize the impact that social problems have on society's members. The pedagogical purpose of this strategy is to involve the student in the everyday effects of sociological issues. Students all too often react to discussions of macroproblems with no more than the question, "So what?" What does it mean for me? My future? This is the reason for the second emphasis on social change and the future. We tried to select excerpts that show how problems and our evaluations of them change and will probably develop. This should involve students in discussion of how society is systematically interrelated and how the future is being determined by today's social forces.

Notice that the chapters follow what has become the traditional structure of dealing with microproblems and deviance and then proceeding to macroproblems. Two significant differences are found here: Chapter 1 is devoted to the problems of scientific definition and research, and Chapter 2, we think, is unique in its discussion of the situation of the individual in modern society.

We tried to achieve the same structure in each chapter with at least one reading each on *definition, impact,* and *solution.* We are aware that our goal was differentially realized because the problem areas are in different stages of sociological development. Here is the overall outline of our goals for each chapter:

1. *Social Definition.* How did the problem get recognized and defined, and what is its current importance? To which other problems is it connected? Which groups are trying to change the situation and which are benefiting from maintaining the status quo?
2. *Impact.* How did the problem affect the interaction between individuals? How does it feel to be caught up in the troubles caused by the problem? How does it limit or distort individuals' possibilities?
3. *So What?* What can we do? What will happen if we don't do anything? Here we consider political-economic trends and policies that will acceler-

ate or ameliorate the condition and discuss current redefinitions or individual resocialization attempts.

John Stimson
Ardyth Stimson
Vincent N. Parrillo

Contents

*Our social welfare programs, though attacked as
extravagant and useless, are actually a minor part of a two-
tiered social policy benefiting the nonpoor more fully than
the poor.*

*Rather than integration, we need additive multiculturalism,
where we recognize and appreciate cultural differences, so
that both sides gain cultural features instead of one side's
losing theirs.*

*Karp and Yoels use the social process of aging to show that
our ideas of old, young, female, and male are related to the
power structure of society. Getting old has been much more
devastating for females than for males.*

*Elder abuse, sometimes called "gram-slamming," is just
beginning to be discovered as a problem. It seems to be a
pattern much like child abuse or abuse of females and
reflects our society's devaluation of the aged.*

*Contrary to appearances, women are politically active, but
they are segregated into the support activities that the public
never sees. Margolis describes the grass-roots, entry-level
experience of most women in political life and shows why
women will not achieve power until this role is changed.*

PART FOUR
FAILURES OF SOCIAL INSTITUTIONS

natural response would be to leave. By definition, those who stay are treated as if they are in need of "support services." The "experts" have thereby created a clientele to serve.

Before each student can perform up to his or her ability, we must get rid of the self-fulfilling prophecy produced by the expectations and definitions of teachers. Bias toward middle-class children has encouraged their best performance but has penalized children from poorer backgrounds.

Defining a particular physical or mental condition as a handicap is a social and political decision. Society, not biology, defines persons as being handicapped. The disability movement is fighting to show that "different" is not necessarily weak or inferior.

The American bureaucratic structure seems to be informal and friendly, yet respectful of authority. To survive, however, translations must be made of many common expressions; for example, you must hear, "That's an interesting idea that needs further developing," as "Let's not discuss it now."

The bureaucracies in modern society were originally created to increase efficiency, but they are now so large and complex that they may soon no longer function at all. Elgin and Bushnell give us 16 reasons why this is a very serious problem. They also give us some possible solutions that would help to maintain the existing form of these bureaucracies.

PART FIVE
CHALLENGES TO THE QUALITY OF LIFE

*The ecosystem contains complicated balances and
interrelationships that we do not yet understand. Our rapid
population growth, or consumption excesses, could trigger a
massive damaging interaction at any time.*

*Water appears to be an endlessly renewable resource, but it
is in finite supply. Each city-dweller uses 150–200 gallons
of water a day, and growing our national food supply uses
110 billion gallons per day. Eventually we may have to
recycle seawater and sewerage to fill our need for water.*

*The president of the Club of Rome, updates the club's
famous "Limits to Growth" study and warns that we have
very little time in which to redirect the world community to a
safer course.*

PART One

THE SOCIOLOGY OF SOCIAL PROBLEMS

1

Definitions and Measurements

What do you think would happen if each person in your class compiled a list of what they thought were the most important social problems? Would any two lists agree? Probably not. There would be even less agreement if you all tried to decide what the two most important problems are.

The lists would probably contain problems like crime, drug abuse, poverty, consumer ripoffs, dirty politics, world hunger, nuclear waste, or nuclear war. How are we to decide which should be attacked first?

Only part of the decision problem is caused by the overabundance of so many different types of problems. The major confusion is that social problem decisions have a large subjective element. We each learn to view problems from our own personal and social positions, and our perceptions and evaluations are often in conflict with people from other parts of society.

The readings in this chapter are concerned with overcoming these built-in biases, learning to see through our culturally acquired value screens, and learning to see problems scientifically.

Manis insists that we must use objective standards in judging the seriousness of problems. We cannot just attack problems that offend our social values. He explains the dangers of ignoring scientific information and proposes that the most serious problems are the ones that cause other problems. Primary problems such as racism and poverty lead to so many other bad effects that they should be judged as being the most serious.

Photographs seem like clear-cut records of reality: seeing is believing, right? Not according to Howard Becker, who describes how intentional and unintentional biases alter our perceptions. He also gives us a lesson in how systematically to check the validity of our observations.

The article about quasi-theories is intended to give one explanation for the fact that our society does not provide the funding it should for research and study of social problems. Our culture already provides answers, or at least excuses and rationalizations, that seem to solve almost all the problem situations. We avoid scientific research by smoothing over the rough areas with culturally honored quasi-solutions.

Reading 1
Assessing the Seriousness of Social Problems

Jerome G. Manis
Western Michigan University

The definition of a concept inevitably influences the nature of the related hypotheses or theory. A well-conceived concept is heuristic and realistic—that is, it generates hypotheses that improve our understanding of phenomena. Such a concept will direct researchers toward significant data. As Max Planck (1962:841) has contended, however, there are many "phantom problems—in my opinion, far more than one would ordinarily suspect—even in the realm of science." It is the recognition of anomalies in "normal science" that results in the collapse of accepted paradigms (Kuhn, 1962). . . .

Exponents of leading sociological perspectives—symbolic interactionism and functionalism—have essentially similar conceptions of social problems. To Blumer (1971:298, 301–302), "social problems are fundamentally products of collective definition . . . A social problem does not exist for a society unless it is recognized by that society to exist." Merton (1971:799) is somewhat more inclusive: "The first and basic ingredient of a social problem consists of a substantial discrepancy between widely shared standards and actual conditions of social life." Although he distinguishes between manifest or recognized and latent or unrecognized discrepancies, his definition centers upon "widely shared standards," i.e., society's norms and values.

One of the shortcomings of the public definition of social problems is the inclusion of possibly spurious or "phantom" conditions. . . . Indeed, the "subjective" definition must include witchhunting, long hair, and possession of marihuana as social problems as long as the public is in opposition to them. So defined, the concern of the sociology of social problems is with social issues or controversies rather than the objective conditions detrimental to human or societal well-being.

A related deficiency of the "public opinion" approach to social problems is its inability to assess the seriousness of social problems. Some advocates of this viewpoint are aware of the limitation.

> . . . it is the values held by people occupying different social positions that provide the rough basis for the relative importance assigned to social problems . . . this sometimes leads to badly distorted impressions of various problems, even when these are judged in the light of reigning values (Merton, 1971:801).

> Nor are public definitions sound guides to the magnitude of social problems. . . . Influential publics, moreover, have little if any basis on which to *compare* the relative seriousness—extent and effects—of problems. . . . This definition of social problems

Reprinted with permission from *Social Problems* 22 (1974): 1–15 by The Society for the Study of Social Problems and the author.

explores certain absurdities. Public recognition is in nearly all respects a bad basis for collective judgment. . . . In spite of these difficulties, the definition stands: A social problem is a condition that has been defined by significant groups as a deviation from some social standard, or breakdown of social organization (Dentler, 1971:14–15).

Despite these admissions of "distortions" and "absurdities," sociologists have continued to use popular values as the only criteria of social problems. . . .

THE IDENTIFICATION OF SOCIAL PROBLEMS

For present purposes, social problems are defined as "those social conditions, identified by scientific inquiry and values as detrimental to the well-being of human societies" (Manis, 1974). Four perspectives or viewpoints appear useful in determining and specifying such conditions. These are: (1) public conceptions; (2) the views of appropriate professionals; (3) sociological knowledge; (4) the norms and values of science. The order in which the categories are presented is based upon their increasing importance as criteria for identifying social problems. Consistent application of these criteria can help to reduce or eliminate the anomalies arising from current definitions of social problems.

Public Conceptions

A basic source of information concerning social problems are the opinions and attitudes of the members of a group or society. This information is necessary for understanding social behavior. As Blumer (1971:301) points out, "the process of collective definition determines the career and fate of social problems, from the initial point of their appearance to whatever may be the terminal point in their course." Though most textbooks accept "collective definition" as the essence of social problems, they do not disclose any evidence for the choice of their topics.

The content of the sociological literature—crime, divorce, alcoholism, etc.— *appears* to be congruent with the views of the populace. However, the justification for their inclusion or for the assessment of their assumed seriousness is not revealed to the reader. The absence of such data is a major deficiency in our knowledge. . . .

Public conceptions of deviance, and of social problems generally, are necessary but insufficient knowledge. Certainly, we need to know what a society abhors and why it does so. We also need to know the consequences of these conceptions. Accepting social values as criteria of "harmful people" or "undesirable conditions" lends an aura of scientific respectability to beliefs which may be based on ignorance or prejudice. Accepting these values as the ultimate criteria of social problems is a specious justification for claims of value-neutrality.

Professional Expertise

At times, public opinion differs substantially from the views of experts. A current example is the widespread antagonism to users of marihuana. The public position seems to be based upon many erroneous beliefs: that it is addictive; that it is debilitating; that it invariably leads to other addictions; that users are sexually depraved. The differing views of physicians, psychiatrists, and sociologists apparently have not greatly altered its popular image.

According to current definitions, marihuana is a social problem since it is contrary to social values. Presumably it is a serious problem if many people are strongly opposed to its usage. The views of trained experts are considered relevant because of their disagreement with the public, not for their technical knowledge. Sociologists may agree with the professional definition—but the public definition is the usual standard for identifying social problems.

There are, of course, many experts; and they are not always in agreement. But in agreement or not, their professional training and intimate contact with conditions viewed by the public as undesirable can provide needed correctives. Sociologists do question the medical perspective of psychiatry. Should they not also raise questions about the category of "crazy people"? The latter conception helps to explain the responses of society to those so identified and the effects of these labels. It is less helpful in the search for social causation and consequences.

Sociologists draw upon the data of other experts and disciplines in their analyses of mental disorder, drop-outs, divorce, and riots. This expertise receives special weight in the analyses but not in the definition of social problems. To be consistent with current definitions, the seriousness of social problems should be based not on the weight of technical data but the extent of popular concern.

To propose that the expert's interpretation be included in defining and assessing social problems is not a claim for their absolute correctness. It is only a means for incorporating more technical knowledge into our inquiries. Such knowledge can help to recognize trivial or spurious social problems as well as to identify serious ones.

Sociological Knowledge

Although social problems are defined in terms of public conceptions, values, and controversies, sociologists do not ignore the causes and the consequences of the "undesirable conditions." Indeed, Blumer (1971:300) has contended that sociologists have concentrated on the latter and have "conspicuously failed . . . to study the process by which a society comes to recognize its social problems." What sociologists actually do is different from what they say about social problems.

The discrepancy stems, I believe, from the unwillingness of researchers to accept the implications of the accepted definition. If the public views busing, atheism, subversives, women's liberation, and radical professors as major social problems, will the textbook writers allocate substantial sections to these topics? If not, why not? . . . Understanding of everyday knowledge is needed by sociology; understanding does not require its endorsement. . . .

The Values of Science

A major justification for the accepted definitions of social problems is the presumed value-neutrality of science. A scientific sociology must avoid any appearance of bias derived from personal values. The aim is laudable. The accepted solution—adopting popular values as the standards for identifying social problems—is a substitution of values, not their elimination. The outcome is an illusory value-neutrality. . . .

That science is a social institution with distinctive norms and values can hardly be questioned. Among the accepted values are the search for knowledge, the empirical testing of belief, the provisional standing of accepted viewpoints, the freedom of critics to dissent and propose new interpretations, and the dissemination of knowledge (Merton, 1967). The socialization of would-be scientists includes the inculcation of these values.

Scientists seldom discuss, since they take for granted, certain underlying values. In totalitarian states, protection of life, safety, subsistence, and freedom of inquiry for the scientist may be uncertain. The institution of science depends upon societal tolerance and support. Obviously, science cannot exist without society and functioning scientists. Is it less obvious to contend that science must value an open, supportive society?

A current value-controversy among scientists concerns the social responsibility of science. To take an extreme illustration, does the nuclear scientist have the obligation to test a fission hypothesis which will set off a continuous, endless, chain reaction (Z-bomb?)? Traditionally, scientists have contended that science can only describe "what is, not should be." Contemporary science is *not* limited to this role of passive observation. The rapid tempo of discovery and, particularly, the creation of new phenomena—synthetic atoms, plastics, nylon, etc.—reflect the intentional innovations which have helped to transform the world around us. These creations have blurred the lines between basic and applied science as well as between science and technology.

The thesis here is that the knowledge and the values of science can provide sociology with needed guidelines for appraising social phenomena. Certainly, scientists neither possess all of the needed knowledge nor agree upon scientific values. Nevertheless, existing knowledge and values are more uniform, more rational, and more fruitful criteria than the divergent beliefs and values of any given society. . . .

Proposing the use of scientific criteria to assess the existence or the severity of social problems need not imply absolutism. Specifying their criteria does not require the crowning of scientists. The concepts, hypotheses, theories, and values of science are open to continuing criticism, revision, or rejection on the basis of rational judgments and knowledge. No implication that science be empowered to coerce society to accept its conclusions is intended. All that is suggested here is to permit the knowledge and values of science to identify and to assess conditions deemed harmful to science and to society.

To summarize, scientific knowledge and values are proposed as criteria for identifying socially harmful conditions. These criteria can help to distinguish spurious from genuine social problems. We also need to consider ways of differentiating minor or trivial social problems from major or serious ones. By seriousness is meant the primacy, the magnitude, and the severity of social problems.

THE PRIMACY OF SOCIAL PROBLEMS

An examination of the interrelationships among social problems provides one way of assessing their importance. To illustrate, let us consider the hypothesis that poverty is associated with higher rates of malnutrition, mortality, desertion, delinquency, drop-outs, addiction, and mental disorder. . . . Viewing poverty as an antecedent to many other social problems is a basis for appraising its importance of primacy.

Social problems which produce or exacerbate other social problems are more serious or critical to society than those which have less effects. On such grounds, Perrucci and Pilisuk (1971:xix) refer to "central" or "underlying" social problems as distinguished from the "peripheral" ones produced by the former. Despite the brevity of their discussion, it is evident that they consider cause-effect relationships as their basic criterion. . . .

Primary social problems are influential social conditions which have multiple detrimental consequences for society. For example, we may predict that a conventional war will result in higher death rates, waste of human and other resources, increases in family disorganization, disruption of careers, and neglected solutions to other undesirable conditions. Racism seems conducive to separatism, conflict, individual alienation, etc. On the basis of their multiplicative influences, war and racism can be viewed as primary social problems; their socially harmful effects may be defined as secondary or tertiary problems. . . .

In the absence of detailed, accurate, and precise knowledge, the proposed distinctions between specific primary and secondary or tertiary social problems remain as hypotheses rather than established conclusions. Even so, they are preferable to such criteria as numbers of concerned citizens or level of their emotional outrage. Not only is the distinction more objective, but it requires empirical data concerning the relationships between problem variables. The formulation of more and improved social indicators would facilitate study of such relationships.

Secondary social problems are less critical for a society than primary ones in

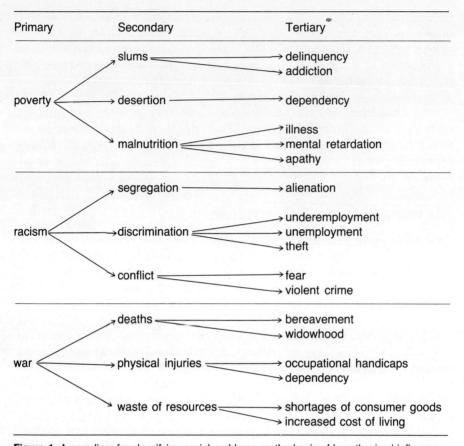

Figure 1. A paradigm for classifying social problems on the basis of hypothesized influences.

that the former are products of the latter. Likewise, tertiary social problems are least important in that they are the products of primary and secondary problems. Secondary social problems may be viewed as intervening variables or as the immediate influences upon tertiary social problems. . . .

THE MAGNITUDE OF SOCIAL PROBLEMS

. . . prevalence and incidence are accepted indicators of the seriousness of social problems. Difficulties arise when attempts are made to compare the magnitude of different phenomena. Some of the suggested difficulties may be exaggerated, particularly when the differences in the units are emphasized. For example, Merton (1971:801) asks, "Shall we conclude that the approximately 9000 murders in 1969 represent about one-fifth as great a social problem as the approximately 56,700 deaths from vehicular accidents in that year?'' Although his response is negative, one may respond, why not? Certainly, the causes differ and the public concern about homicide differs from the public apathy toward traffic fatalities. The consequences *are* similar, as they are also for suicide and for war-related deaths. Vital statistics provide useful sources for appraising the magnitude of social problems.

Another useful comparison can be made of the prevalence of forms of addiction. While the public is more greatly aroused by heroin addiction than by addiction to alcohol or barbituates, it is the resulting legal penalties for the former which compound its seriousness. That there are about ten million alcoholics as compared to several hundred thousand heroin addicts is considered by medical professionals to be the more serious health problem. Should not sociologists adopt similar criteria?

Comparing more divergent conditions, of course, is much more difficult. Assessing the magnitude of poverty requires different standards from those used in appraising the rates of juvenile delinquency. Are equal numbers of the poor and of juvenile delinquents equivalent in seriousness as social problems? Though their differences appear to defy attempts to compare their magnitude, the effort to do so is important. One method of comparing their seriousness would be a consideration of their effects—as noted in the previous section. If poverty is indeed a major source of other problems, we can give its prevalence a greater emphasis or weighting in our deliberations. Furthermore, we can appraise the differential severity of its consequences.

THE SEVERITY OF SOCIAL PROBLEMS

By severity is meant the varying impact, the degree of damage, harshness, or impairment, of social conditions upon the well-being of individuals and society. The harmfulness of some social problems can be assessed more readily than others. Loss of life is clearly a more critical outcome of war than minor injuries. A ten-year prison term is a harsher penalty than a one-year term; these differences of sentence are imposed on the basis of some judgment of differential social injury. In these comments, no implication is intended that assessing severity is a simple or easy task. Here, as elsewhere in this analysis, the aim is to further discussion of the topic.

In the absence of clearcut criteria for defining social problems, evaluation of their severity may be begun with conditions harmful to the physical well-being of individuals. Severity can be ranked from the finality of death, through total, major, and minor incapacity. These are crude but useful categories for assessing impairment. The distinctions are no more arbitrary than those used to distinguish social classes, small groups, or subcultures.

Similar procedures have been applied to the severity of mental disorders. The *American Psychiatric Association* (1952) has considered ''psychiatric impairment'' on terms of mild to severe categories. Their ratings are based on judgments of the individual's ability to function socially and occupationally. Such evaluations are appropriate ways of assessing social problems.

Also similar are the methods used in comparing the severity of crimes. Homicide and aggravated assault are characterized as major crimes while disorderly conduct is not. The alleged criterion is differential harmfulness. On this basis, some sociologists have favored the decriminalization of gambling, homosexual behavior, and other acts which are not clearly detrimental to individuals or to the society. The concept of "crimes without victims" helps to identify trivial or spurious problems.

Closely related to the degree of severity of a social problem is its duration or recurrence. Ignoring their other effects, addictive drugs are considered to be more harmful than non-addictive drugs. Other parallels to this temporal aspect of severity are the medical concern with "chronic" conditions and the penologist's concern with recidivism. Transitory conditions may be considered less severe than continuing or permanent ones. . . .

CONCLUSION

An aim of this discussion has been to emphasize the importance of demonstrable knowledge and reasoned evaluation in identifying and appraising social problems. The knowledge and values of science are less ethnocentric, less erratic, and less influenced by vested interests that those of a majority or significant numbers of a society. Using the views of the latter as the criterion of social problems is a more knowledge-free than value-free definition of social problems.

Adopting scientific knowledge and values as criteria does not imply disregard for public perceptions. Certainly, research is needed to clarify the ways by which individuals come to believe that certain social conditions are undesirable. We need to know more of the processes of collective action, of the influences of mass media and pressure groups, and of the consequences of group reactions. Knowledge of public concerns can reduce the risk of an ivory-towered isolation of sociology.

The effort to determine the seriousness of social problems requires procedures for distinguishing between trivial or spurious and important or genuine ones. That public judgments are made, at times, on the basis of erroneous information or emotionality can hardly be doubted. Such judgments need not be given equality in assessing social problems with those based on facts and reasoned judgments. . . .

To espouse scientific knowledge and values for the appraisal of social phenomena implies no claims of omniscience and certainly not of omnipotence. Similar limitations are applicable to public opinion. The latter is influenced by advertising, political ideologies, religious beliefs, etc. Accepting public opinion as the standard for defining and assessing social problems is incongruent with the rational basis of scientific inquiry.

The place of values remains the central dilemma of the sociological enterprise. Values are involved in the choice of concepts, research topics, and methods of inquiry. They are clearly relevant to the definition of social problems and to assessments of their seriousness. The knowledge values of science provide a more appropriate perspective for sociology than those of "significant numbers" of a given society.

REFERENCES

American Psychiatric Association. 1952. *Diagnostic and Statistical Manual, Mental Disorders.* Washington, D.C.

Blumer, Herbert. 1971. "Social problems as collective behavior." *Social Problems* 18(Winter): 298–306.

Dentler, Robert A. 1971. *Basic Social Problems.* Chicago: Rand McNally.

Kuhn, Thomas S. 1970. *The Structure of Scientific Revolutions.* Chicago: University of Chicago Press.

———. 1974. "The concept of social problems: Vox populi and sociological analysis." *Social Problems* 21:305–315.

Merton, Robert K. 1967. *On Theoretical Sociology.* New York: Free Press.

———. 1971. "Social problems and sociological theory," pp. 793–845 in Robert K. Merton and Robert Nisbet (eds.), *Contemporary Social Problems.* New York: Harcourt Brace Jovanovich.

Perrucci, Robert and Marc Pilisuk (eds.). 1971. *The Triple Revolution Emerging: Social Problems in Depth.* Boston: Little, Brown.

Planck, Max. 1962. "Phantom problems in science," pp. 840–852 in Dagobert D. Runes (ed.), *Treasury of World Science.* New York: Philosophical Library.

Reading 2

Do Photographs Tell the Truth?

Howard S. Becker

Northwestern University

Do photographs tell the truth? Social scientists and photographers are equally concerned with the question, though they come to it by different routes. "Visual sociology" and "visual anthropology" are small but growing movements within those disciplines, and historians (Michael Lesy being the most obvious example) are toying with more imaginative and extensive use of photographs than had been customary. If we are going to use photographs as evidence for social science assertions, we need to know whether they can be trusted as evidence, whether and how they "tell the truth."

Reprinted with permission from *Afterimage* (February 1978):p. 9–13.

Photographers have a much more ambivalent concern with the truth of photographs, and often adopt a strategy that attempts to have it both ways, presenting photographs in a way that intimates, without quite saying, that they convey some important or essential truth about the matter they picture. But the photographers know perfectly well that the pictures represent a small and highly selected sample of the real world about which they are supposed to be conveying some truth. They know that their selection of times, places, and people, of distance and angle, of framing and tonality, have all combined to produce an effect quite different from the one a different selection from the same reality would produce. They worry that, because someone else could have photographed the same subject differently, they will be accused of bias. With that worry in mind, they think defensively and assert before they can be accused of it that their pictures are only a personal view, "just the way it looked to me," that any other personal view would be just as "valid." But they never really mean the disclaimers, either about their own pictures or about any other pictures that have any claim to documentary veracity.

You can easily prove to yourself the uselessness of the "it's-only-personal" disclaimer. Take some photograph that has a strong element of seeming to report on the truth about society or some portion thereof—the FSA photographs are good for the purpose, although they needn't be classics (I often use the photographs my students make). Now tell yourself, or some friends, or anyone who will listen, that you have just discovered that this picture was not made where it appears to have been made or where its caption says it was, or that the people in it are not who they seem to be or are not doing "naturally" what the picture shows them doing. I once upset a class by telling them that the pictures one student had made were phony in that, while they were photographed at O'Hare Field, every person in them was an extra he had hired and whose movements he had choreographed. The response to such an assertion is interesting. I have never known anyone to respond in any way other than to say, "It's not true!," even people who a moment earlier were asserting stoutly that the picture represented a personal view whose truth didn't matter. If we refuse to believe that a photograph does not have the warrant of reality we assumed it did, we must see that part of our response to it was a response to it as evidence of something about the real world and the photographer in it.

Not every photograph will produce such a response of course. Whole genres simply do not raise the issue of truth. No one knows or cares where a Uelsmann construction originated, and if Duane Michals uses models, so what? On the other hand, it would make a great deal of difference to us if we thought that even such obviously "personal" work as Diane Arbus's or Robert Frank's was not shot where it purports to have been or that the people who appear in those images were hired models; and the case is stronger when we think of photographs by W. Eugene Smith or the FSA photographers. Anyone whose response to photographs never includes this reaction need not read further.

Most of us, then, do worry about whether the pictures we make and look at are "true" and can be seen to be true by others who look at them. I want to suggest some ways of thinking about this question that are less confusing than the approaches we commonly take. In doing so, I will rely on some ideas more or less well known to social scientists and will probably violate some photographic sensibilities, but that is the price of escaping the traps we get ourselves into.

What I will propose is not necessarily the best or the only or even a terribly important way of evaluating photographs, nor must all photographs be evaluated by the standards I will describe. But if truth is a factor in our response to a photograph then these standards are relevant to our understanding and judgment of it, and to our aesthetic experience of it as well.

WHAT'S TRUE?

A first clarification requires us to give up the question "Is it true?" In that simple form it is unanswerable, meaningless, and therefore foolish. Every photograph, because it begins with the light rays something emits hitting film, must in some obvious sense be true; and because it could always have been made differently than it was, it cannot be the whole truth and in that obvious sense is false.

To talk about the question more sensibly, we have to refine it. To begin, we can ask, "Is this photograph telling the truth about *what?*" Pictures can ordinarily contain enough information that we can use them to give us evidence about more than one topic. Are Brassai's pictures (in *The Secret of Paris of the 30's*) telling us the truth about Paris, or about Paris in the 1930s, or about the Parisian demi-monde, or about that sort of demimonde in general, or . . . ? So we must first specify what we are getting the truth about.

Even that is not enough. If we know the topic, we still don't know what is being asserted about it. We sometimes feel that the assertions a photograph makes—its "statement"—are so subtle and ineffable that they cannot be reduced to words. No doubt the entire statement cannot be reduced in that way. Much of it is made in a visual language that we don't have any workable rules for translating into words. Further, it contains so much material that reducing it to words would take more work than it is worth. Still, we do not usually feel that we can say nothing at all about the content of the picture. So we need a way of extracting from the image some verbal statements that will help us decide what, if anything, the picture is telling us the truth about, and what the truth is.

Here is a way to proceed. For any picture, ask yourself what question or questions it *might* be answering. Since the picture could answer many questions, we can decide what question we are interested in. The picture will, of course, suggest that some questions are likely to find answers in it. Some of Brassai's photographs clearly answer questions about how Parisian whores did business, while Danny Lyon's pictures (in *The Bikeriders*) answer some of our questions about how members of motorcycle gangs spend their leisure time.

We needn't restrict ourselves to questions the photographs suggest. We can also use them to answer questions the photographer did not have in mind and that are not obviously suggested by the picture. . . . We can thus avoid interminable, unresolvable, and irrelevant questions about the photographer's intent, for, whatever the intent, we can use the photograph to answer questions we want to raise and still not do violence to the work of artist-photographers.

In either case, we choose a question we think the photograph might enable us to answer. We may approach the photograph with the question already in mind or it may come to us as we inspect the image. Either way, we go over the image systematically to see what kind of answer it can give. We may find that it doesn't really answer the question very well, but will answer some other question more satisfactorily, leaving less margin for doubt. The job is to find a question and answer which fit each other, the answer being the answer for that question and vice versa.

The most obvious questions that photographs answer are the most specific. What did those people have on their pantry shelves? What kind of jackets did the members of Lyon's motorcycle gang wear? But we are only interested in such specific information if the subjects of the photograph are celebrities of some kind or intimates of ours, or if the photographs are to be used in a legal proceeding. Normally, we find photographs interesting because they answer questions about something larger than the immediate subject, and photographers usually give us to understand that their images have such broad meaning. Thus, Owens does not call his book *Livermore,* he calls it *Suburbia,* and in so doing intimates (presumably purposefully) that the photographs answer questions about the suburban way of life generally, not just about one suburb. If it were only about that one suburb, we would find the photographs less interesting; few people (other than those who live there) have a deep interest in Livermore, California. Books of documentary photographs often have titles that imply that kind of interesting generalization (think of *The Americans, American Photographs,* or *You Have Seen Their Faces*). But even without such help, we quickly jump to such generalizations, for without them the photographs would never command our attention at all.

So we usually inspect this kind of photograph with an eye to answering some general question about social arrangements or processes. The kinds of questions that concern us are often those social scientists ask. For instance, what are the main themes of the culture of this society? That is the kind of question Ruth Benedict raised in *Patterns of Culture* and *The Chrysanthemum and the Sword,* and I think it a fair way to characterize Robert Frank's book to say that *The Americans* is a kind of answer to such questions about the United States. The list of themes his book gives as an answer, if we should put the question to it, includes (and my list is not exhaustive) such themes as these:

1.   The automobile dominates American society. Americans revere their automobiles and practically live in them.

2. They similarly revere the flag, or at least display it everywhere, in so many and such varied places as to devalue and degrade it.
3. Religious symbolism is likewise omnipresent and thereby meaningless and degraded. Only among blacks is it a living force.
4. Some males—white, upper middle class, middle-aged, or Westerners— are powerful, inspiring fear and deference. Older men are devalued, ignored, and badly treated, as are poor people and members of ethnic minorities.
5. Women are powerless, and get by only on looks and an attachment to a powerful male.

This is not the place for a full analysis of *The Americans*. But the nature of cultural themes is at least one order of question to which it gives answers.

Other photographic work characterizes the way of life of some social stratum, occupational group, or social area by detailing major forms of association among the group's members and placing them in relation to some set of environing forces. Danny Lyon's work does that. Other photographers answer questions that amount to some version of: can such things be? That is, they verify that certain phenomena have actually occurred or existed, so that we know that future talk and theorizing will have to take their existence into account. Insofar as Diane Arbus's published photographs tell us about something beyond herself, they serve that purpose, pointing to the existence of a population of freaks and weirdos ordinarily conveniently forgotten by more "normal" members of American society, a population ignored by both lay and professional theories of how the society works. Or take this question: would small-town American men, farmers and similar working-class people, perform cunnilingus in public on women who are total strangers to them? Most writers about American society would find that unlikely, but a few photographs in Susan Meiselas's *Carnival Strippers,* plus the supporting text, show us that they have, at least often enough for her to photograph it; on the testimony of her informants, the event is commonplace.

Further examples are unnecessary. We can read out of these photographs answers to such questions. The answers, both specific and general, that we find in the photograph can be taken as the propositions whose truth the photograph asserts. Thus, we no longer have to ask such unanswerable questions as "Is Smith's essay on the Spanish village a 'true' picture of life there?" Instead, we can ask specific questions about that life—do the villagers take religious rituals very seriously?— and use the material in the pictures to answer them. The first step in deciding whether pictures tell the truth, then, is to decide what truth they assert by seeing what answers we can extract from them to questions either we or they have suggested. (This way of looking at things emphasizes that pictures do not simply make assertions, but rather that we interact with them in order to arrive at conclusions—in short, that we play an active role in the process, as Dewey long ago argued and a host of other people have reiterated since.)

THREATS TO VALIDITY

Once we know what we think a picture asserts, or can be made to assert, we can ask: is the assertion true? Before I suggest a way of dealing with this problem I want to make a few preliminary remarks.

1. The truth need not be the *whole* truth. It is irrelevant to criticize the assertion we have extracted from a picture because there is some other assertion it will also support, *unless* the two assertions are contradictory. Since pictures often contain a wealth of information, it is not surprising that more than one true thing can be said on the basis of a single image. When this happens, it only means that we are asking different questions, which deserve and get different answers.

2. The truth will ordinarily not be verified by a single photographic image and usually not by any number of photographic images taken by themselves. Photographers and others have fallen into the habit of discussing the question of truth as though it had to be settled with reference to one picture—what can we assert for sure on the basis of this one picture? The answer is usually nothing at all. We generally decide important questions on the basis of an assessment of all kinds of evidence, balancing all the fragments of fact we can assemble to arrive at the best judgment we can make about a proposition. Those fragments will ordinarily include other photographs besides the one we are working with, *and* a variety of textual materials: documents, interviews, and so on.

3. We can never be absolutely sure of the truth of an assertion. Our knowledge is always partial and therefore fallible; we may find a new piece of evidence tomorrow which will show us that the assertion we thought true is, after all, false. Thus, recent investigation of the circumstances of the making of many of the early photographs of American Indians shows that they are grossly inaccurate, because the photographers clothed and posed their subjects according to the way they thought Indians ought to look rather than investigating their lives sufficiently to be able to photograph them as they did look in ordinary life (see Scherer, 1975). This and similar cases show how new information can shift our ideas about the validity of an assertion and thus the degree to which those ideas rest on more than the internal evidence deducible from one photograph.

4. No single standard of proof is acceptable for all social groups and all purposes. Some groups are more skeptical than others, in part because of professional biases (i.e., psychologists are probably more skeptical than anthropologists) and in part depending on whose ox is being gored (proof of something that damages some cause of mine is going to have to be very convincing proof, much more so than in the opposite case). Further, we demand a higher standard of proof if we are going to base some important action on our conclusion. (One reason we are less skeptical about photographic materials may be that we seldom take any important action on their basis.)

With those qualifications, we can think about how to tell whether the assertion we have drawn from a photograph is true. The idea of *threats to the validity* of a proposition was first proposed and much elaborated by Donald Campbell, a psychologist and philosopher of science, and a number of his collaborators. The idea is simple enough. We decide whether a proposition is true (or, perhaps better, whether we ought to believe it) by thinking explicitly of all the reasons we might have to doubt it, and then seeing whether the available evidence requires us to take those doubts seriously. If the evidence suggests that we need not entertain these doubts, that these threats to the validity of our idea are not sound, then we can accept the proposition as true.[1]

Campbell and others have listed a large number of threats to the validity of hypotheses or assertions. Many of them have special reference to the situation of the laboratory experiment; others are more generally applicable. I don't intend to go through their entire list, but rather to generate the beginnings of a similar list applicable to assertions based on photographic materials. We now have available many photographic monographs and essays which make some sort of statement about social life. Inspecting a variety of these works, we can see what doubts we have about them; generalizing those doubts, we can see what the general categories of threats to the validity of photographically derived assertions might be. (Campbell has revised his list several times since its first publication, and the list I will give is likewise provisional, to be extended on the basis of how it works in practice.) When we understand the threats to the validity of our assertion we can compile a catalogue of problems and solutions. Here are some of them.

1. The most obvious threat to the validity of a conclusion based on photographic evidence is the suspicion that the photograph was faked in some way. It might have been retouched; Lesy shows some gross examples of filthy factories, worthy of Lewis Hine, magically turned into spacious sunlit, healthful places of work. The print might be composite of a number of negatives, showing people together who in fact never met. The people and things in the picture might have been specially arranged by the photographer, or by someone else (with or without the photographer's knowledge and consent), as in the case of Arthur Rothstein's "skull" picture. Rothstein photographed a bleached steer skull sitting on some parched earth in North Dakota. He had found the skull nearby and moved it around the square of bare dirt and some nearby grass, looking for the best light and angle. Republican politicians, in an effort to embarrass the Democrats and Franklin Roosevelt, charged that the picture was faked, that the skull had never actually been where Rothstein photographed it. They intimated that he carted the skull around with him looking for likely places to put it so as to dramatize the drought. What they objected to was the implied conclusion that the drought was so bad that cows were simply dying and rotting on the open range.[2]

----

[1]The original statement of the approach is Campbell and Stanley (1966). Some important revisions are suggested in Campbell (1969).

[2]The story is told in Hurley (1972: 86–92).

Retouched photograph in Michael Lesy, from *Real Life: Louisville in the Twenties;* Courtesy of the University of Louisville Photographic Archives, Caulfield & Shook Collection.

The Rothstein story illustrates several points. Whether the picture is "true" depends on what conclusion we draw from it. If we take it as evidence that North Dakota cows were dying of thirst it is probably not true. If we take it as symbolizing a condition of drought, illustrating its severity, then it probably was true. The story also indicates what is required for a picture to be taken as unassailably "true." If we suspect that it has been covertly interfered with by someone so that it does not picture what would have been there without such interference, its value as evidence diminishes. Thus, we may not trust Irving Penn's pictures of Peruvian peasants (in *Worlds in a Small Room*) to tell us what kind of people they are, because Penn tells us that he arranged their poses himself, moving arms, legs, and torsos as he did with fashion models. Whatever we might conclude about peasant life and culture from the way they held themselves before the camera is now suspect, since it might only be Penn's idea of peasants that we see. Conversely, when a picture openly displays the visible signs of having been "doctored" (as in the images in Dawn Ades's *Photomontage*), we find no fault with it; no one is trying to fool us and we know that we must make any inferences with the doctoring in mind.

2. The Rothstein story suggests a second threat to the validity of assertions based on photographs. Photography has an ambiguous status in relation to high art, and many photographers whose work is unabashedly commercial or journalistic also

Unretouched photograph in Michael Lesy, from *Real Life: Louisville in the Twenties;* Courtesy of the University of Louisville Photographic Archives, Caulfield & Shook Collection.

would like it to be taken as "artistic." They are encouraged in this by the overseers of the art photography world who periodically discover artistic merit in work of that kind, so that photojournalists like Cartier-Bresson and W. Eugene Smith are recognized as artists, their work hung in museums, bought and sold by dealers and collectors. No genre of photography seems immune to this. A strong move to take fashion photographs seriously has been launched and even aerial reconnaissance photographs made under Steichen's direction during World War I have received such treatment (see Sekula, 1975).

I don't want to debate the rights and wrongs of this practice here. Some of the people and photographs so ennobled deserve it; many do not. In any event, because photographers, whatever kind of work they are doing, may want to be recognized as artists, we sometimes suspect that they have made their pictures to fit into currently fashionable artistic styles, either technically and compositionally, or with respect to mood and subject matter. Thus, some years ago, Jones and Boruch mounted an exhibition of photographs of a dying California town: boarded up stores, deserted streets, a closed bank. The show received a respectful review from Margery Mann (1964) who, some months later, wrote an aggrieved letter to the editor in which she announced that she had since been to that town and discovered that not a block away from the dying downtown was a brand new thriving downtown, with a new branch of the bank that had closed, two auto dealers, and other signs of prosperity. The photographers seemed to have succumbed to an "artistic" desire for nostalgic stories of the death of the Old West. None of this is a criticism of the photographs or an assertion that they are untrue, only a statement that you cannot conclude from them that the town was dying; the photographers could be faulted only insofar as they had suggested that you could.

The desire to make "art" may, then, lead photographers to suppress details that interfere with their artistic conception, a conception that might be perfectly valid in its own right, but that unsuits the photographs for use as evidence for certain kinds of conclusions. Many social scientists have just this fear about photographs. It is a justified fear, but one relevant not only to photographs or to those photographs made with some artistic intention. Insofar as the artistic intention interferes with the photograph's evidentiary use, it does so by affecting the selection and presentation of details, so that some things are not shown, some details are emphasized at the expense of others and thus suggest relationships and conclusions without actually giving good cause for believing them, and by presenting details in such a way (through manipulation of lighting or the style of printing, for instance) as to suggest one mood rather than another. Since every way of making a photograph, whether for artistic purposes or for presentation as evidence in a courtroom, does all of these things, there is a problem, but it is one every user of photographs has. Further, every form of verbal material poses the same problems, for writing and oral testimony are likewise shaped with some audience in mind and must be interpreted and understood accordingly. So, knowing that the photographer had some artistic intentions does not invalidate the work as evidence; we can still decide that some conclusion is true. Knowing that, however, we will be alerted to certain threats to the validity of our assertions. These threats are not easily summed up, for they depend on whatever artistic conventions and fashions were current when the photograph was made. Knowing that, we can look especially for those kinds of sampling and presentational omissions or biases that might be associated with those conventions.

3. We may suspect that the photographer has inadequately sampled the events that might have been photographed, failing to see all the things relevant to the question and answer we are interested in, or, having seen them, failing to photograph them. One of the chief problems here is access. Can we get access to the full range of relevant activities and, if we can, on what terms can that access be negotiated? What do we have to give in return? When we look at photographs as evidence, we want to know about access and terms. Photographers usually give us information on these points, either explicitly (as in Bruce Davidson's introduction to *East 100th Street* or Smith's lengthy text in *Minamata*) or implicitly, by the evidence of the pictures themselves. It's often said that a photograph records, among other things, the relation of the photographer to the people in the picture, whether that be intimate, friendly, hostile, or voyeuristic. . . . Part of our concern is always to know how much time the photographer spent; we trust the sample more

if we know it was a long time. A week is one thing, a year or two is something else.

Getting permission or freedom to make photographs of people can profitably be viewed as a negotiation between them and the photographer. Each gives something and gets something. Most photographers have developed some way of handling this problem, but it is seldom discussed frankly or at length. What did the photographer trade for permission to do the work? For instance, I have spent two years photographing the people who provide emergency medical services for large outdoor rock concerts in the San Francisco Bay Area. The one rule I had to accept in order to get access with a camera to large parts of the operation was never to photograph, or use a photograph of, a patient's face; the reason is clear and understandable, and I accepted the prohibition as the price of doing the project at all. Nevertheless, people who see the work now cannot answer questions about what kinds of people the patients are or how they feel about the service they are getting, because of the rule I accepted during that negotiation.

A second problem is the photographer's theory. We don't photograph what is uninteresting to us or what has no meaning. What can have meaning and be interesting is a function of the theory we have about what we are investigating. We can usually get an idea of the photographer's theory by investigating both the pictures themselves and the accompanying text. We may decide that the theory has blinded the photographer to things we need to know to decide whether a particular assertion is true. We criticize here, insofar as we make a criticism, not the photographs but the theory or idea that lay behind their making. (See Becker, 1975.)

In any event, an inadequate sample, however it came about, can lead us to feel a serious threat to the validity of the assertion we want to make based on the photographs.

4. Finally, we may suspect that some form of censorship has prevented us from seeing all the pictures we might have seen, and that the ones that have been withheld would have changed our view substantially and perhaps even altered our conclusions. Censorship may be imposed by the state or some subdivision thereof, by a general cultural atmosphere that makes certain photographs unseemly or distasteful, or by photographers themselves out of some personal or political conviction.

Contemporary standards have loosened up so much with respect to "moral" issues that we now see photographs that would not have been made public only a few years ago. A striking example of this is Brassai's new book, which includes his already famous photographs of Paris plus many other photographs made at the same time but presumably considered too raunchy for public exhibition or distribution then, but not now. So we now see the gay bars we didn't see before, the whores and their customers in private, and so on. None of this contradicts what we saw before; it extends and amplifies it just as we might have imagined, without being quite sure we were right, even though our worldly wisdom told us we probably were.

But because we now see these pictures doesn't mean that we don't still have to consider the possibility of censorship. In particular, keep in mind that sex is only one topic which may be censored. There are many others. Anything people don't want known about, and there are millions of such things, may be censored if those who want the matter covered up have the power to do it. In fact, preventing things from being made public is one element of the practice of public relations, and businesses and communities, in particular, often try to keep "unfavorable" material, including photographs, from being made public. Though carried on by private parties rather than the government, and not the result of some general cultural standard, this too has the effect of limiting what we see.

The photographer may similarly limit what we see. In this case, of course, there is a nicer name and a rationale for what is done. We often speak of editing, meaning the weeding out of a small pile of superior pictures from the larger mass of all the photographs. It is unlikely that we would want to see all that material, although it is not, for instance, ridiculous to suggest that proof sheets might be available for independent checking—everyone has found it extremely interesting to see the full range of negatives Walker Evans produced for the FSA. We will frequently find that seeing the larger body of work will not change our ability to make various assertions or the warrant for those assertions. But it might, and we might want to know about that before accepting the answer to some question.

Photographers may also censor their work for reasons of ideology or ethics, as I have done with the faces of rock medicine patients. Without being required to by circumstances, they may decide that they don't wish to show everything, that some things are no one's business or disrespectful to the people being photographed. It is instructive to compare the work of Bill Owens and Roslyn Banish in this respect. Banish (in *City Families*) has treated a somewhat similar subject matter to that Owens worked with (the only difference being that she is interested in the domestic life of city dwellers instead of suburbanites) in a quite different way. Instead of Owens's "candid snapshots," with the one short, snappy statement by the subject appended, she made formal family portraits, to which are appended lengthy interviews, filled with details about the families' lives and aspirations. The much more respectful photographs present the families in a dignified, sober way that emphasizes their respectability and dignity. Owens does not let his people stay so buttoned up; he persuaded them to show a less dignified, more comic side to the camera, and at the same time has not allowed them to speak for themselves at such length. Owens's photographs give us much more information about a variety of topics: (what goes on behind the neat walls of these suburban cottages? Disorder, drinking, bad taste, sloth, and mess?) and much less about a variety of other topics (hopes, dreams, and aspirations). If I had my choice of a basis for understanding families-in-an-environment, I'd like to have both; I can answer more questions more completely from the combination than with either one taken alone. I don't know if it's fair to call Banish's respectful photographic editing or Owens's severe editing of his subjects' words censorship; probably not, but the effect is the same and in each case means that we can have less confidence in the conclusions we draw from the material presented than we might otherwise have.

There will always be reasons good enough for some people not to present all the material they might, whether the reasons are matters of ethics, politics, or just good taste. In seeing what we can conclude, what questions we can answer plausibly, we must take into account whatever we know or suspect about the degree to which this kind of selection occurred. We must recognize that others will regard whatever signs of such selection they discover as weaknesses in the argument we are presenting, and thus we will want to avoid such biases, hide their signs or explain what they are and why they are present.

One final point. Insofar as we take some particular way of doing things as evidence that a suspected threat to the validity of some answer we are drawing from a photograph is not operating, we must be watchful for the possibility that the sign of authenticity itself has been faked. Many photographers now print their photographs with a heavy black line around the border of the print. Among other things, the line indicates that the negative has not been cropped, that all its evidence has been openly and honestly presented to us. But, of course, black lines can be made around parts of a negative. And, more to the point, the device obscures a more serious threat: any ordinarily skillful photographer can frame an image so as to leave out the unwanted details a less skillful person would have had to crop.

CONCLUSION

To repeat, my purpose here has been to begin the discussion, not to conclude it. The list of threats is sketchy, the suggestions for means of dealing with them hardly even suggestive. The way to proceed, I think, is to continue to investigate successful practice—works that convince and succeed in overcoming doubt—in both social science and photography, learning from and generalizing from experiences in both areas.

REFERENCES

Becker, H. S. 1975. "Photography and sociology." *Afterimage* (May –June).

Campbell, D. T. 1969. "Prospective: artifact and control," in R. Rosenthal and R. L. Rosnow (eds.), *Artifact in Behavioral Research*. New York: Academic Press.

——— and J. C. Stanley. 1966. *Experimental and Quasi-Experimental Designs for Research*. Chicago: Rand McNally.

Hurley, F. J. 1972. *Portrait of a Decade*. Baton Rouge: Louisiana State University Press.

Mann, M. 1964. Review. *Artforum* (May).

———. 1964. Letter. *Artforum* (September).

Scherer, J. C. 1975. "You can't believe your eyes: inaccuracies in photographs of North American Indians." *Studies in the Anthropology of Visual Communication* 2: 67–86.

Sekula, A. 1975. "The instrumental image: Steichen at war." *Artforum* (December): 26–35.

Reading 3

Quasi-Theories and Research Origination: Quasi-Theories as Substitute Cures

John Stimson

William Paterson College

Ardyth Stimson

Kean College of New Jersey

NEGOTIATED REALITY

Sociologists continue to uncover and debate the ramifications of W. I. Thomas's statement (1951) that typically we do not make our decisions statistically or scientifically, that we lead our lives by inference. Recent extensions and explorations of the nonscientific nature of social life can be summarized as Negotiated Reality theory—a view that sees the process of daily interaction interrupted by discussion of motivation, causation, or planning only when a problem arises that directly disrupts the normal flow. The immediate goal is to reinstate nondisturbing normality. If the disturbance, or disturber, cannot be labeled and put aside, then reality must be examined and redefined to include it as normal. It is not necessary that any "real" disturbance, or solution, exist: The explanation process, itself, will solve the situation in any case (Mills, 1940; Rains, 1975:5).

Merton (1971) and Blumer (1971) developed "constructionist" descriptions of the collective process of social-problem definition that demonstrated that group values define what is or is not a problem. Hewitt and Hall (1973) have extended the relevance of this perspective by examining the collective definition of the supposed causes and solutions of social problems. They show that quasi-theories exist in all our minds and can be called up to quiet the effects of disturbing events.

There is a strong similarity between the social negotiation of reality process that Hewitt and Hall (1973) describe and the formulation of many applied research programs. We have often found it a battle to propose that an applied research be allowed to try to find answers that others around the table thought they already knew. Hewitt and Hall's description of quasi-theory structure places these conflicts in a meaningful social-psychological context. It can help explain why each person thinks he is an adequate sociologist and how he is supported in this belief by the typical social process of problem solving.

Reprinted with permission from *Sociological Practice* (Spring 1977): 38–48. Copyright © 1977 by Human Sciences Press, 72 Fifth Avenue, New York, NY, 10011.

GOALS

Three main suggestions will be made. First, researchers, especially when hoping to affect policy, must recognize that a powerful competitor really does exist—that there are traditional alternatives to science that more easily alleviate the tension that leads to problem solving. Second, each of these alternatives is a quasi-theory with a specific time-ordered structure of social construction that can be interrupted so that meaningful research can be originated. Finally, research results can find an interested audience among policy makers only if researchers return to a normal conversational style of presentation that argues for "scientific" cures in the same manner in which competing cures are justified.

We will extend Hewitt and Hall's concept by showing that social science research is but a special case within this normal process—a special case that has, perhaps, lost touch with the normal structure of problem discussion and definition. Quasi-theorizing is the normal procedure. Science, for all its organization and supposed protections against introspection, rearranges the usual chronological pattern of problem solution. Science, thereby, places itself at a severe disadvantage during the argumentation that must take place when applied research is either formulated or presented.

QUASI-THEORY STRUCTURE

Hewitt and Hall describe a series of steps with a recognizable structure that directly contradicts scientific procedure. "What is essential to a quasi-theory is its logic, which is one of cause and effect, though quite disarranged temporally if viewed from a scientific viewpoint. The use of quasi-theories involves postulation of a cure, followed by an analysis of cause and effect, that supports the cure" (1973:370). Analysis is post hoc. What represents causal research in this normal talk-structure of problem solution is a "build-around" of justifying definitions. The stages of this process are: (a) choice of a cure (a way to stop the disturbance); (b) definition of what can be cured (i.e., the "real" problem is distinguished from its false aspects, "false" usually meaning those that can't be affected by the chosen cure); (c) selection of examples from cultural and biographical experience that support the efficacy of the cure and the problem definition. . . .

Hall and Hewitt (1970) used the quasi-theory of communication to demonstrate how 1960s political disturbances were explained away before they were properly analyzed. The process moved directly from public notice of conflict to a cure that stated: "We all share the same values and goals, we are just having trouble communicating our common humanity, Americanism or interest in progress, etc." The apparent value conflicts were seldom examined. A solution was selected, ready-made, from the cultural context in order to calm the disturbance.

Two other familiar examples from the political process are quoted by Hall and Hewitt. Real analysis or action has often been avoided by assigning causal power to either "outside agitators" or a "conspiracy by a controlling elite." Quasi-theories are also used to alleviate tension and confusion that can be handled in no other way. When human problems seem to have no solution, a quasi-theory will be submitted, for example, "Time will heal it," or the behavior is ascribed to some invisible unconscious instinct that is "natural." . . .

SOME QUASI-THEORIES THAT REPLACE RESEARCH

The goal of this section is to stimulate an exchange of experiences among sociologists by providing a preliminary list of quasi-theories that we have heard explain away problems that needed research.

1. Some version of the notion that *man is rational,* materialistic, and able quickly to recognize the route to the greatest reward is a concept often used to oversimplify potential research situations. It is used especially in commercial research to explain away labor-management or consumer-intention studies. Its central notion is that "dollar-profit" overrides mere social values or definitions of the situation because it is somehow more basic or natural. This view does not recognize profit as just one value among many. It sees profit as a normal outcome of man's basic utility-seeking efficiency in avoiding unrewarded effort. Advertising research has often shown that, on the contrary, "profit" can be a function of created, manipulated desire. This "thing-rational" notion of man occasionally closes out social problem research, for example, the notion that low pay is the central problem of ghetto life—better salaries would be more motivating and thereby cure everything else. . . .

2. "We can't wait; *immediate action* is needed" has signaled the end of many research proposals (Blalock, 1970:5). It is based on the assumption that the obvious problems are the real problems. It has been an effective call to action *instead of study,* especially when phrased in terms of "a war on . . ." or "a crusade against . . ." by a charismatic political or business leader. There are real time pressures. Problems are urgent, but this does not reduce the need for knowledge before action or excuse the belief that an area is over-simple.

Banfield (who has proposed some research-aborting quasi-theories of his own) does make a telling point when he describes "Incessant Politics and Perpetual Service" as our twin national afflictions (cited in Nisbet, 1974). Nisbet ends his review of *The Unheavenly City* with the hope that the next wave of politicians and administrators will be devoted to the apothegm: "Don't just do something. Sit there!" (1974:152).

The entire Banfield controversy is a good example of a battle of quasi-theories. We remember only the "cures" he has criticized, and what his critics said. Banfield's contribution is his attack on the popular notions that cities are rapidly deteriorating and are "cauldrons of repressed revolt" (in Nisbet, 1974:143–144). Banfield thereby helped to place urbanology back in historical perspective, back into the arena where research might be allowed.

The alternative that Banfield presents, however, supports another series of popular quasi-theories that also preclude research.

3. *Panglossian* quasi-theories are based on the notion that time will cure all. They state that life is difficult and that we are in the grip of major long-term processes (Demographic Transition or Racial Assimilation) that cannot be substantially affected. We are in the best of all possible worlds, considering the changes we are living through. Banfield's urbanology is a current example: "The mere act of *doing for* others, especially when armed with the might and wealth of the democratic state, cannot help but destroy, or set back grievously, processes of an adaptive nature in the [local] areas" (in Nisbet, 1974:150). That is, immigrants must assimilate or poverty cultures must adapt, and artificial assistance can only slow the natural process.

This is the most extreme research killer, and we should remember that it is partly an attempt to destroy the quasi-theory of Perpetual Service. Even Killian, the proponent of sociological pessimism, leaves a place for research: "If the pessimistic sociologist is impelled to be an activist, he can still address himself to the question, 'What sorts of adjustments do individuals and groups make to living in a world that is not and never will be a utopia?'" (Killian, 1971:284).

4. A related quasi-theory develops from the attempt to rank interventions by *measuring the human suffering* that each would alleviate. Crisis intervention is the normal operation of most social-problem practitioners. They are concerned with research and method, in the abstract, but have come to believe that they must alleviate the immediately presented severe symptom before more-lasting change can take place.

The notion of directing immediate action at areas of maximum individual pain is not invalid. It becomes a research-stifling quasi-theory only when extended so that possible *causes* or problems are chosen using an estimate of their destructive impact. We have often seen this orientation in juvenile problems research, for example, a working mother *must* cause such deprivation that the child will be disorganized, or broken homes are so traumatic that they *must* produce delinquency.

The supposed traumatic effects of inadequate housing have probably received more governmental attention than any other form of suffering, but recent study shows that little evidence can be found to support new housing as an effective cure, or even a major correlate, of other problems (Mitchell, 1974). Housing construction has probably been chosen so often because of economic (it stimulates finance and employment) and political (it provides tangible achievements) considerations.

Its appeal to the public, its plausibility, is probably based on a quasi-theory that equates, somehow, a man's castle with his worth. Mitchell comments that "decent housing and a suitable living environment are rapidly being elevated to the status of fundamental human rights" (1974:276). The quasi-theory that accompanies this value states that a man or family cannot function properly, rationally and morally, when this fundamental right or need is violated (i.e., when too much suffering is caused, it is not a motivation toward change, but a degradation).

5. The *"sweet mystery of life"* quasi-theory is used, almost seasonally, during congressional investigations of basic research grants. It states that research on such things as love, marriage, birth, death, etc., is useless because these subjects are so basic that the answers are automatically known by all. An extreme form of this view states that it is better not to study sex or marriage, for example, because it is better to suffer the high divorce rates of today than to risk the disenchanting coldness that might result from scientific analysis. We refer you to Lazarsfeld's work (1969) combating the notion of the obvious and offer only one additional comment. The culture is generous. It offers contradictory advice: He who hesitates is lost! Look before you leap! . . .

6. The *"ask the contact-person"* quasi-theory is mentioned by Blalock (1970) and by Foote (1974). It avoids research by assuming that the person who deals with the situation (salesperson, community organizer, local politician) can easily report the most important variables and the causal structure.

Blalock blames sociologists because "we have not seriously challenged the nonsensical idea that there is little point in analyzing "cold" statistics when real insights are to be obtained by seeing life as it actually is and by getting out and doing things, rather than living in the "ivory tower" (1970:7).

Foote's example explains how marketing research is often cut short by asking the salesperson to act as the expert on the consumer. The answer is always that price is the most powerful variable. Foote points out, however, that the real consumption process is complete by the time the salesperson becomes involved. Price can be the last, and the least important, variable.

Other examples that ignore the fallacy of assuming that participants have a clear view of their surroundings include asking police about crime or social workers about poverty. Contact-people serve symptoms and have developed a set of quasi-theories that is peculiar to their occupational positions.

One result of this acceptance of the contact-person as expert is that most statistics that are regularly collected are designed by, and for, the contact-operators. They are assumed to know the important items that will predict the future and assist understanding of the situation.

7. The *"just ask* those living in the situation" quasi-theory is quite similar, but it is in error for a different reason. People living in even a very difficult situation have usually adjusted or adapted to it. Selltiz and her co-workers base their discussion of exploratory research on this assumption. They suggest that the quickest way to discover the potent variable is to ask strangers, deviants, outcasts, or marginal men. These respondents' views are not as likely to have been neutralized, repressed, or subculturally socialized (Selltiz et al., 1959:65). Again, there is nothing wrong with client or consumer surveys—as long as they are not proposed as causal analyses. . . .

8. Finally, researchers must be careful to avoid activating the quasi-theory of *hopeless overdetermination.* In some areas, especially urban problems and juvenile

delinquency, sociologists have been too convincing in their destruction of simplistic theories. The authors have often lost a committee's attention when trying to lay out a complicated causal structure. This experience demonstrated that quasi-theory structures are important. One cure, or cause, is all that can be handled and justified in one discussion. . . .

The feeling of helplessness that develops in an administrator or lay committee during too complicated a discussion is the surest killer of research proposals. The listener feels justified in retreating to popular quasi-theories when science violates his structure of thought. The analysis has become more threatening than the problem itself, and traditional simplifications are sought, quickly.

The implicit value orientation of this paper is that research can be valid, and that whatever sociology's problems are, more exploratory and descriptive studies will be helpful. This orientation does *not* include the belief that sociologists' theories are the "real" theories and the public's are merely "quasi." The goal is for sociologists to be allowed to research to learn and inform.

REFERENCES

Blalock, Hubert M., Jr. 1970. *An Introduction to Social Research.* Englewood Cliffs, N.J.: Prentice-Hall

Blumer, Herbert. 1971. "Social problems as collective behavior." *Social Problems* 18:298–306.

Foote, Nelson. 1974. "Putting sociologists to work." *American Sociologist* 9:125–134.

Hall, Peter M., and John P. Hewitt. 1970. "The quasi-theory of communication and the management of dissent." *Social Problems* 18:17–27.

Hewitt, John P., and Peter M. Hall. 1973. "Social problems, problematic situations, and quasi-theories." *American Sociological Review* 38:367–374.

Killian, Lewis M. 1971. "Optimism and pessimism in sociological analysis." *American Sociologist* 6:281–286.

Lazarsfeld, Paul F. 1969. "What do attitude surveys tell us?" *Public Opinion Quarterly* 13:378–390.

Merton, Robert K. 1971. "Social problems and sociological theory," pp. 793–845 in Robert K. Merton and Robert Nisbet (eds.), *Contemporary Social Problems.* New York: Harcourt Brace Jovanovich.

Mills, C. Wright. 1940. "Situated actions and vocabularies of motive." *American Sociological Review* 5:904–913.

Mitchell, Robert E. 1974. "Sociological research on the economic myths of housing." *Social Problems* 22:259–280.

Nisbet, Robert. 1974. "The urban crisis revisited," pp. 142–151 in George Riter (ed.), *Social Realities.* Boston: Allyn and Bacon.

Rains, Prudence 1975. "Imputations of deviance." *Social Problems* 23:1–11.

Selltiz, Claire, et al. 1959. *Research Methods in Social Relations.* New York: Holt, Rinehart and Winston.

Thomas, W. I. 1951. *Social Behavior and Personality,* E. H. Volkart, ed. New York: Social Science Research Council.

CHAPTER 2

The Individual in Modern Society: Alienation and Anomie

The transition from life in a simple agricultural town to coping with the pace and complexity of the modern urban-industrial life-style has been recognized as a central cause of many of our problems. What individuals experienced because of this change has been described as disorganization, lawlessness, rootlessness, powerlessness, and meaninglessness.

Melvin Seeman is an expert in analyzing the alienation caused by modern life. He shows us how sociologists and psychologists have defined and used this idea to understand problems as wide ranging as mental and physical illness and political apathy.

One of the paradoxes of sociological analysis is that what seem to be very personal problems often turn out to be caused by the social structure. In Bernikow's descriptions of the many impacts of aloneness, we see that shyness, apathy, and other social disconnections are often caused by our culturally acquired values.

The third selection, by Biggart, describes one of the social values that shapes us into separate individuals concerned primarily with competition. It has often been proposed that a better understanding of our overattachment to success would help us to reduce alienation. Biggart contributes to this understanding through an analysis of our changing ways of "making it" in modern society as they are shown in our popular "success manuals."

Reading 4

Alienation Motifs in Contemporary Theorizing: The Hidden Continuity of the Classic Themes

Melvin Seeman

University of California, Los Angeles

There is a notion abroad that the idea of alienation has had its day. The concept flourished after its postdepression rediscovery in Marx, and became the signature of the subsequent decades when, as Daniel Bell notes (1976:43), the sociology of the '50s and '60s concerned itself with mass society and mass protest, and "the cultural intelligentsia brooded on themes of despair, anomie and alienation." This wave of interest in alienation earned an almost undeniable mark of validity in the late '60s when political protest and civil disorder appeared as a world-wide incarnation of the problem of alienation.

But, just as the fervor of protest has exhausted itself, in many ways the analytic attraction of the concept of alienation seems similarly to have been exhausted. It might be difficult to fully document the decline, but it is my definite impression that there is much less citation involving the concept, and much less fascination with it. In fact, one senses a certain antiquated air surrounding its current use.[1]

. . . Despite the fact that an obituary for alienation was written as long as ten years ago (Lee, 1972), and despite the fact that the signs do appear to point to its decline, my thesis is that alienation is very much alive and well—leading a lively underground life in contemporary research and theory. It survives because, whether explicitly designated with the alienation label or not, the ideas involved in the alienation tradition are indispensable for sociological and psychological analysis. Thus, my argument ultimately goes beyond simply noting how prevalent and variegated the hidden alienations are. The thrust is that *the themes that are classically brought together under the alienation rubric refer to the fundamental ways in which the individual is related to social structure.* . . .

I seek explicitly to show that the root ideas that have been identified as components of the alienation theme—e.g., powerlessness, meaninglessness, social isolation, and self-estrangement (Seeman, 1959; 1972a)—play, if anything, an

---

[1]There are certainly grounds for debate about this premise of the concept's diminished popularity (noting, for example, the recent emergence of a Research Committee on Alienation in the International Sociological Association). It is notoriously hard to obtain, or interpret, objective evidence of a faded romance. I have, however, examined the titles of all articles, notes and comments that have appeared in the past five years (1978–1982) in three major journals (*The American Journal of Sociology, American Sociological Review*, and *Social Psychology Quarterly*) and find, as I expected that there were *no* alienation titles among nearly 1000 publications (575 articles and 371 notes and comments). Nevertheless, I would not insist on this point, in part because the trend is not essential to my central argument that there is a substantial "underground" use of alienation themes.

Reprinted with permission from *Social Psychology Quarterly* 46(3) (1983): 171–184 Abridged.

enlarged role in contemporary theorizing. That enlargement entails two phenomena: first, the range of events to which these aspects of alienation are applied has become truly impressive; and second, that these applications are, in fact, studies of alienation is concealed by the reluctance to name the phenomena in that way. They are "hidden" alienations in that the ideas, but not the name, are employed. In what follows, I treat several dimensions of alienation to document this proposal about the current state of affairs, and then, in a brief coda, comment on the significance of this demonstration concerning the vitality of the alienation theme.

POWERLESSNESS

One of the dominant concerns in the classical literature on alienation is "powerlessness," referring to the person's sense of control over events (or lack of it). This is certainly a primary theme in Marx, where the issues of "free agency" in work and of capitalist domination are at the heart of the discussion of alienated labor. Furthermore, the concept of reification, which has sometimes been proposed as a preferable alternative to alienation (Israel, 1971) carries the same message of powerlessness, since it refers to a world in which social products and institutions that are created by human activity are abstracted and incorrectly conceived as independent things: in reification "people take their places as pawns rather than the origin of institutional arrangements" (Sampson, 1976:393).

This historical derivation understood, it is often startling to observe the extent to which an emphasis on the significance of powerlessness has currently come to dominate seemingly disparate domains of inquiry. A variety of concepts focusing on the individual's sense of control have taken hold in current theorizing. Though one could document this prominence of the powerlessness theme at great length, I present here a small sample of the arenas in which that theme has come to play a crucial role. In each case, I use examples where the word "alienation" is not a part of the author's lexicon, yet the concern for the sense of powerlessness is evident.

1. I have already noted how attractive Rotter's concept of "internal vs. external control" has become (referring to the person's expectancy that his own behavior can, or cannot, have an influence on the outcome of events). And I have noted, too, the affinity of that concept with sociological interests in the powerlessness aspect of alienation, it being a matter of little moment for present purposes whether the person's sense of low control is purported to be the product of capitalist domination, the mass society, fate, luck, bureaucracy, political coalitions, or postindustrial technology.

A substantial share of this work on the sense of control has been done in experimental settings, showing in microcosm the kind of negative effects on learning and performance that one might expect the sense of powerlessness to generate (Lefcourt, 1980). But the most striking recent application of the internal-external control idea has come outside the laboratory, leading to a challenging and potentially revolutionary reconsideration of medical care. The challenge was perhaps most clearly expressed in a well-known book by Norman Cousins (*Anatomy of an Illness*, 1979), a personal account of his recovery from a life-threatening illness. "There was, first of all," he wrote regarding his illness, "the feeling of help-lessness—a serious disease in itself" (1979:153). It was only, he insists, when he rejected the traditional passive doctor-dependent role as patient and insisted upon being an active participant in planning his own care that the body's restorative powers were brought into full play. Thus, the argument holds, the sense of personal control is much more influential than traditional medicine allows.

It is not an easy thesis to document, but the evidence appears to be accumulating that a realistic and active sense of control may, indeed, contribute to recuperation—and perhaps represents a fundamental feature of the well person. Thus, in a field study among institutionalized aged, Langer and Rodin (1976) compared matched groups of nursing home residents where the experimental group was provided with an opportunity to make a choice of a gift (a plant) and be responsible for its care, while the control group had the selection made for them and the care provided by the staff. A simple action, this, choosing one's own plant and caring for it; but the findings indicate that those who did so showed significantly greater improvement in their physical condition as compared with the no-choice control group (see also, Rodin and Langer, 1977).

Similarly, in a longitudinal study (Seeman and Seeman, forthcoming), of Los Angeles County residents involving systematic reinterviewing over a full year, it has been shown that a high sense of mastery (low powerlessness) correlates with superior initial and year-end self-rated health; and the sense of control is also associated with less year-long acute and chronic illness, less bed confinement, and more self-initiated preventive health behavior (e.g., weight control and nonsmoking).

In short, what we see in these investigations (and in numerous parallel ones, [Strickland, 1978]), is what amounts to an extension and radicalization of an early empirical study of alienation (Seeman and Evans, 1962) which explored the hypothesis that tuberculosis patients who felt relatively powerless would know less about their illness. The recent extension (indeed explosion) of interest in the bearing of the sense of control on health exhibits a clear continuity with this initial study, though the word alienation or powerlessness is rarely used. The "radicalization" lies in the fact that it is no longer simply a question of the connection between powerlessness and knowledge about illness, but of the potential role of powerlessness in the person's total health scenario—in physical well-being, doctor-patient relations, the occurrence and management of illness, and recuperation.

2. In the field of mental health, a frequently cited work in recent years is Martin Seligman's book on *Helplessness* (1975). The index carries no listing for "alienation" (or for "powerlessness"); but from start to finish it is an argument for the critical role that the sense of low control plays in the development of anxiety and

depression, in childhood and adolescent personality disorders, and even in psychosomatic death. The work is heavily based on experimental animal studies and on Seligman's own experience as a clinical psychologist. His argument concerning the power of the lack of power is provocative and it is of a piece with the medical revolution already commented upon. It carries the significance of powerlessness into the domain of mental disorder, while strongly reiterating the physical implications: As Seligman remarks, "Helplessness seems to make people more vulnerable to the pathogens, some deadly, that are always around us" (1975:181).

But the argument is also frustrating insofar as it invokes what is, to my mind, a formidable thesis about alienation while not naming it as such and, more important, not using the extensive available literature on powerlessness as a resource. The work, in fact, begins with a classic portrait of bureaucratically engendered powerlessness (parents facing institutionalized unresponsiveness in a children's hospital); but Seligman's inattention thereafter to alienation studies is striking. . . .

3. There are those who will say, however, that these sense of control studies are essentially psychological[2] and are too removed from specifically sociological interests in social systems and in structural analysis. But does that mean that we must look mainly to the psychologists for contemporary interest in alienation as low-sensed control? Hardly. In one form or another, that idea recurs under varied names in the specifically sociological literature, ranging from the microlevel symbolic interactionist branch to the macro-Marxist branch. What, for example, are the "hidden injuries" of social class as depicted by Sennett and Cobb (1972)? Prominent in their portrait is the sensed absence of control, since they depict a working class which, despite advancements and increased income, remains fundamentally deprived. "The fear," they write, "of being summoned before some hidden bar of judgment and being found inadequate effects the lives of people who are coping perfectly well from day to day; it is a matter of a hidden weight . . . a matter of feeling inadequately in control where an observer making material calculation would conclude that the workingman had adequate control" (1972:33–34).

There is, too, the increasingly favored idea of "system blame," an idea that has been used by Portes (1971) to explain lower class left radicalism. Radical

[2]It bears noting that, among psychologists, the reigning theories are, indeed, heavily infused with concepts that bear a close resemblance to the concern in alienation studies with personal and social control. One illustration is Brehm's (1972) theory of "reactance," referring to the individual's inherent motivation to defend a freedom that is threatened. Though Brehm deals mainly in laboratory analogues, the diminished sense of control that is at issue parallels the powerlessness that may have had much to do with the rebellion witnessed in the 1968 Parisian events of May (Seeman, 1972b). That is not the same as saying that powerlessness taken alone provides the explanation of such events, and operates in any simple or linear way (Seeman, 1975), or that powerlessness cannot also generate passivity; but it does assert that Brehm's postulate of "reactance" is not far removed from the classic alienation-as-powerlessness theme. Many well-known theories of behavior, in fact, make much of such constructs regarding the person's perceived control over interaction and its outcomes—as in the Kelley and Thibaut (1978) concept of "fate control," or Bandura's (1977) "self-efficacy."

ideology, he proposes, is not simplistic or irrational, or a function of low education and/or social isolation. Rather, it involves the learning, through normal political socialization, of an established definition of the situation that blames the system (rather than oneself, fate, etc.) for one's deprivations. The notion of system blame, however, is easily recognizable as a variant of powerlessness: it is, by way of example, what blacks in the U.S. are engaging in when they rightly blame discrimination, rather than personal inadequacy, as the source of their inferior status and low achievement (Taylor and Walsh, 1979). The idea of system blame is directly coordinate with the concept of "internal-external control," as has been suggested by Gurin et al., (1978). Their factor analysis of the Rotter I-E scale produced two major factors, one of which they titled "control ideology" (distinguished from a second factor titled "personal control"). The ideology factor basically taps (as would an index of system blame) the individual's beliefs about the degree to which external forces (e.g., institutional practices, legal and political standards, etc.), rather than personal qualities or abilities, shape the distribution of rewards in the society. I take it, thus, that talk about system blame is, in fact, talk about alienation in the powerlessness sense. . . .

MEANINGLESSNESS

I have devoted considerable attention to the powerlessness aspect of alienation, and cannot hope (for reasons of space and reader patience) to present a similarly detailed case for the other varieties of alienation. The same proposition holds, however, for each of them; and I illustrate that point by dealing rather more briefly with three additional aspects of alienation—meaninglessness, social isolation, and self-estrangement—to show how they are widely used but simultaneously unnoticed, and unnamed, as alienation phenomena. . . .

It was . . . more than four decades ago that Hadley Cantril (1941) presented one of the earliest efforts at organized treatment of then-active movements (e.g., Father Divine and Fascism), the key concept in his analysis being "the search for meaning" in a chaotic world.

It is a popular theoretical thread, and we again find this dynamic—the alienation dynamic of meaninglessness—being appealed to by Platt (1980). Platt argues against the interpretation of revolution through "categorical analysis" (meaning such categories as race, social class, relative deprivation, psychological types, etc.), calling attention to the "heterogeneity problem" that categorical analysis cannot accommodate. Thus, he is impressed by the variation that is typical of participants in such collective behavior; and he proposes, therefore, to look for a *subjectively* adequate theory of revolution that can explain both the heterogeneity and the complexity of revolutionary movements. In his view, the key social process that these divergent participants share is the problem of collective meaning-making in a chaotic situation. The root of the matter is that people find themselves in a failing, meaningless society, and it is in revolutionary ideologies and actions that the necessary recovery of meaning is found. Whatever else one might say about this view, it is one more contemporary focus on alienation as meaninglessness.

If this discussion of meaninglessness in modern dress seems suspiciously familiar, there is a very good reason. Though the word is not mentioned, it sounds very much like the classic Durkheimian portrait of "anomie." In his essay on Durkheim, Parsons (1968:316) speaks of anomie as "one of the small number of truly central concepts of contemporary social science," and then proceeds to establish that meaninglessness is the core component of anomie. In that societal condition, the problem is that there is anomic *uncertainty,* a lack of definiteness of expectations. Members find exertion for success "meaningless not because they lack the capacity or opportunity to achieve what is wanted, but because they lack a clear definition of what is desirable" (1968:316–17). In alienation terms, it is not powerlessness but meaninglessness that provides the key to anomie.

Interestingly enough, McHugh (1968) uses both of these variants of alienation—again, without naming them as such—in his effort to depict how people manage to develop orderly definitions of their situations. They manage to do so, he argues, even under conditions that threaten to degenerate into social disorder, and "disorder is anomie" (1968:50). But what does the disorder of an interaction hinge upon? For McHugh, anomie is conceived of as occasions involving the failure of two fundamental rules: whatever the content of an interaction, "the actor invokes the rule that it (must) have intelligible purpose . . . [and] the rule that there must be some means by which purposes can be attained. The disorder of an interaction, then, hinges on a decision by the actor that one or another of these rules is inoperative—that purpose is unintelligible or means unavailable" (1968:51). My translation of this is that anomie involves either meaninglessness or powerlessness, or both. And perhaps more importantly, we see over the range of these examples regarding meaninglessness that this variety of alienation is consistently employed in both microanalyses of intimate interaction and in macrointerpretations of societal crises (revolutions, social movements, etc.)[3]

SOCIAL ISOLATION

There was a time when analysts worried endlessly about the isolated and uprooted citizen of the mass society, and about the loss of "community." That was about the time, not surprisingly, when the worry about alienation also was overtly very much

---

[3]Meaninglessness has also been employed as a key variable in the expanding field of medical sociology. Antonovsky (1979) has proposed that "the sense of coherence" in social affairs (a proxy for alienation as meaninglessness, though neither of these words figure prominently in the analysis) is a critical variable in sustaining a healthful ("salutogenic") lifestyle. Antonovsky also takes considerable pains, and rightly so, to distinguish between the sense of incoherence (meaninglessness) and the sense of low control (powerlessness).

in evidence. Serious doubts about the validity of these worries were generated when research on urban society began to contradict this image of isolation; and as some of the romanticism about the loss of communal life began to fade, so too did a share of romantic interest in alienation itself.

As that word for the imagined trouble began to be suspect, however, an interesting thing happened: the problem of isolation vs. integration became ever more prominent, though now taken more from the positive side. The negative word "alienation" was simply supplanted by the positive concept of "social supports," and we observe these days a massive interest in studies of friendship networks (in anthropology as well as in sociology; see, for example, Gulick, 1973; and Fischer, 1982).

These may be seen, in fact, as studies in the consequences of alienation, as social isolation. One of the most popular hypotheses currently under review in the health field, for example, is the so-called "buffering hypothesis"—namely, the idea that those who are not integrated into supportive social networks suffer a wide range of negative consequences, since the effects of stressful circumstances can be moderated or eliminated for those who are not isolated. Thus, evidence has been developed to show that, for those who are network engaged, the consequences of job loss are minimized (Gore, 1978) and occupational stress takes less toll on health (LaRocco et al., 1980); the evidence even suggests that mortality rates are higher for isolates (Berkman and Syme, 1979). . . .

SELF-ESTRANGEMENT

It takes a little courage to tackle the problem of self-estrangement, an idea whose scope and subtle resonances pose a formidable analytic challenge. A modicum of clarity can be generated if we distinguish three conceptions of self-estrangement: in alliterative language, these are (1) the "despised" self; (2) the "disguised" self; and (3) the "detached" self.

The first of these refers essentially to low self-esteem, to a negatively evaluated discrepancy between the person's preferred ideal and the perceived actual self. This usage is common both in clinical psychology and in sociological social psychology (Gegas, 1982)—but it is of minor importance here, since it is not a version of self-estrangement that is historically associated with sociological interests in alienation.

The notion of a "disguised" self is more *apropos* and more complicated. As one might guess from the label, it has a strong affinity with the Marxian conception of self-estrangement—in particular with the "false consciousness" feature of that conception. In one sense or another, the disguised self involves a "deprivation of awareness" (Touraine, 1973:201)—e.g., the failure to realize one's truly human capabilities, or one's true interests, or one's true feelings (to be, as the saying has it, "out of touch" with one's feelings—as for example, with an overprotective unconsciously rejecting parent).

The third version of self-estrangement also borrows from Marx, but seeks to avoid the massive problems involved in establishing what the "true" human nature, class interests, or feelings are. The self-estrangement of the "detached" self lies in the disjunction between activity and affect—i.e., the individual's engagement in activities that are not rewarding in themselves (Seeman, 1959; as Marx put it, alienated labor which is "only a *means* for satisfying other needs").

We have witnessed over the past decade a virtual rediscovery of this Marxian concern about alienated labor, though the designation of alienation or self-estrangement is rarely used. This is so, for example, in the vast new literature and new programs on the "quality of work" and "job redesign" (O'Toole, 1974; Kanter, 1977). Much of this program on the quality of work has been effected by non-Marxians (though the Marxian message about the evils of degrading and disengaged labor is central) but without the same assumptions or proposed remedies.

Even in specifically sociological contemporary studies bearing on alienation in work, one often has to supply the alienation marker. Some of the best of these studies have lately been done by Melvin Kohn (1981) showing the positive consequences of engagement in "self-directed" work, meaning nonroutinized substantively complex, independently controlled and unsupervised work. That certainly sounds suspiciously like creative and engaging unalienated work, particularly if one assumes (as I do) that there will be a substantial correspondence between the objective description of job qualities and the person's subjective experience of them.

Similar investigations incorporating measures of work circumstances that mirror the theme of alienated labor can be readily adduced, though under a variety of designations—e.g., job decision latitude (Karasek, 1979); or work attachment (Dubin, 1976). Typically, these measures focus on either the worker's degree of independent control over the work process, or on the level of intrinsic satisfactions that are available in task performance (or both). . . .

We return, thus, to the more grandiose version of this paper's theme (hinted at in the introduction). It is not only that the ideas relating to alienation exhibit a clandestine vitality in the literature. It is that they *cannot* disappear, for the reason that they involve primordial issues in sociological analysis. It is possibly even the case that explicit recognition of the continuities involved in the alienation perspective would make more visible the orderliness of the terrain in which sociologists are actually working (the map having been rather fragmented and lost of late). For, the negative word "alienation," when seen in its positive side and in a broad sense, signifies "membership"—meaning the variety of fundamental ways in which the individual is grounded in society: by way of the sense of efficacy, inclusion, meaningfulness, engagement, trust and value commitment.

REFERENCES

Bell, D. 1976. *The Cultural Contradictions of Capitalism*. New York: Basic Books.
Cantril, H. 1941. *The Psychology of Social Movements*. New York: John Wiley.

Cousins, N. 1979. *Anatomy of an Illness*. New York: W. W. Norton.

Dubin, R., R. A. Hedley, and T. C. Taveggia. 1976. "Attachment to work," pp. 281–341 in R. Dubin (ed.), *Handbook of Work, Organizations and Society*. Chicago: Rand McNally.

Fischer, C. S. 1982. *To Dwell Among Friends: Personal Networks in Town and City*. Chicago: University of Chicago Press.

Gegas, V. 1982. "The self-concept." pp. 1–33 in R. H. Turner and J. F. Short, Jr. (eds.), *Annual Review of Sociology* Vol. 8. Palo Alto, Calif.: Annual Reviews.

Gulick, J. 1973. "Urban Anthropology," pp. 979–1029 in John G. Honigman (ed.), *Handbook of Social and Cultural Anthropology*. Chicago: Rand McNally.

Gurin, P., G. Gurin, and B. M. Morrison. 1978. "Personal and ideological aspects of internal and external control." *Social Psychology* 41:275–96.

Israel, J. 1971. *Alienation: from Marx to Modern Sociology*. Boston: Allyn and Bacon.

Kanter, R. M. 1977. *Men and Women of the Corporation*. New York: Basic Books.

Karasek, R. A., Jr. 1979. "Job demands, job decision lattitude and mental strains: Implications for job redesign." *Administrative Science Quarterly* 24:285–308.

Kohn, M. L. 1981. "Personality, occupation and social stratification: A frame of reference," pp. 267–91 in Donald J. Treiman and Robert V. Robinson (eds.), *Research in Stratification and Mobility: A Research Manual*. Vol. 1. Greenwich, Conn.:JAI Press.

Langer, E. J., and J. Rodin. 1976. "The effects of choice and enhanced personal responsibility for the aged: A field experiment in an institutional setting." *Journal of Personality and Social Psychology* 34:191–198.

Lee, A. M. 1972. "An obituary for alienation." *Social Problems* 20:121–129.

Lefcourt, H. 1980. *Advances and Innovations in Locus of Control Research*. New York: Academic Press.

McHugh, P. 1968. *Defining the Situation: The Organization of Meaning in Social Interaction*. New York: Bobbs-Merrill.

O'Toole, J. (ed.). 1974. *Work and the Quality of Life*. Cambridge, Mass.: M.I.T. Press.

Parsons, T. 1968. "Durkheim, Emile" pp. 311–320 in David L. Sills (ed.), *International Encyclopedia of the Social Sciences*. New York: Macmillan and Free Press.

Platt, G. M. 1980. "Thoughts on a theory of collective action: Language, affect and ideology in revolution" pp. 69–94 in Mel Albin (ed.). *New Directions in Psychohistory*. Lexington, Mass.: Lexington Books.

Portes, A. 1971. "On the logic of postfactum explanations: The hypothesis of lower-class frustration as a cause of leftist radicalism." *Social Forces* 59:26–44.

Rodin, J. and E. J. Langer. 1977. "Long-term effects of a control-relevant intervention with the institutionalized aged." *Journal of Personality and Social Psychology* 35:897–902.

Sampson, E. E. 1976. Social Psychology and Contemporary Society. New York: John Wiley.

Seeman, M. 1959. "On the meaning of alienation." *American Sociological Review* 24:783–791.

———. 1972a. "Alienation and engagement," pp. 467–527 in A. Campbell and P. E. Converse (eds.), *The Human Meaning of Social Change*. New York: Russell Sage.

———, and J. W. Evans. 1962. "Alienation and learning in a hospital setting." *American Sociological Review* 27:772–783.

Seligman, M. E. 1975. *Helplessness*. San Francisco: W. H. Freeman.

Sennett, R., and J. Cobb. 1972. *The Hidden Injuries of Class*. New York: Vintage.

Strickland, B. R. 1978. "Internal-external expectancies and health-related behaviors." *Journal of Consulting and Clinical Psychology* 46:1192–1211.

Taylor, M. C., and E. J. Walsh. 1979. "Explanations of black self-esteem: Some empirical tests." *Social Psychology Quarterly* 42:242–253.

Touraine, K. 1967. "L'alienation de l'ideologie a l'analyse." *Sociologie du Travail,* 9:192–201.

Turner, R. H., and L. M. Killian. 1972. *Collective Behavior.* Englewood Cliffs, N.J.: Prentice-Hall.

Reading 5

Alone: Yearning for Companionship in America

Louise Bernikow

Jasper Evian is the pen name of a New York author, divorced 10 years ago. His daughter moved with his former wife to California, and Jasper's longing for his child is constant and dull, like a toothache. In spite of a web of connections to friends, business associates and transient lovers, Jasper suddenly has begun waking up at 4 in the morning consumed by loneliness. "My ambition," he says, "is wholly personal now. I can't understand people pursuing worldly success. All I want to do is fall in love."

Linda, a Dallas bank executive, is driving home on the freeway. She has had a busy day at the office, handled a tricky negotiation, lunched with a colleague, dined with clients. It took years to achieve her current position as the highest-placed woman in the bank. She plans to work at home on Sunday, but she still thinks of Sundays as family days and being alone then is like being a dateless teen-ager on Saturday night. "I've become a workaholic because I'm so lonely," she admits privately.

For several years, drugs were Antonio Rico Harris's best friends. He started smoking marijuana and snorting cocaine, moved on to smoking cocaine and taking angel dust. At Tuum Est, a drug-rehabilitation center on the beach in Venice, Calif., Antonio, 20, puts his hands through his groomed Afro and stretches a basketball-player body on a couch. He has been without drugs for seven months. "People look at me and say, 'What's wrong? You look mad.' I'm not. It just feels like I'm the only person in the world."

As early as the 1830s, Alexis de Tocqueville wrote about the loneliness of Americans, describing the citizens of this country as "locked in the solitude of their own hearts.'' The dictionary defines loneliness as ''an absence of companionship or society,'' but anyone who has ever been lonely—and that's just about everyone—knows that it is not quite so simple. People can be lonely in isolation or lonely in a crowd; lonely because they have no one to be with or lonely because they are with someone they can no longer reach.

Yet Americans are also more than a little ambivalent about loneliness. We view it as something to admire as much as avoid. You can hardly say ''cowboy,'' that venerated American archetype, without adding ''lonesome.'' The private eye, another idealized American hero, is almost always a loner. Schoolchildren are taught to respect Thoreau for going without ''companionship or society'' at Walden Pond. ''The courage to stand alone'' is a long-standing American virtue. Self-made men who battle to victory in business without aid or comfort are pointed out for emulation. (Women are not as often praised, in our history, for going it alone.)

A growing number of social scientists and mental health professionals are now studying contemporary American loneliness. Some say that we are more lonely than in the past; others argue that we just think we are. More persuasive is the evidence that the physical and emotional consequences of loneliness pose greater dangers than anyone thought. Dr. Stephen E. Goldston, director of the Office of Prevention at the National Institute of Mental Health in Washington, an organization not known for its interest in subjects of merely philosophical value, believes that ''persistent and severe'' loneliness can lead to alcoholism, drug abuse and suicide. Recently, his office convened a conference to raise the question of whether such loneliness can be prevented or cured.

And loneliness may have a larger impact on society than we have realized. ''We must do something about any circumstances in which a person can say, 'No one knows who I am or cares to know,' '' says Dr. Philip G. Zimbardo, a psychologist at Stanford University. ''For anyone in such a predicament can turn into a vandal, an assassin or a terrorist.'' The most recent example that comes to mind is that of John W. Hinckley Jr., the wandering loner who pined for the love of a movie star and shot a President just to get her attention.

Current research reveals that the people who are loneliest don't necessarily fit the popular stereotypes. Adolescents appear to be more plagued by loneliness than anyone else; older people, surprisingly, may be less so. Homosexuals may be no more prone to loneliness than heterosexuals. Success seems to offer scant protection against loneliness—especially for women. Geography has little to do with it either. Social psychologists Carin Rubenstein and Phillip Shaver surveyed several rural communities and large metropolises and found no less loneliness in the small friendly towns than in the big, unfriendly cities.

It is not that people have become more isolated in any tangible way. On the contrary, electronic communications and jet-age transportation have made it possible to stay in closer contact than ever before. Rather, there is a sense that our connections are somehow inadequate. The cause of this dissatisfaction is elusive.

To some extent, experts say, it has to do with the ascendance of a culture that places so much emphasis on acquiring possessions and status that most people devote little time or energy to forming and maintaining relationships. Exaggerated expectations created by the idealized versions of life on television, in films and in the scores of "self-help" books on the best-seller lists may also play a role. And because of increasing freedom and mobility, ties to spouses, family, church and community unravel more easily.

The America de Tocqueville traveled through was a rural country in which the ties holding people together were essentially those of family and community. Some of the current alarm stems from looking at the 1980 census and seeing how complete the progressive dissolution of those ties now seems to be. More people live alone today than ever before: almost one fourth of the population. Within this group are a large number of people under 40 who, for a variety of reasons, have chosen not to marry. The women in this group are often the first women in their families to live alone. A generation earlier, they would have become housewives; now they are working or going to school instead. Pursuing a career undoubtedly brings many women new fulfillment. But it may also take a toll that, until recently, has gone largely unexamined.

Many of those who live alone are divorced, separated or widowed, and the rising number of people in this category is also a cause for concern. America's divorce rate is not only the highest in the world, it is also the highest it has ever been: One out of every two marriages now fails. One out of five children lives with only one parent. One out of eight children in a two-parent family lives with one natural parent and one stepparent.

Because life expectancy is increasing, there are more people over 65 than ever before. Currently, they make up 11.3 percent of the population. More than a third of this group are widows, many living alone on limited incomes. In the past, people over 65 with children and grandchildren lived with them or near them. Today, that is uncommon.

Economic conditions have made matters even worse. However alienated people may feel from their work, those who don't have it are likely to be much more lonely than those who do. When mental-health experts point to the stress that unemployment puts on individuals and families, they talk about depression and self-blame, which often accompany feelings of loneliness. In Cleveland, for example, the population has declined 23.6 percent in the past 10 years because of dwindling economic opportunity. Joe Stevens, driving his cab between the airport and a major downtown hotel, says Cleveland has become an especially lonely place for him. One son moved to Houston two years ago and another is planning to go soon. Neither wanted to leave, but neither could find work at home.

Ordinary people cope with loneliness in ordinary ways. They keep the radio or the television on for company. They smile back at the anchorman on the evening news when he says, "See you tomorrow." For companionship and society, they turn to soap operas that offer the illusion of involvement in other people's daily lives. People take tranquilizers and go to bed, read or go to a movie, join churches, evangelical movements or even cults, buy things they don't really want, go to doctors more often than necessary and dial the weather report just to hear a friendly voice. They think loneliness is to be lived with, like the weather. They don't think they are in danger.

Dr. James J. Lynch, a specialist in psychosomatic disease at the University of Maryland School of Medicine, thinks they are wrong. Loneliness is dangerous, he believes, especially to the heart. A broken heart, Dr. Lynch argues, is not a metaphor. His 1977 book, ''The Broken Heart: The Medical Consequences of Loneliness,'' made frightening connections between lack of human companionship and heart disease. A nurse's hand can slow a patient's pounding pulse; the simple routine of pulse-taking often calms arrhythmic heartbeats. People often develop heart ailments when they lose love or companionship. ''The rise of human loneliness,'' he concludes, ''may be one of the most serious sources of disease in the 20th century.''

Since then, Dr. Lynch has been studying other ''loneliness diseases,'' especially hypertension and migraine headaches. In each case, he has found connections between loneliness and illness. His hypertensive patients experienced a steep rise in blood pressure whenever they spoke to anyone. ''These people are out of contact with what is going on. It's like a baby crying inside an adult. Where there is real communication,'' he adds, ''there is no physiological disruption.''

''Pain turned inwards,'' is Dr. Lynch's medical definition of loneliness, and ''ruptured patterns of discourse.'' We are experiencing an epidemic of this, he says, and you see it ''especially in self-destructive diseases like cigarette smoking and drinking.''

Dr. Robert N. Bellah, a Berkeley sociologist, sees the epidemic as a continuation of national tradition, intensified by recent history. A team of interviewers under his direction has been asking people what they believe in and finding that we still hold certain truths to be self-evident.

''Personal freedom, autonomy and independence are the highest values for Americans,'' Dr. Bellah says. ''You're responsible for yourself. We place a high value on being left alone, on not being interfered with. The most important thing is to be able to take care of yourself. As soon as possible, we believe, a child should take care of itself. It's illegitimate to depend on another human being.'' People no longer have communities to which they are irrevocably tied, Dr. Bellah adds. ''Communities are chosen, not given. They're brittle, fragile, with a tremendous turnover.'' And few people are happy with this situation. In fact, Americans are awash in nostalgia for old-fashioned families and small, tightknit communities. Individualism is ''a terrifying demand,'' Dr. Bellah says. Throughout the country, he finds, ''there is an element of loneliness not far below the surface.''

There are profits to be made from all this loneliness. The promise of companionship and society sells everything from banking services ("You have a friend at Chase Manhattan") to real estate (a road sign outside Houston advertising a condominium promises, "You won't be a stranger for long"). The telephone company's advertising aims directly at the lonely. If you want to "reach out and touch someone," you'll have to pay for a long-distance telephone call.

A large and growing industry promises romantic companionship for a price. Increasing numbers of single people are willing to pay $400 or more to subscribe to video dating services. *Intro,* the first national singles magazine, claims an initial circulation of 100,000. To serve an obviously growing market, a black magazine, *Chocolate Singles,* has recently been launched as well. In New York, Dr. Martin V. Gallatin, a sociologist, teaches an adult-education course on "Lover Shopping at Bloomingdale's" and is organizing a lecture called "Be Your Own Matchmaker."

Such high-priced courses and the video dating operations are popular largely because they promise efficiency. Why waste time wading through the unsuitables life turns up when for a few dollars more you can preselect your potential partners? This logic appeals to Frank Matticola, who came to Two's Company, a Houston video dating service, because, he says, he had his "priorities." Two's Company recently opened its doors in a complex not far from the fashionable Galleria area. It's in a one-story row of new buildings and looks as fresh and spare as a dentist's office. Frank is 36, twice divorced, a bit overweight, with a receding hairline and an open face. In his three months in Houston, where he moved from New Jersey, he has taken care of two priorities. First, he got a job as a production superintendent in the oil industry. Second, he found an apartment at Tennis World, a singles complex right near the Two's Company office. This is his first day off in 10 weeks and he has come to take care of his third priority.

He wants "someone to share my free time with, which is very little." As Frank talks, his face softens, the coldness in his language gives way. Frank doesn't want anyone to know it, but he is lonely. Sheepishly, he makes what he thinks is an unfashionable confession: "I miss being married. You get home early and you'd like to have someone there. It's harder after you have been married."

JoAnn is filling out her application in another room. She is 33, has springy blonde curls and half-giggles whenever she speaks. This subject makes her nervous. She has just moved to Houston from Oklahoma, where she was a sales representative. "I didn't know one person," she says, "and I traveled the whole state. I'd come back into Oklahoma City on Friday night and I'd be in my apartment, throwing myself on the floor sobbing, until Monday morning, when I left to go back out on the road." She asked for a transfer. Now, she says, "all the guys I work with are old and married. I just want somebody else to be part of my life. I've thought of adopting as a single parent. I do want more than I have now, whether it be a child or a husband."

She thinks she knows what kind of man would make her feel less alone: "A nice guy with a sense of humor, someone sensitive." Other women enrolled in the service have filled out questionnaires in which they, too, talk about "sensitivity," "being able to express his feelings" and "warmth" as important qualities in a man.

"But JoAnn," her friend Barbara, who has also come to enroll, interrupts, 'you would never date a man who makes less than you, would you?"

"No."

Therein lies a cross fire between the sexes, a stalemate in expectations that explains, in part, why so many men and women who say they are lonely and looking for companionship never seem to find it. JoAnn wants a "New Man," a sensitive, nurturing fellow, and an "Old Man," a powerful breadwinner, at the same time. Frank wants a woman who will be there when he gets home, but most of the women he will meet through Two's Company are professional and ambitious and likely to be working late at their own offices. The manager of Two's Company says that most of the men who go there prefer "independent women"—no "born-again housewives." But further probing reveals that while they may not want to pay all the bills, they are still uncomfortable with many of the consequences of female independence.

Dr. Sol Landau sees the same stalemate at his Mid-Life Services Foundation, an organization he has just set up in an office building near Dadeland, in South Miami. A hearty, expansive man, Dr. Landau had been a practicing rabbi for 17 years. Now, he mostly counsels people in "midlife" and finds the lack of companionship between husbands and wives a direct consequence of the women's movement and the inability of men to change. "Men need to be mentors," he says, "and they're married to women who now need to throw off their mentors. The men I see are threatened by their wives working or going to school. They can still only function from the throne."

Unable to attach themselves seriously to someone else, often because men and women don't know what to expect of each other anymore, a lot of people immerse themselves in their work. The most acute loneliness Dr. Landau sees is in "the most successful men, workaholics, men unconnected to their personal lives." But an increasing number of women now fall into this category as well.

In Houston, Dr. Dale Hill's therapy practice is made up almost exclusively of professional women who see loneliness as their greatest problem. In rural Massachusetts, Dr. Frances Lippmann, a clinical psychologist, says the same: "The women I see still feel that deep loneliness about meeting somebody, no matter how successful they are."

When researchers note that women say they are lonely far more often than men do, they interpret this, in part, as a greater willingness on the part of women to talk about feelings, but it also suggests different expectations of companionship and intimacy. In a recent survey of adolescents prepared for the National Institute of Mental Health, 61.3 percent of the girls, as opposed to 46.5 percent of the boys, said they were lonely.

When the Berkeley sociologist Claude Fischer asked adults whom they talked with about personal matters and whose opinion they considered in making important decisions, he found that women, married or not, were likely to have several confidants. Many unmarried men said the same, but a substantial number indicated that they had no one in whom they could confide. The most significant difference, however, was that married men usually named only their wives as confidants. And the older a man was, the less likely he was to have a friend or relative in whom to confide.

Adolescents, more than others, complain that they feel as if the world were away for the weekend and never coming back. No one to talk to. No one who cares. Dr. Harvey Greenberg, a specialist in adolescent psychiatry and a professor at the Albert Einstein College of Medicine in New York, believes loneliness in adolescents stems from ''a breakdown of family, the fact that there are now lots of only children, lots of older parents and working mothers.'' Some girls are getting pregnant to ''have a baby to take care of as protection against loneliness.''

Although a large measure of loneliness is normal in adolescence—''the specific psychological task of adolescence is mourning the loss of the omnipotent parent''—Dr. Greenberg finds today's teen-agers ''encouraged by a garbage culture with no values, nothing to latch onto; they're preoccupied with themselves. Kids need a mentor or patron. Teachers used to do this, but they do it less now because they're worn down, angry, bitter and paranoid.'' Dr. Greenberg adds that loneliness in adolescents is an important factor in the increase in teen-age suicide, which has risen 300 percent over the last 25 years.

The elderly, on the other hand, may not be as badly off as we expect. A Harris poll conducted last year showed that 65 percent of nonelderly persons considered loneliness ''a serious problem'' for the aged. But only 13 percent of people over 65 agreed. This may have something to do with lessening expectations in old age. But it may also show, according to Dr. Anne Peplau, a psychologist at the University of California at Los Angeles, that ''older adults value privacy and independence. They view living alone as an achievement rather than a sign of rejection by others.'' Friends, she says, are more important to older people, in terms of companionship, than children or relatives. Indeed, several studies have found greater loneliness among single elderly people living with relatives than among those who live alone or with friends.

Dr. Peplau, who has been studying loneliness and aging, finds gender differences significant in terms of how people handle loneliness. ''Men rely on wives and girlfriends for social relationships, for intimacy. If their wives die before they do, men are in trouble. Women usually have both a heterosexual relationship and a reliance on friends. They seem to keep making friends throughout the life cycle. If friends die or move away, women replace them. Men don't as often.''

Dr. Peplau thinks women have greater social skills and are better able than men to adjust to widowhood and old age. Four women at Wynmoor Village, a retirement community in Cocoanut Creek, Fla.—all widowed and in their 60's—don't necessarily agree. It's small comfort to them to know that men in their circumstances stand a greater chance of becoming ill or dying.

"I walk into the apartment, close the door and something happens to me," Honey Albert says. "I feel nauseous. It's not because I don't have friends. I can be with you all day," she tells Gloria Winetsky, "and I'm still lonely."

Gloria Winetsky shifts on the couch. Her experience is different. She is not lonely and she thinks that a large part of the reason is that she was less dependent on her husband when he was alive than her friends were on theirs. She arrived in Florida thinking, "Here is where you pick up your life," and she has done it. She is self-reliant and generally pleased with the quality of her friendships.

Shirley Moses, an energetic, dark-haired woman, is pouring coffee. "Your children don't take away your loneliness," she says, "only your contemporaries." But her contemporaries don't seem able to do it, in fact. "I play cards with eight people and none of them gives a damn about me," she admits. "You can't ever find a place for yourself on Sunday." The others agree.

"The worst loneliness is going out with couples," Shirley Moses says. "You feel part of you is missing." As a result, these women stay away from the organized activities at Wynmoor Village that attract couples. Married women, they say, don't want them around. They're guarding their husbands.

When Honey Albert moved to Florida, she said to herself: "I'm not going to spend the rest of my life alone in an apartment." She went to the swimming pool and introduced herself to everyone. One of the women laughs as Honey Albert tells of dashed expectations and failed resolve. Didn't she put up signs, too, inviting people to coffee? Honey denies it.

Listening to the widows argue, it is clear how easily discouraged anyone can be when attempts to break out of loneliness find no support; how much simpler it might seem to resign yourself to a life alone in your apartment.

Our increasing loneliness is not only a yearning for companionship. People feel alone when they don't belong to something larger, when they don't feel connected to a "family" or a "community."

"A lot of men not raising their kids," says Dr. Paul Lippmann, a New England psychoanalyst, "are so lonely for those kids, but they have all kinds of tricks not to think about it." Although people often marry or have children to avoid loneliness, family therapists are concerned about the widespread inability of parents to be intimate with either each other or their children. Guy Berley, a family therapist at the Johnson County Mental Health Facility outside Kansas City, Kan., calls it "distancing behavior"—children putting themselves at a remove from their parents, and parents from their children. Working mothers, however, don't seem to him to cause or experience increased loneliness in their families. "It can be a good thing," he says. "The women are making a needed economic contribution to the family and they feel better about themselves."

Working has traditionally offered opportunities for companionship and society, but increasing numbers of people work alone and some suffer immensely because of it. This was made clear one recent sunny Sunday morning in Houston. Volunteers were answering the crisis-line telephone in a small, partitioned office. Most of the volunteers had come to work at the crisis line because they were new to town and this was their way of being around other people.

A man called, weeping. He didn't give his name. His wife, he said, had left him because "I blew up and hit her." The volunteer on the telephone suggested he find someone to talk to, perhaps a friend at work. He was silent. Then he said, "I can't. Where I work I stare at dials all day. There's no one around."

Gilley's bar is just outside Houston, in Pasadena. In the movie "Urban Cowboy," John Travolta enjoyed a lot of companionship and society at Gilley's, competitive though it was. Now someone at the door takes a few dollars from you and you bump almost immediately into a row of video games. You can't buddy up to the bar—there is no space around it—but you can hide out alone with Pac-Man. Or you can hover around the edges of the dance floor while the band plays "Cotton-Eyed Joe"—which is what Bob White is doing.

Trim, wearing high-heeled boots, tight shirt and jeans, White looks like a lonesome cowboy but is, in fact, an enterprising furniture trucker out of North Carolina. He has a wife back home and he sees her about every two weeks. Nights on the road, he goes stir-crazy with loneliness. "I lay up in the Days Inn Motel with the TV on and I can't stop thinking about my first wife leaving me and maybe this one's going to leave and I've got to get out and be around where there's people." Why, then, stay on the road? "Because I wouldn't make even $5 an hour back in North Carolina."

Thomas J. Peters is wearing running shoes and swiveling back and forth in his chair. He has a small office on the third floor of the Stanford Business School, where he lectures, and he knows a lot about loneliness in American business. The "unbelievable and deep-felt need to be part of something is rarely met in the working world," he says. The few corporations that do meet this need are the best-run companies in America. The "magic," he says, "at I.B.M., Hewlett-Packard or Procter & Gamble comes from creating a sense of community or family."

Peters thinks the Japanese do much better at making workers feel part of a community at work. As a result, "you've got Honda workers racing around straightening out windshield wipers in their free time while General Motors workers sit silently watching a piece of junk go by and don't do anything about it because they know they won't be listened to."

"Look at middle management in the auto industry," Peters says. "There are five layers between the first line worker and the chairman at Toyota, and there are 17 at Ford. Middle management has no job. You're sitting there manipulating numbers, going bugeyed looking at the computer display, worrying about abstractions like profits and writing reports to ace out the people next to you. It's bound to be a god-awful lonely existence."

Companies create a sense of family, Peters says, "with hokey stuff, Mickey Mouse things like company picnics." Like Tupperware holding a weekly ceremony in which almost all its saleswomen win awards. Or the I.B.M. sales branch that staged an event at the Meadowlands in New Jersey, the sales force running through the players' entrance, their names in lights on the big board. "I.B.M.," Peters says, "probably gives its employees more community within the corporate environment than most of us have outside where we work. You move from I.B.M., San Jose, to I.B.M., Armonk, N.J., and you probably don't know you've moved, except for the temperature difference."

People concerned about loneliness talk in terms of disease. They speak of a nationwide "epidemic." They search for a cure. But the desert seems a more appropriate metaphor. And out there in the desert of eroding families and unfulfilled hunger to connect with other people, oases are being discovered or built.

Crystal Lugo found one. She lived in a section of East Los Angeles that, she says, "was all retired people. There was no one to talk to." She watched soap operas and talked on the telephone. Then her marriage broke up and she was left with a 4-month-old daughter. A social worker told her about the community's Displaced Homemaker's Program. Now, she is learning office skills, but she is also learning how to be with people. "The people in the program are all used to staying home. We're scared. We don't have any confidence." This is a precarious solution because the program, federally funded, is in danger of being cut next year.

Alan Leavitt, program chief of mental-health services for the city of San Francisco, says his city is "the last refuge of the lonely" and points out that San Francisco has the highest mortality rate from cirrhosis of the liver in the country. If alcoholism and drug abuse are good indicators of loneliness, he is right. But Toby Marotta finds an oasis in San Francisco.

In little more than a decade, Marotta says, the city has gone from being one of the country's loneliest places to being "a community replacing the family for gay men. A dozen years ago, there were few social institutions apart from sex-oriented ones, the bars and bathhouses, almost all private businesses, illicit." A homosexual man arriving in San Francisco would go to the Tenderloin, which is like Times Square. "He'd feel despicable," Marotta says, "he'd be surrounded by ugliness. Today, he would go to the Castro."

Marotta, a trim, earnest, light-haired man, speaks as though he were lecturing at Harvard, from which he did in fact, receive a doctoral degree in government and education. He is the author of several books relating to homosexuality. The Castro (the neighborhood around Castro Street), he explains, is a real community. The bars are bright and airy, with plate-glass windows. Although they used to be "places where you went to score, like singles bars," now they exude almost a family atmosphere. Patrons know the bartenders. The crowd is the same every week. They offer low-priced meals.

In the community around the bars, Marotta says, "connections are no longer solely sexual.'' He cites a long list of institutions, beginning with musical choruses and ending with an array of self-help groups. The Castro is thriving in difficult economic times, partly because of the high proportion of men who, Marotta says, ''have money, mobility and no dependents.''

Because they tend to be more sexually active than heterosexuals, fewer homosexual men suffer the loneliness that comes from never being physically intimate with another person, according to Marotta. ''Gay culture facilitates sexual connections,'' he says, although he admits that homosexual life can leave another kind of emptiness, ''the loneliness that comes from not being known, from being unable to sustain emotional relationships.''

Mildred Murray has found yet another kind of oasis. A bustling 68-year-old woman, she has been divorced three times and is not interested in another marriage. A year ago, she was living in a trailer on property owned by one of her three sons. ''I thought I had it licked by the tail,'' she says, ''but I started feeling very lonely. All my friends died off or I just lost touch with them.'' She heard about a new program in southern California matching senior citizens with each other as housemates. Gene was a widower living in his own home in Van Nuys. Neither of them had ever thought about such an unconventional arrangement, but they decided to try it. Mildred Murray asked permission of each of her three sons.

The night she moved in, she lay staring at the bedroom door. ''I knew he was clean, but I didn't know if he was a moral person.'' A year later, she can't imagine living any other way. Sometimes, she makes Gene's bed and cooks his meals. She likes visiting her children or taking a trip and ''not having to report to him.'' She is not lonely, but many of her friends are. ''One of them's so lonely, she's at the senior citizens' center all day long. I,'' Mildred Murray boasts, ''am always just in and out of there.''

The people creating such oases have several things in common. They don't deny their loneliness, they don't castigate themselves for being alone, and they recognize the need to build bridges to others, rather than waiting for their loneliness simply to go away. Too many of us, however, are ambivalent about the spaces between us. We want independence and a faithful lover, we want the support of a family but not its demands, we want a community but we don't want to conform to its codes.

Historically, too, we swing from one extreme to the other. The reigning ideal of the 1950s was the family as a self-contained society. In the 60s, it was a group culture. In the 70s, beating a retreat from so much togetherness, the cultural ideal became the solitary individual pursuing his or her own best career and being his or her own best friend. The pendulum is swinging again. The language of the 80s tends to be a rather cold language of connection. We speak of ''networking'' and ''interfacing,'' but underneath that we're really looking for people we can depend on, people who will laugh at our jokes and listen to our nightmares. We don't really want to interface with our networks. We want to cuddle our grandmothers and take walks with our lovers. Above all, we want someone to talk to.

Reading 6

Rationality, Meaning, and Self-management: Success Manuals, 1950–1980

Nicole Woolsey Biggart

University of California, Davis

One of the most widespread themes in Max Weber's work is rationalization, the increasing application of reason and technique to social structures and relations which accompanied the movement from traditional to industrialized society in the West (Eisen, 1978; Kalberg, 1980). Modern organization theory referred to as "neo-Weberian" has focused mainly on the formal structural effects of rationalization, usually by developing Weber's ideal-type of bureaucracy (March and Simon, 1958; Perrow, 1979) or by exposing its limits (Bennis, 1966; Gouldner, 1954; Merton, 1957). Less attention has been paid to the idea of rationality as a methodical way of life and as the systematization of meaning patterns (Schlucter, 1979:14). It is clear, however, that Weber was concerned with the subjective understandings of individuals living and working within impersonal structures created for reasons of economic efficiency, rather than for human needs or moral purpose. In his political writings, for example, Weber (1921) described bureaucracy as an "iron cage" in which people feel trapped by rational arrangements over which they have no control. The "iron cage"—or "the system" as many people call it—seems immutable and appears to define all possibilities for meaningful action.

The rationalization of the workplace (and society at large) that Weber observed at the beginning of the 20th century is largely complete in the industrialized West. What have been the implications of this process, not just for such organizational attributes as specialization and hierarchy, but for workers' experience in a society dominated by large enterprises and an ethic of objective rationality?[1] In this paper I explore one indicator of the impact of rationalization on work life: popular success manuals published in the United States from 1950 to 1980. "How to succeed" books are a useful barometer of changing trends in the popularly approved routes to meaning and success, and were available in the United States even before the Industrial Revolution. Artifacts of popular culture, including popular books, allow social scientists unobtrusive entrance into dominant social meanings (Webb and

[1]Several theorists have attempted to clarify Weber's various usages of "rationality" and the types of rationality to which he referred. In this paper I am concerned with the historical movement toward social action that is instrumental, occurs in a means-end calculus, and has the properties of formal reasoning. It is most often referred to as "formal" (Eisen, 1978), or "objective" rationality (Kalberg, 1980).

Reprinted with permission from *Social Problems* 30(3) (February 1983):298–311 by The Society for the Study of Social Problems and by the author.

Weick, 1979), as well as the opportunity to study how social understandings assume practical forms. Best-selling success manuals are both an indication of what workers, primarily middle-class men,[2] perceive as their opportunities for fulfillment, and evidence of the techniques by which they believe occupational success may be achieved.

Four formulas in best-selling advice books have captured the attention of a mass audience of middle-class U.S. workers since 1950: (1) success-through-striving, (2) entrepreneurial schemes, (3) manipulation techniques, and (4) displacement of the success goal. These four themes directly reflect the socially approved work opportunities defined by an advanced industrial system; they show no evidence of protest against what Marxist scholars have described as an alienated work life (Aronowitz, 1973; Braverman, 1975). Furthermore, these manuals demonstrate that workers have internalized instrumental rationality—in other words, they view themselves as objects to be controlled and manipulated. As a result, workers apply to themselves the techniques and routines of modern organizational activity; that is, they "self-manage."

In this paper I first briefly summarize the changing ideals of success in the United States from the colonial period until the Second World War, and the relation of these ideals to then-existing socio-economic structures. Then I describe those success manuals that have been overwhelmingly popular since 1950, outlining their different models of success and formulas for achievement. Finally, I suggest how success formulas help explain the experience of middle-class workers.

IMAGES OF SUCCESS: 1750–1950

Success books are a uniquely North American expression of a belief in self-reliance, the value of education, and hard work in achieving mobility.[3] Although advice books have been a popular genre in the United States since Benjamin Franklin's *Poor Richard's Almanac* (1958) first appeared in 1732, both the messages and images have changed considerably since then. Numerous literary critics and social historians have plotted these changes, often by examining heroes in popular fiction, as well as advice books (Cawelti, 1965; Chenoweth, 1974; Huber, 1971; Kennedy,

---

[2]Most success books, until recently, were written specifically for men. With the exception of what I describe as "striving" books, which addressed men and women in all statuses, modern success manuals usually speak to persons aspiring to middle-class positions. Striving books, however, had the largest sales of all success books and can be presumed to have been read by many middle-class workers, particularly since they stressed middle-class values.

[3]This belief is North American and not shared in the same way by European cultures where a feudal history of ascription and rigid class structures still tempers the way in which people seek and define success. Upwardly mobile Europeans obscure their lowly origins, while North Americans are likely to advertise them as evidence of personal superiority (Cawelti, 1965:2).

1949; Weiss, 1969; Wyllie, 1954).[4] These studies reveal three success models, which overlap chronologically: the Protestant ethic, the character ethic, and the personality ethic.

1.) *The Protestant ethic* dominated cultural ideas from the colonial period to the early 19th century. Success meant status, virtue, and wealth, and the route to its achievement was economic restraint and piety. Worldly success and religious practice were inseparable. Material riches were a sign of God's favor, not evidence of individual superiority. The model person was "the man of action who was also the man of God" (Brooks, 1958:5). This image "assumed a static, hierarchical social order within which success was the attainment of a respectable competence in this world and eternal salvation in the world to come" (Cawelti, 1965:4). This image was also consonant with the early capitalism of a mercantile and agrarian elite. The accumulation of material goods was not for consumption or pleasure, however. Rather, as stewards of God's bounty, people were obligated to conserve and multiply wealth through savings and reinvestment. Weber's own study of this cultural ideal, *The Protestant Ethic and the Spirit of Capitalism* (1958), demonstrates how Puritan values provided meaning for self-denial to an emerging middle class, while simultaneously serving the growth of entrepreneurial capitalism.

2.) *The character ethic,* which was first articulated in the early 19th century and became dominant by 1900, was a transformation of the Protestant ethic. It suggested that getting ahead was a matter of cultivating one's self, developing character traits conducive to entrepreneurship such as foresight, integrity, and good judgment. Success was more narrowly defined to mean wealth; the achievement of social status and salvation were secondary goals. Success was no longer a signal from God; instead, wealth was viewed as the reward of individual accomplishment and industry, not inherited capability or heavenly favor (Wyllie, 1954:170). Typical expressions of the character ethic were "rags-to-riches" stories, self-improvement manuals, and biographical narratives of heroes who, against great odds, put together industrial empires. The formula for success, in addition to developing character, was initiative, competitiveness, and perseverance. In its 19th century formulation the character ethic promoted individual entrepreneurship, but with increasing industrialization the philosophy of self-improvement began to mold itself to the opportunities and needs of the large corporation. By the turn of the century, an acceptable alternative to entrepreneurial success became working one's way up the corporate hierarchy (Cawelti, 1965:169; Wyllie, 1954:168).

3.) *The personality ethic,* which took hold in the 1930s, also evolved from its predecessor (Huber, 1971). Like the character ethic, it defined success as wealth, but it developed further formulas for achievement in large-scale corporate and

---

[4]Wyllie (1954) provides a useful bibliography of primary sources. See Chenoweth (1974) for secondary sources on the analysis and history of success manuals.

government workplaces. But where the character ethic stressed effort and initiative, the personality ethic promoted the selling of the self. During the Depression, it became apparent that hard work, while important, was not enough. Dale Carnegie's *How to Win Friends and Influence People* (1936), the first important book to espouse the personality ethic, offered formulas for making people likable and charmingly persuasive. It dominated the success literature for years, eventually selling over 7 million copies, and was still in print in 1982. The personality ethic also completed the redefinition of success-oriented behavior from self-denial to indulgence.[5] The stimulation of consumption was important to the development of domestic markets (Bell, 1976; Ewen, 1976), and modern self-help books moved toward "an overriding emphasis on the pursuit and use of wealth" (Cawelti, 1965:169).

FORMULAS FOR SUCCESS: 1950–1980

The Data

Many books are published each year that offer a formula for success or give advice, but only a handful capture the imagination of a mass audience. I have restricted my analysis to hard-cover books which were best-sellers in the United States between 1950 and 1980; rather than analyze the changes in what was published, I have analyzed the changes in what was sought and read. This assumes that people were reasonably aware of the books' general lines of argument before purchasing them— either because of the title, heresay, or publicity. Sales, undoubtedly, were partly a reflection of promotion budgets, and it has been impossible to correct for this influence. Also, I have not included paperback sales, which are an important indicator of how lasting an influence many works have had, as well as an indication of total "reach." Some books were issued only in paperback, other in hard cover first. Earlier works often had hard-cover editions only. I chose to analyze only hard-cover best sellers, a choice that eliminates difficulties in comparison, but undoubtedly distorts the data somewhat.

I established an arbitrary criterion for a book having achieved a mass audience: any book that was listed on *The New York Times* best-seller list for a least eight weeks I considered to have been sufficiently popular to indicate mass public sentiment. Of the 20,000 to 30,000 new titles published annually in the United States (*Bowker Annual*), only 20 to 40 books achieve this notoriety each year. *The New York Times* compiled their best-seller lists from reports from 125 to 1,400 U.S. bookstores. Typically, 10 books were on the list each week in the non-fiction

---

[5]Lowenthal's (1961) classic "The Triumph of Mass Idols," a content analysis of magazine biographies, showed how publishers during this period moved from stories about "idols of production" to "idols of consumption."

category until 1978, when the list was lengthened to 15 books; for the sake of consistency, I have included only books that were among the top 10. *The New York Times'* lists are similar to the annual best-seller lists compiled by *Publisher's Weekly* since 1950, but include a few more volumes. The inclusion or exclusion of

Table 1   Best-Selling Success Books: 1950–1980 (Arranged by Category)

Success-Through-Striving Books
   The Art of Real Happiness (Peale and Blanton, 1950), 1950[a]
   A Guide to Confident Living (Peale, 1948), 1950
   The Power of Positive Thinking (Peale, 1952), 1952
   TNT: The Power Within You (Bristol, 1954), 1954
   Love or Perish (Blanton, 1956), 1956
   Stay Alive All Your Life (Peale, 1957), 1957
Entrepreneurial Scheme Books
   How I Turned $1,000 Into a Million in Real Estate in My Spare Time (Nickerson, 1959), 1959
   How I Made $2,000,000 in the Stock Market (Darvas, 1960), 1960
   How to Avoid Probate (Dacey, 1965); 1966.
   Anyone Can Make A Million (Shulman, 1966); 1967.
   The Money Game (Smith, 1969), 1969
   You Can Profit From A Monetary Crisis (Browne, 1974) 1974
   How to Prosper During the Coming Bad Years (Ruff, 1979), 1979
   How You Can Become Financially Independent by Investing in Real Estate (Lowry, 1977), 1980
   Crisis Investing (Casey, 1980), 1980
Manipulation Manuals
   Games People Play (Berne, 1964), 1965–67
   Body Language (Fast, 1970), 1970
   I'm OK—You're OK (Harris, 1970), 1972–73
   Winning Through Intimidation (Ringer, 1973), 1975–76
   Power! How to Get It, How to Use It (Korda, 1975), 1975–76
   Looking Out For Number One (Ringer, 1977), 1977–78
Displacement Books
   How to Live 365 Days A Year (Schindler, 1954), 1955–56
   The Peter Principle (Peter and Hull, 1969), 1970
   The Peter Prescription (Peter, 1972), 1972
   TM: Discovering Inner Energy and Overcoming Stress (Bloomfield et al., 1974), 1975
   The Relaxation Response (Benson, 1975), 1976
   How To Be Your Own Best Friend (Berkowitz and Newman, 1973), 1974
   Your Erroneous Zones (Dyer, 1976), 1977
   Pulling Your Own Strings (Dyer, 1978), 1979
   The Sky's The Limit (Dyer, 1980), 1980

[a] Years in parentheses are publication dates. Years after parentheses are dates of appearance on best-seller list for at least eight weeks.

specific books in the categories I define below can be argued, but I believe the general trends in popular interest are discernable.[6]

Thirty books met my criteria for extraordinary popularity (Table 1). Their formulas for success fall generally into four categories, which I call success-through-striving, entrepreneurial schemes, manipulation manuals, and displacement books. The first three categories are descendants of success ideals articulated in earlier periods; the fourth, displacement books, seems to represent a new cultural phenomenon. All, however, reflect contemporary work conditions in U.S. society.

Success-Through-Striving

The personality ethic established by Dale Carnegie in 1936 developed in the years after the Second World War into a "striving" formula. Striving books emphasized the opportunities for financial success, and sometimes organizational status, in the expanding economy after the war. More importantly, they suggested that dreams of success were more important than success itself, and that striving was its own reward (Chenoweth, 1974:138). Norman Vincent Peale and Smiley Blanton's *The Art of Real Happiness* (1950) and Peale's *A Guide to Confident Living* (1948) were best-sellers in 1950 and started a trend in success literature that completely dominated the U.S. market until 1958. Peale's *The Power of Positive Thinking* (1952) outsold every non-fiction book in the mid-fifties except the Bible (Weiss, 1969: 224). Peale preached a secular religion as a basis for success, and emphasized proper outlook rather than hard work. By simply thinking successfully readers could control their fate. "Your life, or mine, is not determined by outward circumstances, but by the thoughts that habitually engage the mind" (Peale and Blanton, 1950:68). "Believe in yourself! Have faith in your abilities! Without a humble but reasonable confidence in your own powers you cannot be successful or happy" (Peale, 1952:1). Striving books often suggested praying for success and, curiously, described prayer as a rational technique. "It is a mistake to think that the laws of efficiency do not apply to prayer" (Peale, 1948:81).

Claude M. Bristol's *TNT: The Power Within You* (1954) preached appropriate outlook also, but relied less on religious authority. "I will—I will—I will—I will! Say this to yourself again and again, and mean it! Look into the mirror and say it."

---

[6]There are five books that I considered including but did not. The first, *How to Succeed in Business Without Really Trying* (Mead, 1952), is a humorous novel consistent with the advice of "striving," but it is a fiction work, not an advice book. *Up the Organization* (Townsend, 1970) and *Management* (Drucker, 1974) both address themselves to top managers and primarily discuss how to run an organization, not how to manage a career. Whyte's *The Organization Man* (1956) and Maccoby's *The Gamesman* (1976), which outline the prototypical white-collar workers of the 1950s and 1970s, are not advice books, but their findings are wholly consistent with the conclusions I draw from popular success manuals. Whyte's "organization men" no doubt read striving books, and one can envision Maccoby's "gamesmen" employing some of the tactics described by manipulation manuals.

The last of the striving books to become a best-seller was Peale's *Stay Alive All Your Life* (1957). It offered a stronger version of his earlier formula for transforming the world through thought.

> Most people underrate themselves. To counteract the crippling effect of such downgrading on yourself, practice optimistic enthusiasm about your own possibilities. When you vigorously reject the concept of personal limitations and become enthusiastic about your own life it is astonishing what new qualities will suddenly appear within you. You can then *do* and *be* what formerly would have seemed quite impossible. (1957:26)

Success-through-striving books promoted pleasant demeanor, optimism, and cooperative qualities such as "getting along" with superiors. This formula suited the needs of corporate life in the 1950s and justified the lives of the "organization men" described by Whyte (1956:129): "The young men have no cynicism about the 'system,' and very little skepticism—they don't see it as something to be bucked, but as something to be cooperated with." Indeed, the credibility of innocuous advice was probably sustained because of the economic boom of the period that made widespread entrepreneurial and corporate mobility possible.

> Corporations have been expanding at a great rate, and the effect has been a large-scale deferral of dead ends and pigeonholes for thousands of organization men. With so many new departments, divisions, and plants being opened up, many a young man of average ability has been propelled upward so early—and so pleasantly—that he can hardly be blamed if he thinks the momentum is a constant. (Whyte, 1956:130)

Entrepreneurial Scheme Books

In 1959 a new type of success manual, entrepreneurial scheme books, emerged to offer advice for making money independent of organizations. The early books were testimonials of moderately successful people who devised strategies for making fortunes through investment. All started with relatively little money or expertise and thus served as role models. Their premise was that if they could be successful investors, so could the reader. *How I Made $2,000,000 in the Stock Market* (Darvas, 1960) was written by a dancer, *Anyone Can Make a Million* (Shulman, 1966) by a doctor, and *How I Turned $1,000 into a Million in Real Estate in My Spare Time* (Nickerson, 1959) by a writer. None were professional investors when they began.

Subsequent, best-selling entrepreneurial scheme books were written by professional financial advisors. Adam Smith, a pseudonym for New York investment counselor George J. W. Goodman, explained the "new economics" in *The Money Game* (1969) and encouraged readers to enter into financial dealing. Success in all of these works was defined only in terms of money.

It is part of the ethos of this country that you *ought* to be rich. You ought to be, unless you have taken some specific vow of poverty such as the priesthood, scholarship, teaching, or civil service, because money is the way we keep score. This feeling has been a long time in the making. It goes away sometimes in depressions, when briefly wealth becomes suspect and poverty is not dishonorable. The rest of the time, poverty is very close to criminal. (Smith, 1969:301)

Investment books are not simply the product of periods of economic growth. During periods of recession in the 1970s books were published giving advice, not only on how to protect assets, but on how to take advantage of economic downturns. Harry Browne's *You Can Profit from a Monetary Crisis* (1974:11) was typical: "Every crisis is an opportunity . . . it's a time to be prudent, to be ready, to meet the future and take advantage of it." Several other investment books with this theme were also popular during the seventies.

The one financial advice book with a different message was Richard Dacey's *How to Avoid Probate* (1965), a best-seller in 1966. This was a legal guide that showed middle-class people how to protect their estates from probate taxes. While not concerned directly with success, it did reflect the growing public distrust of large institutions. Entrepreneurial scheme books encouraged people to look outside of the corporate reward system. They claimed that the average person's best hope for a successful life was independent wealth and freedom from organizations.

Manipulation Manuals

Manipulation manuals appeared in the mid-sixties and, like entrepreneurial scheme books, continued to be popular in the early 1980s. Where investment advice books stress success outside of an organization, manipulation manuals address the desire for organizational mobility, as well as independent success. These books have only a tenuous relationship to the cheery gospel of confidence proposed in the earlier striving works, however. Manipulation manuals offer an insidious formula based on superior knowledge and personal skill, and they advocate hard work in climbing to the top of the hierarchy or in amassing a fortune. These books attest to growing competition for jobs and confirm what Lasch (1979) identified as the "ethic of self-preservation." According to Lasch, the modern individual suffers from chronic insecurity because it is no longer possible to have confidence in the economic or social order. The individual is released from any morality except the morality of self-preservation. Manipulation manuals are an expression of this ethic and rely on psychological durability and Machiavellian tactics; personal qualities of character and formulas are irrelevant or secondary.

The first of these books to emerge was not actually a success manual, but significant in that it was the first popular psychology book to attract public attention and because its methodology has since been widely used in business and government. *Games People Play* (1964), by Dr. Eric Berne, dissected the most routine social interactions, revealing them to be a form of highly structured intercourse with predetermined scripts. Berne gave the term transactional analysis, or TA, to his technique for understanding "what's really happening" in conversation. TA provided another best seller, *I'm OK—You're OK* (Harris, 1970); both books, although not specifically written for business audiences, were the vanguard of a new organizational consulting era. Organizational psychologists applied TA to corporate intercourse and taught managers how to use it to gain the results they wanted. TA has been used to teach employees how to "handle" difficult customers, to conduct interviews, and to manage conflict. These books did not advocate manipulation, but revealed the techniques that were later perfected by others with manipulative intent. Many spin-off volumes openly advocated the use of TA or gamesmanship for getting ahead.

Where Berne and Harris analyzed verbal communication, Julius Fast, in *Body Language* (1970), analyzed the non-verbal messages present in behavior. Fast taught readers what a given stance, approach, or sitting position meant, and how to manipulate situations with their bodies.

> When a man's territorial defenses are weakened or intruded upon, his self-assurance tends to grow weaker. In a working situation the boss who is aware of this can strengthen his own position of leadership by intruding spatially on the man under him. The higher-up who leans over the subordinate's desk throws the subordinate off balance. The department head who crowds next to the worker while inspecting his work makes the worker uneasy and insecure. (1970:53)

More recent manipulation manuals are far more strident. In *Winning Through Intimidation* (1973:27) real estate salesman Robert J. Ringer dismisses the traditional success methods. "I learned that striving for a positive mental attitude will get you nowhere unless you have the ammunition to back it up." He proposed that success seekers supplement good attitude and hard work with intimidation, and forget ethics as irrelevant.

> When it was over I wasn't always the most popular guy at the [real estate] closing, but after my education at Screw U., I had decided that I would rather have the seller taking my name in vain as I walked away with my chips, than have him remarking what a nice guy I was as I walked away without my hand. (1973:216)

Winning Through Intimidation and its sequel, *Looking Out for Number One* (1977), were each on the best-seller list for over a year.[7]

While Ringer's books were oriented toward entrepreneurs like himself,

---

[7]Ringer had another best-seller, *Restoring the American Dream* (1979), but this was an expression of his *laissez-faire* economic philosophy, not a success manual per se.

Michael Korda's *Power! How to Get It, How to Use It* (1975) was written for corporation employees. Korda asserted that upward mobility is only for the scheming and insensitive. *Power!* teaches readers how to out-maneuver opponents by such techniques as moving to the power position at cocktail parties, getting a corner office and painting it blue ("the power color"), and developing a "firm, trustworthy gaze, and a confident, relaxed mouth" (1975:17). He tells readers to avoid Florsheim shoes and involuntary facial tics, as they suggest weakness.

> It is possible to prevent involuntary twitching at the corners of the mouth by applying Zylocaine anesthetic ointment before an important meeting, but the effect is temporary, and if too much ointment is used the lips become numb and speech is slurred. (i975:17)

Like the striving and entrepreneurial scheme books, manipulation manuals assume that the reader's goal is financial success. But manipulation manuals address a more educated audience in a more competitive environment, and ethical constraints are weakened, if not totally absent. Peale promoted prayer and did not stress hard work; manipulation manuals dismiss morality and urge constant attention to one's career. Achievement is still a goal of U.S. workers, but as the competition has grown, the tactics have become more fierce.

Displacement Books

Not all workers are willing to engage in manipulative techniques, and not everyone can be upwardly mobile in hierarchically organized work places. One book which achieved popularity in the 1950s rationalized a lack of success. Written by John Schindler, a doctor, *How to live 365 Days a Year* proposed dropping out of competition to preserve one's mental health.

> For the individual who is caught in his job, the only answer is to sneak enjoyment in through the back door; to make himself as cheerful as possible; and to be upset by the irritations of the job as little as possible. (Schindler, 1954:150)

With the exception of this one book, displacement books did not achieve popularity until the 1970s. They became best sellers about the same time as the more strident manipulation manuals, and offered two choices: coping or narcissism. Coping books, like Schindler's, present surrender and resignation as rational alternatives to the "rat race." Narcissism books direct the pursuit of success to non-work areas. Both types of displacement books help readers create an identity separate from their role as a worker, extremely difficult in a society that all but equates personal worth with occupational success.

One coping book, *How to Be Your Own Best Friend* (1973), was written by two psychoanalysts, Berkowitz and Newman. They advocated seeking happiness within the self by self-praise and self-compassion, a non-competitive tactic. In addition, this book destroys the self-made man model and rejects the power of positive thinking.

> Someone who thinks he can do anything he has a "mind" to do is not in contact with himself. It is an arrogant belief because it sets no limits. . . . When we use our willpower to achieve goals that do not spring out of us, but which we set for the sake of pleasing others or to fulfill a fantasy about who we are, we create a kind of monster, a mechanical man in which our living self is trapped. (1973:25)

Laurence Peter and Raymond Hull (1969:25) used humor to present their message that corporate misery is achieved through the "Peter Principle:" "In a hierarchy every employee tends to rise to his level of incompetency" and, therefore, to a level of unhappiness. Peter stated his position more explicitly in *The Peter Prescription* (1972:99), identifying the problem of overachievement as the product of a high-pressure society. "Civilized man has built a system of entrapment wherein he continually strives for more and cannot refuse a challenge, however meaningless." Those who refuse to fall into the trap are glorified for their superior insight. Peter turns a lack of upward mobility into a reward; corporate climbers ("processionary puppets") are pathological, or at best, misguided.

Two books help the individual cope by teaching physical techniques that soothe the mind. *The Relaxation Response* (Benson, 1975) and *TM: Discovering Inner Energy And Overcoming Stress* (Bloomfield *et al.*, 1974) teach meditation to the tired, anxious, and distracted, and offer a way out of a difficult, competitive world. Meditation has since become an acceptable technique for temporarily running away, or at least for coping with stress more effectively. These books were best sellers, but there are dozens of imitations written for specific segments of the middle-class market. The meditation movement purports to enable people to achieve inner harmony and to become united with the disjointed self.

Wayne Dyer's three best sllers, *Your Erroneous Zones* (1976), *Pulling Your Own Strings* (1978), and *The Sky's the Limit* (1980), advocate self-development, but not in support of a financial success model. Dyer tells readers to seek non-material rewards of their own choice and to reject institutionalized definitions of approval. "You may be surprised to hear this, but failure does not exist. Failure is simply someone else's opinion of how a certain act should have been completed" (1976:133).

Although I do not list them here because they do not deal with success directly, books promoting diets, exercise, and other leisure activities are an extension of the displacement ethic. Leisure pursuits, particularly non-competitive ones, create attainable goals and outlets for frustrated people. For example, Jim Fixx's *The Complete Book of Running* (1977:32), suggests that running helps individuals adjust to the world: "To learn the meaning of not winning in running is to learn the meaning of not winning elsewhere in our lives . . . failures seem less poisonous" (1977:32).

DISCUSSION

Success books first appeared in the 18th century. The breakdown of traditional social orders in North America at the time had at least two important effects on workers. First, a person's traditional place in the occupational structure was no longer assured. Ascription was increasingly replaced by an achievement ethic that granted (and demanded) the opportunity to make one's place in the world, and simultaneously to be evaluated according to the status of that place. Second, the Age of Reason established the idea that the social and physical worlds operate according to laws, not supernatural forces. People began to see themselves as engineers of society and masters of their own fate within it. Success manuals were a response to both the need to define one's social status and the belief that, with the application of proper principles, it was possible to do so fruitfully.

Although industrialized societies offer diverse positions in their occupational structures, every society has in fact held up images of the ideal—the type of position to which one *ought* to aspire (Klapp, 1962). These ideals of success orient individuals toward their pursuit, thereby controlling behavior by controlling aspirations. As Weber (1958) and others have suggested, the popular ideal has typically supported the needs of the economic system. Thus, the Protestant ethic and the character ethic served the development of entrepreneurial capitalism; the personality ethic served the emerging corporate capitalism of the 20th century by expanding the vision of success to include corporate mobility, and by prompting consumption.

Underlying all of these ideals of success has been a strong middle-class belief in meritocracy, the idea that social rewards are distributed in proportion to individual worth: the most able become top executives; those less deserving find their relative places in the social hierarchy. The widespread belief in this meritocratic ideology has put great pressure on the individual to succeed: success represents not just material rewards but a certification of one's self.

According to Marxist scholars, however, support for the economic structure of advanced capitalism by middle-class workers might be in jeopardy because of the increasing rationalization of professional, clerical, and technical work. Mills referred only briefly to this phenomenon in *White Collar* in 1951, when striving books were popular. He attributed white-collar workers' frustration to bureaucratic organization with its "centralization of decision" and "formal rationality" that deprive the corporate workers of "Any total view and understanding of its process" (1951:226). Recent scholars claim the process has evolved much further and see the source of disenchantment in the work itself, not just in attributes of bureaucratic organization. Aronowitz (1973:306) cites the contradiction between 'the expectations generated by [middle class] training and the boredom and rote of their tasks." Technical and managerial workers have also been thrown into impersonal mass labor markets and compete for work just as manual laborers. Braverman (1974) claims this is an additional source of disillusionment:

Feeling the insecurity of their role as sellers of labor power and the frustrations of a controlled and mechanically organized workplace, they begin, despite their remaining privileges, to know those symptoms of dissociation which are popularly called "alienation" and which the working class has lived with for so long that they have become part of its second nature. (1974:408)

While middle-class work has become more rationalized and frustrating, there has been no rebellion against the economic structure. Rather, modern advice books suggest that middle-class workers accept the legitimacy of the system, and privatize their concerns in ways that do not threaten the social order.[8] The existing capitalist structure can accommodate three worker strategies: (1) fighting to improve one's position by climbing the organizational ladder to a more rewarding job; (2) seeking success independently of the corporate (or government) system; and (3) accepting one's position as alienating and turning to other pursuits for meaning. These three strategies are evident in the four categories of success books that have achieved mass audiences since 1950. *Success-through-striving* books support the traditional choice of working one's way to the top of the hierarchy. Those who believe that mobility in the organizational world is possible must accept the challenge to fight their way up the ladder or accept themselves as mediocre, defeated by others more capable than themselves. *Entrepreneurial scheme books* represent the second socially approved alternative, "making it" on one's own. Although difficult even in a thriving economy, independent success in the face of great obstacles is a powerful dream. Sennett and Cobb (1972:237) see the desire for autonomous work as an attempt to be free from organizational judgment and to have the opportunity to personally claim an accomplishment, something rarely possible in offices where work is usually interdependent.

Manipulation manuals are evidence of both of these strategies, but exaggerate and distort traditional values of self-reliance and ingenuity to respond to a brutally competitive environment.[9] Working "for the money," and not the satisfaction, has been the only alternative for most middle-class women and blue-collar workers, but for middle-class men it has not been a socially acceptable choice. This third possibility, however, may become acceptable if only a few can have satisfying work within large organizations; the advance of technology, a more educated workforce, and new competition from women and minorities seem to assure that competition will be even greater for relatively fewer "good" jobs. And despite a resurgence of

[8]At least not organized rebellion. White-collar crime has, of course, been attributed to this process (Sutherland, 1949).

[9]Although manipulation manuals and success-through-striving books are both based on a "keep on trying" theme, they derive from two behaviorist theories of interpersonal relations. Striving books advocate a positive reinforcement theory that establishes good will in order to gain power; readers are encouraged to take the role of the other and to develop empathy as a means of controlling the situation. Manipulation manuals advocate negative reinforcement, such as intimidation, in order to gain a superior position in interaction.

an entrepreneurial ethic in the 1980s, few can aspire to great success as small businessmen in an economy of limited competition.

Displacement books represent a turn toward resignation. Although the occasional U.S. thinker, such as Thoreau (1893), has encouraged retreat from the larger society, this has never been an enduring theme in U.S. social thought. The massive popularity of coping books suggests, however, that increasing numbers of middle-class workers are seeking relief from the stress of the work place and meaning outside the world of work. Although largely dismissed as representative of a benign leisure cult, displacement books are more appropriately viewed within the context of the middle-class work system and the alternatives that system makes possible.

This suggests, as well, that it is in the interest of corporations to encourage the leisure demands of their middle-level employees or risk frustrating an important segment of their workforce. Non-work pursuits in no way alleviate the alienation of middle-class work, but alienation is thereby submerged and directed outside the work place.

CONCLUSION: THE RISE OF SELF-MANAGEMENT

Social scientists have developed a great body of literature on the larger social-structural and organizational effects of rationalization processes. Less effort has been devoted to studying the effects of rationalized arrangements on the life experience of actors. However, the writings of historians such as Braudel (1979) and Le Roy Ladurie (1979) suggest that the texture of the average person's daily existence has changed radically in the last few centuries. Pre-industrial people oriented themselves to the traditionally defined activities of their status, and to, primarily, religious values—what Weber called "ultimate ends."[10] Their lives were experienced as integrated wholes: work, play, and religion were not segmented into different places and times. Activities in all spheres were conducted with the same people and in accord with values known and accepted by all.

Set free from traditional limits, modern individuals are also set free from traditional patterns of meaning in which experience is fulfilling if it corresponds with shared beliefs. Having few defined paths, people today are expected to create their own. However, as success books suggest, modern individuals do not pursue meaning willy-nilly, but do so in patterned ways that reflect larger social arrangements. Despite a contemporary ideology that stresses individualism and self-actualization, they orient their aspirations towards the possibilities of life in organizations and in the market place, and the limits on experience they impose. Success in a rationalized world, paradoxically, represents relative freedom from rationalization. Entrepreneurial success grants autonomy from large-scale workplaces, and execu-

[10]According to Kalberg (1980:1176), Weber foresaw the erosion of ideals with the systematization of daily life: "He saw the fading away of . . . the autonomous and free individual whose actions were given continuity by their reference to ultimate ends."

tive status grants a measure of discretion and a wider organizational view than is possible for specialized workers.

It is ironic, too, that in the pursuit of success, people today employ the method of modern organizational life: they self-manage. Early success books, while guides to individual behavior, sought to help individuals find their place in society or in the world beyond. They offered self-help techniques, but always in tandem with religious or ethical pursuits such as devotion or the development of character, and usually in reference to moral ideas about the type of person necessary to society. Success books since 1950, however, are purely instrumental and make no reference to interests beyond the individual, or to values other than self-preservation and wealth. They have become pure technique and imply or advocate that people view themselves as objects to be manipulated. The extraordinary popularity of success books demonstrates that objective rationality applied to the self is widely accepted as legitimate and efficacious. The meaning of life, these books suggest, is increasingly viewed as the proper managment of one's life course. The most successful people are those who have self-managed best in the organization or in the market. Ultimate ends have been replaced by a belief in calculus: the rationalized methods originally applied to machines, material, and workers, have been applied to the self, in the form of career- or stress-management.

REFERENCES

Aronowitz, Stanley. 1973. *False Promises*. New York: McGraw-Hill.

Bell, Daniel. 1976. *The Cultural Contradictions of Capitalism*. New York: Basic Books.

Bennis, Warren. 1966. *Changing Organizations*. New York: McGraw-Hill.

Benson, Herbert. 1975. *The Relaxation Response*. New York: William Morrow.

Berkowitz, Bernard, and Mildred Newman, with Jean Owen. 1973 *How to Be Your Own Best Friend*. New York: Random House.

Berne, Eric. 1964. *Games People Play*. New York: Grove Press.

Blanton, Smiley. 1956. *Love or Perish*. New York: Simon & Schuster.

Bloomfield, Harold H., Michael Peter Cain, and Dennis T. Jaffe. 1974. *TM: Discovering Inner Energy and Overcoming Stress*. New York: Delacorte Press.

Bowker Annual of Library and Book Trade Information. 1950–1980. New York and London: R. R. Bowker.

Braudel, Fernand. 1979. *The Structures of Everyday Life*, Vol. 1. New York: Harper & Row.

Braverman, Harry. 1974. *Labor and Monopoly Capital*. New York: Monthly Review Press.

Bristol, Claude M. 1954. *TNT: The Power Within You*. Englewood Cliffs, N.J.: Prentice-Hall.

Brooks, Van Wyck. 1958. *America's Coming of Age*. Garden City, N.Y.: Doubleday/Anchor. [1915]

Browne, Harry. 1974. *How You Can Profit from a Monetary Crisis*. New York: Macmillan.

Carnegie, Dale. 1936 *How to Win Friends and Influence People*. New York: Simon & Schuster.

Casey, Douglas R. 1980. *Crisis Investing*. New York: Harper & Row.

Cawelti, John G. 1965. *Apostles of the Self-made Man*. Chicago: University of Chicago Press.

Chenoweth, Lawrence. 1974. *The American Dream of Success*. North Scituate, Mass.: Duxbury Press.

Dacey, Norman F. 1965. *How to Avoid Probate*. New York: Crown.

Darvas, Nicolas. 1960. *How I Made $2,000,000 in the Stock Market*. New York: American Research Council.

Drucker, Peter. 1974. *Management*. New York: Harper & Row.

Dyer, Wayne W. 1976. *Your Erroneous Zones*. New York: Funk and Wagnalls.

———. 1978. *Pulling Your Own Strings*. Boston: G. K. Hall.

———. 1980. *The Sky's the Limit*. New York: Simon & Schuster.

Eisen, Arnold. 1978. "The meanings and confusions of Weberian 'rationality'." *British Journal of Sociology* 29 (March):57–70.

Ewen, Stuart. 1976. *Captains of Consciousness*. New York: McGraw-Hill.

Fast, Julius. 1970. *Body Language*. New York: M. Evan.

Fixx, James F. 1977. *The Complete Book of Running*. New York: Random House.

Franklin, Benjamin. 1958. *Poor Richard's Almanac* (1732). New York: David McKay.

Gouldner, Alvin. 1954. *Patterns of Industrial Bureaucracy*. Glencoe, Ill.: Free Press.

Harris, Thomas A. 1970. *I'm OK—You're OK*. New York: Harper.

Huber, Richard M. 1971. *The American Idea of Success*. New York: McGraw-Hill.

Kalberg, Stephen. 1980. "Max Weber's types of rationality: Cornerstones for the analysis of rationalization processes in history." *American Journal of Sociology* 85 (March):1145–1179.

Kennedy, Gail (ed.). 1949. *Democracy and the Gospel of Wealth*. Boston: D. C. Heath.

Klapp, Orrin E. 1962. *Heroes, Villains, and Fools: The Changing American Character*. Englewood Cliffs, N. J.: Prentice-Hall.

Korda, Michael. 1975. *Power! How to Get It, How to Use It*. New York: Random House.

Lasch, Christopher. 1979. *The Culture of Narcissism*. New York: W. W. Norton.

Le Roy Ladurie, Emmanuel. 1979. *Montaillou*. New York: Random House.

Lowenthal, Leo. 1961. "The triumph of mass idols," pp. 109–140 in Leo Lowenthal (ed.), *Literature, Popular Culture, and Society*. Englewood Cliffs, N.J.: Prentice-Hall.

Lowry, Albert J. 1977. *How You Can Become Financially Independent by Investing in Real Estate*. New York: Simon & Schuster.

Maccoby, Michael. 1976. *The Gamesman,* New York: Simon & Schuster.

March, James, and Herbert Simon. 1958. *Organizations*. New York: John Wiley.

Mead, Edward Shepherd. 1952. *How to Succeed in Business Without Really Trying*. New York: Simon & Schuster.

Merton, Robert. 1957. *Social Theory and Social Structure*. New York: Free Press.

Mills, C. Wright. 1951. *White Collar*. New York: Oxford University.

Nickerson, William. 1959. *How I Turned $1,000 into a Million in Real Estate in My Spare Time*. New York: Simon & Schuster.

Peale, Norman Vincent. 1948. *A Guide to Confident Living*. Englewood Cliffs, N.J.: Prentice-Hall.

———. 1952. *The Power of Positive Thinking*. Englewood Cliffs, N.J.: Prentice-Hall.

———. 1957. *Stay Alive All Your Life*. Englewood Cliffs, N.J.: Prentice-Hall.

————, and Smiley Blanton. 1950. *The Art of Real Happiness* Englewood Cliffs, N.J.: Prentice-Hall.

Perrow, Charles. 1979. *Complex Organizations.* Glenview, Ill.: Scott, Foresman.

Peter, Laurence J. 1972. *The Peter Prescription.* New York: William Morrow.

————, and Raymond Hull. 1969. *The Peter Principle.* New York: William Morrow.

Ringer, Robert J. 1973. *Winning Through Intimidation.* Greenwich, Conn.: Fawcett.

————. 1977. *Looking Out for Number One.* New York: Funk and Wagnalls.

————. 1979 *Restoring the American Dream.* New York: QED.

Ruff, Howard J. 1979. *How to Prosper During the Coming Bad Years.* New York: Warner Books.

Schindler, John A. 1954. *How to Live 365 Days a Year.* Englewood Cliffs, N.J.: Prentice-Hall.

Schlucter, Wolfgang. 1979. "The paradox of rationalization: On the relation of ethics and world." pp. 11–54 in Guenther Roth and Wolfgang Schlucter (eds.), *Max Weber's Vision of History, Ethics, and Methods.* Berkeley: University of California Press.

Sennett, Richard, and Jonathan Cobb. 1972. *The Hidden Injuries of Class.* New York: Random House.

Shulman, Morton. 1966. *Anyone Can Make a Million.* New York: McGraw-Hill.

Smith, Adam (pseudonym for George J. W. Goodman). 1969. *The Money Game.* New York: Random House.

Sutherland, Edwin H. 1949. *White-Collar Crime.* New York: Holt, Rinehart and Winston.

Thoreau, Henry David. 1893. *Walden, or Life in the Woods.* Boston and New York: Houghton Mifflin.

Townsend, Robert. 1970. *Up the Organization.* New York: Alfred A. Knopf.

Webb, Eugene, and Karl Weick. 1979. "Unobtrusive measures in organizational theory: A reminder." *Administrative Science Quarterly* 24 (December):650–659.

Weber, Max. 1921. *Gesammelte Politische Schriften.* Munich: Drei Masken Verlag.

————. 1958. *The Protestant Ethic and the Spirit of Capitalism* (1930). New York: Scribners.

Weiss, Richard. 1969. *The American Myth of Success.* New York: Basic Books.

Whyte, William H. 1956. *The Organization Man.* New York: Simon & Schuster.

Wyllie, Irving. 1954. *The Self-made Man in America.* New York: Free Press.

PART Two

TWO

SOCIAL AND INDIVIDUAL DISORDER

CHAPTER 3

Drug Abuse and Sexual Expressions

How an individual's behavior is judged depends on society's definition of the situation in which it takes place. Even killing another person is not always wrong; it depends on the societal perception of the circumstances. These ideas change over time. Whether a specific behavior should be accepted or punished and corrected depends on the era in which it occurs. What was once unthinkable often becomes accepted.

A good example of this is transsexualism, the feeling that one's true personality is that of the opposite sex. Transsexualism has recently become accepted as a condition that should be corrected. If, however, a few years ago, a male felt strongly that he was truly a female and had himself castrated, he would probably have been institutionalized in a mental facility. Society did not accept his changed condition.

Billings and Urban show us how societal acceptance develops and sometimes even redefines the original problem. They explain that the medical profession has lumped together and labeled a diverse group of sexual deviants as having a condition that can be surgically corrected. It has become accepted that a physician can "change the sex" of a patient using cosmetic surgery.

Adler and Adler describe the process through which very young children, those from only a few months to eight years of age, are taught by their families to become marijuana users. The changing social meanings of the drug's use is vividly illustrated by reading how these "tinydopers" are socialized. This demonstrates an interesting social value paradox. Even though the parents studied view their actions as being acceptable, the rest of society sees them as being deviant.

Gray's entry deals with the complex relationship between our values about sex and violence. We now know that if men who are already angry toward women are exposed to some types of pornography, they will become even angrier, and perhaps violent. The solution to this problem involves the social role definitions that are at the root of men's feelings of anger toward women. In other words, society's unrealistic role expectations for men cannot possibly be met, and this leads to feelings of frustration and anger.

Reading 7

The Socio-Medical Construction of Transsexualism: an Interpretation and Critique

Dwight B. Billings

University of Kentucky

Thomas Urban

Yale University

There is hardly a more dramatic instance of contemporary professional authority than so-called "sex-change" surgery. Physicians perform cosmetic surgery yet certify that their patients have undergone a change of sex. Courts acknowledge this claim by allowing transsexuals to be issued new birth certificates in most states. Our study of sex-change surgery reveals that these physicians heal neither the body nor the mind, but perform a moral function instead. After conducting a surgical rite of passage, physicians are accorded moral authority to sponsor passage from one sexual status to another. Public acceptance of sex-change surgery attests both to the domination of daily life and consciousness by professional authority as well as the extent to which many forms of deviance are increasingly labeled "illness" rather than "sin" or "crime" (Friedson, 1970). Furthermore, and in a curious way, the stress by "phallocentric medicine" (Wilden, 1972:278) on the presence or absence of a penis as the definitive insignia of gender challenges the politics of the women's movement and the intellectual thrust of the behavioral sciences, which assert that anatomy need not define destiny. Sex-change surgery privatizes and depoliticizes individual experiences of gender role distress.

We show that transsexualism is a socially constructed reality which *only* exists in and through medical practice. The problem of transsexual patients does not lie "in their minds," as sex-change proponent John Money (1972:201) puts it. Money's statement typifies medicine's reification of transsexualism as a psychological entity. In contrast, we believe transsexualism is a relational process sustained in medical practice and marketed in public testimony such as Money's (1972:204) description of the "warm glow" of sexual fulfillment available through surgery. The legitimation, rationalization, and commodification of sex-change operations have produced an identity category—transsexual—for a diverse group of sexual deviants and victims of severe gender role distress. . . .

MEDICAL EXEMPLARS AND PROFESSIONAL MOTIVATIONS

The treatment of hermaphrodites, persons born with sexual organs of both sexes, set several precedents for sex reassignment of transsexuals. Surgical techniques for reconstructing genital abnormalities and standards developed to determine the direc-

Reprinted with permission from *Social Problems* 29(3) (February 1982): 266–282 by The Society for the Study of Social Problems and by the authors.

tion of hermaphroditic sex assignment were both applicable to transsexualism. Some physicians who treated hermaphrodites stressed chromosonal characteristics; surgeons generally stressed the nature of the external genitalia. From their study of 105 cases of hermaphoditism, Money et al. (1957) proposed that up to the age of two-and-a-half years, the external genitalia should be the principal determinant for sex assignment; in persons older than two-and-a-half, surgery should conform to the established direction of gender role socialization. By reporting dramatic instances among hermaphrodites of chromosonal men who have been successfully socialized as women, and vice versa, they demonstrated the independence of biological sex and gender. Money et al. (1955:290) claimed, however, that gender "is so well established in most children by the two-and-a-half years that it is then too late to make a change of sex with impunity."[1] They acknowledged that sex reassignment could be made in later years if hermaphrodites themselves felt some error had been made in their assigned sex—a concession that proved important for the treatment of transsexuals.

Money et al.'s claim that all the hermaphroditic children in their sample were "successfully" reassigned from one sex to another before the age of two-and-a-half provided the only empirical support for gender role fixity. Only five children in their sample of 105 were reassigned after this age, though four were judged by unspecified criteria as "unsatisfactory." Anomalies were soon reported, though these studies are rarely cited in the transsexual literature (Berg et al., 1963). Dewhurst and Gordon (1963) reported 15 successful cases of reassignment among 17 hermaphroditic children up to 18 years of age. Thus, there were at least as many cases in medical literature of patients successfully altering their gender roles as there were cases of those who did not.

Psychiatrist Ira Pauley (1968), a proponent of sex change, acknowledged that such anomalies cast some doubt on the otherwise considerable clinical evidence for gender role fixity—a theory crucial to the argument that psychotherapy is ineffective for transsexuals (Benjamin, 1966). Pauley claimed, however, that psychiatrist Robert Stoller had clarified the apparent contradiction. Stoller (1964a,b) re-directed attention from "gender role" to "core gender identity," arguing that those rare individuals who appear to change identity later in life do not really do so. Rather, he argued, they have always had a third (hermaphroditic) gender identity—"not male or female but both (or neither)" (Stoller, 1964b:456). Apparent cases of reversals of early socialization were thus discounted.

Clinical experience with hermaphrodites thus established three points: (1) the refinement of surgical techniques for genital reconstruction; (2) the theory that gender role learning is independent of physical anatomy and is fixed at an early age; and (3) the policy that, since self-identification is more important than external genitalia, "rare requests" from adult hermaphrodites for sex reassignment should be given "serious evaluation" (Money et al., 1955).

[1]Subsequently, Money et al. (1957) compared gender role learning in humans to "critical imprinting" in some animal species which, they argued, begins in the first year of life.

Psychiatrists and plastic surgeons at Johns Hopkins University provided another precedent for sex-change operations with a series of studies of patients requesting cosmetic surgery. Here was an established field of medicine where doctors performed operations upon demand without medical justification. Yet Edgerton et al. (1960–61:139) found that 16 percent of their sample of patients demanding elective surgery were judged psychotic, 20 percent neurotic and 35 percent had personality trait disorders. Meyer et al. (1960:194) found that of 30 patients studied, one was diagnosed psychotic, two were severely neurotic, eight had obsessive personalities, and four were schizoid; and 14 others were judged at tending toward obsessional schizophrenia. Most patients rejected psycho-therapy, however, as an alternative to surgery. The researchers concluded from post-operative interviews that "psychological improvement" and patient satisfaction resulted from surgery. Even "severely neurotic and technically psychotic patients" were judged to benefit from such operations (Edgerton et al., 1960–61:144).

With the publication of these findings, and those on hermaphrodites, the medical rationales for sex-change surgery were in place. Johns Hopkins University became the most prominent center for the surgical treatment of transsexualism in the United States in the 1970s. Psychologist John Money, psychiatrist Eugene Meyer, and plastic surgeon Milton Edgerton formed the nucleus of the Johns Hopkins team.

Three factors motivated physicians to fight attempts to declare sex-change operations illegal:

1. The paramount role of the physician as healer was stressed (Benjamin, 1966:116). Early defenses stressed patients' intense anguish and the duty of physicians "to ease the existence of these fellow-men" (Hamburger, 1953:373).

2. The opportunity for ground-breaking research in psychiatry was recognized. Robert Stoller (1973a:215) referred to transsexuals as "natural experiments" offering "a keystone for understanding the development of masculinity and femininity in all people."[2] Surgeons, too, were interested in sharpening their skills. Several told us in interviews that they regard sex-change surgery as a technical *tour de force* which they undertook initially to prove to themselves that there was nothing they were surgically incapable of performing. Plastic surgeons, especially, found sex-change surgery strategically important for expanding their disciplinary jurisdiction.[3]

3. An over-abundance of surgeons in the United States has resulted in competi-

[2]Some experiments were not so "natural." University of Minnesota researchers, for instance, were curious about the effects of high estrogen dosage and surgery on "profound psychopaths." Not surprisingly, they concluded that "if there is one follow-up conclusion that can be made with assurance at this stage, it is that estrogen and sex-reassignment surgery do not alter the sociopathic transsexual" (Hastings, 1974).

[3]Such operations "represented a unique experience and challenge to perfect techniques heretofore restricted to the treatment of congenital malformations and traditionally the province of the urologist and gynecologist, rather than the plastic surgeons" (Money and Schwartz, 1969:255). The desire for jurisdictional expansion and prestige among lower status medical specialties—in this case, plastic surgery and psychiatry—is especially "conducive to the 'discovery' of a particular deviant label" as Pfohl (1977:310) shows in the case of the "discovery" of child abuse by pediatric radiologists.

tion for patients and an increasing number of "unnecessary" operations (Bunker, 1970), many of which are performed on women in the course of their sexual maturation and functioning (Corea, 1977). Although medicine is a "market profession," it is not socially legitimated as a business enterprise (Larson, 1977). Nevertheless, sex-change surgery is profitable: reassignment operations alone cost around $10,000 in the late 1970s. Related elective surgery, consultation fees, and weekly estrogen treatments push the cost even higher.[4]

Legitimating the Search: Etiology, Diagnosis and Treatment

News of Johns Hopkins University's program touched off a renewed wave of opposition within medicine in the late 1960s.[5] Psychoanalysts in private practice led the attack. Using a variety of analytic techniques to support their position that persons demanding castration were *ipso facto* mentally ill, they labeled transsexuals as "all border-line psychotics" (Meerloo, 1967:263), or victims of "paranoid schizophrenic psychosis" (Socarides, 1970:346) or "character neurosis" (Stinson, 1972:246). They attacked surgery as non-therapeutic. If patients' requests represented "a surgical acting out of psychosis" (Volkan and Bhatti, 1973:278), then surgeons were guilty of "collaboration with psychosis" (Meerloo, 1967:263). The *Journal of Nervous and Mental Disease* devoted an entire issue in 1968 to the topic and concluded that the issues of etiology, diagnosis, and treatment were still unresolved and that the term "transsexualism" itself had won premature acceptance in the literature. The report concluded: "What [transsexualism] means in contradistinction to 'transvestite' or 'homosexual' is not clear" (Kubie and Mackie, 1968:431). Such criticism threatened the professional security of sex-change physicians and raised the question of whether patients could consent to such operations since psychotics cannot legally do so.

In response, sex-change proponents legitimated surgical treatment by (1) constructing an etiological theory which stressed the non-psychopathic character of the illness and (2) rationalizing diagnostic and treatment strategies. Although some physicians asserted that biological predispositions for transsexualism might yet be discovered, most stressed early socialization in their etiological accounts. Recalling the hermaphrodite literature, Money and Gaskin (1970–71:251) spoke of the "virtually ineradicable" effects of ambivalent gender role learning at an early age.

---

[4]Physicians' fees alone—apart from hospitalization—for 628 patients and 169 operations at Stanford University's sex-change clinic totaled $413,580.00. This figure excludes the cost of psychiatric counseling and other operations (e.g., rhinoplasty, augmentation mamoplasty, and thyroid cartilage shaves) which patients usually demand. Some private practitioners have performed up to 1000 sex-change operations. Restak (1980:11) calls sex-change surgery a "$10 million growth industry."

[5]Other university hospitals, such as the University of Minnesota's, began surgical treatment at roughly the same time but avoided public disclosure (Hastings, 1969). In addition, a few operations were secretly performed in the 1950s at the University of California at San Francisco (Benjamin, 1966:142) We have learned that Cook County Hospital in Chicago was performing sex-change operations as early as 1947, predating Jorgensen's famous European surgery by five years.

Stoller (1967:433) claimed that male transsexualism was the predictable outcome of a particular family situation involving "too much contrast with mother's body for too long and a father who is absent and so does not interrupt the process of feminization." The result is a son so strongly identified with his mother that he not only *wishes* to be like her, but comes to believe that he *is* like her despite incongruous genitals. Stoller conceptualized transsexualism as an identity issue—not a neurotic perversion—resulting "from the same kinds of forces necessary for normal development" (1973b:216). In contrast to neurotic perversions such as transvestism, Stoller contended that transsexualism was "not a product of neurosis, i.e., of conflict and compromise, any more than is the core masculinity in normal men or feminity in normal women" (1973b:219).

Thus, physicians defended themselves against the charge of "collaboration with psychosis" by claiming to resolve surgically their patients' bitter conflicts between self-image and body-image. Arguing that "psychiatric name-calling" adds little to understanding (Baker and Green, 1970:89), they replaced the language of perversions with a new language to describe patient demand for sex-change surgery. These demands were referred to as a "single theme" (Hoopes et al., 1968), a "principal theme" (Pauley, 1968), an "*idée fixe*" (Money and Gaskin, 1970–71), an "intensive desire" (Forester and Swiller, 1972), and an "intense conviction or fixed idea" (Sturup, 1976).[6]

Within this etiological framework, physicians were confident they could diagnose transexualism accurately. While critics charged that "transsexualism represents a wish, not a diagnosis" (Socarides, 1970), Baker and Green (1970:90) asserted that "transsexualism is a behavioral phenomenon unique unto itself. We believe that although it is related to other anomalies of psychosexual orientation and shares features in common with them, it can, nevertheless, be differentiated." Male transsexualism, upon which attention was fixed,[7] was identified as a point on a clinical continuum along with effeminate homosexuality and transvestism. Although the boundaries "are sometimes ill defined" (Baker and Green, 1970:90) and the "transition zones are blurry" (Money and Gaskin, 1970–71:254), Fisk (1973:8) summarized the following behavioral guidelines for recognizing the "true transsexual":

1. A life-long sense or feeling of being a member of the "other sex."
2. The early and persistent behavioristic phenomenon of cross-dressing, coupled with a strong emphasis upon a total lack of erotic feeling associated with cross-dressing.
3. A disdain or repugnance for homosexual behavior.

[6]They attempted a further semantic shift by questioning the term "delusional," arguing that the request for sex-change surgery, given medical technology, is no more delusional than the request to go to the moon, given modern space technology (Knorr et al., 1969).

[7]There was considerably less agreement on the etiology and diagnosis of female transsexualism, partly because there is no concept of female transvestism. Clinicians at the University of California at Los Angeles found female transsexuals harder to identify than male transsexuals (Stoller, 1972), while the Johns Hopkins University clinic reported the opposite (Money and Gaskins, 1970–71). An influential theory of female transsexualism was offered by Pauley (1969a).

Once physicians were satisfied that they were dealing with patients whose sanity was intact, and that they were not catering to perverse wishes for self-destruction, then the best indicator of transsexualism was the intensity of a patient's desire for surgery. They assumed such persistence would distinguish a male trans-sexual from an effeminate homosexual or a transvestite who—while behaviorally similar—nonetheless "values his penis and abhors the thought of its loss" (Baker and Green, 1970:91). The lack of erotic motivation, along with evidence of a *life-long* identity pattern, were taken as further proof of transsexualism. Correspondingly, ideal treatment consisted of (1) careful psychiatric screening to assess personality stability and the fixity of gender identity; (2) an extensive period of hormone treatment to develop secondary anatomical characteristics of the cross-sex; (3) at least one year of supervised cross-gender living to guarantee stability and commitment; and, finally (4) surgery (Baker and Green, 1970; Edgerton et al., 1970; Hastings, 1969; Koner et al., 1969; and Money, 1972). Physicians were urged to standardize patient management policies and a number of quantitative diagnostic instruments, such as Lindgren and Pauley's (1975) "Body Identity Scale" were developed to rationalize patient selection.[8] Scientistic accounts of transsexual treatment largely succeeded in silencing critics, for, as Habermas (1979:184) among others have demonstrated, "the formal conditions of [scientistic]justification themselves obtain legitimating force" in the justification of norms and actions in modern culture.

A SUCCESS STORY: SELLING TRANSSEXUALISM

The first physicians to "discover" and treat transsexuals were totally unprepared for the experience (Ihlenfeld, 1973b:64). Their "inexperience and *naïveté*" (Fisk, 1973) was not surprising since "there [were] no textbooks to consult, no authorities to lean on and to quote" (Benjamin, 1966:105). Often they were required to make decisions unrelated to their professional training. By the late 1960s, sex-change proponents began publicly to extol the benefits of sex reassignment in books, journals, newspapers, magazines, and world lecture tours. Although its role is rarely acknowledged in the truncated histories of transsexual treatment presented in medical journals, the Erikson Educational Foundation of Baton Rouge, Louisiana, made three important contributions to the social movement to incorporate sex change in medical jurisdiction:[9]

[8]The strategic political value of rationalization/standardization is also apparent. In 1977, at the Fifth International Gender Dysphoria Syndrome Symposium in Norfolk, Virginia, we heard a leading physician argue for a committee to prepare policy guidelines by saying: "If we have such a committee we can hold the American Medical Association and the American College of Surgeons in abeyance."

[9]Freidson (1970:254) has noted the contributions of such crusading lay interest groups to the professional construction of illness. These "flamboyant moral entrepreneurs" function like advocacy organizations in movements to define social problems (Blumer, 1971; Spector and Kitsuse, 1977). They seek public support for the application of the label of illness to behaviors (such as excessive drinking) not otherwise defined as illness, e.g., alcoholism (Conrad, 1975).

1. Socialization. The Erikson Educational Foundation brought transsexualism to the attention of the public and the medical world by (1) annually sponsoring international medical symposia; (2) helping to send physicians and behavioral scientists such as Leo Wolman, Ira Pauley, and John Money (a foundation board member) around the world to discuss the new "disease"; (3) sponsoring workshops at medical schools, colleges and national meetings of professional associations; and (4) disseminating information about transsexualism through films and pamphlets to physicians, psychologists, lawyers, police, clergy, and social workers. Such efforts aroused public sympathy for transsexuals. In one of her daily "Dear Abby" newspaper columns, Abigail Van Buren told a distressed wife who discovered her husband cross-dressing that he was a possible candidate for surgery who should consult the Erikson Educational Foundation. She affirmed her belief in surgical reassignment, saying: "I believe that knowledge, skill, and talent are divinely inspired and that those scientists, physicians, and surgeons whose combined efforts have made sex-change surgery possible, do so with God's guidance" (Van Buren, 1977:C-10). Similarly, Ann Landers (1979:B-5) wrote that "those who want the surgery should have it."

2. Patient advocacy and services. The foundation created a National Transsexual Counseling Unit in conjunction with the San Francisco policy department and issued identification papers to transsexuals otherwise subject to police harassment.[10] The foundation obtained funding for individual sex-change operations from private insurance carriers, city and state welfare agencies, and vocational rehabilitation programs. It established a national referral network for patients, which identified over 250 sympathetic, competent doctors. From 1968 to 1976 it circulated a *Newsletter* to more than 20,000 subscribers, which cited and summarized medical and scientific reports on transsexualism.

3. Grants. The foundation made grants through the Harry Benjamin Foundation to individual researchers and to several gender clinics, including the one at Johns Hopkins University.

Physicians often complain that transsexual patients are unrealistic about the benefits of surgery. Many "harbor unrealistic expectations for an immediately blissful life, exciting and romance-filled" (Green, 1970:1602). In other contexts (e.g., arguing their patients' competence to give informed consent) physicians defend their patients' senses of reality, but here they acknowledge that "rarely does such a patient initiate a realistic discussion about the obvious problems that follow surgery: legal, social, economic, and emotional. The fact that there is pain conected with the surgery takes some patients rather by surprise" (Hastings, 1974:337).

Physicians fail to comprehend that medical claims themselves are one source of such dreams and misunderstandings. Benjamin (1966) claimed an astonishing

---

[10]The foundation convinced the Pennsylvania Health Department to issue authorization permits for presurgical cross-dressing, and it lobbied successfully throughout the United States for new birth certificates for post-operative patients.

success rate for reassignment surgery. Only one of the 51 patients he examined after surgery was judged "unsatisfactory." He wrote glowing accounts of these "twice-born" patients: "To compare the Johnny I knew with the Joanna of today is like comparing a dreary day of rain and mist with a beautiful spring morning, or a funeral march with a victory song" (1966:153). Similarly, readers of the *Erikson Education Foundation Newsletter* (1969:1) learned of anonymous transsexuals for whom "new life is brimming over with hope and happiness." Physicians offered men more than just the chance to be rid of their dreaded male insignia—they were promised the experience of female sexuality. A representative of the University of Virginia gender clinic told the *National Enquirer* (1979:1) that "following a sex-change operation, the new female is able to function normally with the exception of having babies." Money (1972:204) claimed that the owner of an "artificial vagina" from Johns Hopkins University "enjoys sexual intercourse, experiencing a pervasive glow of erotic feeling and in some instances, a peak of climatic feeling that corresponds to the orgasm of former days." Human experiences such as sexual fulfillment and gender role comfort were thus transformed into luxury commodities available at high prices from U.S. physicians; victims of aberrant gender role conditioning and other sexual deviants were induced to seek gratification in a commodified world of "artificial vaginas" and fleshy, man-made penises.

Physicians now admit that " 'transsexualism' was apparently made so appealing that doctors report patients saying, 'I want to be a transsexual' " (Person and Oversey, 1974:17). Early followup reports discourage patient wariness. Pauley (1968:465) reviewed 121 post-operative cases and concluded unequivocally that "improved social and emotional adjustments is at least 10 times more likely than an unsatisfactory outcome."[11] Ihlenfeld's (1973a) evaluation of 277 post-operative patients was only three pages long; Gandy's (1973) study of 74 patients consisted of two pages and a table. All the reports were superficial.[12] Relying entirely on patients' self-reports that they would "do it all again," researchers neglected the lesson of cognitive dissonance research which suggests that post-operative patients could ill afford to be critical of such a profound alteration as genital amputation.[13]

FOLLOW-UP EVALUATIONS AND THE DISCOVERY OF "THE CON"

Early follow-up studies, which minimized complications and stressed post-operative adjustment, were important for the legitimation of sex-change operations.

[11]Compare also Baker and Green (1970), Edgerton et al. (1970), Hoenig et al. (1971), Money and Gaskin (1970–71), and Randall (1969).

[12]In the most extensive review of follow-up literature to date, Tiefer and Zitrin (1977) report that of 10 unpublished and 19 published reports, 24 were "preliminary," "anecdoctal," or "brief." Of the five studies rated "excellent," only two were by U.S. physicians—with a combined sample of 38 patients—despite the fact that thousands of operations have been performed in the United States.

[13]Thus, one patient with a "terrible sense of foreboding" immediately after surgery, when asked whether he had done the wrong thing, responded: "But if I did, it's done and I have to find some way to adjust to it" (quoted in Money and Wolff, 1973:248). See also Stoller and Newman (1971:26).

Gradually, however, a number of disquieting items surfaced in the medical literature, including what appears to be a "polysurgical attitude" among post-operative
transsexuals demanding repeated forms of cosmetic surgery (Pauley, 1969b:47) and
many surgical complications. In 1977, the Stanford University gender clinic,
thought by many professionals to perform the finest sex-change surgery in the
country, reported that their two-stage female-to-male conversion took an average of
3.5 operations and that half of their male-to-female conversions involved complications (Norburg and Laub, 1977). Post-operative complications reported in medical
journals include: breast cancer in hormonally treated males; the need for surgical
reduction of bloated limbs resulting from hormones; repeated construction of vaginal openings; infections of the urinary system and rectum; hemorrhaging; loss of
skin grafts; post-operative suicides and suicide attempts; persistent post-operative
economic dependency; patient demands to reverse surgery; chronic post-operative
depression, psychosis, and phobia; sexual dysfunctions; and pre- and post-operative
prostitution, often necessitated by the high cost of treatment. Some sex-change
patients threatened "to shoot the genitials of the surgeon with a shotgun" (Laub and
Fisk, 1974); others filed legal suits, euphemistically referred to by Money (1972:
208) as "a psychopathically litiguous disposition."[14]

As the frequency and range of complications become known, physicians were
shocked by a bizarre revelation: transsexuals had routinely and systematically lied.
Since transsexualism is initially self-diagnosed and because there are no organic
indications of the "disease," physicians are dependent upon the accuracy and
honesty of patients' statements for diagnosis as well as for their understanding of the
illness. Deception became so commonplace that Stoller (1973a:536) complained:
"Those of us faced with the task of diagnosing transsexualism have an additional
burden these days, for most patients who request sex reassignment are in complete
command of the literature and know the answers before the questions are asked."
The psychiatrist's task was to judge how well patients' self-reported life histories fit
the criteria for transsexualism established in the medical literature. Since the reputa-
ble clinics treated only "textbook" cases of transsexualism, patients desiring surgery, for whatever personal reasons, had no other recourse but to meet this evaluation standard. The construction of an appropriate biography became necessary.
Physicians reinforced this demand by rewarding compliance with surgery and
punishing honesty with an unfavorable evaluation. The result was a social process
we call "the con."

An elaborate and well-informed patient grapevine, indirectly facilitated by the
Erikson Educational Foundation's patient services, conveyed tips on each clinic's
evaluative criteria and on "passing":

> Unlike the old medical saw that claims the last time you see a textbook case of anything
> is when you close the textbook, we began to see patients that appeared to be nearly

---

[14]Compare Hastings (1974), Levine et al., (1976), Markland (1973), Meyer and Hoopes (1974),
Randall (1971), and Tiefer and Zitrin (1977) for reports on complications.

identical—both from a subjective and historical point of view. . . . Soon it became conspicuously and disturbingly apparent that far too many patients presented a pat, almost rehearsed history, and seemingly were well versed in precisely what they should or should not say or reveal. Only later did we learn that there did and does exist a very effective grape-vine. (Fisk, 1973:8)

In many instances, the con involved outright deception. For example, a physician warned the Fifth International Gender Dysphoria Symposium in 1977 to watch for a male-to-female post-operative transsexual posing as the mother of young, male candidates in order to corroborate their early socialization accounts of ambivalent gender cues and over-mothering. More often, the process was less direct. Fisk (1973:9) acknowledges "the phenomenon of retrospectively 'amending' one's subjective history. Here, the patient quite subtly alters, shades, rationalizes, denies, represses, forgets, etc., in a compelling rush to embrace the diagnosis of transsexualism." Many patients were as familiar with the medical literature as physicians were.[15]

As early as 1968, Kubie and Mackie (1968:435) observed that patients demanding surgery "tailor their views of themselves and their personal histories to prevailing 'scientific' fashions." Kubie and Mackie warned other physicians that such persons "must present themselves as textbook examples of 'transsexuals' if they are to persuade any team of physicians to change them." This advice went largely unheeded until, gradually, in follow-up conversations, some model patients admitted having shaped biographical accounts to exclude discrediting information, including homosexual and erotic, heterosexual pasts. One patient revealed: "When I assumed the feminine role, I really researched and studied the part, and in essence, I have *conned you and otherwise charmed you* into believing me" (Roth, 1973:101, emphasis added).[16]

Jon Meyer (1973:35), director of Johns Hopkins University's gender clinic, complained that "the label 'transsexual' has come to cover such a 'multitude of sins.'" Meyer (1974) acknowledged that among the patients who had requested and sometimes received surgery at Johns Hopkins were sadists, homosexuals, schizoids, masochists, homosexual prostitutes, and psychotic depressives. Stanford University physicians, too, admitted that among the patients they had operated on were transvestites, homosexuals, and psychotics—all previously viewed as distinct from transsexuals (Fisk, 1973). . . .

[15]In addition to bibliographies and summaries of technical literature published in the *Erikson Education Foundation Newsletter* and Benjamin's (1966) book addressed to laymen, autobiographies of famous transsexuals are an additional resource for patient socialization. See Jorgensen (1967), Martino (1977), and Morris (1974).

[16]Physicians' efforts to be open and sympathetic to their patients, despite their need for reliable information, facilitated "the con." Edgerton et al. (1970:44) advised their colleagues: "It is not difficult for the surgeon to establish a good relationship with transsexual patients—but to do so, he must deal with the patient as a member of the psychological sex chosen by the patient.

IMPLICATIONS FOR CRITICAL THEORY

Forms of illness are always more than biological disease; they are also metaphors, bearing existential, moral, and social meanings (Sontag, 1978). According to Taussig (1980:3), "the signs and symptoms of disease, as much as the technologies of healing, are not 'things-in-themselves,' are *not only* biological and physical, but *are also* signs of social relations disguised as natural things, concealing their roots in human reciprocity." Even with negotiated illnesses which often lack a basis in biology, the reified disease language of natural science obscures their social origins (Holtner and Marx, 1979:137). Disease-talk is about things, not social interaction. Patients whose subjective histories are subsumed under the unifying rhetoric of transsexualism win operations but no language adequate to express the disparate and diverse desires which lead them to body mutilation. These remain private, inchoate, unspeakable.[17]

Critical theorists describe the ideal therapy situation as a paradigm of non-distorted communication (Habermas, 1968:214). Rather than "treat human beings as the quasi-natural objects of description," the goal of communication is patients' self-reflection and emancipation from the reified pseudo-language of neurotic symptoms (Apel, 1977:310).

> The real task of therapy calls for an archaeology of the implicit in such a way that the processes by which social relations are mapped into diseases are brought to light, de-reified, and in doing so liberate the potential for dealing with antagonistic contradictions and breaking the chains of oppression. (Taussig, 1980:7).

According to this view, therapy promises either to provide patients with sufficient self-understanding to criticize society and struggle politically against the crippling effects of social institutions or to provide new fetishes and easily commodifiable solutions to personal troubles (Kovel, 1976–77).

Transsexual therapy, legitimated by the terminology of disease, pushes patients toward an alluring world of artificial vaginas and penises rather than toward self-understanding and sexual politics. Sexual fulfillment and gender role comfort are portrayed as commodities, available through medicine. Just as mass consumer culture, whose values are illusive, offers commodities whose "staged appearance" are removed from the mundane world of their production (Schneider, 1975:213), surgically constructed vaginas are abstracted from the pain and trauma of operating rooms and recovery wards.

Critical theorists claim that the illusions of consumerism can be as pathological for individuals as the neuroses and psychoses symptomatic of the earlier period of capitalist industrial production (Lasch, 1978). Today, in late-capitalist consumer culture, frenzied rituals of buying contradict the puritanical self-denial characteristic of the nineteenth century. We express our identity as much by the things we buy as

[17]See Janice Raymond (1979) for an opposing critique of sex change as an attempt by certain men to benefit from and coopt women's newly won privileges which result from feminist consciousness and struggle.

the work we do. Commodities promise escape from alienation and the fulfillment of our needs. Critics compare the temporary solace of consumer spending with the transitory euphoria of a drug-induced trance (Schneider, 1975:222). Similarly, transsexuals are in danger of becoming surgical junkies as they strive for an idealized sexuality via surgical commodities. This is what physicians refer to as a "poly-surgical attitude" among post-operative patients (Pauley, 1969a). Male-to-female patients especially are caught up in an escalating series of cosmetic operations—including genital amputation—to more closely approximate ideal female form. They routinely demand breast implants and operations to reduce the size of the Adam's apple. Edgerton (1974) reports that 30 percent of his patients also sought rhinoplasty (nose reconstruction), others demand injection of Teflon to modulate vocal pitch and silicon to alter the contours of face, lips, hips, and thighs. Surgeons reduce the thickness of ankles and calves and shorten limbs. In their desperation to pass, male-to-female patients try to effect a commodified image of femininity seen in television advertising. In so doing, many patients are themselves transformed into commodities, resorting to prostitution to pay their medical bills.[18]

While it is difficult to assess the ultimate worth of consumer products, we can try to discern the false promises implicit in their appeal. In the absence of adequate follow-up research, it is impossible to assess the lasting value of sex-change surgery, though recent studies suggest an almost invariable erosion of the transsexual fantasy following an initial "phase of elation" lasting two to five years after surgery (Meyer and Hoopes, 1974). Johns Hopkins University physicians stopped performing sex-change operations in 1979 on the grounds that the patients they operated on were no better off than a sample of transsexual patients who received psychotherapy but not surgery (Meyer and Reter, 1979). Other prominent clinics, however, continue to perform surgery (Hunt and Hampson, 1980).

The following excerpt from a letter written by one transsexual who underwent surgery expresses the disappointment and anguish of some patients:

> No surgery can possibly produce anything that resembles a female vagina. The operation is a theft. [The surgically remodelled tissue] is nothing but an open wound. It needs dilation to keep it open and if dilated too much becomes useless for intercourse. Such an open wound lacks protective membranes and bleeds under pressure. . . . A piece of phallus with an open wound below and a ring of scrotum hanging is all it is. . . . Who calls that an artificial vagina is nothing but a bandit looking for ignorant and credulous people to exploit them. (quoted in Socarides, 1975:130)

The evidence suggests that Meyer and Hoopes (1974:450) were correct when they wrote that "in a thousand subtle ways, the reassignee has the bitter experience that he is not—and never will be—a real girl but is, at best, a convincing simulated female. Such an adjustment cannot compensate for the tragedy of having lost all chance to be male and of having, in the final analysis, no way to be really female."

[18]For the correlation between financial dependency during reassignment and prostitution, see Hastings (1974), Levine et al. (1975), Meyer (1974), and Norburg and Laub (1977).

THE POLITICS OF SEX REASSIGNMENT

Taussig (1980:7) shows that "behind every disease theory in our society lurks an organizing realm of moral concerns." In this paper we have examined both physicians' and patients' motives for sex-change surgery. We conclude that at the level of ideology, sex-change surgery not only reflects and extends late-capitalist logics of reification and commodification, but simultaneously plays an implicit role in contemporary sexual politics.

The recognition that, in this day and age, the fulfillment of human desire is less a matter of public discussion than a technical accomplishment of social administration (Habermas, 1973:253) applies equally to sex changes. Medicine brushes aside the politics of gender to welcome suffering patients—many fleeing harassment for sexual deviance[19]—into pseudo-tolerant gender-identity clinics. Yet these clinics are implicitly political and, indirectly, intolerant.

With reproduction and sexual functioning falling under medical jurisdiction, physicians have played crucial roles in maintaining gender organization (Ehrenreich and English, 1973). In providing a rite of passage between sexual identities, sex-change surgery implicitly reaffirms traditional male and female roles. Despite the mute testimony of confused and ambivalent patients to the range of gender experience, individuals unable or unwilling to conform to the sex roles ascribed to them at birth are carved up on the operating table to gain acceptance to the opposite sex role.[20]

Critical theorists contend that, in the United States, hegemonic ideology absorbs and domesticates conflicting definitions of reality (Gitlin, 1979:263). But rather than support contemporary movements aimed at reorganizing gender and parenting roles and repudiating the either/or logic of gender development (Chodorow, 1978, 1979; Ehrensaft, 1980), sex-change proponents support sex-reassignment surgery. By substituting medical terminology for political discourse, the medical profession has indirectly tamed and transformed a potential wildcat strike at the gender factory.[21]

[19]For physician reports of harrassed patients, see Benjamin (1971:77), Edgerton et al. (1970:43), Meyer and Hoopes (1974:450), and Randall (1971:157).

[20]Physicians' remarks on the prevention of transsexualism make the political implications of sex change overt: deviations from traditional roles are potentially harmful to children. Benjamin (1971:76) warns that male children's curiosity about female clothing "should never be made light of by parents" and Richard Green (1969:33) warns of "sissy behavior during childhood" and of "playing house.'" Accepting Stoller's theory of the dominating mother as the principal agent of transsexual socialization, Green contends that "goals of family therapy are for the husband and wife to gain some perspective on the second-class status of the husband and on the significance of their unbalanced roles in shaping their son's personality." Similarly, Newman and Stoller (1971:301) report success in effecting a "therapeutically induced Oedipus complex" on a "very feminine boy" by encouraging the child to assert his male identity by first beating a doll and then expressing aggression toward his mother and sister.

[21]Said one politically aware transsexual quoted by Feinbloom (1976:159): "As long as society insists on requiring everyone to fit in a strict two-gender system, the whole transsexual thing will always be a game, to hide what I've been or what I want to be. If the women's movement is so into freeing up the definitions of gender, why not start with us?"

REFERENCES

Apel, Karl-Otto. 1977. "The a priori of communication and the foundation of the human-
ities," pp. 292–315 in Fred Dallmayr and Thomas McCarthy (eds.), *Understanding and
Social Inquiry*. Notre Dame, Ind.: University of Notre Dame Press.

Baker, Howard, and Richard Green. 1970. "Treatment of transsexualism." *Current Psychiatry Therapy* 10:88–99.

Benjamin, Harry. 1954. "Transsexualism and transvestism as psycho-somatic and somato-
psychic syndromes." *American Journal of Psychotherapy* 8:219–239.

──────. 1966. *The Transsexual Phenomenon: All the Facts About the Changing of Sex
Through Hormones and Surgery*. New York: Warner Books.

──────. 1971. "Should surgery be performed on transsexuals?" *American Journal of Psychotherapy* 80:74–82.

Berg, Ian, Harold Nixon, and Robert MacMahon. 1963. "Change of assigned sex at puber-
ty." *Lancet* 12:1216–1217.

Bunker, John P. 1970. "Surgical manpower: A comparison of operations and surgery in the
United States and in England and Wales." *New England Journal of Medicine.*
282.1:135–143.

──────. 1979. "Feminism and difference: Gender, relation and difference in psychoanalytic
perspective." *Socialist Review* 9:51–69.

Corea, Gena. 1977. The Hidden Malpractice: How American Medicine Mistreats Women.
New York: Jove.

Dewhurst, C. J., and R. R. Gordon. 1963. "Change of sex." *Lancet* 12:1213–1216.

Edgerton, Milton T. 1974. "The surgical treatment of male transsexuals." *Clinics in Plastic
Surgery* 1:285–323.

──────, Wayne Jacobson, and Eugene Meyer. 1960–61. "Surgical-psychiatric study of
patients seeking plastic (cosmetic) surgery." *British Journal of Plastic Surgery* 13:136–
145.

──────, Norman J. Knorr, and James R. Callison. 1970. "The surgical treatment of transsexual patients." *Plastic and Reconstruction Surgery* 45:38–46.

Erikson Educational Foundation Newsletter. 1969. "Life Begins Again" Spring:1.

Feinbloom, Deborah Heller. 1976. *Transvestites and Transsexuals: Mixed Views*. New York:
Delacorte.

Fisk, Norman. 1973. "Gender dysphoria syndrome (The how, what, and why of a disease),"
pp. 7–14 in Donald Laub and Patrick Gandy (eds.), *Second Interdisciplinary Symposium of Gender Dyphoria Syndrome*. Palo Alto, Calif: Stanford University Press.

Forester, B. M., and H. Swiller. 1972. "Transsexualism: Review of syndrome and presentation of possible successful therapeutic approach." *International Journal of Group Psychotherapy* 22:343–351.

Freidson, Eliot. 1970. *Profession of Medicine: A Study in the Sociology of Applied Knowledge*. New York: Dodd, Mead.

Gandy, Patrick. 1973. "Follow-up on 74 gender dysphoric patients treated at Stanford," pp.
227–229 in Donald Laub and Patrick Gandy (eds.), *Second International Symposium on
Gender Dysphoria Syndrome*. Palo Alto, Calif.: Stanford University Press.

Green, Richard. 1969. "Childhood cross-gender identification," pp. 23–36 in Richard
Green and John Money (eds.), *Transsexualism and Sex Reassignment*. Baltimore: Johns
Hopkins University Press.

————. 1970. "A Research Strategy." *International Journal of Psychiatry* 9:269–273.

Habermas, Jurgen. 1968. *Knowledge and Human Interests*. Boston: Beacon Press.

————. 1973. *Theory and Practice*. Boston: Beacon Press.

————. 1979. *Communication and the Evolution of Society*. Boston: Beacon Press.

Hamburger, C., G. K. Sturup, and E. Dahl-Iversen, 1953. "Transvestism." *Journal of the American Medical Association* 152:391–396.

Hastings, Donald W. 1966. "Transsexualism and transvestism." *Journal of the American Medical Association* 197:594–600.

————. 1969. "Inauguration of a research project on transsexualism in a university medical center," pp. 243–252 in Richard Green and John Money (eds.), *Transsexualism and Sex Reassignment*. Baltimore: Johns Hopkins Press.

————. 1974. "Postsurgical adjustment of male transsexual patients." *Plastic Surgery* 1:335–344.

Holzner, Burkhart, and John H. Marx. 1979. *Knowledge Application: The Knowledge System in Society*. Boston: Allyn and Bacon.

Hoopes, J. E., N. J. Knorr, and S. R. Wolf. 1968. "Transsexualism: Considerations regarding sexual reassignment." *Journal of Nervous and Mental Disease* 147:510–516.

Hunt, D. Daniel, and John Hampson. 1980. "Follow-up of 17 biologic male transsexuals after sex reassignment surgery." *American Journal of Psychiatry* 137:432–438.

Ihlenfeld, Charles. 1973a. "Outcome of hormonal-surgical, intervention on the transsexual condition: Evolution and management," pp. 230–233 in Donald Laub and Patrick Gandy (eds.), *Proceedings of Second Interdisciplinary Symposium on Gender Dysphoria Syndrome*. Palo Alto, Calif.: Stanford University Press.

————. 1973b. "Thoughts on the treatment of transsexuals." *Journal of Contemporary Psychotherapy* 6:63–69.

Jorgensen, Christine. 1967. *A Personal Autobiography*. New York: Bantam.

Knorr, Norma, Sanford Wolf, and Eugene Meyer. 1969. "Psychiatric evaluation of male transsexuals for surgery," pp. 271–280 in Richard Green and John Money (eds.), Transsexualism and Sex Reassignment. Baltimore: Johns Hopkins University Press.

Kovel, Joel. 1976–77. "Therapy in late capitalism." *Telos* 30:73–92.

Kubie, Lawrence S., and James B. Mackie. 1968. "Critical issues raised by operations for gender transmutations." *Journal of Nervous and Mental Disease* 147:431–443.

Landers, Ann. 1979. "Sex-change operations are more than cosmetic." *The Raleigh Register*, January 21: B-5.

Larson, Magali Sarfatti. 1977. *The Rise of Professionalism: A Sociological Analysis*. Berkeley: University of California Press.

Lasch, Christopher. 1978. *The Culture of Narcissism*. New York: W. W. Norton.

Laub, Donald R., and Norman M. Fisk. 1974. "A rehabilitation program for gender dysphoria syndrome by surgical sex change." *Plastic and Reconstruction Surgery* 53:388–403.

Levine, Edward, Charles Shaiova, and F. M. Mihailovic. 1975. "Male to female: The role of transformation of transsexuals." *Archives of Sexual Behavior* 4:176–185.

Lindgren, Thomas, and Ira Pauley. 1975. "A body image scale for evaluating transsexuals." *Archives of Sexual Behavior* 4:640–657.

Martino, Mario. 1977. *Emergence*. New York: New American Library.

Meerloo, Joost. 1976. "Change of sex and colloraboration with the psychosis." *The American Journal of Psychiatry* 124:263–264.

Meyer, Eugene, Wayne Jacobson, Milton Edgerton, and Arthur Canter. 1960. "Motivational patterns in patients seeking elective plastic surgery." *Psychosomatic Medicine* 22:193–201.

Meyer, Jon K. 1973. "Some thoughts on nosology and motivating among 'transsexuals,'" pp. 31–36 in Donald Laub and Patrick Gandy (eds.), *Proceedings of Second Interdisciplinary Symposium on Gender Dysphoria Syndrome.* Palo Alto, Calif.: Stanford University Press.

————. 1974. "Clinical variants among applicants for sex reassignment." *Archives of Sexual Behavior* 3:527–558.

————, and John E. Hoopes. 1974. "The gender dysphoria syndromes: A position statement on so-called 'transsexualism.'" *Plastic and Reconstructive Surgery* 54:444–451.

————, and Donna Reter. 1979. "Sex reassignment: Follow-up." *Archives of General Psychiatry* 36:1010–1015.

Money, John. 1972. "Sex reassignment therapy in gender identity disorders." *International Psychiatry Clinics* 8:198–210.

————, and Ronald Gaskin. 1970–71. "Sex reassignment." *International Journal of Psychiatry* 9:249–269.

————, Joan Hampson, and John Hampson. 1955. "Hermaphroditism: Recommendations concerning assignment of sex, change of sex, and psychologic management." *Bulletin of the Johns Hopkins Hospital* 96–97:284–300.

————, Joan Hampson, and John Hampson. 1977. "Imprinting and the establishment of gender role." *Archives of Neurology and Psychiatry* 77:333–336.

Morris, Jan. 1974. *Conundrum.* New York: New American Library.

National Enquirer. 1979. "Sex-change operation left me trapped between a man and woman." October 30:1.

Newman, Lawrence, and Robert Stoler. 1971. "The oedipal situation in male transsexualism." *British Journal of Medical Psychology* 44:295–303.

Norburg, Martha, and Donald Laub. 1977. "Review of the Stanford experience: Implications for treatment." Paper presented at the Fifth International Gender Dysphoria Symposium, Norfolk, Virginia, February 12.

Pauley, Ira B. 1968. "Current status of change of sex operation." *Journal of Nervous and Mental Disease* 47:460–471.

————. 1969a. "Adult manifestations of female transsexualism," pp. 59–90 in Richard Green and John Money (eds.), *Transsexualism and Sex Reassignment.* Baltimore: Johns Hopkins University Press.

————. 1969b. "Adult manifestations of male transsexualism," pp. 37–58 in Richard Green and John Money (eds.), *Transsexualism and Sex Reassignment.* Baltimore: Johns Hopkins University Press.

Person, Ethel, and Lionel Oversey. 1974. "The transsexual syndrome in males, I and II." *American Journal of Psychotherapy* 28:4–20, 174–193.

Randall, John. 1971. "Indications for sex reassignment surgery." *Archives of Sexual Behavior* 1:153–161.

Raymond, Janice. 1979. *The Transsexual Empire: The Making of the She-Male.* Boston: Beacon Press.

Roth, Helen N. 1973. "Three years of ongoing psychotherapy of a transsexual patient," pp. 99–102 in Donald Laub and Patrick Gandy (eds.), *Proceedings of Second Interdisciplinary Symposium on Gender Dysphoria Syndrome.* Palo Alto, Calif.: Stanford University Press.

Schneider, Michael. 1975. *Neurosis and Civilization: A Marxist/Freudian Synthesis.* New York: Seabury Press.

Socarides, Charles. 1970. "A psychoanalytic study of the desire for sexual transformation ('transsexualism'): The plaster-of-Paris man." *International Journal of Psycho-Analysis* 51:341–349.

_____. 1975. Beyond Sexual Freedom. New York: Quadrangle.

Sontag, Susan. 1978. *Illness as Metaphor.* New York: Farrar, Straus, and Giroux.

Stinson, G. 1972. "A study of twelve applicants for transsexual surgery." *Ohio State Medical Journal* 68:245–249.

Stoller, Robert J. 1964a. "A contribution to the study of gender identity." *International Journal of Psycho-Analysis* 45:220–226.

_____. 1964b. "The hermaphroditic identity of hermaphrodites." *Journal of Nervous and Mental Disease* 139:453–457.

_____. 1967. "Etiological factors in male transsexualism." *Transactions of the New York Academy of Sciences* 86:431–433.

_____. 1973a. "Male transsexualism: Uneasiness." *American Journal of Psychiatry* 130:536–539.

_____. 1973b. "The male transsexual as 'experiment.'" *International Journal of Psycho-Analysis* 54:215–225.

Sturup, Charles. 1976. "Male transsexuals: A long-term follow-up after sex reassignment operations." *Acta Psychiatry* 53:51–63.

Taussig, Michael T. 1980. "Reification and the consciousness of the patient." *Social Science Medicine* 14:3–13.

Van Buren, Abigail. 1977. "Male athlete would rather be a woman." *Paris News* (Paris, Kentucky), November 10:A-10.

Volkan, Vanik, and Tajammul Bhatti. 1973. "Dreams of transsexuals awaiting surgery." *Comprehensive Psychiatry* 14:269–279.

Wilden, Anthony. 1972. *System and Structure: Essays in Communication and Exchange.* London: Tavistock.

Reading 8

Tinydopers: A Case Study of Deviant Socialization

Patricia A. Adler
Peter Adler
University of California, San Diego

Marijuana smoking is now filtering down to our youngest generation; a number of children from 0–8 years old are participating in this practice under the influence and supervision of their parents. This phenomenon, *tinydoping* raises interesting questions about changes in societal mores and patterns of socialization. We are not concerned here with the desirability or morality of the activity. Instead, we will discuss the phenomenon, elucidating the diverse range of attitudes, strategems and procedures held and exercised by parents and children.

An examination of the history and cultural evolution of marijuana over the last several decades illuminates the atmosphere in which tinydoping arose. Marijuana use, first located chiefly among jazz musicians and ghetto communities, eventually expanded to "the highly alienated young in flight from families, schools and conventional communities" (Simon and Gagnon, 1968:60; see also Goode, 1970; Carey, 1968; Kaplan, 1971; and Grinspoon, 1971). Blossoming in the mid-1960s, this youth scene formed an estranged and deviant subculture offsetting the dominant culture's work ethic and instrumental success orientation. Society reacted as an angry parent, enforcing legal, social and moral penalties against its rebellious children. Today, however, the pothead subculture has eroded and the population of smokers has broadened to include large numbers of middle class and establishment-oriented people.

Marijuana, then, may soon take its place with alcohol, its "prohibition" a thing of the past. These two changes can be considered movements of moral passage:

> Movements to redefine behavior may eventuate in a moral passage, a transition of the behavior from one moral status to another. . . . What is attacked as criminal today may be seen as sick next year and fought over as possibly legitimate by the next generation. (Gusfield, 1967:187. For further discussions of the social creation of deviance, see also Matza, 1969; Kitsuse, 1962; Douglas, 1970; and Becker, 1963.)

Profound metamorphoses testify to this redefinition: frequency and severity of arrest is proportionately down from a decade ago; the stigma of a marijuana-related

Reprinted with permission from *Symbolic Interaction* 1 (2) (Spring 1978): 90–105.

arrest is no longer as personally and occupationally ostracizing; and the fear that using grass will press the individual into close contact with hardened criminals and cause him to adopt a deviant self-identity or take up criminal ways has also largely passed.

The transformation in marijuana's social and legal status is not intrinsic to its own characteristics or those of mood-altering drugs in general. Rather, it illustrates a process of becoming socially accepted many deviant activities or substances may go through. This research suggests a more generic model of social change, a sequential development characteristic of the diffusion and legitimation of a formerly unconventional practice. Five stages identify the spread of such activities from small isolated outgroups, through increasing levels of mainstream society, and finally to such sacred groups as children.[1] Often, however, as with the case of pornography, the appearance of this quasi-sanctioned conduct among juveniles elicits moral outrage and a social backlash designed to prevent such behavior in the sacred population, while leaving it more open to the remainder of society.

Most treatment of pot smoking in the sociological literature have been historically and sub-culturally specific (see Carey, 1968; Goode, 1970; Grupp, 1971; Hochman, 1972; Kaplan, 1971; and Simon and Gagnon, 1968), swiftly dated by our rapidly changing society. Only Becker's (1953) work is comparable to our research since it offers a generic sequential model of the process for becoming a marijuana user.

The data in this paper show an alternate route to marijuana smoking. Two developments necessitate a modification of Becker's conceptualization. First, there have been many changes in norms, traditions and patterns of use since the time he wrote. Second, the age of this new category of smokers is cause for reformulation. Theories of child development proposed by Mead (1934), Erikson, (1968) and Piaget (1948) agree that prior to a certain age children are unable to comprehend subtle transformations and perceptions. As we will see the full effects and symbolic meanings of marijuana are partially lost to them due to their inability to differentiate between altered states of consciousness and to connect this with the smoking experience. Yet this does not preclude their becoming avid pot users and joining in the smoking group as accepted members.

Socialization practices are the final concern of this research. The existence of tinydoping both illustrates and contradicts several established norms of traditional childrearing. Imitative behavior (Piaget, 1962), for instance, is integral to tinydoping since the children's desire to copy the actions of parents and other adults is a primary motivation. Boundary maintenance also arises as a consideration: as soon

---

[1]The period of childhood has traditionally been a special time in which developing adults were given special treatment to ensure their growing up to be capable and responsible members of society. Throughout history and in most cultures children have been kept apart from adults and sheltered in protective isolation from certain knowledge and practices (see Aries, 1965).

as their offspring can communicate, parents must instruct them in the perception of social borders and the need for guarding group activities as secret. In contrast, refutations of convention include the introduction of mood-altering drugs into the sacred childhood period and, even more unusual, parents and children get high together. This bridges, often to the point of eradication, the inter-generational gap firmly entrenched in most societies. Thus, although parents view their actions as normal, tinydoping must presently be considered as deviant socialization.

METHODS

Collected over the course of 18 months, our data include observations of two dozen youngsters between the ages of birth and eight, and a similar number of parents, aged 21 to 32, all in middle-class households. To obtain a complete image of this practice we talked with parents, kids and other involved observers (the "multi-perspectival" approach, Douglas, 1976). Many of our conversations with adults were taped but our discussions with the children took the form of informal, extemporaneous dialogue, since the tape recorder distracts and diverts their attention. Finally, our study is exploratory and suggestive; we make no claim to all-inclusiveness in the cases or categories below.

The Kids

The following four individuals, each uniquely interesting, represent many common characteristics of other children and adults we observed.

"Big Ed": The Diaperdoper. Big Ed derives his name from his miniature size. Born three months prematurely, now three years old, he resembles a toy human being. Beneath his near-white wispy hair and toddling diapered bottom, he packs a punch of childish energy. Big Ed's mother and older siblings take care of him although he often sees his father who lives in a neighboring California town. Laxity and permissiveness characterize his upbringing, as he freely roams the neighborhood under his own and other children's supervision. Exposure to marijuana has prevailed since birth and in the last year he advanced from passive inhalation (smoke blown in his direction) to active puffing on joints. Still in the learning stage, most of his power is expended blowing air into the reefer instead of inhaling. He prefers to suck on a "bong" (a specially designed waterpipe), delighting on the gurgling sound the water makes. A breast fed baby, he will go to the bong for oral satisfaction, whether it is filled or not. He does not actively seek joints, but Big Ed never refuses one when offered. After a few puffs, however, he usually winds up with smoke in his eyes and tearfully retreats to a glass of water. Actual marijuana inhalation is minimal; his size renders it potent. Big Ed has not absorbed any social restrictions related to pot use or any awareness of its illegality, but is still too young to make a blooper as his speech is limited.

Stephanie: The Social Smoker. Stephanie is a dreamy four-year-old with quite good manners, calm assurance, sweet disposition and a ladylike personality and appearance. Although her brothers are rough and tumble, Stephanie can play with the boys or amuse herself sedately alone or in the company of adults. Attendance at a progressive school for the last two years has developed her natural curiosity and intelligence. Stephanie's mother and father both work, but still find enough recreational time to raise their children with love and care and to engage in frequent marijuana smoking. Accordingly, Stephanie has seen grass since infancy and accepted it as a natural part of life. Unlike the diaperdoper, she has mastered the art of inhalation and can breathe the smoke out through her nose. Never grasping or grubbing for pot, she has advanced from a preference for bongs or pipes and now enjoys joints when offered. She revels in being part of a crowd of smokers and passes the reefer immediately after each puff, never holding it for an unsociable amount of time. Her treasure box contains a handful of roaches (marijuana butts) and seeds (she delights in munching them as snacks) that she keeps as mementos of social occasions with (adult) "friends." After smoking, Stephanie becomes more bubbly and outgoing. Dancing to records, she turns in circles as she jogs from one foot to the other, releasing her body to the rhythm. She then eats everything in sight and falls asleep—roughly the same cycle as adults, but faster.

When interviewed, Stephanie clearly recognized the difference between a cigarette and a joint (both parents use tobacco), defining the effects of the latter as good but still being unsure of what the former did and how the contents of each varied. She also responded with some confusion about social boundaries separating pot users from non-users, speculating that perhaps her grandmother did smoke it but her grandfather certainly did not (neither do). In the words of her father: "She knows not to tell people about it but she just probably wouldn't anyway."

Josh: The Self-gratifier. Everyone in the neighborhood knows Josh. Vociferous and outgoing, at age five he has a decidedly Dennis-the-Menace quality in both looks and personality. Neither timid nor reserved, he boasts to total strangers of his fantastic exploits and talents. Yet behind his bravado swagger lies a seeming insecurity and need for acceptance, coupled with a difficulty in accepting authority, which has led him into squabbles with peers, teachers, siblings and parents.

Josh's home shows the traditional division of labor. His mother stays home to cook and care for the children while his father works long hours. The mother is always calm and tolerant about her youngster's smart-alec ways, but his escapades may provoke an explosive tirade from the father. Yet this male parent is clearly the dominating force in Josh's life. Singling Josh out from his younger sister and brother, the father has chosen him as his successor in the male tradition. The parent had himself begun drinking and smoking cigarettes in his early formative years, commencing pot use as a teenager, and now has a favorable attitude toward the early use of stimulants which he is actively passing on to Josh.

According to his parents, his smoking has had several beneficial effects. Considering Josh a "hyper" child, they claim that it calms him down to a more normal speed, often permitting him to engage in activities which would otherwise be too difficult for his powers of concentration. He also appears to become more sedate and less prone to temper tantrums, sleeping longer and more deeply. But Josh's smoking patterns differ significantly from our last two subjects. He does not enjoy social smoking, preferring for his father to roll him "pinners" (thin joints) to smoke by himself. Unlike many other tinydopers, Josh frequently refuses the offer of a joint saying, "Oh that! I gave up smoking that stuff." At age five he claims to have already quit and gone back several times. His mother backs this assertion as valid; his father brushes it off as merely a ploy to shock and gain attention. Here, the especially close male parent recognizes the behavior as imitative and accepts it as normal. To others, however, it appears strange and suggests a surprising sophistication.

Josh's perception of social boundaries is also mature. Only a year older than Stephanie, Josh has made some mistakes but his awareness of the necessity for secrecy is complete; he differentiates those people with whom he may and may not discuss the subject by the experience of actually smoking with them. He knows individuals but cannot yet socially categorize the boundaries. Josh also realizes the contrast between joints and cigarettes down to the marijuana and tobacco they contain. Interestingly, he is aggressively opposed to tobacco while favoring pot use (this may be the result of anti-tobacco cancer propaganda from kindergarten).

Kyra: The Bohemian. A worldly but curiously childlike girl is seven-year-old Kyra. Her wavy brown hair falls to her shoulders and her sun-tanned body testifies to many hours at the beach in winter and summer. Of average height for her age, she dresses with a maturity beyond her years. Friendly and sociable, she has few reservations about what she says to people. Kyra lives with her youthful mother and whatever boyfriend her mother fancies at the moment. Their basic family unit consists of two (mother and daughter), and they have travelled together living a free life all along the West Coast and Hawaii. While Josh's family was male dominated, this is clearly female centered, all of Kyra's close relatives being women. They are a bohemian group, generation after generation following a hip, up-to-the-moment, unshackled lifestyle. The house is often filled with people, but when the visitors clear out, a youthful, thrillseeking mother remains, who raises this daughter by treating her like a sister or friend. This demand on Kyra to behave as an adult may produce some internal strain, but she seems to have grown accustomed to it. Placed in situations others might find awkward, she handles them with precocity. Like her mother, she is being reared for a life of independence and freedom.

Pot smoking is an integral part of this picture. To Kyra it is another symbol of her adulthood; she enjoys it and wants to do it a lot. At seven she is an accomplished smoker; her challenge right now lies in the mastery of rolling joints. Of our four examples, social boundaries are clearest to Kyra. Not only is she aware of the necessary secrecy surrounding pot use, but she is able socially to categorize types of people into marijuana smokers and straights. She may err in her judgment occasionally, but no more so than any adult.

Stages of Development

These four and other cases suggest a continuum of reactions to marijuana that is loosely followed by tinydopers.

From birth to around 18 months a child's involvement is passive. Most parents keep their infants nearby at all times and if pot is smoked the room becomes filled with potent clouds. At this age just a little marijuana smoke can be very powerful and these infants, the youngest diaperdopers, manifest noticeable effects. The drug usually has a calming influence, putting the infant into a less cranky mood and extending the depth and duration of sleep.

After the first one and a half years, the children are more attuned to what is going on around them: they begin to desire participation in a "monkey see, monkey do" fashion. During the second year, a fascination with paraphernalia generally develops, as they play with it and try to figure it out. Eager to smoke with adults and older children, they are soon discouraged after a toke (puff) or two. They find smoking difficult and painful (particularly to the eyes and throat)—after all, it is not easy to inhale burning hot air and hold it in your lungs.

But continual practice eventually produces results, and inhalation seems to be achieved somewhere during the third or fourth year. This brings considerable pride and makes the kids feel they have attained semi-adult status. Now they can put the paraphernalia to work. Most tinydopers of this age are wild about "roachclips," itching to put their joints into them as soon as possible after lighting.

Ages four and five bring the first social sense of the nature of pot and who should know about it. This begins as a vague idea, becoming further refined with age and sophistication. Finally, by age seven or eight kids have a clear concept of where the lines can be drawn between those who are and aren't "cool," and can make these distinctions on their own. No child we interviewed, however, could verbalize about any specific effects felt after smoking marijuana. Ironically, although they participate in smoking and actually manifest clear physical symptoms of the effects, tinydopers are rationally and intellectually unaware of how the drug is acting upon them. They are too young to notice a change in their behavior or to make the symbolic leap and associate this transformation with having smoked pot previously. The effects of marijuana must be socially and consensually delienated from non-high sensations for the user to fully appreciate the often subtle perceptual and physiological changes that have occurred. To the youngster the benefits of pot smoking are not at all subtle: he is permitted to imitate his elders by engaging in a social ritual they view as pleasurable and important; the status of adulthood is partially conferred on him by allowing this act, and his desire for acceptance is fulfilled through inclusion in his parents' peer group. This constitutes the major difference in appreciation between the child and adult smoker.

Parents' Strategies

The youth of the sixties made some forceful statements through their actions about how they evaluated the Establishment and the conventional American lifestyle. While their political activism has faded, many former members of this group still feel a strong commitment to smoking pot and attach a measure of symbolic significance to it. When they had children the question then arose of how to handle the drug vis-à-vis their offspring. The continuum of responses they developed ranges from total openness and permissiveness to various measures of secrecy.

Smoking Regularly Permitted. Some parents give their children marijuana whenever it is requested. They may wait until the child reaches a certain age, but most parents in this category started their kids on pot from infancy. These parents may be "worried" or "unconcerned."

Worried. Ken and Deedy are moderate pot smokers, getting high a few times a week. Both had been regular users for several years prior to having children. When Deedy was pregnant she absolutely refused to continue her smoking pattern.

> I didn't know what effect it could have on the unborn child. I tried to read and find out, but there's very little written on that. But in the "Playboy Advisor" there was an article: they said we advise you to stay away from all drugs when you're pregnant. That was sort of my proof. I figured they don't bullshit about these types of things. I sort of said now at least somebody stands behind me because people were saying, "You can get high, it's not going to hurt the baby."

This abstinence satisfied them and once the child was born they resumed getting high as before. Frequently smoking in the same room as the baby, they began to worry about the possible harmful effects this exposure might have on his physical, psychological, and mental development. After some discussion, they consulted the family pediatrician, a prominent doctor in the city.

> I was really embarrassed, but I said, "Doctor, we get high, we smoke pot, and sometimes the kid's in the room. If he's in the room can this hurt him? I don't want him to be mentally retarded." He said, "Don't worry about it, they're going to be legalizing it any day now—this was three years ago—it's harmless and a great sedative."

This reassured them on two counts: they no longer were fearful in their own minds, and they had a legitimate answer when questioned by their friends.[2]

---

[2]Particularly relevant to these "justifications" is Scott and Lyman's (1968) analysis of accounts, as statements made to relieve one of culpability. Specifically, they can be seen as "denial of injury" (Sykes and Matza, 1957) as they assert the innocuousness of giving marijuana to their child. An "excuse" is further employed, "scapegoating" the doctor as the one really responsible for this aberration. Also, the appeal to science has been made.

Ken and Deedy were particularly sensitive about peer reactions:

> Some people say, "You let your child get high?!" They really react with disgust. Or they'll say, "Oh you let your kids get high," and then they kind of look at you like, "That's neat, I think." And it's just nice to be able to back it up.

Ken and Deedy were further nonplussed about the problem of teaching their children boundary maintenance. Recognizing the need to prevent their offspring from saying things to the wrong people, they were unsure how to approach this subject properly.

> How can you tell a kid, how can you go up to him and say, "Well you want to get high, but don't tell anybody you're doing it"? You can't. We didn't really know how to tell them. You don't want to bring the attention, you don't want to tell your children not to say anything about it because that's a sure way to get them to do it. We just never said anything about it.

They hope this philosophy of openness and permissiveness will forestall the need to limit their children's marijuana consumption. Limits, for them, resemble prohibitions and interdictions against discussing grass: they make transgressions attractive. Both parents believe strongly in presenting marijuana as an everyday occurrence, definitely not as an undercover affair. When asked how they thought this upbringing might affect their kids, Deedy offered a fearful but doubtful speculation that their children might one day reject the drug.

> I don't imagine they'd try to abuse it. Maybe they won't even smoke pot when they get older. That's a big possibility. I doubt it, but hopefully they won't be that way. They've got potheads for parents.

Unconcerned. Alan and Anna make use of a variety of stimulants—pot, alcohol, cocaine—to enrich their lives. Considered heavy users, they consume marijuana and alcohol daily. Alan became acquainted with drugs, particularly alcohol, at a very early age and Anna first tried them in her teens. When they decided to have children the question of whether they would permit the youngsters to partake in their mood-altering experiences never arose. Anna didn't curtail her drug intake during pregnancy; her offspring were conceived, formed and weaned on this steady diet. When queried about their motivations, Alan volunteered:

> What the hell! It grows in the ground, it's a weed. I can't see anything wrong with doing anything, inducing any part of it into your body any way that you possibly could eat it, smoke it, intravenously, or whatever, that it would ever harm you because it grows in the ground. It's a natural thing. It's one of God's treats.

All of their children have been surrounded by marijuana's aromatic vapor since the day they returned from the hospital. Alan and Anna were pleased with the effect pot had on their infants; the relaxed, sleepy and happy qualities achieved after inhaling pot smoke made child-rearing an easier task. As the little ones grew older they naturally wanted to share in their parents' activities. Alan viewed this as the children's desire to imitate rather than true enjoyment of any effects:

> Emily used to drink Jack Daniels straight and like it. I don't think it was taste, I think it was more of an acceptance thing because that's what I was drinking. She was also puffing on joints at six months.

This mimicking, coupled with a craving for acceptance, although recognized by Alan in his kids, was not repeated in his own feelings toward friends or relatives. At no time during the course of our interview or acquaintance did he show any concern with what others thought of his behavior; rather, his convictions dominated, and his wife passively followed his lead.

In contrast to the last couple, Alan was not reluctant to address the problem of boundary maintenance. A situation arise when Emily was three, where she was forced to learn rapidly:

> One time we were stopped by the police while driving drunk. I said to Emily—we haven't been smoking marijuana. We all acted quiet and Emily realized there was something going on and she delved into it. I explained that some people are stupid and they'll harm you very badly if you smoke marijuana. To this day I haven't heard her mention it to anyone she hasn't smoked with.

As each new child came along, Alan saw to it that they learned the essential facts of life.

Neither Alan nor Anna saw any moral distinction between marijuana smoking and other, more accepted pastimes. They heartily endorsed marijuana as something to indulge in like "tobacco, alcohol, sex, breathing or anything else that brings pleasure to the senses." Alan and Anna hope their children will continue to smoke grass in their later lives. It has had beneficial effects for them and they believe it can do the same for their kids:

> I smoked marijuana for a long time, stopped and developed two ulcers; and smoked again and the two ulcers went away. It has great medicinal value.

Smoking Occasionally Permitted. In contrast to uninterrupted permissiveness, other parents restrict marijuana use among their children to specific occasions. A plethora of reasons and rationalizations lie behind this behavior, some openly avowed by parents and others not. Several people believe it is okay to let the kids get high as long as it isn't done too often. Many other people do not have any carefully thought-out notion of what they want, tending to make spur-of-the moment decisions. As a result, they allow occasional but largely undefined smoking in a sporadic and irregular manner. Particular reasons for this inconsistency can be illustrated by three examples from our research:

1. **Conflicts between parents** can confuse the situation. While Stella had always planned to bring her children up with pot, Burt did not like the idea. Consequently, the household rule on this matter varied according to the unpredictable moods of the adults and which parent was in the house.

2. Mike and Gwen had trouble **making up their minds.** At one time they thought it probably couldn't harm the child, only to decide the next day they shouldn't take chances and rescind that decision.

3. Lois and David didn't waver hourly but had **changing ideas over time.** At first they were against it, but then met a group of friends who liked to party and approved of tinydoping. After a few years they moved to a new neighborhood and changed their lifestyle, again prohibiting pot smoking for the kids.

These are just a few of the many situations in which parents allow children an occasional opportunity to smoke grass. They use various criteria to decide when those permissible instances ought to be, most families subscribing to several of the following patterns:

Reward. The child receives pot as a bonus for good behavior in the past, present or future. This may serve as an incentive: "If you're a good boy today, Johnny, I may let you smoke with us tonight," or to celebrate an achievement already completed like "going potty" or reciting the alphabet.

Guilt. Marijuana can be another way of compensating children for what they aren't getting. Historically, parents have tried to buy their kids off or make themselves loved through gifts of money or toys but pot can also be suitable here. This is utilized both by couples with busy schedules who don't have time for the children ("We're going out again tonight so we'll give you this special treat to make it up to you") and by separated parents who are trying to compete with the former spouse for the child's love ("I know Mommy doesn't let you do this but you can do special things when you're with me").

Cuteness. To please themselves parents may occasionally let the child smoke pot because it's cute. Younger children look especially funny because they cannot inhale, yet in their eagerness to be like Mommy and Daddy they make a hilarious effort and still have a good time themselves. Often this will originate as amusement for the parents and then spread to include cuteness in front of friends. Carrying this trend further, friends may roll joints for the little ones or turn them on when the parents are away. This still precludes regular use.

Purposive. Giving marijuana to kids often carries a specific anticipated goal for the parents. The known effects of pot are occasionally desired and actively sought. They may want to calm the child down because of the necessities of a special setting or company. Sleep is another pursued end, as in "Thank you for taking Billy for the night; if he gives you any trouble just let him smoke this and he'll go right to bed." They may also give it to the children medicinally. Users believe marijuana soothes the upset stomach and alleviates the symptoms of the common cold better than any other drug. As a mood elevator, many parents have given pot to alleviate the crankiness young children develop from a general illness, specific pain or injury. One couple used it experimentally as a treatment for hyperactivity (see Josh).

Abstention. Our last category of marijuana smoking parents contains those who do not permit their children any direct involvement with illegal drugs. This leaves several possible ways to treat the topic of the adults' own involvement with drugs and how open they are about it. Do they let the kids know they smoke pot? Moreover, do they do it in the children's presence?

Overt. The great majority of our subjects openly smoked marijuana in front of their children, defining marijuana as an accepted and natural pastime. Even parents who withhold it from their young children hope that the kids will someday grow up to be like themselves. Thus, they smoke pot overtly. These marijuana smokers are divided on the issue of other drugs, such as pills and cocaine.

1. **Permissive.** One group considers it acceptable to use any drug in front of the children. Either they believe in what they are doing and consider it right for the kids to observe their actions, or they don't worry about it and just do it.

2. **Pragmatic.** A larger, practically oriented group differentiated between "smokable" drugs (pot and hashish) and the others (cocaine and pills), finding it acceptable to let children view consumption of the former group, but not the latter. Rationales varied for this, ranging from safety to morality:

Well, we have smoked hashish around them but we absolutely *never ever* do coke in front of them because it's a white powder and if they saw us snorting a white powder there goes the drain cleaner, there goes the baby powder. Anything white, they'll try it; and that goes for pills too. The only thing they have free rein of is popping vitamins.

Fred expressed his concern over problems this might engender in the preservation of his children's moral fibre:

If he sees me snorting coke, how is he going to differentiate that from heroin? He gets all this anti-drug education from school and they tell him that heroin is bad. How can I explain to him that doing coke is okay and it's fun and doesn't hurt you but heroin is something else, so different and bad? How could I teach him right from wrong?

3. Capricious. A third group is irregular in its handling of multiple drug viewing and their offspring. Jon and Linda, for instance, claim that they don't mind smoking before their child but absolutely won't permit other drugs to be used in his presence. Yet in fact they often use almost any intoxicant in front of him, depending on their mood and how high they have already become.

In our observations we have never seen any parent give a child in the tinydoper range any kind of illegal drug other than marijuana and, extremely rarely, hashish. Moreover, the treatment of pot has been above all direct and open: even those parents who don't permit their children to join have rejected the clandestine secrecy of the behind-closed-doors approach. Ironically, however, they must often adopt this strategy toward the outside world; those parents who let it be known that they permit tinydoping frequently take on an extra social and legal stigma. Their motivation for doing so stems from a desire to avoid having the children view pot and their smoking it as evil or unnatural. Thus, to de-stigmatize marijuana they stigmatize themselves in the fact of society.

REFERENCES

Adler, Peter, and Patricia A. Adler. 1979. "Symbolic interactionism," in Patricia A. Adler, Peter Adler, Jack D. Douglas, Andrea Fontana, C. Robert Freeman and Joseph Kotarba, *An Introduction to the Sociologies of Everyday Life.* Boston: Allyn and Bacon.

Adler, Patricia A., Peter Adler, and Jack D. Douglas. Forthcoming. "Organized crime: Drug dealing for pleasure and profit," in Jack D. Douglas (ed.), *Deviant Scenes.*

Aries, Phillipe. 1965. *Centuries of Childhood: A Social History of Faimly Life.* New York: Vintage.

Becker, Howard S. 1953. "Becoming a Marijuana user." *American Journal of Sociology* 59 (November).

_____. 1963. *Outsiders,* New York: Free Press.

Carey, James T. 1968. *The College Drug Scene.* Englewood Cliffs, N.J.: Prentice-Hall.

Douglas, Jack D. 1970. "Deviance and respectability: The social construction of moral meanings," in Jack D. Douglas (ed.), *Deviance and Respectability.* New York: Basic Books.

_____. 1976. *Investigative Social Research.* Beverly Hills, Calif.: Sage Publications.

Erikson, Erik. 1968. *Identity, Youth and Crisis.* New York: W. W. Norton.

Goode, Erich. 1969. *Marijuana,* New York: Atherton.

_____. 1970. *The Marijuana Smokers.* New York: Basic Books.

Grinspoon, Lester. 1971. *Marihuana Reconsidered.* Cambridge, Mass.: Harvard University Press.

Grupp, Stanley E. (ed.). 1971. *Marihuana.* Columbus, Ohio: Charles E. Merrill.

_____. 1973. *The Marihuana Muddle.* Lexington, Mass.: Lexington Books.

Gusfield, Joseph R. 1967. "Moral passage: The symbolic process in public designations of deviance," *Social Problems* 15:2 (Fall).

Hochman, Joel S. 1972. *Marijuana and Social Evolution*. Englewood Cliffs, N.J.: Prentice-Hall.

Kaplan, John. 1971. *Marihuana: The New Prohibition*. New York: Pocket Books.

Kituse, John I. 1962. "Societal reactions to deviant behavior." *Social Problems*. 9:3 (Winter).

Lyman, Stanford, and Marvin B. Scott. 1968. "Accounts," *American Sociological Review* 33:1.

———. 1970. *A Sociology of the Absurd*. New York: Appleton-Century-Crofts.

Matza, David. 1969. *Becoming Deviant*. Englewood Cliffs, N.J.: Prentice-Hall.

Mead, George H. 1934. *Mind, Self and Society*. Chicago: University of Chicago Press.

Piaget, Jean. 1948. *The Moral Judgment of the Child*. New York: Free Press.

———. 1962. *Play, Dreams and Imitation in Childhood*. New York: W. W. Norton.

———, and B. Inhelder. 1969. *The Psychology of the Child*. New York: Basic Books.

Simon, William, and John H. Gagnon. 1968. "Children of the drug age," *Saturday Review*, September 21.

Sykes, Gresham, and David Matza. 1957. "Techniques of Neutralization," *American Sociological Review* 22 (December).

Reading 9

Exposure to Pornography and Aggression Toward Women: The Case of the Angry Male

Susan H. Gray

New York Institute of Technology

WHAT IS PORNOGRAPHY? AND WHO CONSUMES IT?

Defining pornography is the key problem in the debate over, and study of, its effects. Neither the president's commission nor the U.S. courts have come up with a definition acceptable to all. The president's commission examined all sexually explicit materials, including books, manuscripts, photographs and films. The mildest material it considered was depictions of nudity. Believing that the word "pornography" denoted disapproval, the president's commission preferred the words "obscenity" or "sexually explicit materials." Court definitions of obscenity, the legal term for pornography, have ranged from material which on the whole appeals to prurient interests and has no redeeming social value (*Roth* v. *United States*, 1957) to a reluctance to define obscenity and a delegation of that task to local

Reprinted with permission from *Social Problems* 29 (4) (April 1982): 387–398 by The Society for the Study of Social Problems and by the author.

communities (*Miller* v. *California,* 1973). Women Against Pornography targets any materials depicting violence towards women, and has included under this broad category *Vogue* magazine fashion spreads by photographer Richard Avedon and a Warner Brothers billboard advertisement, later discontinued, which read: "I'm black and blue from the Rolling Stones and I love it."[1] Most contemporary research on pornography studies both soft-core and hard-core materials. Although the distinction between soft-core and hard-core is sometimes fuzzy, "soft-core" generally refers to depictions of nudity or semi-nudity, or depictions of sexual activity without explicit photographs or descriptions of genitals. "Hard-core" generally refers to depictions of nudes engaged in implied sexual activity with a focus upon the genitals. For the purpose of this paper, I define pornography as both soft-core and hard-core depictions of sexual behavior, be they found in magazines, books, films or audiotapes.

Most consumers of pornography are young, married men. They are college educated, politically liberal, high consumers of the mass media in general, and had an average income of $12,000 in 1970 (Nawy, 1973; Wilson and Abelson, 1973). About a quarter of all men have been exposed to sado-masochistic materials. Men use pornography most often as means of enhancing the responsiveness and enjoyment of sexual intercourse with a stable partner. Younger consumers without a stable partner usually use pornography to masturbate (Nawy, 1973; Wilson and Abelson, 1973).

Malamuth and Spinner (forthcoming) analyzed the content of photographs, drawings and cartoons in *Playboy* and *Penthouse* magazines from 1973 to 1977 to see if there had been changes in the number of portrayals of violence against women. They found that violent portrayals have been increasing in both of these periodicals, although they never exceeded 10 percent of all the cartoons and 5 percent of the photographs and drawings. One of Malamuth and Spinner's criteria of sexual violence was scenes that depicted sado-masochism, a form of sexual expression which can take place between consenting adults and is not necessarily exploitative or violent against women. Changing fashions in sexual expression may account for the increase that Malamuth and Spinner found. On the other hand, Diamond (1980) suggests an increasing violence in pornography represents a patriarchal response to increases in the social power of women.

Smith (1976) studied "adults-only" paperback fiction available in "adult" bookstores in the United States and found violent themes in about one third of the 428 books he reviewed. The violence was not always physical, but included blackmail and mental coercion, usually committed by men against women. Typically, the woman was forced to participate in an initially unwanted sexual act and began by protesting but ended up pleading for more, her sexual passion unleashed. . . .

---

[1] See Bullough and Bullough (1977) for further discussion of the problem of defining pornography.

ANGER, HARD-CORE PORNOGRAPHY, AND AGGRESSION

Several studies show that aggression levels in previously angered males are raised by exposure to hard-core pornography, but that aggression is not raised in non-angered males (Meyer, 1972; Baron, 1974, 1978; Donnerstein et al., 1975). Pornography facilitates the expression of anger if anger toward a particular target already exists. Violence is facilitated either through teaching an angered man to view women poorly (the behaviorist model) or through encouraging a cathartic release of anger.

Portrayals of violence without sexual content can facilitate the expression of anger as well as can portrayals of sexually related violence. In Meyer's (1972) study, undergraduate male students were angered by painful electric shocks, which they thought were the result of negative evaluations by another student (gender unspecified) of their performance on a task. The angered students were then shown a violent film segment (a knife fight scene in *From Here to Eternity*), a segment from a hard-core "stag" movie, an exciting but non-violent and sexually neutral film segment (a cowboy saddling and riding a half-broken horse), or not shown any film. Subjects who viewed the violent film clip gave the most electric shocks to the person that had angered them. Viewers of the "stag" film gave more shocks than did viewers of the cowboy clip or those who saw no film. A difficulty of experiments such as this is that retaliatory behavior toward a specific person is different from displaced retaliation toward a more general target. Hurting a known or an unknown person because a woman aroused your anger in a pornographic novel or film is different from hurting the specific person who hurt you. The relationship between these two expressions of anger is not clear from the data available.

Angered men need not be exposed to explicit sexual materials to interpret them sexually. An early study of male sex offenders shown drawings with ambiguous sexual connotations found that the offenders were capable of producing their own pornographic content (Linder, 1953). A more recent study of undergraduates found that angered men rated cartoons with both exploitative and non-exploitative sexual themes from *Playboy* as higher in sexual content than did non-angered men (Baron, 1978). Angered men can easily attribute their arousal to sexual stimuli, rather than to their anger. Where there is no explicit sexual stimuli in the immediate environment, an angered man will conjure up some, if necessary.

The strength of the pornographic stimulus affects whether an angered man acts aggressively. When angered and then subsequently aroused by hard-core pornography, men have difficulty distinguishing between anger and sexual arousal. Soft-core pornography is less likely to trigger subsequent aggression in angered men. Sexual arousal through soft-core pornography either distracts attention from previous anger or defuses anger through recognition of the incompatibility of sexual arousal with aggression (Baron, 1974; Donnerstein et al., 1975).

Men can be distracted from their anger by hard-core as well as soft-core pornography. Zillman and Sapolsky (1977) angered male college students and then exposed them to either neutral photographs (furniture, scenery and abstract art), soft-core pornography, or hard-core pornography. Both soft-core and hard-core materials defused anger, and subjects exposed to either were no more likely to retaliate against the researcher than were the subjects exposed to neutral photographs.

Baron and Bell (1977) found that aggression by angered men was inhibited after exposure to strongly arousing pornography. They point out that it is not just a question of whether pornograpy is soft-core or hard-core, but whether the themes are tenderness (aggression-inhibiting) or wildness and impulsivity (aggression-facilitating). The issue is further complicated by studies which examine anger and exposure to pornography in reverse order. Men who are shown hard-core pornography and then angered attribute their arousal to anger, rather than sexuality, thus facilitating their aggression (Donnerstein et al., 1975). Anger can also be increased because men are distracted by their anger from a source of sexual stimulation. As the studies reviewed here show, men who are not previously or subsequently angered usually do not become aggressive when exposed to hard-core or soft-core pornography.

In a society in which responses to anger other than aggression are permitted (e.g., seduction), aggression need not be the main response of angered men. Laboratory research subjects sitting in front of a machine which they believe they can use to administer electric shocks to victims do not have many other behavioral options for discharging arousal. Yet, as the studies discussed above show, even with behavioral options curtailed, men confronted with highly arousing pornography usually remain non-aggressive in front of such machines—provided they have not been angered. For angered men, sexuality and aggression are more compatible, particularly where there is difficulty distinguishing anger from sexual arousal and where the sexual arousal does not distract from or diffuse the anger.

PORNOGRAPHY AND AGGRESSION: THE LONG-TERM EFFECTS

Studies of pornography usually measure its effects immediately or 10 minutes after exposure, though some attention has also been given to long-term effects.

People exposed to hard-core pornography who are not angered do not become aggressive over time. In a study of married couples over a 12-week period, Mann et al. (1973) found that viewing weekly hard-core pornographic films with themes including sado-masochism produced no significant changes in sexual behavior, other than an increase in sexual behavior on film-viewing nights. Pornography can also become boring over time, resulting in lowered interest in and response to it (Howard et al., 1973).

There is evidence that pornography gradually erodes inhibitions against aggression toward both men and women. Male subjects in Baron and Bell's (1973) study initially gave weaker electric shocks to female victims than to male victims. When Donnerstein and Hallam (1978) gave men a second opportunity to shock a woman who had angered them, the men's inhibitions decreased drastically after a 10-minute wait in which they sat quietly, if they had previously been shown hard-core films.[2] There has been too little research on the long-term effects of exposure to pornography in potentially deviant or already deviant men. However, there is some evidence that long-term exposure is not detrimental to men who are chronically angry towards, or incompetent with, adult women.

Goldstein and Kant have studied rapists and pedophiles (child molesters) admitted to a state hospital in California (Goldstein, 1973; Goldstein and Kant, 1974; Kant and Goldstein, 1970).[3] Rapists and pedophiles reported less exposure to pornography during adolescence and adulthood than the general male population. Not only did rapists report that the pornography they found most exciting was the portrayal of non-violent heterosexual intercourse, but they had less exposure to these portrayals and to photographs or movies of fully-nude women, oral sex, or sado-masochistic activity than the general male population. Rapists had more exposure than the general male population to photographs of explicit sexual acts while they were six to 10 years old, but these photographs did not necessarily portray violence. Goldstein and Kant (1974) theorized that pornography performs an educational function for men during their formative years; deprived of information about sex, rapists and pedophiles have few stimuli which portray society's definition of the "normal sex act." The rapists and pedophiles studied found it more difficult to talk about sex and had fewer sources of sexual information, such as parental explanations.

Goldstein and Kant found that rapists and pedophiles did not initiate the postures or acts they found most exciting in pornography, but used portrayals of these acts for more general sexual arousal and masturbation. Hard-core pornography was

[2]In a contradictory study by Jaffe et al. (1974), men were not initially inhibited in their aggression toward women, but gave more intense electric shocks to women than to men. These were research subjects who had *not* been previously angered, but had been strongly aroused. However, a further study by Donnerstein (1980) revealed that when men are exposed to *both* pornography and violence in the same film, more aggression is exhibited toward men than toward women, both on the first and second opportunity. Even with previously angered men, therefore, aggression toward women may still be inhibited under highly arousing conditions, although not consistently so. Men who are aggressive toward other men, after exposure to pornography and violence, may be acting because of the way they see men treat women in violent pornographic materials. This aggressive behavior would indirectly benefit, rather than harm, women.

[3]Another way to gauge the long-term effects of the widespread availability of pornography on sexually deviant men is to examine statistical information from Denmark. Since the Danish ban on pornographic literature was repealed in 1967, sex offences have been decreasing in Copenhagen (Kutchinsky, 1973). However, prosecutions have also decreased as a greater tolerance has developed for behavior such as "peeping" or verbal indecency. Rape has remained fairly stable over the last few decades, with only several dozen cases reported in Copenhagen each year. Child molestation has decreased. These statistics reveal no harmful social consequences of the repeal.

not an incitement to rape or child molestation. But violence and brutality, *whether associated with sex or not,* were often mentioned as disturbing—particularly to rapists. Violence and brutality—not sexuality—were the stimuli for aggression.

> We must consider that sex offenders are highly receptive to suggestions of sexual behavior congruent with their previous formed desires and will interpret the material at hand to fit their needs. . . . [The question becomes] whether the stimulus most likely to release anti-social behavior is one representing sexuality or one representing aggression. (Goldstein and Kant, 1974:109)[4]

A related study by Kercher and Walker (1973) found that convicted rapists exposed to slides containing non-rape sexual cues were not aroused any more than were men from the general population. Moreover, the rapists rated the slides less appealing than the general population. Avel, Blanchard, Barlow, and Mavissakian (1975) and Abel, Barlow, Blanchard, and Guild (1977) studied the relationship between exposure to audiotaped narration of rape scenes and arousal patterns in rapists. Although they concluded that arousal patterns are idiosyncratic, the rapists they studied did become more sexually aroused by narrations of rape and aggression than did non-rapists. Both Abel, Barlow, Blanchard, and Guild (1977) and Barbaree et al., (1979) suggest that narrations of violent sex do not arouse rapists any more than do narrations of sex between mutually consenting partners. Rather, narrations of violent sex fail to inhibit arousal to the extent that force inhibits the arousal of normal males, or enables them to suppress their arousal.

TYPES OF ANGER, FANTASY, AND IMAGES OF WOMEN

Research to date suggests that anger is a greater social problem than pornography, especially when anger is directed toward those less powerful. Anger is most dangerous in men who are unable to effectively distinguish between aggression, the control of women, and sexual arousal. The goals of social change might be better served by focusing on the source of anger in men, and by helping men to deal with

---

[4]Groth and Birnbaum (1979) also conclude that rape is related more to the need to express anger than to consumption of pornography. However, a study of sexual offenders by Davis and Braucht (1973) did find a small relationship between childhood exposure to pornography and later rape, statutory rape or homosexual prostitution (r = +0.26). Part of the control population in Davis and Braucht's research consisted of members of religious organizations, men who were probably less likely to consume or to admit to the consumption of pornography, thereby affecting the comparative statistic on the general male population's use of pornography. In addition, in any retrospective study, it is unclear whether or not there is a direct causal relationship between early exposure to pornography and sexual deviance. The amount of early exposure to pornography may be a reflection of a character already likely to become involved in sexual offenses. Finding that sexual offenders are consumers of pornography is like finding that many heroin addicts at one point also smoked marijuana. It does not demonstrate that one is an outgrowth of the other.

that anger, than by focusing on pornography. Anger not validated by pornography will be validated elsewhere if supported by cultural values. Recent "horror" films such as *I Spit on Your Grave* depict violence against "liberated," independent women (Ebert, 1981).

It is unrealistic to hope to eliminate all anger in men toward women; it is equally unrealistic to hope to eliminate pornography. A complex relationship exists between sex and anger. Both sex and anger involve one person who has less power than the other or others. Relationships between men and women in western culture are generally power relationships. The struggle between men and women for power is often arousing to both, but most people do not translate that arousal into violence.

Nevertheless, the relationship between sex and anger is an important one. What many researchers have not considered is that anger takes different forms. Studies on pornography and aggression in angered men often view anger superficially as a factor leading to erosion of self-esteem in the laboratory. This superficial anger may be a different kind of anger than the anger manifested by chronically disturbed men. The deep anger in disturbed men is a potentially unresolved component of psychoanalytic development (Stoller, 1975). Deep anger may stimulate more socially destructive behavior than the superficial anger stimulated in experimental laboratories. To view the effects of pornography on this deep anger we have only the indirect evidence from studies of sex offenders. An important question is whether those with unresolved deep anger are those more likely to attack women when their superficial anger is stimulated in the laboratory or in everyday life. To stimulate superficial anger in the laboratory, I feel, could help those with deep anger to quickly get in touch with their feelings. The routine insults of everyday life, including the thwarting of expectations derived from pornography, perhaps provide this stimulus for the rapist. More information is needed on the process, and the extent, to which everyday incidents put people in touch with their deep anger.

It has been argued that the consumption of pornography is a cathartic device to discharge momentary aggressive impulses (English, 1980). But pornography can also be a tool for validating a deeper anger toward women. This may be one reason why soft-core pornography generally distracts men who are angry, but hard-core pornography is less likely to do so. If superficially induced anger puts men in touch with a deeper anger, partially validated by pornography, then pornography becomes more dangerous than we might otherwise believe. The process by which men are put in touch with deep anger must become a central question in the debate over pornography.

I believe that non-angered men perceive both soft-core and hard-core pornography as fantasy. Most people can distinguish between fantasy and reality. For those who cannot, it is the unresolved anger and not the pornography which creates the fundamental problem. Artistic media, such as films, novels or even advertising, often employ fantasy, and its creators expect it to be recognized as such. That a particular portrayal is not realistic, or expresses anger toward a group of people, is usually not an effective argument for the portrayal's danger to society. In situations in which lack of realism is a danger to society (e.g., propaganda or racist literature and films), it is usually because consumers cannot easily separate reality from fiction. Both soft-core and hard-core pornography may often be crude—a form of low culture rather than high culture—but they are nevertheless, I believe, folk art forms. Like comic books or murder mysteries, pornography is a manifestation of popular culture, created by members of a society. Should we ask that pornography be more realistic than other forms of fiction? That some of the literature previously labelled pornographic is now regarded as quality literature, rather than pornography, makes the answer to this question particularly difficult. The dividing line between low-brow and high-brow art can be vague.

I believe that the content of most sexual fantasies is not inherently bad simply because it is silly, or angry, or not representative of the "real" sex life of most people—or even because it may shape reality. In sex, there can be elements of objectification, of dominance and submission, of competition, lovelessness and pain. Some people may prefer to repress these in their sex lives; others may take delight in expressing them. But pornography reveals the options, both exploitative and non-exploitative—options which are there independent of the existence of pornography. Often revealing to consumers what they like, pornography is equally capable of demonstrating what they do not like.

If pornographic images of women are often derogatory, and validate anger, the images of consumers of pornography are often equally so. Consumers are portrayed as tragic figures involved in the exploitation of male sexual desire by female workers in the pornography industry who seek avenues for economic upward mobility. This exploitation is degrading to both the seller and the buyer, as are many other forms of commercial enterprise when the business ethic takes precedence over all else.

If some people nevertheless find the images of women in pornography repulsive, it is futile to try to change images of women by reducing the amount of pornography available. Suppression rarely changes social images over time; more often it drives them underground, thereby giving them a tantalizing flavor. Suppression could even encourage a more extreme pornographic genre.

THE FUTURE OF PORNOGRAPHY

Future research on pornography should endeavor to: (1) provide a more uniform definition of pornography; (2) investigate systematically the link between sexual arousal, anger and aggression when a greater range of behavioral options are presented; (3) decide whether to focus on the general male population or a population with greater pathology when investigating angered men; and (4) create unobtrusive measures of arousal and a mechanism for the male subject to differentiate between specific women and unknown and unseen female targets. Greater coordination of research efforts in these ways would help clarify the extent to which angered men are dangerous when exposed to pornography. At present, the move towards suppression of extreme forms of pornography is not supported by solid empirical evidence of the harmful effects of pornography.

Johnson and Goodchilds (1973) suggest an alternative to suppression: a pornography more clearly in line with both feminist and humanist values. In this genre, neither sex would be manipulated or used as an object, as they are in conventional pornography. English (1980) has speculated on a pornography in which older women pair with younger men, body types become more variable, and sexual expression becomes less phallocentric, thereby making pornography more appealing to female consumers. Some would argue that this would no longer be pornography.

Faust (1980) has argued that women have their own distinct pornographic genre in escapist romantic fiction whose heronies are often alternately raped and seduced. Brownmiller (1975), on the other hand, insists that there can be no female equivalent of pornography, a male invention. In Brownmiller's sense of pornography as domination, escapist romantic fiction is an exercise in masochism and contrary to humanist and/or feminist values. The content of pornography might be changed if those with humanist and feminist values became involved in its production, thereby creating a new market among feminist and humanist consumers. There is no reason to expect, however, that traditional pornography would not continue to be in demand as well.

If the relationship between exposure to pornography and the degree of violence against women is the key issue in the debate over pornography, it must be recognized that themes of violence have become an integral part of most of our media. A disturbed mind will find exciting stimuli wherever it looks. The amount of violence depicted in pornography is less than the amount of violence shown on television in the United States (Dienstbier, 1977). Dienstbier has pointed out the irony in U.S. society's massive exposure to violence in the media with lower exposure to violence in real life, coupled with society's lower exposure to pornography in the media and higher exposure to sex in real life.

We are not likely to eliminate the anger underlying male violence against women completely. To the extent which we do not, pornography can always evoke that anger. Psychoanalysts claim that a certain amount of frustration and anger is necessary to create a separate ego identity. Without that frustration and developmental anger, normal forms of loving and normal expressions of sexuality would not occur (Stoller, 1975). If we view these expressions as desirable, but if that same anger, when unresolved, produces violence against women,[5] we need cultural mechanisms to encourage socially acceptable forms of resolving this anger or directing it more appropriately: better communication in interpersonal relations,

---

[5]As Chodorow (1978) points out, contemporary family organization contributes to lack of respect for women as well.

changes in the rigid role expectations and notions of masculinity which lead to pain and anger when they cannot be lived up to, and improved education for men about the nature of being a woman and about female sexuality. Without these, violence toward women can find its expression with or without pornography. With these mechanisms, pornography may once again be viewed as just another form of fantasy, probably not dangerous and maybe no longer attractive to men who are no longer angry.

REFERENCES

Abel, Gene G., David H. Barlow, Edward B. Blanchard, and Donald Guild. 1977. "The components of rapists' sexual arousal." *Archives of General Psychiatry* 34:895–903.

———, Edward B. Blanchard, David H. Barlow, and Matig Mavissakian. 1975. "Identifying specific erotic cues in sexual deviations by audiotaped descriptions." *Journal of Applied Behavior Analysis* 8: 247–260.

Amoroso, Donald M., and Marvin Brown. 1973. "Problems in studying the effects of erotic material." *Journal of Sex Research* 9: 187–195.

Barbaree, H. E., W. L. Marshall, and R. D. Lanthier. 1979. "Deviant sexual arousal in rapists." *Behaviour Research and Therapy* 17: 215–222.

Baron, Robert A. 1974. "Aggression-inhibiting influences of heightened sexual arousal." *Journal of Personality and Social Psychology* 30: 318–322.

———.1978. "Aggression-inhibiting influences of sexual humor." *Journal of Personality and Social Psychology* 36: 189–197.

———. 1979. "Heightened sexual arousal and physical aggression: An extension to females." *Journal of Research in Personality* 13: 91–102.

———, and Paul A. Bell. 1973. "Effects of heightened sexual arousal on physical aggression." Paper presented to the annual convention of the American Psychological Association, Montreal, August.

———, and Paul A. Bell. 1977. "Sexual arousal and aggression by males: Effects of type of erotic stimuli and prior provocation." *Journal of Personality and Social Psychology* 35: 79–87.

Brownmiller, Susan. 1975. *Against Our Will: Men, Women and Rape*. New York: Bantam.

Bullough, Vern, and Bonnie Bullough. 1977. *Sin, Sickness and Sanity: A History of Sexual Attitudes*. New York: New American Library.

Chodorow, Nancy. 1978. *The Reproduction of Mothering: Psychoanalysis and the Sociology of Gender*. Berkeley: University of California Press.

Commission on Obscenity and Pornography. 1970. *The Report of the Commission on Obscenity and Pornography*. Washington, D.C.: U.S. Government Printing Office.

Davis, Keith, and G. Nicholas Braucht. 1973. "Exposure to pornography, character and sexual deviance: A retrospective survey." *Journal of Social Issues* 29: 183–196.

Diamond, Irene. 1980. Pornography and repression: A reconsideration." *Signs* 5: 686–701.

Dienstbier, Richard A. 1977. "Sex and violence: Can research have it both ways?" *Journal of Communication* 27: 176–188.

Donnerstein, Edward. 1980. "Pornography and violence against women: Experimental studies." *Annals of the New York Academy of Science* 347: 277–288.

Donnerstein, Edward, and John Hallam. 1978. "Facilitating effects of erotica on aggression against women." *Journal of Personality and Social Psychology* 36: 1270–1277.

Donnerstein, Edward, Marcia Donnerstein, and Ronald Evans. 1975. "Erotic stimuli and aggression: Facilitation or inhibition?" *Journal of Personality and Social Psychology* 32: 237–244.

Dworkin, Andrea. 1981. *Pornography: Men Possessing Women*. New York: Putnam.

Ebert, Roger. 1981. "Why movie audiences aren't safe anymore." *American Film* 6 (March): 54–56.

English, Deidre. 1980. "The Politics of Porn." *Mother Jones* 5(April): 44–45.

Faust, Beatrice. 1980. *Women, Sex and Pornography: A Controversial Study*. New York: Macmillan.

Goldstein, Michael J. 1973. "Exposure to erotic stimuli and sexual deviance." *Journal of Social Issues* 29: 197–219.

_____, and Harold S. Kant. 1974. *Pornography and Social Deviance*. Berkeley: University of California Press.

Gordon, John. 1980. "On sex and sexism." *Inquiry 3* (May 5): 29–31.

Groth, A. Nicholas, and H. Jean Birnbaum. 1979. *Men Who Rape: The Psychology of the Offender*. New York: Plenum.

Hentoff, Nat. 1979. "The new legions of erotic decency." *Inquiry* 3 (December 10): 5–7.

Howard, James L., Myron B. Liptzin, and Clifford B. Reifler. 1973. "Is pornography a problem?" *Journal of Social Issues* 29: 133–145.

Jaffe, Yoran, Neil Malamuth, Joan Feingold, and Seymour Feshbach. 1974. "Sexual arousal and behavioral aggression." *Journal of Personality and Social Psychology* 30: 759–764.

Johnson, Paula, and Jacqueline D. Goodchilds. 1973. "Pornography, sexuality and social psychology." *Journal of Social Issues* 29: 231–238.

Kaminer, Wendy. n.d. "Women against pornography: Where we stand on the first amendment." Mimeographed. Women against pornography, 358 W. 47 Street, New York, N.Y.

Kant, Harold S., and Michael J. Goldstein. 1970. "Pornography." *Psychology Today* 4 (December): 59–61, 76.

Kercher, Glen A., and C. Eugene Walker. 1973. "Reactions of convicted rapists to sexually explicit stimuli." *Journal of Abnormal Psychology* 81: 46–50.

Kutchinsky, Bert. 1973. "The effect of easy availability of pornography on the incidence of sex crimes: The Danish experience." *Journal of Social Issues* 29: 163–181.

Lederer, Laura (ed.). 1980. *Take Back the Night: Women on Pornography*. New York: William Morrow.

Lindner, Harold. 1953. "Sexual responsiveness to perceptual tests in a group of sexual offenders." *Journal of Personality* 21: 364–374.

Malamuth, Neil M., and James V. P. Check. 1980. "Penile tumescence and perceptual responses to rape as a function of victim's perceived reactions." Journal of Applied Social Psychology 10: 528–547.

_____, and Barry Spinner. Forthcoming. "A longitudinal content of analysis of sexual violence in the bestselling erotica magazines." *Journal of Sex Research*.

_____, Scott Haber, and Seymour Feshbach. 1980. "Testing hypotheses regarding rape: Exposure to sexual violence, sex differences and the normality of rapists." *Journal of Research in Personality* 14: 121–137.

————, Maggie Heim, and Seymour Feshbach. Forthcoming. "Sexual responsiveness of college students to rape depictions: Inhibitory and disinhibitory effects." *Journal of Personality and Social Psychology.*

————, Ilana Reisin, and Barry Spinner. 1979. "Exposure to pornography and reaction to rape." Paper presented to the annual convention of the American Psychological Association, New York City, August.

Mann, Jay, Jack Sidman, and Sheldon Starr. 1973. "Evaluating social consequences of erotic films: An experimental approach." *Journal of Social Issues* 29: 113–131.

Meyer, Timothy. 1972. "The effects of sexually arousing and violent films on aggressive behavior." *Journal of Sex Research* 8: 324–331.

Nawy, Harold. 1973. "In the pursuit of happiness? Consumers of erotica in San Francisco." *Journal of Social Issues* 29: 147–161.

The New York Times. 1977. "Judge in Wisconsin calls rape by boy 'normal' reaction." May 27, p. A9.

Rosen, Raymond C., and Francis J. Keefe. 1978. "The measurement of human penile tumescence." *Psychophysiology* 15: 366–376.

Smith, Don D. 1976. "The social content of pornography." *Journal of Communication* 26: 16–24.

Stoller, Robert J. 1975. *Perversion: The Erotic Form of Hatred.* New York: Pantheon.

Wilson, W. Cody, and Herbert I. Abelson. 1973. "Experience with and attitudes toward explicit sexual materials." *Journal of Social Issues* 29: 19–39.

Zillman, Dorf, and Barry S. Sapolsky. 1977. "What mediates the effect of mild erotica on annoyance and hostile behavior in males?" *Journal of Personality and Social Psychology* 35: 587–596.

Cases cited

Miller v. *California,* 413 U.S. 15, 1973.

Roth v. *United States,* 354 U.S. 476, 1957.

CHAPTER 4

Deviance, Crime, and Violence

Organized terrorism is not new. It has existed for centuries. Demaris traces the evolution of modern political terrorism from its beginnings in early religious conflict and economic anarchism. The original Terrorist Brigade was proud of both its name and the fact that only those who opposed its revolution were harmed. Today's terrorists on the other hand, do not make this distinction: bombs are planted where anyone can be killed.

Victims of rape face a twofold problem. First, there is the physical and emotional damage experienced at the time of the attack. Next, there is the trauma that results when others fail to believe that the alleged victims were, in fact, assaulted as they describe. In our society, sex and violence are a much greater part of everyday life than we are inclined to recognize. Holmstrom and Burgess call our attention to common and often unnoticed occurrences of "forced sex." Their data indicate we tend to see force as being justified in many sexual encounters, which inhibits women from proving that the violence they experienced was not "normal" or provoked.

Although it is violent crimes that create the most fear and get the most attention, white-collar and corporate crimes may cause even more damage to our society. For many years, consumer groups fought to prove that the Corvair automobile was unsafe and even lethal. John DeLorean discusses how executives made a series of decisions that kept General Motors producing the Corvair even though its design flaws were well known. According to DeLorean, those who consider themselves to have high moral standards have been known to make irresponsible and immoral decisions.

Cressey argues that our traditional treatment programs for convicted criminals perpetuate and worsen crime. By segregating criminals behind walls, we reinforce prisoners' identities as wild, different, and alien. We are supporting crime factories; the only results are more criminals. Cressey suggests that the development of prison industries, modeled on industrial factories, would be more productive for society and the inmates. Instead of exaggerating their differences, work in prison industries would give prisoners more in common with those "outside" in normal society.

Reading 10

Political Terrorism

Ovid Demaris

Political terrorism is a by-product of the Industrial Revolution, a disorder created by the destruction of the ancient patterns of life. A society that had been largely agrarian was thrust suddenly into a world of machines and factories, of labor and capital. The resulting displacement of populations, the deterioration of the environment, and the disruption of an entire way of life fed the fires already ignited by political repressions and the writings of intellectuals who inspired the violent deeds that have been with us ever since.

Although terrorism's philosophical underpinnings antedate the last two centuries (organized and irregular warfare are almost as old as the human race), religious and economic anarchism are the true antecedents of modern political terrorism.

For example, the Cathari, or Albigensians, and other gnostic heresies held that the universe was totally corrupt, unreal, and without meaning: only the world of the spirit was important, and all authority of a temporal nature was denied. Accused of immorality, devil worship, blood sacrifice, and heresy, they were persecuted by the Catholics. St. Dominic, the founder of the Dominican Brothers, preached the destruction of Cathari by terror. The wholesale massacre of both heretics and Christians was excused on the theory that "God will know His own."

The Anabaptists believed they belonged to the Community of Saints. They denied the rule of church and state, considering them unnecessary, since they were in direct contact with God. Authority was evil because it stood between man and the divine light within him. The existing society had to be destroyed so that the new order could be established, with its laws revealed by the inner light of the prophet or leader. This was the first time that anarchical philosophy embraced the total leadership of an inspired individual.

Plague, economic disaster, heavy taxation, and religious strife added to the misery of the people of Switzerland, Germany, and the Low Countries. This allowed Jan Mathys and his disciple John of Leiden to arouse the Anabaptists to a fever pitch. The city of Münster was sacked, and all records of contracts and debts were destroyed and all books and manuscripts were burned. They established a sommunal state, seizing food, clothing, all worldly goods, and placed them in a common store.

After Mathys was killed leading a sortie, John of Leiden instituted a reign of terror accompanied by polygamy and sexual excess. When Münster was retaken in 1535, John of Leiden was tortured to death. The Anabaptist revolt had many

Reprinted with permission from *Brothers in Blood* (New York: 1977), pp. 377–387.

features later found in anarchistic movements: belief in the healing properties of violent destruction, the importance of violence as an end in itself, and the belief in the dream of building an entirely new social order on the ruins of the old. As in the cases of the Albigensians and the Peasants' Revolt, Anabaptist terror led not to the desired end but to the destruction of their society, the death of their leaders, and the eradication of their movement by counterterror of unbelievable fury.

The Inquisition and the Dominican order were instruments of organized terror, but the Jesuits provided the closest parallel to today's concept of terrorist groups. Founded by Ignatius Loyola in 1533, the Society of Jesus was called by Loyola "the little battalion of Jesus." Organized to combat the Reformation and to propagate the Roman Catholic faith among the heathen, it grew into one of the largest and best-organized groups of terrorists in history. The Jesuits were the shock troops of the Counter Reformation. Their casuistical principles and the nature of their secret society caused them to be damned and feared by both Protestants and Catholics.

Their belief in the "sovereignty of the people" and "tyrannicide" was anarchical in theory and action. God had vested sovereignty in the people, who voluntarily delegated it to the monarch. The people were free to reassert their prerogatives and depose the monarch whenever he failed to govern in accordance with their wishes. In the Jesuits' judgment, this failure occurred when the sovereign either adopted Protestantism or seemed likely to do so. Under the casuistical principle that the end justifies the means, killing a ruler who had turned away from the church was a sacred duty—not a crime.

Whenever the society deemed it necessary to eliminate a king, prince, or other important personage, the Jesuit assassin was prepared in a ceremony called the Blessing of the Dagger. Next to the Dark Chamber where Jesuit novices were initiated was a small room called the Cell of Meditation. A painting was placed in the center of an altar, covered with a veil and surrounded by torches and lamps of a scarlet color. A casket covered with hieroglyphics and bearing a representation of a lamb (symbolic of Christ) on its lid was placed on a table. The brother chosen for the "deed of blood" came here to receive his instructions. When he opened the casket, he found a dagger wrapped in a linen cloth. An officer of the order removed the dagger, kissed it, sprinkled it with holy water, and then handed it to a deacon, who attached it to a rosary and hung it around the neck of the chosen one, informing him that he was the elect of God and telling him the name of his victim.

Then a prayer was offered for his success: "And Thou, invincible and terrible God, who didst resolve to inspire our elect and thy servant with the project of exterminating [the name of the victim], a tyrant and heretic, strengthen him, and render the consecration of our brother perfect by the successful execution of the great work. Increase, O God, his strength a hundredfold, so that he may accomplish the noble undertaking, and protect him with the powerful and divine armor of thine elect and saints. Pour on his head the daring courage which despises all fear, and fortify his body in danger and in the face of death itself.''

The veil was then removed from the painting and the elect beheld a portrait of Jacques Clément, the young Dominican monk who had assassinated Henry III of France, surrounded by a host of angels carrying him to celestial glory. The implication was clear; the current elect would also be wafted to the side of a grateful God once his mission was accomplished.

A crown, symbolic of the heavenly crown he was about to win, was placed on his head. "Deign, O Lord of Hosts, to bestow a propitious glance on the servant thou has chosen as thine arm, and for the execution of the high decree of thine eternal justice. Amen."

The technique was not unlike that employed by the Old Man of the Mountain, who used to drug some of his young assassins into a deep sleep and transport them to his secret pleasure garden, persuading them when they awoke that he had brought them to Paradise itself. Drugged again, they would awake in the everyday world, now forever convinced that their master could reward them with eternal Paradise after death if they did his bidding while they were alive. How far removed is all this from today's URA? Kozo Okamoto, the sole surviving terrorist of the Lod Airport massacre, wanted to commit suicide because "we soldiers after we die want to become the three stars of Orion. The revolution will go on, and there will be many stars."

The Jesuits' powers grew quickly and their terroristic methods caused such fear that they came into conflict with civil and religious authorities in most countries where they operated. The Jesuits were driven from France in 1594, from England in 1579, from Venice in 1607, from Spain in 1767, and from Naples in 1768. They were finally suppressed by Pope Clement XIV in 1773 and not revived until they had turned away from terrorist tactics.

Gradually the concept of anarchy moved from the religious realm to the economic. Nineteenth-century pamphleteers exemplified the shift in their demands for social justice. One wrote, "Magistrates, provosts, beadles, mayors—nearly all live by robbery . . . they all batten on the poor . . . the stronger robs the weaker." Another said, "I would like to strangle the nobles and the clergy, every one of them. . . . Good working men make the wheaten bread but they never chew it; no, all they get is the sifting from the corn, and from good wine they get nothing but the dregs and from good clothing nothing but the chaff. Everything that is tasty and good goes to the nobles and the clergy." . . .

There was something romantic about the Russian czar-killers of the late nineteenth century. Unlike the propaganda-conscious terrorist groups of today, who shy away from the word *terrorist,* the members of the Terrorist Brigade were proud of the label. They brought the word *terrorist* into common political usage. They believed that political murder "shakes the whole system to its foundations," but the assassination of Czar Alexander II only meant greater repression. Then the assassination of the czar's uncle, Duke Sergei, followed by the execution of the responsible terrorist led to the October Revolution and its savage repression. The brigade disintegrated in 1908 when it learned that its leader was a member of the secret police.

The Terrorist Brigade was immortalized by Albert Camus in his play *The Just Assassin*. It is the story of a young revolutionary who is chosen to kill the head of the secret police. The plan calls for him to throw a bomb into the target's carriage, but as the carriage draws closer, the terrorist can see that the police official is holding two small children on his lap. Bomb in hand, he turns and runs away, having decided that the deed must be done another day. Agreeing with his decision, his comrades say, "Even in destruction, there's a right way and a wrong way—and there are limits."

There are academicians today who point to this example when they want to show that terrorism has undergone a radical transformation in recent years. Their thesis is that terrorists used to operate under a code of honor, that their murders were strategic and for a cause.

"Until about the middle of the twentieth century, terrorism was most often a modernist version of the older politics of assassination—the killing of particular people thought to be guilty of particular acts," Michael Walzer wrote in the *New Republic* on August 30, 1975. "Since that time terrorism has most often taken the form of random murder, its victims unknown in advance and, even from the standpoint of the terrorists, innocent of any crime. The change is of deep moral and political significance, though it has hardly been discussed. It represents the breakdown of a *political code* worked out in the late 19th century and roughly analogous to the laws of war, developed at the same time."

The code made a distinction between combatants and noncombatants. "In former times," says Walzer, "children, passers-by and sometimes even policemen were thought to be uninvolved in the political struggle, innocent people whom the terrorist had no right to kill. He did not even claim a right to terrorize them; in fact his activity was misnamed—a minor triumph for the forces of order. But today's terrorists earn their title. They have emptied out the category of innocent people; they claim a right to kill anyone; they seek to terrorize whole populations."

Examples to the contrary would fill another book. Bombings during the nineteenth century killed hundreds of "innocent" people. Two incidents come immediately to mind: the Haymarket and Wall Street bombings. The following sentiment was expressed by French poet Laurent Tailhade: *Qu'importe les victimes si le geste est beau?* ("What do the victims matter if the gesture is fine?")

The best description of a terrorist can be found in Sergei Nechayev's *Revolutionary Catechism:*

> The revolutionary is a dedicated man. He has no personal inclinations, no business affairs, no property, and no name. Everything in his life is subordinated towards a

single exclusive attachment, a single thought, and a single passion—the revolution. . . . He has torn himself away from the bonds which tie him to the social order and to the cultivated world, with all its laws, moralities, and customs. . . . The revolutionary despises public opinion . . . morality is everything which contributes to the triumph of the revolution. Immoral and criminal is everything that stands in his way. . . . Night and day he must have but one thought, one aim,—merciless destruction . . . he must be ready to destroy himself and destroy with his own hands everyone who stands in his way.

Anarchists who advocate violence, whether Anabaptists or Baader-Meinhof gang members, have spilled a great deal of blood, innocent or otherwise. They preach terrorism for its own sake, the destruction of the old system and the building of the new. "We are not in the least afraid of ruins," said Spanish anarchist leader Buenaventura Durutti. "We are going to inherit the earth. There is not the slightest doubt about it. . . . We carry a new world, here in our hearts."

The words are representative of the ideal of anarchism and symbolic of the reality. In the end it was the Fascist who built on the ruins of Spain and the people were subjected to dictatorship.

Anarchist philosophic beliefs and anarchist violent actions are separated by a chasm. The philosophy teaches that man is naturally good and made evil only by laws and governments, that given a stateless condition his reason and primitive sense of right and wrong would assert themselves, permitting all to live peacefully and cooperatively in bliss.

The contradictions of idealism and coercion have caused splits within all anarchical movements. It is perhaps the reason why such movements have never made a successful revolution. Their political theories are based on the false assumption that love and violence are synonymous.

Terrorism also has failed as a tactic because it is ineffective against a ruthless tyranny or strong democracy. Unlike organized revolution, it has never overthrown or even seriously threatened a totalitarian state. What limited success it has achieved has been against parliamentary monarchies and weak democracies. Only in countries like Spain in 1936 and the Weimar Republic has it been possible for unaided terrorism to achieve results commensurate with the effort expended.

The strategy of terrorism is to generate fear, to employ that weapon in a special and complicated sort of way. Terrorism is an illusionist's trick. The power of the terrorist is unreal. Revolution, like war, has been described as the strategy of the strong, while terrorism, being the work of a small elite, is the strategy of the weak. Terrorism is a weapon used by those who lack strength to act directly. The strategy is to achieve its goal not through its acts but through the enemy's response to them. For terrorism is merely the first step in a revolutionary struggle. It is a psychological assault intended to produce a psychological result. It can be fear, frustration, anger, helplessness. Whatever the reaction, the idea is to provoke the government into embarking on a course of action the terrorist desires. In other words, the terrorist is in the peculiar position of having to undertake actions he does not desire, such as hijackings and the murder of innocent people, in order to provoke one he does desire—for example, a brutal police repression. The objective is to reveal the hidden weakness, evil, or corruption of the existing government—to unmask the beast, as it were. In revealing the real face behind the mask, the terrorist hopes to enlist the support of the people, which is the next step toward achieving conditions propitious for revolutionary guerrilla warfare.

The terrorist has been compared to a magician who tricks his mark into watching his right hand while his left hand, unnoticed, makes the switch. The strategy of deliberately killing the innocent is a risky one. The act may appear particularly horrifying to the public because it seems so pointless. The reaction could turn the terrorists into enemies of the people as well as of the government. Che Guevara was opposed to terrorism for precisely this reason. He argued that it hinders "contact with the masses and makes impossible unification for action that will be necessary at a critical moment." In this treatise on guerrilla warfare, he dealt with terrorism in a single paragraph.

On the other hand, Carlos Marighella had much to say about it in his *Mini-Manual of the Urban Guerrilla:* "Terrorism is an arm the revolutionary can never relinquish. Bank assaults, ambushes, desertions, diverting of arms, the rescue of prisoners, executions, kidnapping, sabotage, terrorism and the war of nerves are all cases to point. . . . The government has no alternative except to intensify repression." The aim, he says, is to escalate the situation so that people "will refuse to collaborate with the authorities and the general sentiment is that the government is unjust." The idea is to show that the capitalist state depends for its continued existence upon the use of violence and its own terror. This is the conventional wisdom of a wide spectrum of terrorist groups—IRA, FLQ, ERP, RAF, ETA, URA, ALN, MIR, FAR, PLO, PFLP, PDFLP, ALF, ELF, TPLA—a veritable alphabet soup of terror, not to mention the separatist movements active all over the globe.

The most successful terrorism is that practiced by governments to sustain their power. Yet even a mild form of repression can boomerang in a colonialist situation, as happened in Ireland and Israel. Great Britain defeated itself, as France did in Algeria. A motley band of Algerian nationalists calling themselves the National Liberation Front (or, by its French initials, FLN) was able to persuade a mixed indigenous population, with no history of its own, to think of itself as the citizenry of a separate nation. The FLN's strategy was to pressure the French into reacting in a way that would demonstrate the unreality of the French claim that there was no distinct Algerian nation, that it was genuinely a part of France. French reaction to random violence was to treat all persons of non-European origin as suspects, even to transferring army units of Muslim Algerian troops into mainland France and replacing them in Algeria by European troops, thereby signaling the end of Algérie Français. When people began to feel excluded from the existing community, their sympathies went to the FLN, which was able to shift from terrorism to organized guerrilla warfare.

The terrorist tactics used in colonial countries seldom succeed against an indigenous government, which is far more reluctant to relinquish its hold than a colonial power with a country of its own to which it can withdraw. The Israelis, who are fighting on home ground, with their backs to the sea, have no place to which to retreat. In Uruguay, once the model democracy of Latin America, the terror of the Tupamaros not only failed but led directly to a repressive military dictatorship.

Despite their inherent weakness, terrorists nonetheless have scored many political successes in the last few decades. They have caused enough damage to intimidate and blackmail powerful governments. Technology—jet travel, satellite communication, lightweight bazookas, plastic bombs, compact automatic weapons— has enabled them to invade the political arena and to express their ideological goals on a more organized level than in the past. Also, world opinion is on their side. Imperialism is now regarded as immoral, even by the United Nations. The colonial empires are dissolving so quickly that it is almost impossible to keep count. This is in part the result of costly wars in Indochina, Indonesia, and Algeria and in part of centrifugal pressures from dissident ethnic minorities. The breakup of large heterogeneous countries into smaller national units has been accelerated by terrorism carried out in the name of oppressed ethnic minorities seeking self-rule.

The United Nations had 51 members in 1945; by 1960 there were 82; there are now 138 and another 20 nations are not members. Indications are that there may be 200 or even 300 politically independent nations in the world by the end of the century.

Brian Jenkins wrote in a Rand Corporation report:

> The resultant international system is likely to resemble the political complexity of Renaissance Italy, in which major kingdoms, minor principalities, tiny states, independent city republics, Papal territories, and bands of *condottieri* engaged in incessant, but low-level, warfare with one another. Medieval Europe, and India in the seventeenth and eighteenth centuries also come to mind. . . . The world that emerges is an unstable collection of nations, mini-states, autonomous ethnic substates, governments in exile, national liberation fronts, guerrilla groups aspiring to international recognition and legitimacy via violence, and a collection of ephemeral but disruptive terrorist organizations, some of which are linked together in vague alliances, some perhaps the protégé of foreign states. It is a world in which the acronyms of various self-proclaimed revolutionary fronts may take their place in international forums alongside the names of countries. It is a world of formal peace between nations—free of open warfare except, perhaps, for brief periods—but of a higher level of political violence, of increased internal insecurity.

Although most terrorists identify with Mao and Castro, few have the patience to go into the mountains for decades if necessary to wage their revolution. Mao

developed the modern theory of guerrilla fighting. He formulated a series of relationships that differed from existing military strategies and earlier Marxist theories
of revolution. Contrary to the Marxists, his emphasis was on military power.
Political power depends on military power; or, as Mao put it, "political power
grows out of the barrel of a gun." Although his forces were initially inferior, Mao
reasoned that the superior political motivation of his guerrillas, strengthened by the
political support of the Chinese peasants, made it possible for them to survive
military reverses. The strategy was to wage a protracted military campaign that
would eventually wear down the enemy.

By politicizing and mobilizing people who would be mere bystanders in a
conventional conflict, Mao introduced a relationship between military action and
propaganda. The effect that any violent action has on the people watching may even
exceed the importance of the conflict itself. Terrorism is that principle applied on
the grandest scale.

Reading 11

Rape and Everyday Life

Lynda Lytle Holmstrom
Ann Wolbert Burgess

Studies of rape victims frequently rely on reported cases. This approach is very
sensible for studying certain problems, such as the reactions of institutions to the
victim. However, to rely exclusively on reported cases is to run the risk of overemphasizing rapes by strangers as well as overemphasizing the image of rape as
bizarre and unusual. Rape can be viewed as a part of everyday life. Research
designs not based either in a hospital or in the criminal justice system are necessary
in order to understand more fully this aspect of rape. Several categories of known
rapists have been studied, including dates and husbands.

There is a history of research on male sexual aggression in dating. A classic
study of college dating was published in 1957 by Clifford Kirkpatrick and Eugene
Kanin. While not using the term *rape* (a reasonable choice given the year of the
study), they asked women on a university campus whether they had been sexually
"offended" during the academic year. The results showed that "20.9 percent were
offended by forceful attempts at intercourse and 6.2 percent by 'aggressively forceful attempts at sex intercourse in the course of which menacing threats or coercive
infliction of physical pain were employed.' "[1] A replication study published twenty

---

[1]Clifford Kirkpatrick and Eugene Kanin. "Male sex aggression on a university campus," *American
Sociological Review* 22 (1957):53.

years later reports similar findings regarding the incidence and frequency of male sexual aggression at a large midwestern state university. The main change after two decades was in the type of dyad where the male sexual aggression occurred. The earlier research found that aggression was more apt to occur among long-term dyads (i.e., couples who were steady dates, pinned, engaged); the replication study found that the offensive episodes were more apt to occur among less involved dyads (i.e., the casual dates). The authors speculate on the reasons for this change.[2] An even more recent study by Phyllis Meighen (done in the Northeast) also shows considerable evidence of coerciveness (and ambiguity) in sexual relations in the context of college dating.[3]

Sexual aggression by husbands is a more recent topic. The law has been changed recently in a number of states. But even today, in most states, the law states that a husband, by definition, cannot rape his wife; that is, forced sexual intercourse with one's wife is legal. The "legal fiction," as judges sometimes call it, is that the wife consents at the time of marriage to all future sex with her husband. Nevertheless, many men do *in fact* rape their wives. Marital rape is now receiving attention from activists, lawyers, and researchers; recently, a historic Oregon trial of a husband received wide coverage by the news media.

David Finkelhor and Kersti Yllo have done research on the problem of marital rape, although they prefer to use the less threatening term of "forced sex" in marriage. They limit their current analysis to cases of marital sex involving *physical* coercion and draw their sample from a New England family planning agency. One interesting finding is that forced sex can occur both in marital relationships that are generally violent and in those that otherwise are violence-free.[4]

Perhaps the most comprehensive social research on marital rape so far has been done by Diana Russell. By contemporary standards, she uses a reasonably conservative definition of rape. She reserves the term for physically forced vaginal, oral, and anal sex, as well as forced digital penetration. And she distinguishes between rape achieved by physical force, by threat of physical force, and when the woman is unable to consent (e.g., is unconscious, drugged).

Russell's findings on the prevalence of wife rape are quite striking. An important methodological point is that Russell's study attempts a statistically random sample of women from the general population. With a reasonably conservative definition of rape and approaching a random sample, she reports: "Eighty-seven women in our sample of 930 women eighteen years and older were the victims of at least one completed or attempted rape by their husbands or ex-husbands. This

---

[2]Eugene J. Kanin and Stanley R. Parcell, "Sexual agression: A second look at the offended female," *Archives of Sexual Behavior* 6 (1977):67–76.

[3]Phyllis Meighen, "Sexual assault against women" (Department of Sociology, Boston College, Chestnut Hill, Mass., n.d.).

[4]David Finkelhor and Kersti Yllo, "Forced sex in marriage: A preliminary research report," *Crime and Delinquency* 28 (1982):459–78.

constitutes 14 percent of the 644 women [in the sample] who had ever been married.''[5] This figure of 14 percent becomes even more striking when one realizes that it means one of every seven women ever married. Rape by an intimate, like rape by a stranger, is traumatic. Russell speaks forcefully of the suffering of these wives.

The important point is that researchers are expanding the kinds of populations being studied in detail and the questions that are being asked. Victimization surveys have been around for some time and serve a useful purpose. But now there are random samples of a general population or of a subgroup (college students) in which the respondents are being asked different questions about rape and sexual assault than they were before. Several studies are now teaching us more about unreported cases, cases in which the rapist is well known to the victims, and about victims of attempted rape. The broader range of resulting information can lead us to change our ideas about rape—what it is and what causes it. Increasingly people are talking of the connections between rape and current definitions of ''normal'' sexuality.

A common approach to rape, both among the public and researchers, is to view it as a deviant or a sick act. Yet while rape may be extreme behavior, more and more feminists and researchers have commented upon some of the similarities between rape and certain current ideals of ''normal'' heterosexuality. Attention is given to the merging of sex and violence in ordinary everyday life. U.S. society is a multifaceted one in which there is not one sexuality but many, including versions with expression of gentleness and mutuality. Despite this variety, the fact remains that a main—perhaps the dominant—view of sexuality currently in our society is that of a male sexuality *combining* sex and violence.

Early on, Susan Griffin called attention to the merging of sex and violence in the United States:

Many men appear to take sexual pleasure from nearly all forms of violence. Whatever the motivation, male sexuality and violence in our culture seem to be inseparable. James Bond alternately whips out his revolver and his cock, and though there is no known connection between the skills of gun-fighting and love-making, pacifism seems suspiciously effeminate.[6]

Griffin's point is that power and violence have become eroticized in our culture not just for a few crazed individuals, but as a general male cultural ideal.

Analysts from other English-speaking countries have also talked of the connections between rape and currently typical male-female relations. Lorenne Clark and Debra Lewis, writing of the Canadian experience, analyze the pervasiveness of coercive sexuality. ''Rape is only an extreme manifestation of the coercive sexuality that pervades our entire culture. It is an inescapable by-product of a system in

[5]Diana E. H. Russell, *Rape in Marriage* (New York: Macmillan. 1982), p. 57.
[6]Susan Griffin, ''Rape: The all-American crime,'' *Ramparts* 10 (1971):28.

which sexual relationships are also power relationships."[7] Paul Wilson, writing of the Australian scene, comments, "It is difficult to isolate rape as an act of random violence outside normal heterosexual relations."[8] He notes that Australians, perhaps even to a greater extent than Americans, have a cultural system emphasizing female passivity and chastity, and masculine sexual prowess.

The above analyses, which have existed for some time now, make intuitive sense when one looks at how we are surrounded in our culture by entities such as the mass media that promote a combining of sex and violence. The question, however, is how well these analyses hold up empirically. Recent studies of "normal" populations do support these analyses.

Mary Koss and Cheryl Oros studied sexual experiences among a normal college population. The sample consisted of 3,862 university students (91 percent white, 7 percent black, 2 percent Hispanic and native American) in classes that were selected randomly from the course schedule. The data support the idea that rape is on a *continuum* with what our culture now defines as normal male behavior and that there is a *continuum* of sexual aggression. For example, 70.5 percent of the women said they had had a man misinterpret the degree of sexual intimacy they desired; 21.4 percent said they had had sexual intercourse with a man when they did not feel like it because of being continually pressured by his arguments; 30.2 percent said they had had a man use some degree of physical force (arm twisting, holding the woman down, etc..) to try to get them to kiss or pet when they did not feel like it; 8.2 percent said they had had sexual intercourse when they did not feel like it because the man used some degree of physical force (arm twisting, holding the woman down, etc.); and 6 percent said they had been raped.[9]

Neil Malamuth (with various coauthors) has carried out a series of studies investigating empirically whether "normal" men have a proclivity to rape. He asked subjects—male college students from the United States and Canada—about the likelihood that they personally would commit rape if it were guaranteed they would not be caught. On the average, in the various studies, approximately 35 percent indicated some likelihood that they would rape. Malamuth then made comparisons between his subjects and convicted rapists. The literature shows that convicted rapists are especially apt to believe rape myths and to have high sexual arousal by depictions of rape. In the Malamuth study, the author divided the college students into those with a lower and a higher likelihood of raping. The subjects who indicated a higher likelihood showed a greater similarity to convicted rapists in regard to their acceptance of rape myths and their sexual arousal by rape depictions.

[7]Lorenne M. G. Clark and Debra J. Lewis, *Rape: The Price of Coercive Sexuality* (Toronto: The Women's Press, 1977), p. 124.

[8]Paul R. Wilson, *The Other Side of Rape* (St. Lucia: University of Queensland Press, 1978), p. 55.

[9]Mary P. Koss and Cheryl J. Oros, "Sexual experiences survey." *Journal of Consulting and Clinical Psychology* 50 (1982):456.

The data suggest that many males in a normal population do have a proclivity to rape.[10]

Especially sobering are the findings of Jacqueline Goodchilds and her coworkers in their studies of adolescent sexual socialization. Their subjects were 432 teenagers in Los Angeles (half were male, half female: approximately one-third were exactly 16 years old; one-third were Anglo, one-third were black, and one-third Hispanic). Two themes are especially relevant in this discussion. First, the males perceived the world in sexual terms more than the females. For example, female teenagers perceived things such as dress, actions, and where people go in a less sexualized way. They were less likely to define the above as cues that a person desired sexual relations, while male teenagers were more apt to perceive males' and females' motivations as sexual.[11] The possibilities for differing perceptions of a given act in the dating scene obviously are very high. A second theme in their work (presented in another paper, using data about the Anglos) has to do with the question of when force is seen as appropriate. The researchers obtained very different answers about force, depending on whether they asked the question abstractly or concretely. When they asked, "Under what circumstances is it OK for a guy to hold a girl down and force her to have sexual intercourse?" 82 percent of males and females said it was never OK. But when asked about specific situations (e.g., "the girl had led the guy on," or "the couple have dated a long time"), the percentage of teenagers who then said that forced sex was never OK dropped dramatically to 34 percent. The important point is that in various sexual scenarios, force is seen as justified.[12]

Empirical studies make it clear that violence and sex are intertwined in a multiplicity of ways in our society, even in normal populations. Sometimes, violence itself is eroticized; sometimes, it is merely a means to sex; and in some cases, sex is a means to violence. These empirical studies, taken as a group, suggest that rape is on a continuum with what many people today regard as "normal" heterosexuality. Working with offenders or victims, clinicians still may find it useful to conceptualize rape more as something pathological than as an exaggeration of "normal" sexuality. Nevertheless, as studies on more diverse populations accumulate, what is so striking are the continua in "normal" heterosexual behavior from mutual to unilaterally imposed and from nonviolent to violent.

[10]Neil M. Malamuth, "Rape proclivity among males," *Journal of Social Issues* 37 (1981):138–157.

[11]Gail Zellman, Paula B. Johnson, Roseann Giarrusso, and Jacqueline D. Goodchilds, "Adolescent expectations for dating relationships: Consensus and conflict between the sexes," paper presented at the American Psychological Association meeting, New York, September 1979, p. 12.

[12]Roseann Giarrusso, Paula Johnson, Jacqueline Goodchilds, and Gail Zellman, "Adolescents' cues and signals: Sex and assault," paper presented at the Western Psychological Association meetings, San Diego, April 1979.pp. 5–6.

CAUSES OF RAPE

A contributing factor to the occurrence of rape is that men can get away with it. Elsewhere in our writings we have addressed more directly the issue of the reasons for rape. We have suggested that rapists are driven by a combination of motives. We see rapists as motivated simultaneously by power, anger, and sexuality. And in a pair or group rape, there may be the fourth motive of seeking male camaraderie. Our data from victims (who reported their victimization) and Nicholas Groth's data from rapists (who were convicted) suggest that power, anger, and sexuality are *all* present, in varying degrees, in all rapes, or at least in all reported rapes. And, at least in reported rapes, sexuality does not appear as the dominant motivation.[13] Perhaps additional motives, such as a sense of entitlement to sexual services, will be added to the list—either for some or for all rapists—as more becomes known through research utilizing different kinds of samples

Much previous work (including much of our own) on the causes of rape has focused on the psychological aspects or on the micro-sociological level. It is important not to look only at the psychological level of analysis. A crucial question to ask is, *What are the ideological and social structural conditions that are conducive to producing such motivations in a significant segment of the male population?* What conditions, moreover, are conducive to creating widespread acceptance among the general population of such behavior? Considerable work now exists on both the ideological and social structural support for rape.

The belief system in our society *supports* and *promotes* rape in many ways. Victims have difficulty convincing others—police, hospital personnel, prosecutors, judges, and jurors—that they were victimized. Some victims have difficulty convincing their husbands. Authorities, family and friends, and the general public often have in their minds an image of rape that does not acknowledge many rape scenarios as rape.

Research studies now document that ideological support for the commission of rape exists widely in the general society. Martha Burt's recent work on "rape culture" is perhaps most notable. Burt is interested in whether people in the general population believe such rape myths as "Only bad girls get raped," "Any healthy woman can resist a rapist if she really wants to," and "Rapists are sex-starved, insane, or both."[14] Her data were obtained by interviews with a random sample of 598 adults in Minnesota. The results show that many people do believe many of the rape myths, and their attitudes toward rape are strongly associated with other strongly held attitudes. Among these other attitudes, the person's acceptance of

[13]A. Nicholas Groth, Ann Wolbert Burgess, and Lynda Lytle Holmstrom, "Rape: Power, anger, and sexuality," *American Journal of Psychiatry* 134 (1977):1239–1243.

[14]Martha R. Burt, "Cultural myths and supports for rape," *Journal of Personality and Social Psychology* 38 (1980):217.

interpersonal violence is found to be the strongest attitudinal predictor of his/her acceptance of rape myths.

There are suggestions in the literature that rapists are likely to believe rape myths. Diana Scully and Joseph Marolla explore the statements of convicted rapists using as part of their framework the concept "vocabulary of motive." They divide their sample of convicted rapists into admitters and deniers (those who admitted having raped and those who denied). Deniers described the *victim* in a way that made their own behavior seem more appropriate or justified. For example, one denier said of his victim, "She semi-struggled but deep down inside I think she felt it was a fantasy come true." The important theoretical point Scully and Marolla make is that "deviant actors do not invent lies but rather their vocabularies are drawn from the surrounding culture and are a reflection of what they have reason to expect others will find acceptable."[15] The surrounding culture in many ways sees forced sex as acceptable.

Analysts looking at the social structural support for rape have focused on stratification by gender, by racial or ethnic group, and by class. Currently, stratification by gender is perhaps the most widely discussed. Numerous people have observed that in our society men have more power, status, and so forth than women, both in the realm of interpersonal relations and in the stratification system of the broader society. Men's possession of (or, in some cases, desire for) greater power contributes to the rape of women. In turn, rape and the fear of rape support men's power. This power differential is what Susan Brownmiller, the widely quoted feminist journalist, is getting at when she says:

> Man's discovery that his genitalia could serve as a weapon to generate fear must rank as one of the most important discoveries of prehistoric times. . . . From prehistoric times to the present, I believe, rape has played a critical function. It is nothing more or less than a conscious process of intimidation by which *all men* keep *all women* in a state of fear. [Emphasis in the original.][16]

She has been criticized for this thesis. Leaving aside the issue of whether the process is conscious, we believe there is considerable insight in the statement. Brownmiller would have been more correct, however, had she said instead that rape is one way in many (but not all) societies that men *as a class* oppress and control women *as a class*. In our society, for example, men as a class wield power over women as a class, and one mechanism used is rape and the fear of rape. Certainly

---

[15]Diana Scully and Joseph Marolla, "Convicted rapists' construction of reality: The denial of rape," paper presented at the American Sociological Association meetings (San Francisco, September 1982), pp. 13, 4.

[16]Susan Brownmiller, *Against Our Will: Men, Women, and Rape* (New York: Simon & Schuster, 1975), pp. 14–15.

many individual men do not identify with or sympathize with notions that rape is desirable. For that matter, many individual men do not identify with various other traditionally masculine themes. The fact remains that "macho" values have become institutionalized. Male-dominated patterns of aggressive behavior and male-dominated institutions oppress and control women. The criminal justice system is a perfect example. The criminal justice system is a masculine world—both ideologically and social-structurally—and female rape victims do not fare well in it. This is the kind of institutionalized handicap that women continually face in our society.

There is a long history of analysis of the connection between race and rape, particularly as it involves interracial rape between whites and blacks. Analyses tend to focus on conditions in the South during and shortly after slavery and on the legacy of this history. One theme is the connection between the portrayal of black men as rapists, and therefore deserving of lynching, and of black women as bad and therefore deserving of sexual victimization. Gerda Lerner notes the historical situation: "The myth of the black rapist of white women is the twin of the myth of the bad black woman—both designed to apologize for and facilitate the continued exploitation of black men and women. Black women perceived this connection very clearly and were early in the forefront of the fight against lynching." Recently Angela Davis observed that "the historical knot binding Black women—systematically abused and violated by white men—to Black men—maimed and murdered because of the racist manipulation of the rape charge—has just begun to be acknowledged to any significant extent."[17]

Interest has recently broadened to include other racial/ethnic groups. Joyce Williams and Karen Holmes have looked at the intertwining of sexism and racism among three ethnic/racial groups. Researching in San Antonio, they have been sensitized to the intricate relations between the Anglos, blacks, and Mexican-Americans. In Williams and Holmes' racial-sexual stratification theory, "rape is viewed as a convergence of racism and sexism in a social system where life chances (positive and negative) are determined largely by sex and/or race-ethnicity."[18] To this statement they should have also added social class. The important point in their work is that power in U.S. society is both white and male. The fact of white patriarchy works itself in many convoluted ways into the relations between races and, for that matter, between males and females within each racial group.

The various authors mentioned above differ in whether they focus on sexism, racism, socioeconomic class, or some combination of these. They also differ in the degree to which they look at intraracial or at interracial rape. And within the latter, the focus may be on rape perpetrated by the dominant group against the minority or

[17]Gerda Lerner, ed., *Black Women in White America: A Documentary History* (New York: Pantheon, 1972), pp. 193–194; Angela Y. Davis, *Women, Race, and Class* (New York: Random House, 1981), p. 173.

[18]Joyce E. Williams and Karen A. Holmes, *The Second Assault: Rape and Public Attitudes* (Westport, Conn.: Greenwood Press, 1981), p. xii.

on that perpetrated by the minority against a member of the dominant group. The body of literature taken as a whole strongly suggests that to come to a general understanding of rape one must analyze the power structure of the society, and that stratification by gender, race-ethnicity, and socioeconomic class are all important.

A comparative example—the case of Ingham, a small town in the sugar cane area of north Queensland, Australia—also suggests the importance of stratification by gender, race-ethnicity, and *socioeconomic class*. Schultz's analysis of pack (group) rape in Ingham focuses on "organized rape as a social institution." She states: "Since 1972 organized pack rapes involving up to thirty-two men and one or two women have been taking place up to four times a week in this small, tropical town which has won awards for its neatness." The organized rapes started with a small group and later evolved into a more generalized pattern: "More general group rapes started as a social activity at the cabarets which are held evey Saturday night in one of the Ingham hotels. . . . At such functions the group organizers would decide on the woman for the night."[19]

Schultz's analysis shows the complex way the town's power structure perpetuates these organized rapes. It indicates the importance of stratification by gender (e.g., a very "masculine town," utter contempt for women), by socioeconomic class (e.g., great social distance between the town's elite, who could perhaps do something about the problem, and the women most liable to be victims), and by racial/ethnic group (e.g., a correlation between ethnicity and class in the town).

It seems clear from numerous analyses (based on a variety of types of data) that rape is, in large measure, a battle over power. Rape is fostered by certain sets of power relationships. It is important to emphasize that the relationship between power and rape is a complex one. Also, the arena (political, economic, familial) in which people have or do not have power may be important. Consider, for example, the complexities in stratification by gender. Certainly one can find societies where the men wield economic and political power and also rape women: our own society is such an example. But men may also rape when women wield such power. Peggy Reeves Sanday, using anthropological data, reports that in 12 percent of the societies where females have political and economic power or authority, one finds that rape is institutionalized or reported as frequent.[20] Another example of complexity is stratification by race. Most rapes are intraracial. But in some cases, men with power use interracial rape in a way that reinforces their power (e.g., white men raping black women). In other cases, men without much power in the broader society use interracial rape as a way to retaliate against the dominant group (e.g., black men raping white women). Thus, an analysis of rape should be sensitive to the intricacies and complexities of power relationships.

[19]Julianne Schultz, "The Ingham case," in Wilson, *The Other Side of Rape*, pp. 112, 115.
[20]Peggy Reeves Sanday. *Female Power and Male Dominance: On the Origins of Sexual Inequality* (New York: Cambridge University Press, 1981), pp. 164–167.

The above analyses suggest that certain ideologies and social structural arrangements encourage rape. If this is so, then one would predict that the rape rate would vary from society to society, and that the rates would correlate with types of societies. Sanday has recently done an interesting study of rape and follows this general approach. Sanday's interest is in the sociocultural context of rape, and in her comparative study she uses the Murdock and White standard cross-cultural sample. She finds, first, wide variation cross-culturally in the incidence of rape. Second, she contrasts "rape-free" and "rape-prone" societies, and then concludes: "Rape in tribal societies is part of a cultural configuration that includes interpersonal violence, male dominance, and sexual separation. In such societies, as the Murphys . . . say about the Mundurucu: 'men . . . use the penis to dominate their women.'" Sanday suggests that such a configuration develops when a society suffers from decreasing food resources, migration, or other situations that encourage dependence on the destructive capacities of males rather than on the fertility capabilities of females:

> When people perceive an imbalance between the food supply and population needs, or when populations are in competition for diminishing resources, the male role is accorded greater prestige. . . . Rape is part of a broader struggle for control in the face of difficult circumstances. Where men are in harmony with their environment, rape is usually absent.

She suggests that this finding is instructive for our society, in which "more men than we like to think feel that they do not have mastery over their destiny."[21]

Reading 12

How Moral Men Make Immoral Decisions

J. Patrick Wright (as told by John Z. DeLorean)

. . . Never once while I was in General Motors management did I hear substantial social concern raised about the impact of our business on America, its consumers or the economy. When we should have been planning switches to smaller, more fuel-efficient, lighter cars in the late 1960s in response to a growing demand in the marketplace, GM management refused because "we make more money on big

[21]Peggy Reeves Sanday, "The socio-cultural context of rape: A cross-cultural study." *Journal of Social Issues* 37 (1981):25.

cars." It mattered not that customers wanted the smaller cars or that a national balance-of-payments deficit was being built in large part because of the burgeoning sales of foreign cars in the American market.

Refusal to enter the small car market when the profits were better on bigger cars, despite the needs of the public and the national economy, was not an isolated case of corporate insensitivity. It was typical. And what disturbed me is that it was indicative of fundamental problems with the system.

General Motors certainly was no more irresponsible than many American businesses. But the fact that the "prototype" of the well-run American business engaged in questionable business practices and delivered decisions which I felt were sometimes illegal, immoral or irresponsible is an indictment of the American business system.

Earlier in my career, I accepted these decisions at GM without question. But as I was exposed to more facets of the business, I came to a realization of the responsibilities we had in managing a giant corporation and making a product which substantially affected people and national commerce. It bothered me how cavalierly these responsibilities were often regarded.

The whole Corvair case is a first-class example of a basically irresponsible and immoral business decision which was made by men of generally high personal moral standards. When Nader's book threatened the Corvair's sales and profits, he became an enemy of the system. Instead of trying to attack his credentials or the factual basis of his arguments, the company sought to attack him personally. This move failed, but, in the process, GM's blundering "made" Ralph Nader.

When the fact that GM hired detectives to follow and discredit Nader was exposed, the system was once again threatened. Top management, instead of questioning the system which would permit such an horrendous mistake as tailing Nader, simply sought to preserve the system by sacrificing the heads of several executives who were blamed for the incident. Were the atmosphere at GM not one emphasizing profits and preservation of the system above all else, I am sure the acts against Nader would never have been perpetrated.

Those who were fired no doubt thought they were loyal employees. And, ironically, had they succeeded in devastating the image of Ralph Nader, they would have been corporate heroes and rewarded substantially. I find it difficult to believe that knowledge of these activities did not reach into the upper reaches of GM's management. But, assuming that it didn't, top management should have been held responsible for permitting the conditions to exist which would spawn such actions. If top management takes credit for a company's successes, it must also bear the brunt of the responsibility for its failures.

Furthermore, the Corvair was unsafe as it was originally designed. It was conceived along the lines of the foreign-built Porsche. These cars were powered by engines placed in the rear and supported by an independent, swing-axle suspension system. In the Corvair's case, the engine was all-aluminum and air-cooled (compared to the standard water-cooled iron engines). This, plus the rear placement of the engine, made the car new and somewhat different to the American market.

However, there are several bad engineering characteristics inherent in rear-engine cars which use a swing-axle suspension. In turns at high speeds they tend to become directionally unstable and, therefore, difficult to control. The rear of the car lifts or "jacks" and the rear wheels tend to tuck under the car, which encourages the car to flip over. In the high-performance Corvair, the car conveyed a false sense of control to the driver, when in fact he may have been very close to losing control of the vehicle. The result of these characteristics can be fatal.

These problems with the Corvair were well documented inside GM's Engineering Staff long before the Corvair ever was offered for sale. Frank Winchell, now vice-president of Engineering, but then an engineer at Chevy, flipped over one of the first prototypes on the GM test track in Milford, Michigan. Others followed.

The questionable safety of the car caused a massive internal fight among GM's engineers over whether the car should be built with another form of suspension. On one side of the argument was Chevrolet's then General Manager, Ed Cole, an engineer and product innovator. He and some of his engineering colleagues were enthralled with the idea of building the first modern, rear-engine, American car. And I am convinced they felt the safety risks of the swing-axle suspension were minimal. On the other side was a wide assortment of top-flight engineers, including Charles Chayne, then vice-president of Engineering; Von D. Polhemus, engineer in charge of Chassis Development on GM's Engineering Staff; and others.

These men collectively and individually made vigorous attempts inside GM to keep the Corvair, as designed, out of production or to change the suspension system to make the car safer. One top corporate engineer told me that he showed his test results to Cole but by then, he said, "Cole's mind was made up."

Albert Roller, who worked for me in Pontiac's Advanced Engineering section, tested the car and pleaded with me not to use it at Pontiac. Roller had been an engineer with Mercedes-Benz before joining GM, and he said that Mercedes had tested similarly designed rear-engine, swing-axle cars and had found them far too unsafe to build.

At the very least, then, within General Motors in the late 1950s, serious questions were raised about the Corvair's safety. At the very most, there was a mountain of documented evidence that the car should not be built as it was then designed.

However, Cole was a strong product voice and a top salesman in company affairs. In addition, the car, as he proposed it, would cost less to build than the same car with a conventional rear suspension. Management not only went along with Cole, it also told the dissenters in effect to "stop these objections. Get on the team, or you can find someplace else to work." The ill-fated Corvair was launched in the fall of 1959.

The results were disastrous. I don't think any one car before or since produced as gruesome a record on the highway as the Corvair. It was designed and promoted to appeal to the spirit and flair of young people. It was sold in part as a sports car. Young Corvair owners, therefore, were trying to bend their car around curves at high speeds and were killing themselves in alarming numbers.

It was only a couple of years or so before GM's legal department was inundated with lawsuits over the car. And the fatal swath that this car cut through the automobile industry touched the lives of many General Motors executives, employees and dealers in an ironic and tragic twist of fate.

The son of Cal Werner, general manager of the Cadillac Division, was killed in a Corvair. Werner was absolutely convinced that the design defect in the car was responsible. He said so many times. The son of Cy Osborne, an executive vice-president in the 1960s, was critically injured in a Corvair and suffered irreparable brain damage. Bunkie Knudsen's niece was brutally injured in a Corvair. And the son of an Indianapolis Chevrolet dealer also was killed in the car. Ernie Kovacs, my favorite comedian, was killed in a Corvair.

While the car was being developed at Chevrolet, we at Pontiac were spending $1.3 million on a project to adapt the Corvair to our division. The corporation had given us the go-ahead to work with the car to give it a Pontiac flavor. Our target for introduction was the fall of 1960, a year after Chevy introduced the car.

As we worked on the project, I became absolutely convinced by Chayne, Polhemus and Roller that the car was unsafe. So I conducted a three-month campaign, with Knudsen's support, to keep the car out of the Pontiac lineup. Fortunately, Buick and Oldsmobile at the time were tooling up their own compact cars, the Special and F-85, respectively, which featured conventional front-engine designs.

We talked the corporation into letting Pontiac switch from a Corvair derivative to a version of the Buick-Oldsmobile car. We called it the Tempest and introduced it in the fall of 1960 with a four-cylinder engine as standard equipment and a V-8 engine as an option.

When Knudsen took over the reins of Chevrolet in 1961, he insisted that he be given corporate authorization to install a stabilizing bar in the rear to counteract the natural tendencies of the Corvair to flip off the road. The cost of the change would be about $15 a car. But his request was refused by the Fourteenth Floor as "too expensive."

Bunkie was livid. As I understand it, he went to the Executive Committee and told the top officers of the corporation that, if they didn't reappraise his request and give him permission to make the Corvair safe, he was going to resign from General Motors. This threat and the fear of the bad publicity that surely would result from Knudsen's resignation forced management's hand. They relented. Bunkie put a stabilizing bar on the Corvair in the 1964 models. The next year a completely new and safer independent suspension designed by Frank Winchell was put on the Corvair. And it became one of the safest cars on the road. But the damage done to the car's reputation by then was irreparable. Corvair sales began to decline pre-cipitously after the waves of unfavorable publicity following Nader's book and the many lawsuits being filed across the country. Production of the Corvair was halted in 1969, four years after it was made a safe and viable car.

To date, millions of dollars have been spent in legal expenses and out-of-court settlements in compensation for those killed or maimed in the Corvair. The corpora-tion steadfastly defends the car's safety, despite the internal engineering records which indicated it was not safe, and the ghastly toll in deaths and injury it recorded.

There wasn't a man in top GM management who had anything to do with the Corvair who would purposely build a car that he knew would hurt or kill people. But, as part of a management team pushing for increased sales and profits, each gave his individual approval in a group to decisions which produced the car in the face of the serious doubts that were raised about its safety, and then later sought to squelch information which might prove the car's deficiencies.

The corporation became almost paranoid about the leaking of inside informa-tion we had on the car. In April of 1971, 19 boxes of microfilmed Corvair owner complaints, which had been ordered destroyed by upper management, turned up in the possession of two suburban Detroit junk dealers. When the Fourteenth Floor found this out, it went into panic and we at Chevrolet were ordered to buy the microfilm back and have it destroyed.

I refused, saying that a public company had no right to destroy documents of its business and that GM's furtive purchase would surely surface. Besides, the $20,000 asking price was outright blackmail.

When some consumer groups showed an interest in getting the films, the customer relations department was ordered to buy the film, which it did. To prevent similar slip-ups in the future, the corporation tightened its scrapping procedures.

Reading 13

Warehousing Criminals

Donald R. Cressey
University of California, Santa Barbara

Psychiatrists have clinical evidence suggesting that capital punishment causes murder. Some people kill in the hope that their crime will energize the state into killing them.

This psychological fact illustrates the workings of a general principle long ago discovered by sociological criminologists: A nation's program for dealing with criminals is always reflected in the country's crime rates. If a society tries to control crime by rewarding conformity, citizens will keep the crime rate down by rewarding each other for good conduct. If a society tries to control crime by terrorizing its citizenry, the citizens will terrorize each other.

In *Beyond the Punitive Society,* the proceedings of a conference on Skinnerian principles, Harvey Wheeler put the matter succinctly and well:

> Just as prisons teach criminals how to be criminals, not how to be good citizens, so punishment teaches persons how to punish; how to punish themselves by haranguing themselves with guilt feelings, as well as how to punish others retributively. The result is a society characterized by punishing; repressive behavior produces a suppressive society.

The idea that prisons are schools of crime, in the sense that they provide opportunities for naïve youngsters to learn new tricks from old cons, has been overplayed. The damage done by prisons is much more direct, subtle, and devastating. Every prison is a crime factory because it models how all criminals, not just those locked behind its walls, are supposed to behave. The prison, like the police officer's armament, the decorum of the courtroom, and the dinginess of the county jail, is a symbol of authoritarianism, coercion, condemnation, and rejection. The symbolic message sent by towering walls, razorsharp barbed fences, armed men on catwalks, and cages of reinforced steel suggests that criminals are uncommitted, alien, wild. Because America has increasingly been broadcasting this message, it is not surprising that our criminals have become increasingly violent. Ironically enough, in the last decade legislators and other government officials have responded to the ensuing violence with violence—more and more citizens are being punished by confinement behind walls of concrete and steel.

Americans are strong believers in the idea that the state should hurt criminals by depriving them of their liberty, perhaps because imprisonment as punishment for crime was invented by the radicals of the American Revolution. Today, close to four hundred thousand adults are confined in America's state and federal prisons, up from under two hundred thousand ten years ago. Most will be discharged within a decade, but others will take their places. Altogether, we will imprison over a million people in the next decade, not counting those locked in county jails for short terms. No other Western nation has an imprisonment rate this high.

Despite their love of incarceration, Americans do not want to pay the price of locking up so many citizens. It costs at least $50,000 to build a cell these days, and to keep a prisoner in a cell requires another $1,000 to $2,000 a month. We need a solution to the dilemma that surfaces whenever someone (usually an economist) notes that as the state increases the cost of crime for criminals (longer and harsher prison terms for more offenders), it increases its own economic costs proportionately because it must build, man, and maintain new prisons, pay board-and-room costs of prisoners for longer terms, and pay for increased police and court work as well.

Deterrence policy, long championed by political conservatives, asks that pain be inflicted on criminals as a means of repressing crime—the assumption being that hurting criminals will reduce crime rates both by reforming offenders (specific deterrence) and by terrorizing bystanding citizens so much they will be afraid to violate the law (general deterrence). The psychology underlying this policy, which is the backbone of contemporary criminal law and its administration, has long been discounted by psychologists. Economists, however, like considerable numbers of the general public, continue to subscribe to the hedonistic doctrine that individuals calculate potential costs and benefits in advance of action and regulate their conduct accordingly. The implication is that undesirable acts will not be performed if enough pain is attached to them and if the amount of pain thus attached is made knowable to all, so that prospective criminals can make rational calculations. The upshot, of course, is a tendency to increase punishment (the cost of committing crime) whenever the crime rate seems too high. This tendency now requires more money than even the advocates of deterrence policy are willing to pay.

Influential contemporary liberals (some call them neoconservatives) also have effected policies that are dramatically increasing the costs of punishing criminals. One such policy inflicts the pain of imprisonment on criminals not for its utility but simply because criminals deserve to suffer ("just deserts," "retribution," "vengeance"). Noting that discretionary practices permit discrimination against the poor, liberals also have replaced indeterminate sentences with mandatory, flat, and presumptive sentences. Finally, liberals have begun locking criminals up for purposes of "incapacitation" (warehousing), rather than for either utilitarian or retributive purposes. All three policies, singly and in combination, are being used to imprison more people for longer terms, thus driving state costs out of sight.

It is reasonable, then, to expect economists and others to give their attention to ways of cutting down the costs of punishment while increasing the assumed costs of committing crimes. Some recommend more frequent use of gassing, hanging, and electrocution. Others recommend that we once again banish criminals to a distant land, as Britain once transported criminals first to her American colonies and then, after the Revolution, to her Australian colonies. Still others, like Tom J. Farer, also recommend self-governing distant colonies but with a difference—these colonies would, like the penal colony in French Guiana made famous by Henri Charrie's *Papillon,* be compounds with armed guards at the perimeters.

Transportation of criminals at first cut Great Britain's punishment costs. The Transportation Act of 1718 declared that its purpose was both to deter criminals and to supply colonies with labor. In 1786, after the American colonies had become independent, the policy of transportation to Australia was adopted, and this practice continued until 1867. It was abandoned because it was strenuously opposed by Australians, because it did not seem to produce general deterrence, and because it became too expensive.

Looking back, it cannot be denied that Britain's transportation program was a success. After all, the United States and Australia are now exemplars of democracy, with liberty and justice for all. There is something good about nations whose constitutions were written by the descendants of convicts.

POLICING THE PERIMETERS

But the stories of other penal colonies have no such happy endings. Russia has used Siberia as a penal colony since 1823. Witold Krassowski and I long ago showed, in a 1958 issue of *Social Problems,* that life in Soviet labor camps is not exactly a bean feast, a fact also documented in Alexander Solzhenitsyn's *One Day in the Life of Ivan Denisovich.* These camps, where inmates govern inmates while armed guards patrol the perimeters, seem more like what Farer is proposing than do the Australian and American colonies.

Farer has unwittingly called for more prisons that are run as Attica, San Quentin, and Smokey Mountain are now being run. These and other penitentiaries have the nightmarish character, the hopelessness, the unspeakable humiliations, and the deadly violence Farer mentions. So do Soviet labor camps. Significantly enough, prisons and labor camps have these features precisely because prisoners are left largely alone to conduct their own affairs, as would be the inmates in Farer's guarded compounds.

Until recently, guards in most American prisons functioned like traditional police officers, protecting inmates from each other by arresting and taking misbehaving inmates to disciplinary court for conviction, sentencing, and punishment. In a few prisons, which were said to be "treatment oriented," guards borrowed from the child-rearing techniques of middle-class people and thus controlled inmates by giving love and affection to those who were behaving, and withdrawing love and affection from inmates who were not. Today, guards rarely use either of these control systems, nor have they invented new police methods. They have withdrawn to the walls, as the guards of Farer's compounds would do. As a consequence, inmates are robbing, raping, assaulting, and killing each other as never before.

There are at least four different ways to make sense of the fact that prison guards and their bosses new concentrate on perimeter control, rather than on keeping the prison crime rate down. Each of the four is relevant to Farer's plan for a prison colony "with an easily guarded periphery," a colony that is, like a trust territory, "being prepared for self-determination" through "technical and capital assistance," supervised "democratic elections," and punishment by state officials, not residents, "in case of grave abuse."

The first is to observe that in contemporary prisons, as in Farer's future camps, guards have no obligation to assist inmates. State officials insist only that criminals be warehoused under conditions not constituting cruel and unusual punishment. Accordingly, residents are provided with food, shelter and clothing, an occasional low-paying job, and technical assistance in the form of meager academic and vocational training for those who demand it. That's it. The deterrence policy of conservatives, like the just deserts and incapacitation policies of liberals, insists on nothing more. Guards ignore the needs of inmates because everyone else is ignoring their needs.

Second, haphazard policing in contemporary prisons—the same kind of policing Farer recommends for his compounds—is a way of supplementing the psychological pain stemming from restricted liberty with the bodily pain inflicted by inmates on other inmates. Among unpoliced prisoners, the crime rate is high, but not because the prisoners "are too sick, too emotionally and psychologically crippled to perform necessary social functions." The crime rate is high because most prisoners are bad guys who have track records of violence. Guards are prohibited from beating, choking, cutting, or clubbing inmates, and instances of guard brutality are now rare, despite stories to the contrary. But guards can, and do, retreat to the periphery, thus letting inmates do their dirty work.

Third, poor policing in prisons is valuable to guards and other prison workers because it maximizes inmate divisiveness, thus discouraging inmates from joining forces in attempts to overpower the staff. Armed guards at the perimeters also provide such discouragement, but, if we can believe our Pentagon generals, it is not safe to rely on retaliatory and defensive weapons alone. "If they are fighting each other, they aren't fighting me," a warden told me long ago. They are not banding together to foment revolution either.

The fourth way to make sense of poor prison policing is to recall that a state's crime policies and crime rates are always closely interlaced. Perhaps contemporary guards' withdrawal to the walls is, like proposals for penal colonies whose inmates are to be prepared for "self-determination," a way of encouraging inmates to govern themselves according to the principles underlying the deterrence, incapacitation, and vengeance system of justice dominating official structures in the United States. Using these principles, state officers try to reform offenders by hurting them, try to keep crime rates down by inflicting exemplary punishments, try to give offenders their due by hurting them as much as they have hurt others, and try to incapacitate offenders so they cannot again hurt others, at least for a time. The United States has a high crime rate because many of its citizens, acting as individuals, try to do precisely the same things. American prisons have an even higher crime rate because inmates also ape American criminal justice processes, but do so in the absence of counteracting influences such as humanitarian socialization processes and effective police departments.

PREVENTING CRIME

Crime prevention, whether inside or outside a prison, requires more than merely arresting, convicting, and hurting wrongdoers. There must be preaching and practicing of brotherly love, racial equality, and forgiveness rather than hate. Crime prevention also requires positive programs for cutting the roots of crime and criminality, including programs for giving more and more citizens a larger and larger stake in the economic and political institutions. Penal colonies, whether on the British model (America, Australia), on the Soviet model (labor camps), or on the model used by Howard B. Gill in the Norfolk Prison Colony of Massachusetts during the 1920s (Farer's model), cannot do these things.

Last winter, when federal and state governments were trying to raise about $10 billion for prison construction, Chief Justice Warren Burger recommended that the new prisons should be "factories with fences around them" rather than mere "human warehouses." The rhetoric is right. If prisons would use inmate labor for production, imprisonment costs would go down. For that matter, if we repealed statutes that limit prison industrial production, as the Chief Justice recommended, prisoners might even be persuaded to build their own new prisons, saving even more money. Who knows, an occasional prisoner might even acquire conventional work habits, give up a life of crime, and live happily ever after. As a *Wall Street Journal* editorial put it on December 17, 1981, "On the average, it is probably expecting too much of prisons to do more than segregate criminals as a way of protecting the rest of us. Still, there is always the individual who would benefit from the opportunities Justice Burger has in mind."

A half-dozen years before the Chief Justice gave his speech, Canada introduced a penitentiary industry system modeled on outside industry rather than on traditional prison factories. Only a handful of inmates have been employed, but the plan is to build factories at several prisons and to concentrate on profits rather than on training or rehabilitation. Candidates for jobs must apply in the same manner as they do in private industry, and must be qualified for the position if they are to obtain it. Hours of work are similar to those in private industry. Inmates are paid the federal minimum hourly wage. From their earnings, they pay the prison for room, board, and clothing, and they also pay income taxes as well as fees for unemployment insurance and the Canada Pension Plan (social security).

Maturation of these "factories with fences around them" should be watched closely by U.S. officials. Using inmate labor under fair conditions is a promising way to cut down the costs of punishment. It should be noted, however, that proposals for prison factories, like proposals for penal colonies, do nothing to challenge either our practice of punishing so many citizens or the absurd assumptions on which this practice is based. Every prison and every penal colony, regardless of its program, is a punitive institution. Every prison and every penal colony, no matter how cheap its program, is therefore a symbol of a society's failure to prevent crime by positive, nonpunitive, interventionist means.

Sir Thomas More hurled an angry question at his fellow Englishmen: "What other thing do you do than make thieves and then punish them?" Now, four and a half centuries later, too many Americans are responding, "Nothing."

PART **Three**

SOCIAL INEQUALITY

CHAPTER 5

Ethnic Discrimination and Poverty

In the first selection, William J. Wilson offers valuable insight into both the historical and the contemporary processes causing the social problems for urban minorities. After considering the effects of racial discrimination, migrant flows, changes in ethnic demography, and structural changes in the economy, Wilson argues that cultural values do not determine behavior or success but rather grow out of specific circumstances and life chances, reflecting one's position in the class structure.

Diana M. Pearce examines "The Feminization of Poverty," that is, the alarming increase in the proportion of female-headed households living in poverty. Her article increases our understanding of both the reasons behind this trend and the qualitative differences experienced by white and black women.

William Ryan's tongue-in-cheek title, "How to Keep the Poor Always with Us," is an indictment of our two-tiered social spending programs. When it comes to poverty programs, we actually spend very little money compared with the amounts spent on social programs benefiting the nonpoor. Consequently, our heavy spending to prevent poverty and our "stingy" spending to eliminate poverty has hampered our effectiveness in resolving this problem.

In the final selection in this chapter, Harry C. Triandis speaks of the benefits to everyone through pluralistic interdependence. If the majority develops additive multiculturism instead of the minority psychologically integrating through subtractive multiculturalism, he argues, our rewards include greater acceptable choices, as we master the social skills to enjoy different social settings and life-styles. This would mean improved life chances for all and ultimately a more equal society.

Reading 14

Inner-City Dislocations

William Julius Wilson

University of Chicago

The social problems of urban life in advanced industrial America are, in large measure, viewed as problems of race. Joblessness, urban crime, addiction, out-of-wedlock births, female-headed families, and welfare dependency have risen dramatically in the past several decades. Moreover . . . the rates reflect an amazingly uneven distribution by race. These problems are heavily concentrated in urban areas, but it would be a mistake to assume that they afflict all segments of the urban minority community. Rather . . . these problems disproportionately plague the urban underclass—a heterogeneous grouping of families and individuals in the inner city that are outside the mainstream of the American occupational system and that consequently represent the very bottom of the economic hierarchy. It is my view that the increasing rates of social dislocation in the inner city cannot be explained simply in terms of racial discrimination or in terms of a "culture of poverty," but should be viewed as having complex and interrelated sociological antecedents, ranging from demographic changes to the problems of societal organization. . . .

There is no doubt that contemporary discrimination has contributed to or aggravated the social and economic problems of the black poor. But is discrimination greater today than it was in 1948, when black unemployment (5.9 percent) was less than half the rate in 1980 (12.3 percent), and when the black/white unemployment ratio (1.7) was almost a quarter less than the ratio in 1980 (2.1)? There are obviously many reasons for the higher levels of black joblessness since the mid-1950s, but to suggest contemporary discrimination as the main factor is, as I shall soon show, to obscure the impact of major demographic and economic changes and to leave unanswered the question of why black unemployment was lower not after, but prior to, the mid-1950s. . . .

[T]he problem is to unravel the effects of contemporary discrimination, on the one hand, and historical discrimination, on the other. Even if all contemporary discrimination were eliminated, the problems of social dislocation in the inner city would persist for many years, until the effects of historical discrimination disappeared. However, a full appreciation of the legacy of historical discrimination is impossible without taking into account other historical and contemporary forces that have helped shape the experiences and behavior of impoverished urban minorities.

One of the major consequences of historical discrimination is the presence of a large black underclass in our central cities, plagued by problems of joblessness and other forms of social dislocation. Whereas blacks made up 23 percent of the population of central cities in 1977, they constituted 46 percent of the poor in those cities.

In accounting for the historical developments that contributed to this concentration of urban black poverty, I will draw briefly upon Stanley Lieberson's recent and original study *A Piece of the Pie: Black and White Immigrants Since 1880.* On the basis of a systematic analysis of early U.S. censuses and various other data sources, Lieberson showed that in many areas of life, including the labor market, blacks in the early twentieth century were discriminated against far more severely than the new immigrants from Southern, Central, and Eastern Europe. However, he cautions against attributing this solely to racial bias. The disadvantage of skin color—the fact that the dominant white population preferred whites over nonwhites—is one that blacks have certainly shared with the Chinese, Japanese, American Indians, and other nonwhite groups. Nonetheless, even though blacks have experienced greater discrimination, the contrast with the Asians does reveal that skin color per se "not an insurmountable obstacle." Indeed, Lieberson argues that the greater success enjoyed by Asians may well be explained largely by the different context of their contact with whites. Because changes in immigration policy cut off Asian migration to America in the late-nineteenth and earlier-twentieth century, the Japanese and Chinese populations—in sharp contrast to blacks—did not reach large numbers and therefore did not pose as great a threat to the white population. Lieberson concedes that the "response of whites to Chinese and Japanese was of the same violent and savage character in areas where they were concentrated," but he also notes that "the threat was quickly stopped through changes in immigration policy."

Furthermore, the discontinuation of large-scale immigration from Japan and China enabled these groups to solidify networks of ethnic contact and to occupy particular ocupational niches. The 1970 census records 22,580,000 blacks and only 435,000 Chinese and 591,000 Japanese. "Imagine," Lieberson exclaims, "22 million Japanese Americans trying to carve out initial niches through truck farming!"

THE IMPORTANCE OF MIGRANT FLOWS

If different population sizes accounted for a good deal of the difference in the economic success of blacks versus Asians, they also helped determine the dissimilar rates of progress of urban blacks and the new Europeans. The dynamic factor behind these differences, and perhaps the most important single contributor to the varying rates of urban ethnic progress in the twentieth century, is the flow of migrants. Changes in U.S. policy first halted Asian immigration to America and then curtailed the new European immigration. However, black migration to the urban North continued in substantial numbers several decades after the new European immigration had ceased. Accordingly, the percentage of northern blacks who are recent migrants substantially exceeds the dwindling percentage of Europeans who are recent migrants. . . .

The flow of migrants made it much more difficult for blacks to follow the path of the Asians and new Europeans, who had overcome the negative effects of discrimination by finding special occupational niches. Only a small percentage of a group's total work force can be absorbed in such specialties when the group's population increases rapidly or is a sizable proportion of the total population. Furthermore, the flow of migrants had a harmful effect on the earlier-arriving or longer-standing black residents of the North. Lieberson insightfully points out that

> sizable numbers of newcomers raise the level of ethnic and/or racial consciousness on the part of others in the city; moreover, if these newcomers are less able to compete for more desirable positions than are the longer-standing residents, they will tend to under-cut the position of other members of the group. This is because the older residents and those of higher socioeconomic status cannot totally avoid the newcomers, although they work at it through subgroup residential isolation. Hence, there is some deterioration in the quality of residential areas, schools, and the like for those earlier residents who might otherwise enjoy more fully the rewards of their mobility. Beyond this, from the point of view of the dominant outsiders, the newcomers may reinforce stereotypes and negative dispositions that affect all members of the group.

In sum, because substantial black migration to the North continued several decades after the New European and Asian migration ceased, urban blacks, having their ranks constantly replenished with poor migrants, found it much more difficult to follow the path of the new Europeans and the Asian immigrants in overcoming the effects of discrimination. The net result is that as the nation entered the last quarter century, its large urban areas continued to have a disproportionate concentration of poor blacks who, as I shall show, have been especially vulnerable to recent structural changes in the economy.

It should also be emphasized, however, that black migration to urban areas has been minimal in recent years. Indeed, between 1970 and 1977, blacks actually experienced a net outmigration of 653,000 from the central cities. In most large cities, the number of blacks increased only moderately; in some, in fact, the number declined. As the demographer Philip Hauser pointed out, increases in the urban black population during the 1970s were "mainly due to births." This would indicate that, for the first time in the twentieth century, the ranks of blacks in our central cities are no longer being replenished by poor migrants. This strongly suggests, other things being equal, that urban blacks will experience a steady decrease in joblessness, crime, out-of-wedlock births, single-parent homes, and welfare dependency. In other words, just as the Asian and new European immigrants benefited from a cessation of migration, there is now reason to expect that the cessation of black migration will help to upgrade urban black communities. In making this observation, however, I am in no way overlooking other factors that affect the differential rate of ethnic progress at different periods of time, such as structural changes in the economy, population size, and discrimination. Nonetheless, one of the major obstacles to urban black advancement—the constant flow of migrants—has been removed.

Hispanics, on the other hand, appear to be migrating to urban cities in increasing numbers. The status of Hispanics vis-à-vis other ethnic groups is not entirely clear because there are no useful figures for 1970 on their type of residence. But data collected since 1974 indicate that their numbers are increasing rapidly in central cities, as a consequence of immigration as well as births. Indeed, in several large cities (including New York, Los Angeles, San Francisco, San Diego, Phoenix, and Denver) Hispanics apparently outnumber black Americans. Accordingly, the rapid growth of the Hispanic population in urban areas, accompanied by the opposite trend for black Americans, could contribute significantly to different outcomes for these two groups in the last two decades of the twentieth century. Specifically, whereas blacks could very well experience a decrease in their rates of joblessness, crime, out-of-wedlock births, single-parent homes, and welfare dependency, Hispanics could show a steady increase in each of these problems. Moreover, whereas blacks could experience a decrease in the ethnic hostility directed toward them, Hispanics, with their increasing visibility, could become victims of increasing ethnic antagonism.

The flow of migrants also has implications for the average age of an ethnic group. The higher the median age of a group, the greater is representation in the higher-income and professional categories where older individuals are more heavily represented. It is not mere coincidence, then, that younger ethnic groups, such as blacks and Hispanics, who are highly concentrated in age groups where unemployment and violent crime are prevalent, also tend to have high unemployment and crime rates, even if other factors are considered. In 1980, ethnic groups differed significantly in median age, ranging from 23.2 years for blacks and Hispanics to 31.3 years for whites. Only 21.3 percent of all American whites were under age 15, compared with 28.7 percent for blacks and 32 percent for Hispanics.

In the nation's central cities in 1977, the median age was 30.3 years for whites, 23.9 for blacks, and 21.8 for Hispanics. One cannot overemphasize the importance of the sudden increase of young minorities in the central cities. The number of central-city black teenagers (16–19 years old) increased by almost 75 percent from 1960 to 1969, compared with an increase of only 14 percent for whites in the same age group. Furthermore, young black adults (ages 20 to 24) in the central city increased in number by two-thirds during the same period—three times the increase for comparable whites. From 1970 to 1977, the increase in the number of young blacks slackened off somewhat but was still substantial. For example, the number of young blacks (ages 14 to 24) in the central cities of our large metropolitan areas (populations above 1 million) increased by 22 percent from 1970 to 1977; young Hispanics, by 26 percent. The number of young whites in these central cities, however, decreased by 7 percent.

On the basis of these demographic changes alone, one would expect blacks and

Hispanics to account disproportionately for the increasing social problems of the central city. Indeed, in 1980, 55 percent of all those arrested for violent and property crimes in American cities were younger than 21.

Age is also related to out-of-wedlock births, female-headed homes, and welfare dependency. Teenagers accounted for almost half of out-of-wedlock births in 1978. Moreover, 80 percent of all out-of-wedlock black births in 1978 were to teenage and young-adult (ages 20 to 24) women. Further, the median age of female householders has decreased significantly in recent years because of the sharp rise in teenage and young-adult female householders. (In 1970, young black-female householders, ages 14 to 24, having children under 18 years old constituted 30.9 percent of all black female householders with children under age 18; by 1979, their proportion had increased to 37.2 percent, compared with increases from 22.4 to 27.9 percent for comparable white families and from 29.9 to 38.3 percent for comparable Hispanic families.) Finally, the explosion of teenage births has contributed significantly to an increase in the number of children on AFDC (aid to families with dependent children) from 35 per 1,000 children under age 18 in 1960 to 113 per 1,000 in 1979.

In short, recent increases in crime, out-of-wedlock births, female-headed homes, and welfare dependency are related to the explosion in numbers of young people, especially among minorities. However, as James Q. Wilson pointed out in his analysis of the proliferation of social problems in the 1960s, a decade of general economic prosperity, "changes in the age structure of the population cannot alone account for the social dislocations" in those years. Wilson argues, for instance, that from 1960 to 1970 the rate of serious crime in the District of Columbia increased by more than 400 percent, heroin addiction by more than 1,000 percent, welfare rates by 100 percent, and unemployment rates by 100 percent; yet the number of young persons between 16 and 21 years of age increased by only 32 percent. Also, the number of murders in Detroit increased from 100 in 1960 to 500 in 1971, "yet the number of young persons did not quintuple."

Wilson, drawing from published research, notes that the "increase in the murder rate during the 1960s was more than ten times greater than what one would have expected from the changing age structure of the population alone," and that "only 13.4 percent of the increase in arrests for robbery between 1950 and 1965 could be accounted for by the increase in the number of persons between the ages of ten and twenty-four." Speculating on this problem, Wilson advances the hypothesis that the abrupt increase in the number of young persons had an "exponential effect on the rate of certain social problems." In other words, there may be a "critical mass" of young persons such that when that mass is reached or is increased suddenly and substantially, "a self-sustaining chain reaction is set off that creates an explosive increase in the amount of crime, addiction, and welfare dependency."

This hypothesis seems to be especially relevant to densely populated inner-city neighborhoods, especially those with large public housing projects. The 1937

United States Housing Act provided federal money for the construction of housing for the poor. But, as Roncek and colleagues pointed out in a recent article in *Social Problems,* opposition from organized community groups trying to prevent public housing construction in their neighborhoods "led to massive, segregated housing projects, which become ghettos for minorities and the economically disadvantaged." As large poor families were placed in high-density housing projects in the inner city, both family and neighborhood life suffered. Family deterioration, high crime rates, and vandalism flourished in these projects. In St. Louis, for example, the Pruitt-Igoe project, which housed about 10,000 children and adults, developed serious problems only five years after it opened and became so unlivable that it was closed in 1976, less than a quarter-century after it was built.

If James Q. Wilson's critical-mass theory has any validity, it would seem to be readily demonstrated in densely populated inner-city neighborhoods having a heavy concentration of teenagers and young adults. As Oscar Newman showed in *Defensible Space,* the population concentration in these projects, the types of housing, and the surrounding population concentration have interactive effects on the occurrence and types of crimes. In other words, the crime problem, generally high in inner-city neighborhoods, is exacerbated by conditions in the housing projects. But as Lee Rainwater has suggested, in his book *Behind Ghetto Walls,* the character of family life in the federal housing projects "shares much with the family life of lower-class Negroes" elsewhere. The population explosion of young minorities in already densely settled inner-city neighborhoods over the past two decades has created a situation whereby life in inner-city neighborhoods closely approximates life in the projects. In both cases, residents have greater difficulty recognizing their neighbors and, therefore, are less likely to be concerned for them or to engage in reciprocal guardian behavior. The more densely a neighborhood or block is populated, the less contact and interaction among neighbors and the less likely the potential offenders can be detected or distinguished. Events in one part of the neighborhood or block tend to be of little concern to those residing in other parts. And it hardly needs emphasizing that what observers call "the central city crisis" derives in part from the unprecedented increase in these neighborhoods of younger blacks, many of whom are not enrolled in school, are jobless, and are a source of delinquency, crime, and ghetto unrest.

It should be pointed out, however, that the cessation of black migration to the central cities and the steady black outmigration to the suburbs will help relieve the population pressures in the inner city. Perhaps even more significant is the fact that in 1977 there were overall 6 percent fewer blacks in the age group 13 and under than there were in 1970. In metropolitan areas there were likewise 6 percent fewer blacks in that age group; and in the central cities, there were 13 percent fewer black children age 13 or younger. Similarly, between 1970 and 1977, white children in this age group decreased by 14 percent overall, by 17 percent in metropolitian areas, and by 24 percent in the central cities. By contrast, Hispanic children age 13 or younger *increased* during this period—18 percent overall, 16 percent in metro-politan areas, and 12 percent in the central cities. Thus, just as the change in migration flow could contribute to differential rates of ethnic involvement in certain types of social problems, so too could changes in the age structure. In short, whereas whites and blacks—all other things being equal—are likely to experience a decrease in such problems as joblessness, crime, out-of-wedlock births, family dissolution, and welfare dependency in the near future, the growing Hispanic popu-lation is more likely to show increasing rates of social dislocation.

ECONOMIC CHANGES AND ETHNIC CULTURE

The changes brought about by the cessation of migration to the central cities and by the sharp drop in the number of black children under age 13 seems to make it more likely that the economic situation of urban blacks as a group will noticeably improve in the near future. However, the present problems of black joblessness are so overwhelming (less than 30 percent of all black-male teenagers and only 62 percent of all black young-adult males [ages 20 to 24] were employed in 1978) that perhaps only an extraordinary program of economic reform can possibly prevent a signifi-cant segment of the urban underclass from being permanently locked out of the mainstream of the American occupational system.

In focusing on different explanations of the social dislocation in the inner city, I have yet to say anything about the role of ethnic culture. Even after considering racial discrimination, migrant flows, changes in ethnic demography, and structural changes in the economy, a number of readers will still maintain that ethnic cultural differences account in large measure for the disproportionate and rising rates of social dislocation in the inner city. But any cultural explanation of group behavioral differences must deal with, among other things, the often considerable variation within groups on several aspects of behavior. For example, whereas only 7 percent of urban black families having incomes of $25,000 or more in 1978 were headed by women, 85 percent of those having incomes below $4,000 were headed by women. The higher the economic position of black families, the greater the percentage of two-parent households. Moreover, the proportion of black children born out of wedlock . . . is partly a function of the sharp decrease in fertility among married blacks (i.e., two-parent families) who have a higher economic status in the black community. By treating blacks and other ethnics as monolithic groups, we lose sight of the fact that *high-income* blacks, Hispanics, and Indians have *even fewer* children than their counterparts in the general population.

Nonetheless, in the face of some puzzling facts concerning rates of welfare and crime in the 1960s, the cultural explanation seems to hold validity for some observ-ers. From the Great Depression to 1960, for example, unemployment accounted in large measure for welfare dependency. During this period, the correlation between the nonwhite-male unemployment and the rate of new AFDC cases was very nearly perfect. As the nonwhite-male unemployment rate increased, the rate of new AFDC cases increased; as the former decreased, the latter correspondingly decreased. Commenting on this relationship in his book *The Politics of a Guaranteed Income*, Daniel P. Moynihan stated that "the correlation was among the strongest known to social science. It could not be established that the men who lost their jobs were the ones who left their families, but the mathematical relationship of the two statistical series—unemployment rates and new AFDC cases—was astonishingly close." However, the relationship suddenly began to weaken at the beginning of the 1960s, had vanished by 1963, and had completely reversed itself by the end of the decade—a steady decline in the rate of nonwhite-male unemployment and a steady increase in the number of new AFDC cases.

Some observers quickly seized on these figures. Welfare dependency, they argued, had become a cultural trait; even during an economic upswing, welfare rates among minorities were increasing. Upon closer inspection, though, one sees that even though nonwhite-male unemployment did drop during the 1960s, the percentage of nonwhite males who dropped out of the labor force increased steadily throughout the decade, thereby maintaining the association between economic dislocation and welfare dependency. The importance of labor-force participation in explaining certain types of social problems was also demonstrated in a recent empirical study relating labor-market opportunities to the increasing rate of crime among youths, reported in the *Journal of Political Economy:*

> The labor force/not-in-the-labor-force formulation has greater explanatory power than the non-working formulation, demonstrating the importance of participation rates relative to unemployment rates in explaining crime rates. This point is reinforced when one observes that during the middle and latter sixties, crime rates rose while unemployment rates declined. It is the decline in the participation rate which provides an explanation of the rise in crime during this period.

A well-founded sociological assumption is that different ethnic behaviors and different ethnic outcomes largely reflect different opportunities for, and external obstacles against, advancement—experiences that are in turn determined by different historical and material circumstances and by different times of arrival and patterns of settlement. In addition, even if one can show that different values are related to differences in ethnic group behavior, mobility, and success, this hardly constitutes a full explanation. By revealing cultural differences, we reach only the first step in a proper sociological investigation; analysis of the social and historical basis of those differences remains to be done. In the words of Stephen Steinberg, "only by adopting a theoretical approach that explores the interaction between cultural and material factors is it possible to assess the role of values in ethnic mobility without mystifying culture and imputing a cultural superiority to groups that have enjoyed disproportionate success."

In short, cultural values do not *determine* behavior or success. Rather, cultural values grow out of specific circumstances and life chances and reflect one's position in the class structure. Thus, if lower-class blacks have low aspirations or do not plan for the future, this is not ultimately because of different cultural norms but because the group is responding to restricted opportunities, a bleak future, and feelings of resignation originating from bitter personal experience. Accordingly, as Steinberg persuasively argues, behavior described as social-pathological and associated with lower-class ethnics should not be analyzed as a cultural aberration but as a symptom of class inequality. If impoverished conditions produced exceedingly high rates of crime among first-generation Irish, Italians, and Jews, what would have been the outcome of these groups had they been mired in poverty for five to ten generations like so many black families in the United States?

Adaptive responses to recurrent situations take the form of behavior patterns, norms, and aspirations. As economic and social opportunities change, new behavioral solutions originate, form patterns, and are later upheld and complemented by norms. If new conditions emerge, both the behavior patterns and the norms eventually undergo change. As Herbert Gans has put it: "some behavioral norms are more persistent than others, but over the long run, all of the norms and aspirations by which people live are nonpersistent: they rise and fall with changes in situations."

ALLIES NEEDED

To suggest that changes in social and economic situations will bring about changes in behavior patterns and norms raises the issue of public policy: how to deal effectively with the social dislocations that have plagued the urban underclass over the past several decades. Space does not permit a detailed discussion of public policy and social dislocations in the inner city, but it must be emphasized that any significant reduction of inner-city joblessness, and of the related problems of crime, out-of-wedlock births, single-parent homes, and welfare dependency, will call for a program of socioeconomic reform far more comprehensive than what Americans have usually regarded as appropriate or desirable.

A shift away from the convenient focus on "racism" would probably result in a greater appreciation and understanding of the complex factors that account for recent increases in the social dislocations of the inner city. Although discrimination undoubtedly still contributes to these problems, in the past twenty years they have been more profoundly affected by shifts in the American economy that have both produced massive joblessness among low-income urban minorities and exacerbated conditions stemming from historical discrimination, the continuous flow of migrants to the large metropolises, changes in the urban-minority age structure, and population changes in the central city. For all these reasons, the urban underclass has not significantly benefited from race-specific policy programs (e.g., affirmative action) that are designed only to combat discrimination. Indeed, the economic and social plight of the underclass calls for public policies that benefit all the poor, not just poor minorities. I have in mind policies that address the broader, and more difficult to confront, problems of societal organization, including the problems of generating full employment, achieving effective welfare reform, and developing a comprehensive economic policy to promote sustained and balanced urban economic growth. Unless these problems are seriously addressed, we have little hope that public policy can significantly reduce social dislocation in the inner city.

I am reminded, in this connection, of Bayard Rustin's plea in the early 1960s—that blacks ought to recognize the importance of *fundamental* economic reform and the need for an effective and broad-based interracial coalition to achieve it. It is evident—more now than at any time in the last half of the twentieth century—that blacks and other minorities will need allies to effect a program of reform that can improve the conditions of the underclass. And since an effective political coalition will partly depend upon how the issues are defined, the political message must underscore the need for socioeconomic reform that benefits *all* groups in society. Civil rights organizations, as one important example, will have to change or expand their definition of racial problems in America and broaden the scope of their policy recommendations. They would, of course, continue to stress the immediate goal of eliminating racial discrimination; but they will have to recognize that low-income minorities are also profoundly affected by problems in social organization that go beyond race (such as structural changes in the economy) and that the dislocations which follow often include increased joblessness, rising crime, family deterioration, and welfare dependency.

Reading 15

The Feminization of Ghetto Poverty

Diana M. Pearce

The "other America" is a changing neighborhood: men are moving out; women and their children are moving in. This dramatic change is not a reaction to recent fluctuations in the economy, but instead reflects long-term structural shifts both in the labor market and in marriage and childbearing practices. Today, three-quarters of the poor are women and children.

The poverty *rate* for female-headed households has remained steady over the

Published by permission of Transaction, Inc. from SOCIETY, vol. 21, no. 1, copyright © 1983, by Transaction, Inc.

past decade, with just under one-third of these families living in poverty. But because a significant number of male-headed households have left poverty, and because the number of households headed by women has increased, the proportion of *poor* families that are maintained by women has risen in the 1970s from 36 percent to more than 50 percent. Moreover, there is evidence that the trend is accelerating. Between 1969 and 1978, there was an annual net increase of 100,000 female-headed families in poverty, but in the two years between 1978 and 1980, the net increase each year was approximately 150,000. Furthermore, according to Reynolds Farley and Suzanne Bianchi, families headed by women have experienced a decline in economic status over the past two decades, with their average income dropping from 77 percent to 62 percent of the average income of white husband-and-wife families, and from 63 percent to 47 percent of black husband-and-wife families.

These trends are appearing even more strongly in the black community. Although the proportion of the poor who are black did not change during the 1970s, the proportion who were in families headed by women increased. Indeed, the decade of the seventies saw a dramatic shift of the burden of poverty among blacks from male-headed to female-headed families. The number of black families in poverty who were maintained by men declined by 35 percent, while the number maintained by women *increased* by 62 percent. In the course of one decade, black female-headed families increased from about one-half to three-fourths of all poor black families.

Some elements of the experience of being poor are common to all women; that is, they are a function of gender. Others, however, are the effect of race, though even these are experienced differently by men and women, as we shall see.

Though poor women share many characteristics in common with poor men (such as low education, lack of market-relevant job skills, or location in job-poor areas), the greater rates of poverty among women can be traced to two distinctly female causes. First of all, women who head their families often bear most or all of the economic burden of raising the children. Secondly, because of sex discrimination, occupational segregation in a segmented labor market, and sexual harassment, women who seek to support themselves and their families through paid work are disadvantaged in the labor market.

If a woman is married, even if she is employed outside the home, she shares substantially in the resources obtained by her husband. That transfer drops off dramatically when the parents no longer live together. In 1975, for example, only 25 percent of the women eligible actually received child support, and for more than half of those, the annual income from child-support payments was less than $1,500. If the parents were never married, the picture is even worse; only 5 percent of these fathers provide child support. Ironically, a woman is better off if her husband is dead, for widows are the best protected against income loss following the loss of a spouse and are therefore least likely to be poor. However, receipt of such transfers is unlikely to provide much of a bulwark against poverty; the average amount as of 1978 was about $1,800, and the duration is generally only a few years.

Accordingly, many women seek income through paid employment. For all too many, this goes against their lifelong expectations and preparations. Although it is true that most women today expect to work or have worked, sex-role socialization in general and vocational preparation in particular do not prepare women to be the *primary* breadwinner. Instead, the traditional emphasis has been on jobs, rather than careers, and on making job choices that emphasize flexibility and adaptibility, rather than income potential. Thus, women faced with the necessity of being the sole source of support for themselves and their children are handicapped.

These handicaps are reinforced by a highly discriminatory labor market. Despite increased attention given this problem—including litigation and legislation—continuing levels of *occupational segregation* of women stand in marked contrast to the decline of racial segregation in employment and education. Women who work full time continue to earn only 59 cents on the dollar earned by men who work full time. And while we do not know with precision the magnitude of the problem, it is increasingly evident that large numbers of women experience sexual harassment and thereby incur heavy economic, as well as personal, costs in lost recommendations, denied promotions, abrupt dismissals, and demotions.

BEING BLACK, FEMALE, AND POOR

The inequality experienced by women in the labor market has been conceptualized by some as confinement to the secondary sector of a dual labor market. According to the dual-economy theory, jobs and industries are readily divided into primary and the secondary sectors, and this division is reinforced by barriers that make it difficult for workers to move from one sector to another. In the primary sector, jobs are characterized by good pay and fringe benefits, job security, a high degree of unionization, good working conditions, and due process in job rights. In contrast, the secondary sector includes work in marginal industries; these jobs are low-paying, often seasonal or sporadic, less likely to be unionized, and offer little protection against the vagaries of either the individual employer or the ups and downs of the marketplace.

The duality of the labor market is complemented and reinforced by a parallel duality in the welfare system. There is a primary welfare sector in which benefits are conferred as a right, often (but not always) because they have been "earned." One is not stigmatized by receipt of these benefits, nor must one demonstrate poverty or suffer degrading, detailed investigations of one's lifestyle. The benefits are more generous, often with minimum or national levels set by the federal government. Not only are benefit levels relatively generous, but one does not have to exhaust one's resources to qualify; nor are benefits reduced in proportion to other income. Examples of primary-welfare-sector benefits include unemployment compensation and social security.

In contrast, the secondary welfare sector is characterized by benefits that are much lower, on the average, and highly variable across states and even across localities within a state. Since such benefits are a privilege, not received by right, they may be revoked arbitrarily and for different reasons in different places. They may be, and usually are, reduced in proportion to other income. Receipt of welfare, in the eyes of the public and many recipients, is stigmatizing and demoralizing.

For those in the secondary sector of either the labor market or the welfare system, escape is difficult. This is especially so for women and minorities. For a variety of reasons, the welfare system and related training and jobs programs (such as WIN and CETA) do not overcome the labor-market barriers faced by women. For example, training is often for traditionally female occupations, such as clerical work or food service, occupations that do not pay wages adequate to support a woman and even one child. The stubborn obsession with getting women off welfare and into jobs as quickly as possible, with no attention to their special needs (e.g., for child care or fringe benefits that include adequate health insurance), has long-term results that are counterproductive. Those who accept or are forced to take economically marginal jobs in the secondary sector quickly find that they do not have access to the primary welfare sector when they lose or are laid off from these jobs. They are then forced to depend on impoverished secondary-welfare-sector programs. Thus, the interlocking secondary welfare system and secondary labor market reinforce a vicious circle of welfare dependency and marginal work.

Women and minorities are concentrated in the secondary welfare sector. As shown in Table 1, whereas men are slightly overrepresented and women underrepresented in the primary welfare sector, there is a severe sex discrepancy in the secondary sector. Less than half of white men receive secondary-sector benefits according to their proportion in the population, while three times the number of white women—and six times the number of black women—receive income from the secondary welfare sector according to their proportions in the population.

Many, of course, receive income from earnings as well as from transfer programs, but since the receipt of primary-sector benefits is strongly associated with previously held primary-sector *jobs,* the figures in Table 1 indicate implicitly the effect of differential participation not only in the primary and secondary welfare sectors, but also in the primary and secondary labor markets. (Theoretically, one could receive income from primary as well as from secondary welfare programs, but Census Bureau data show that few actually do.)

If one compares poverty rates across gender and race categories, several conclusions suggest themselves. First, the poverty rate for those receiving benefits (and perhaps, also, earnings) in the secondary sector (67.7 percent) is more than eleven times the rate for those in the primary sector (5.5 percent). Second, within each

Table 1 Primary Versus Secondary Welfare Sectors, 1978

	All Household Heads		Primary Sector[a]		Secondary Sector[b]	
	Percentage	Poverty Rate	Percentage	Poverty Rate	Percentage	Poverty Rate
Men[c]						
White	79.2	4.7	81.5	4.0	30.2	35.7
Black	6.2	11.8	7.3	7.2	10.1	36.9
Subtotal	85.4	5.3	88.8	4.3	40.3	36.1
Women[d]						
White	10.4	23.5	8.9	10.4	28.7	66.8
Black	4.2	50.6	2.3	32.3	30.9	75.8
Subtotal	14.6	31.4	11.2	15.1	59.6	71.2
Total	100.0		100.0	5.5	100.0	67.7

[a]Includes unemployment and workmen's compensation, veterans' benefits.
[b]Includes all types of cash public assistance (aid to families with dependent children, general assistance, etc.)
[c]Both male-only and husband-and-wife households.
[d]Female householder, no husband.
Source: U.S. Census Bureau, *Characteristics of the Population below the Poverty Level: 1978,* Series P-60, No. 124.

sector, the poverty rates are greater for blacks than for whites, and greater for women than for men; but the gender differentials are greater than the racial ones. In this connection, the differences in poverty rates between black and white men within each sector are quite small, whereas there is a substantial added disadvantage to being both black and female. The "double" disadvantage experienced by black women is actually, in quantitative terms, a geometrically increasing "quadruple" disadvantage.

SPECIAL EFFECTS

It is clear from the data that although much of the economic gulf is accounted for by gender, black women experience considerable further disadvantages associated with race. These disadvantages can be grouped into three areas for purposes of discussion: trends in racial desegregation in various areas, demographic trends, and welfare programs.

Considerable occupational desegregation has been experienced by both men and women. This has meant an exodus from extremely low-paying jobs (often irregular and part-time), particularly in household service, that have been race/sex "occupational ghettoes." But because *sex* segregation levels, which have always been higher than those of race, have remained quite high, and because the wages of women have remained at less than 60 percent of men's wages, black men have benefited more from the racial desegregation of occupations than black women. Thus, statistics purporting to show that black women are closing the gap on white women faster than black men are on white men are misleading. The use of white women as a benchmark is inappropriate, for it eliminates the effects of gender. If one compares the progress of black men and black women to that of white men, then at present rates black men will catch up to white men in 35 years, but it will take black women 135 years to achieve occupational parity with white men.

In other areas, there have been parallel developments. For example, as Robert Crain and Rita Mehard have pointed out, school desegregation has opened up opportunities for black students of both sexes and, therefore, has resulted in increased achievement levels. Continued sex segregation of vocational programs, however, has the consequence of channeling women students into lower-paying occupations. For obvious economic reasons, housing desegregation has been experienced disproportionately by two-parent, two-income black families. In sum, racial desegregation has had a much greater impact on families with a male householder.

More than 40 percent of black families, and more than 50 percent of those with children, are headed by a single parent (almost all of which are women.) This is partly related to high divorce rates, but several other factors have contributed to the growth of single-parent homes. One of these is the high ratio of out-of-wedlock births—now at about 55 percent for blacks. Many of these children are born to teenagers. Black women tend to marry or remarry at lower rates than white women, and they tend to remain single longer if they do marry. This is, in part, because of a shortage of black men of marriagable age. For example, the ratio (in the resident population) of black women to men, ages 20 to 49 is 1.16 (the white ratio is 1.01); in other words, there are sixteen "extra" black women for every hundred black men.

This imbalance in the sex ratio is the result of several factors, including higher levels of suicide and homicide among black men and an incredible incarceration rate for young black men—phenomena that are directly related to very high levels of poverty, underemployment, and unemployment. While it is true that *being a single parent* causes poverty, it is also clear that the widespread poverty among young black men, and their less-than-cheerful prospects for future economic stability, is an important *cause* of the formation of single-parent households among blacks. The converse also holds, so that marriage is as much the result of economic security, well-being, and upward mobility as it is the cause of economic-well-being among families. In this connection, Farley and Bianchi find that the black community is not becoming polarized along traditional class lines (such as occupation or education), but that there is a polarization along *marital-status* lines. Two-parent families are increasing their economic status while families headed by women become poorer, opening up a different kind of schism in black America.

All of the factors noted above play a part in the racial differences seen in patterns of welfare use. Keeping in mind that these differences are relative, and that there is high degree of overlap among the factors, I will briefly examine some of the differences between white and black women who are welfare recipients.

White women tend more often to be divorced (as opposed to being single or separated). They also tend to come to welfare with more resources (including education, work experience, and even ownership of a house and/or a more favorable residential location vis-à-vis job opportunities. On the other hand, white women are also less likely to be employed and are more likely to go on welfare as a result of the loss of a husband's earnings. Because of this combination of more immediate need and yet greater "long-run" resources, white women not only tend to be on welfare for shorter periods of time, they are also more fully dependent during the time that they are on welfare. In contrast, more black women come to welfare as a result of unemployment and underemployment. Whereas white women often leave welfare because they have obtained a job or remarried (or both), black women are less likely to find a job—at least one providing sufficient income to support themselves and their family—and are less likely to marry or remarry.

In sum, white women tend more often to use welfare for shorter periods of time, even though welfare accounts for most (if not all) of their income while they are on welfare. Black women who head households, in contrast, are more likely to use welfare for longer periods of time, but in conjunction with earnings and other sources of income (e.g., child support), and are less likely to be totally dependent upon welfare, particularly over a period of years. Again, it should be remembered that these racial differences are relative. It should be emphasized, too, that the differences between women householders who use welfare and those that do not are not all that great. Data reported by Martin Rein and Lee Rainwater show that among those who were heavily dependent on welfare over a seven-year period, almost 30 percent of annual income came from earnings, while among low-income families who did not use welfare during that period, about 70 percent of annual income came from earnings. Phillip AuClaire estimates that about 58 percent of the annual income of long-term welfare recipients who were also employed came from earnings.

THE WORKHOUSE WITHOUT WALLS

Black women experience quantitatively more poverty than either black men or white women, no matter what the circumstances or income source. But there is also an important qualitative difference not made explicit by the above discussion. The various causes of white women's poverty can be traced back to a single, fundamental source—sexism, perpetuated mainly by white men. Only in a sexist society can the breakup of a marriage actually improve the economic well-being of the father, cause the mother and children to suffer a large drop in economic status, and permit most fathers to provide little or no support to their children. The low wages afforded women of equal education and experience cannot be explained away as anything except sex discrimination. The poverty of black women, in contrast, is related to more complex factors. Black men are rarely in the position of employers and, therefore, are hardly able to determine the wage scales of women vis-à-vis men. And for many black men, their own high rates of unemployment and low income make the question of sharing income with their children and their children's mothers moot. Thus, in addition to the sources of poverty experienced by all women—the economic burden of children, labor-market discrimination and duality, a welfare system that provides penurious benefits and no training/support system—black women experience directly and, through black men, indirectly the effects of racial discrimination.

A further qualitative difference experienced by black women is that their poverty has a more permanent, or at least, indefinite quality. They, of course, bear the burden of poverty in the black community, a community that as a whole has long had much more poverty than the white community. Thus, because of the greater economic resources in the white community, white women stand a much greater chance of leaving poverty through marriage than black women. Black women are more likely to experience what I have called the ''workhouse without walls,'' in which they support themselves through a combination of earnings, welfare, child support, and other transfers, whether concurrently or serially.

It is evident that, within the black community, there is a growing gulf between two-parent, two-earner families and families headed by women. It is also clear that the high unemployment rates among black youth which contribute to the formation of single-parent families, together with the sexism in the labor/welfare system which locks women householders into poverty, are resulting in increasing proportions of black children being born into and/or growing up in families that must struggle every day with poverty.

Reading 16

How to Keep the Poor Always with Us

William Ryan

Hardly a day goes by on which some expert doesn't remind us smugly that we really can't expect to cure social ills like poverty simply by "throwing federal dollars at them." These experts are apt to go on and explain that we're wasting billions of the taxpayers' dollars on social programs that don't do a damned bit of good. The tax Scrooges among them add the caution that this sentimental waste of good money is threatening to put us all in the poorhouse. In order to engage in any serious consideration of social-welfare and social-policy issues, one must pay some attention to the implications of this rhetoric and, in addition, acquire some knowledge of the relevant facts.

What is it, exactly, that these hard-nosed sophisticates want us to understand by these assertions? Let me try to make their claims a bit more explicit:

- First of all, they expect us to believe that we have been pouring hundreds of billions into social-welfare programs to help the poor. (In the minds of many, the broad term "social welfare" is directly absorbed into the everyday meaning of "welfare" or "relief.")
- They make the further claim that, despite these efforts, the poor remain poor, and their spoken or unspoken explanation is that this is principally because their individual problems or deficiencies cannot be remedied simply by spending money on them.
- Finally, they paint a grim picture for their audience, one showing that all this extravagant generosity to the poor is producing a mounting burden of federal taxes, which is bringing the average American to his knees.

What is the reality behind this rhetoric? While it is literally true that about half the federal outlay budget falls under the general rubric of social welfare, we must recognize how inclusive this category is. The fact is that about half of all this money is spent on retirement checks, mostly Social Security payments. The large majority of the recipients of these checks do not belong to the group that most people have in mind when they talk about "the poor." Over twenty million senior citizens receive these checks on the third of every month, the average amount for a retired couple today being something over $500. It must be fairly obvious that the majority of these older persons stay afloat somewhat above the official poverty line precisely because we throw these federal dollars at them.

Reprinted with permission from *Equality* (New York: Vintage, 1981), pp. 116–117 by Random House, Inc.

The two next-largest chunks of the money listed under social welfare are payments to the providers of Medicare services (hospitals, physicians, druggists, and so forth) and grants to the states to help support health, education, and social services—ranging from foster home placement to crippled-children's programs to school lunches.

When we get down to the amount of federal money that goes to welfare recipients, the "poor" in most people's minds, the figure gets quite small. In 1977 it was a bit over $12 billion, out of a total "social welfare" budget of over $250 billion; currently, it is probably about $15 billion. About half of the recipients of this largesse are children in AFDC families, the other half are the aged, blind, and disabled who are not eligible for Social Security. This munificient sum represents, not half the federal budget, but a bit more than 2 percent of it. So, it can be seen that what we call "throwing dollars at poverty" represents only a tiny slice of the budgetary pie. Even during the height of the so-called war on poverty, when the federal budget was racing past the $200 billion mark, the Office of Economic Opportunity, which administered the antipoverty programs, never had an annual budget as large as $2 billion. When it comes to throwing dollars at poverty, there aren't many dollars left, and it doesn't take anyone very long to do the throwing.

Is it true that this spending on social welfare is extravagant and useless? As I argued earlier, some of these programs are effective in reducing inequality somewhat, while others have little or no effect. (Many included under the heading of social welfare are not really relevant to the issue; these include the costs of medical care to members of the armed services, research grants to social scientists, and across-the-board subsidies to medical schools, calculated on the basis of the total number of students enrolled.) The items that are instrumental in reducing inequality to a measurable though relatively small extent are those that I have identitied as the relatively "universalistic" social-insurance programs, such as Social Security and unemployment compensation. Cash Social Security benefits to the retired, the disabled, and the surviving spouses and children of breadwinners who died young and weekly compensation checks to the unemployed amounted in 1978 to over $100 billion. Analogous programs—military and civil service retirement, veterans' pensions, railroad retirement pensions, the black-lung program for disabled miners, and the like—add another $30 billion. Medicare accounted for an additional $25 billion. That was almost $160 billion in direct and indirect benefits, going to over 35 million persons. Again, it must be quite obvious that, without this kind of support in the form of social-insurance benefits, most of those 35 million would be in very bad financial trouble indeed. Just considering the elderly, it is beyond the question that there are millions of senior citizens, now supported at some minimal level of dignity and security, who would otherwise be living in unbearable poverty. That is the human meaning of throwing one kind of dollar at social problems. To say that all this has no effect on income inequality and the elimination—or, better, the prevention—of poverty is simply ridiculous.

The exceptionalistic programs, such as welfare and SSI, it is quite true, don't even begin to eliminate poverty. The reason is plain to see: we don't throw enough dollars. To the hapless people dependent on these programs, who number over fifteen million, the majority of them children, we are shamelessly, cruelly stingy.

Of all the individuals who receive benefits from social-welfare programs, a bit more than two-thirds receive some kind of social insurance; the rest receive welfare. We spent ten times as much on social insurance as on welfare. It is rather remarkable, when you come to think of it, that Americans do not appear at all to begrudge the huge amounts we spend on social insurance (essentially to *prevent* poverty) but are brought to the point of outraged frenzy by the relatively small amount we spend on welfare recipients whom we *imprison* in poverty. I say "imprison" advisedly because, obviously, the level of welfare grants guarantees that those who receive them will remain in the lowest depths of poverty.

The grain of truth, then, in the "throwing dollars" charge is that inadequate public assistance—the tiny neglected corner of social welfare—far from solving the poverty problem, is one of its main causes.

The argument that social spending creates spiraling federal taxes, which are bankrupting the average American, is also fallacious. First of all, federal income taxes are not, as we are so frequently told, spiraling up and up. They have remained remarkably stable in relation to income. In absolute figures, of course, taxes go up every year, but they do so at just about the same rate as does gross income. In 1960 federal income taxes were equivalent to 10.5 percent of all personal income; by 1970 the figure had risen to 11.0 percent; by 1977 it had dropped back to 10.6 percent; in 1978 the figure again stood at 11.0 percent; in 1979, at 10.9 percent. In other words, the scarecrow of ballooning federal taxes is a myth.

As for the share of the federal tax burden specifically earmarked for public assistance programs, the average family earning $350 a week spends about $4 a week for all public assistance programs combined (as compared, for example, with $15 a week for national defense). To suggest a more concrete measure of our spending on welfare, for every federal and state tax dollar we spend to support the 7.5 million children on AFDC, we spend over two on liquor and over fifteen on gasoline. This is not to deny that these children are, in fact, a tax burden to the average worker. Many people argue that this is unfair, that it is the responsibility of the natural parents to support these children. But I wonder how long the argument would rage if we all realized how light that burden is. For the average worker, earning $250 a week, the money taken from him for AFDC to support "other men's children," by way of the federal tax deduction, is about fourteen cents a day—the cost of about four cigarettes. All this venom and rage over the cost of four cigarettes a day!

This, then, is the general background. Three questions come to mind:

- How did all this come about?

- What is the purpose of retaining what Alvin Schorr called our two-tiered social-welfare system—universalistic social insurance for the majority and exceptionalistic welfare programs for the despised minority?
- If Americans are ready to support universalistic programs with relatively little grumbling and resentment, why have we not been able to move even further in this direction (as every other industrialized country in the world did long ago)?

The first question can be answered briefly by sketching vignettes of three periods in the history of American social policy—the long period before 1929, the years of the Great Depression in the 1930s, and the decade of the 1960s.

For generations, relief—as it was called—was meager, fragmented, localized, and directed at persons who apparently couldn't make it in the hurly-burly of the free market. Some of these unfortunates were seen as relatively blameless—the ill, widows and orphans, the elderly without families. Others were seen as incompetent and lazy—the drunkard, the malcontent who wanted higher wages than employers were willing to pay, the "town bum," who was found even in the smallest village. The most basic survival needs of such persons (excluding, whenever possible, the incompetent and lazy) were met primarily by private charities, supplemented by a small amount of local tax money, spent in part for small cash grants, in part to support the grim institutions known as poorhouses or county farms—institutions that remain alive in the memories of many living persons. In 1890 the total amount of tax money spent for such purposes in the entire country was $41 million, mostly by local municipalities.

During these years, the Fair Play ideology was riding high and was closely mirrored in most social arrangements, including philanthropy. The poor, the ill, and the aged, worthy and unworthy alike, were the losers in the great race of life. There were prominent professors and intellectuals who argued that these misfits, nature's marked losers, should simply be allowed to die "for the good of the race," but the great majority of Americans rejected so harsh a solution and made a half-hearted commitment to keep the poor from actually dying of starvation.

It took the Great Depression to bring about a major change both in social-welfare-policy thinking and also in the attitudes and beliefs of the average American. All through those grim years everyone knew many solid, hard-working, righteous people who were unaccountably (and, it began to seem, permanently) impoverished. The able-bodied pauper became commonplace; he was one's uncle or cousin or friend or neighbor and could hardly be branded as improvident or shiftless. There was only one way to distinguish him with certainty from the town bum of one's childhood, and that was to clearly establish a new and more respectable category—the *unemployed*.

In this way the problem of pauperism and idleness—of deviant men who *wouldn't* work—was distinguished from the problem of unemployment—of righteous men who *couldn't find* work. The issue of impoverishment was evaded. The issue of equality never even came up. The issue of jobs was made central, and joblessness was redefined in much more universalistic terms—as a mass phenomenon unrelated to personal characteristics and clearly the result of events external to the individual unemployed person. Programs were rapidly developed that were public, legislated, national in scope, and often directed toward a much larger segment of the population than those traditionally seen as "the poor." The federal government entered for the first time into the arena of cash relief payments. Federally funded programs to provide work were established, such as the Public Works Administration, the Works Progress Administration, and the Civilian Conservation Corps. The implicit *duty* of all to work was becoming something like a *right* to work (for a very low wage, of course).

The Social Security Act of 1935 included near-revolutionary provisions for income cushioning that were designed ultimately to protect almost the entire *working* population—social security and unemployment compensation. Both programs were directly related to the experience of work—unemployment insurance if you were laid off from your job, social security pensions based on your having worked most of your life until the age of sixty-five.

For the poor who could not reasonably be defined as able-bodied and eligible for work—again, the traditional widow with small children, the aged, the disabled, the blind—means-tested categorical assistance programs were included, now organized in a more universalistic fashion in some respects, but retaining all the exceptionalistic features of old-fashioned relief.

During the same years, an equally significant piece of legislation, the Wagner Act, guaranteeing labor unions the rights to organize and to engage in collective bargaining, finally gave full legal recognition to the reality that employer-employee relationships were not a series of one-to-one contracts, but that the work force of a firm was a collective entity that could act as such.

The crisis of the Great Depression, then, produced a remarkable upsurge of universalism in thinking about social problems and a dramatic alteration in developments in official social policies. Even the essentially exceptionalistic programs established at that time, and still with us as our public assistance welfare programs, were pushed in the direction of universalism, in that after 1935 the welfare program was national in scope, under federal supervision and with a dramatic increase in public funding.

The next major event, the so-called war on poverty, occurred in the 1960s, following a rediscovery of want in the midst of affluence and the growth of the civil rights movement. The theorizing and the rhetoric accompanying the declaration of war against poverty were, interestingly enough, deeply imbued with universalistic themes. There was a rapid jelling of a consensus about the target to be attacked, namely, the "opportunity structure," the structural barriers built into the fabric of society that kept the poor penned in poverty. But, as the experts translated the rhetoric into actual programs, the target changed subtly but dramatically. All the major poverty programs—Head Start, Adult Education, Manpower Training, Concerted Social Services—were specifically aimed, not at the "opportunity structure," but at the poor themselves. The goal, of course, became the elimination of undesirable internal deficiencies of individuals. The war on poverty was announced in ringing tones with the vow that we would pursue the war to its bitter end. The bitter end was that poverty won.

For forty years now, since our brief romance with openly universalistic programs, we have persisted with our two-tiered social policy, while the rest of the world has far outstripped us in developing social insurance and other universalistic approaches. And it is important to note that variations of this two-tiered system are evident in many other areas of our life. Take housing, for example. Public housing and its alternatives, such as leased housing and rental assistance, are straightforward means-tested programs for the certifiable poor. For middle-income and well-to-do people, we also have housing-assistance programs, but they are almost invisible in their universality—I refer, of course, to income tax exemptions for mortgage interest payments and real estate taxes. These are available to everyone, with no test of eligibility (other than the minor matter of financial capacity to own one's home), and the consequent savings are a direct subsidy to the homeowner from the federal government in precisely the same sense that the relatively low rents in public housing projects are a subsidy to their tenants. The tax deductions that constitute a subsidy to homeowners, however, involve a far greater sum of money than the amount invested in the housing-assistance programs for the poor. But, of course, we homeowners simply take this as our right, our natural entitlement. It never occurs to us that the government is giving us something for nothing.

Transportation offers another example. Public investment in transportation for the poor—that is, public transportation systems—has been minuscule in comparison with the enormous investment in subsidizing interstate highways, airlines, trucking companies, and expressways that conveniently carry commuters to their suburbs.

The general principle seems to be that if a service or social program benefits the well-to-do at least as much as the poor, and preferably a good deal more, it will be organized along universalistic lines. The development of public fire and police departments, of state and national parks and other recreation areas, of polio vaccination, and of sewage disposal systems illustrates this point.

Movement toward universalism, on the other hand, is aborted, transformed, or somehow thwarted and crippled, when it involves any threat of real advance toward greater equalization in the distribution of economic well-being, or even toward the lesser goal of eliminating extreme poverty. I don't believe that public attitudes account for the persistence of exceptionalistic programs. For one thing, as I suggested, the public is dramatically more positive and generous in its attitude toward our universalistic social-insurance programs. In discussions of them we rarely are confronted with the spitefulness that almost always emerges in reaction to any mention of "the poor" or of "welfare people."

Although Americans have been confused and deceived in various ways, they seem almost instinctively committed to universalistic approaches to social policy. Social Security, for example, is now a sacrosanct institution in American life, and any proposal to alter its nature—to make it a voluntary rather than an all-inclusive legislated program, for example—meets with violent disapproval. For as long as there have been records of public opinion on the issue, at least fifty years, Americans have been overwhelmingly in favor of some national program of medical care like federal health insurance.

So true is this that many exceptionalistic programs, designed intentionally or unintentionally to preserve inequality, are set before the public as universalistic schemes. A good example is the Nixon administration's Family Assistance Plan, devised by Daniel P. Moynihan as a substitute for our present public assistance program, and presented to the public under the guise of a "reform" that would institute a "guaranteed annual income." It was, of course, nothing of the kind; it was even more selective than our present system, included provisions for what amounted to forced labor at less than minimum-wage rates, even for mothers of young children, and set income levels far below the government's own poverty line. It was, however, decorated with some universalistic ornaments, such as national administration and standards, the elimination of specific categories, and the inclusion of the working poor, and those universalistic features were its major selling points. The scheme—one of the most insidious attacks on poor people in our history—was narrowly defeated, primarily because of intensive lobbying efforts by poor people's organizations led by George Wiley; yet to this day it is referred to by political columnists and other observers as the progressive Nixon-Moynihan guaranteed-income plan. This probably illustrates why truth-in-labeling laws are so necessary for the protection of consumers.

Nevertheless, gradual movement toward more universalism in social-policy and social-welfare programming contains within itself the seeds of change, the potential leverage for increased equality in our society, depending on the acuteness with which the programs that ultimately emerge are analyzed and explained to the general public. The growing demand for some kind of national health-care program, and the increasing response to this demand on the part of politicians, is a case in point. Such a universalistic program would almost certainly reduce inequality in two ways—it would help to equalize the health *status* of all, and it would reduce the *economic* burden of health care for the great majority of the population.

Reading 17

Additive Multiculturalism: A Specific Proposal

Harry C. Triandis
University of Illinois

Rather than integration, as it is conceived by the popular press, we need *additive multiculturalism*. I hope that the future of pluralism is additive multiculturalism. I borrowed the idea, by analogy, from Lambert's[1] discussion of additive and subtractive bilingualism. Lambert argues that when an English Canadian learns French he adds to his capacities; when a French Canadian learns English there is danger of assimilation into the vast North American culture and loss of the French identity. Whites who learn about black subjective culture and learn to appreciate the positive features of black culture become enriched. Asking blacks to become culturally white is subtractive multiculturalism. As Taylor (1974) wrote, perhaps too strongly, integration as advocated today is a white idea about how blacks would become psychologically white. That conception is *subtractive multiculturalism*. The way to reduce conflict is not for one side to lose what the other side gains, but for both sides to gain.

Some of the negative features of American society—including anxiety over achievement, which results in much "Type A behavior" and a third of a million deaths from heart attacks each year—might be reduced if we adopt a more relaxed outlook, often found among blacks. (I am personally in need of reform, in this respect, as much as anyone else.) The pace is frantic. Too often we are in the situation of the passenger on an airplane who hears the pilot say, "I have excellent news: our speed is breaking all records. Now for the bad news: we are lost." Perhaps we should contemplate whether our crime, pollution, suicide, and divorce rates are where they should be. In any case, we need to understand the feelings associated with each kind of multiculturalism. Desirable pluralism permits everyone to have additive multiculturalist experiences. Ideally, pluralism involves enjoyment of our ability to switch from one cultural system to another. There is a real sense of accomplishment associated with the skill to shift cultures. The balanced bilingual/bicultural person, or even more, the multicultural person, gets kicks out of life that are simply not available to the monolingual/monocultural person. There is a thrill associated with the competence to master different environments, to be successful in different settings. The person who delights in different social settings,

Reprinted with permission from "The future of pluralism," *Journal of Social Issues* 32 (1976):179–208.
[1]W. E. Lambert, "Culture and language as factors in learning and education," paper presented at the Symposium on Cultural Factors in Learning, Bellingham, Washington, 1973.

different ideologies, different life-styles, simply gets more out of life. There are now effective ways to train people to appreciate other cultures (Brislin and Pedersen, 1976). We must use these procedures in our schools to broaden the perspective of most students.

At the simplest level, we find this broadening in the appreciation of different foods. Contrast the meat and potatoes diet of some people with the diet of those who have the means to explore the multinational cuisine of a large city. The ability to appreciate the full range of music produced in different parts of the world is another example. But, food and music appreciation are not as difficult to learn as the subtle ways of human interaction, and particularly intimacy. To be able to become intimate with many kinds of people who are very different is a great accomplishment. This should be the goal of a good education, and the essential step forward to a pluralist society.

A good education also means an education which is adjusted to the needs of the minority as well as the majority groups. Castañada, James, and Robbins (1974) outlined some of the ways in which schools must change to provide the best learning environments for Latin-background, black, and Native American children. Castañada, for instance, points out that frequently teachers punish behaviors that are learned in the child's home, thus making the school environment noxious. The Spanish-American emphasis on family, the personalization of interpersonal relations, the clear-cut sex-role differentiation, and so on create a particular way of thinking, feeling, and learning. A teacher who is not aware of these cultural influences can easily lose contact with a child. For example, teaching a Spanish-background child may be improved if the teacher sits close to the child, touches a lot, hugs, smiles, uses older children to teach younger children, involves the children in group activities, sends work to the child's home so the parents can get involved, arranges for Mexican foods to be cooked in class, teaches Spanish songs to all children, and so on. Similarly, if monocultural American children understood why Native Americans have values stressing harmony with nature rather than its conquest, a present rather than a future time orientation, giving one's money away rather than saving it, respect for age rather than emphasis on youth, such children would broaden their perspective. The dominant American culture will profit from inclusion of such conceptions in its repertoire of values: Harmony with nature is much more conducive to the respect that ecology imposes on technology in the post-industrial era, respect for old age may be much more functional in a nation where the majority is old as it will be soon, a present orientation may be more realistic in a society that can no longer afford to grow rapidly because of energy and resource limitations, and so on. The majority culture can be enriched by considering the viewpoints of the several minority cultures that exist in America rather than trying to force these minorities to adopt a monocultural, impoverished, provincial viewpoint which may in the long run reduce creativity and the chances of effective adjustment in a fast-changing world.

Such goals are equally viable for minority and majority members provided we respect each other's cultural identity. We must not ask blacks to become culturally white. We must not ask them to lose their identity. Integration in the form of becoming like us implies by definition that their culture is inferior. Rather, what we want is to find more common superordinate goals and methods of interdependence that give self-respect to all. We need to be creative if we are to discover such methods.

In his 1969 presidential address to SPSSI Tom Pettigrew (1969) asked whether we should be racially separate or together. After almost ten years I still find his analysis compelling. Yet I also sympathize with black writers who, like Taylor (1974), disagree with Pettigrew's position. Taylor has argued that dependent people cannot be integrated in an equalitarian society. Integration, he argued, can imply loss of identity and inferiority. He insists that only after power is equalized can we have racial justice. Similarly, Ron Katanga has stated: "We can't be independent unless we have something to offer; we can live with whites interdependently once we have black power" (cited by Pettigrew in Epps, 1974). Taylor (1974) is optimistic and gives us some examples of power shifting to blacks: He tells us that in Atlanta the NAACP agreed to the busing of only 3000 instead of 30,000 students in exchange for 9 out of 17 administrative positions in the school system, including the positions of superintendent and assistant superintendent of instruction. The argument is that power can lead to decisions that will improve the quality of education of the black children of Atlanta and that is better than mere integration. Taylor[2] is also impressed by discussions among administrators of the Massachusetts Institute of Technology to transfer a substantial portion of the M.I.T. group life insurance from a white-controlled to two black-controlled insurance companies. His argument is that only when the power gap between the races is made much smaller is contact likely to lead to harmony. Thus, as a first step toward pluralism, he visualizes what he calls "empowerment strategies" for blacks to acquire power. He also emphasizes the importance of institutional racism much more than individual prejudice, as a barrier to pluralism.

I agree with Taylor. I see no good reason to expect mere integration as advocated today to lead to additive multiculturalism. To reach additive multiculturalism I see the need for a three-pronged strategy.

1. Blacks and other minorities must seek power. They need to develop a flexible, imaginative approach to acquiring it. To get power they need resources. They do have one important resource—a common fate. If they manage to communicate within each community the importance of concerted action for improving their position in American society, they will be able to engage in balance-of-power politics and thus acquire more resources than they now have.

[2]D. A. Taylor, personal communication, 1976.

2. To learn about another culture one must be secure in one's own identity. The essence of additive multiculturalism is that those who have a firm identity—the well-established mainstream of America—must do the learning. And they should learn not only about blacks, but also about Spanish-speakers, Native Americans, and other ethnic minorities that exist in significant numbers in the U.S. To be educated in this country should mean that one is able to have good, effective, and intimate relationships with the ten or more important cultural groups that exist here. Specifically, whites must learn to interact effectively with blacks. Right now, given the status of blacks and whites in this country, whites have no good reasons to learn how to get along with blacks. Unlike the American who if he is to visit Paris should learn a bit of French, since otherwise he may not get much champagne or perfume, whites have little motivation to get along with blacks.

Note that I am emphasizing that learning to get along means learning new interaction skills. But this is exactly what additive pluralism is all about. It is being able to get along not only with one's own group but also with other groups. New techniques for culture learning (Seelye, 1975; Triandis, 1975, 1976; Brislin and Pedersen, 1976; Landis, Day, McGrew, Thomas, and Miller, 1976) are becoming available. These techniques can train people to engage in interactions where the rewards exceed the cost for both persons, with a large variety of ethnic groups. By extension some of these techniques can be used to improve relationships between men and women, old and young, and so on. In short, whenever the life experiences of a group are sufficiently different from the experience of another group, the gap in subjective cultures requires an effort to reduce misunderstandings. Each group must learn more about the perspective of the other groups than happens now.

3. There is an urgent need for programs that guarantee jobs to every American who is capable of working. Our data show the largest gap in subjective culture not between blacks and whites but between unemployed blacks and employed blacks. Current estimates of unemployment rates among young black males exceed 50 percent. This is a totally unacceptable rate. A program of guaranteed jobs for those who can work, negative income tax for those who earn too little, job supportive services (such as public nurseries), and welfare payments for the old and disabled, may eventually cost less than the $200 billion spent on various forms of welfare ("Progress Against Poverty," 1976). Such a program can benefit both whites and blacks (though blacks will be helped proportionately more), the costs can be diffused through the income tax structure, and it is consistent with the dominant values of this society—it puts people to work (Rothbart, 1976). I would add one more most important benefit: It creates the preconditions for successful contact. Given the importance of having a job within the American status system, the elimination of the unequal rates of unemployment via elimination of most unemployment would immediately reduce one of the important dissimilarities that make successful interracial contact difficult. I must emphasize that our evidence (Triandis, 1976), as well as that of Feldman (1974), suggests that working class blacks are very similar in their subjective cultures to working class whites; the discrepancies in subjective culture occur among the unemployed. Thus, by eliminating this category we would move toward another precondition of successful contact. Finally, by integrating the unemployed into the economy, we would create some commitment to the successful operation of the whole economic system, and a variety of superordinate goals.

For the guaranteed jobs plan to have the desired effects, however, these jobs must be identified not as government-jobs-specially-made-to-take-care-of-the-unemployment-problem but as legitimate jobs. This means that a variety of avenues toward full employment must be created simultaneously—stimulation of the private sector, identification of activities that have national priority (such as conservation projects), job training, and other programs.

WE NEED MORE RESEARCH

Consider a theoretical model that describes black/white contact. There might be n dimensions on which two groups might be different. In the case of assimilated blacks, n tends to be close to zero; they differ little from whites. In the case of blacks with ecosystem distrust, it may be a very large number.

Now consider m dimensions specifying the conditions under which contact is likely to lead to "successful" interpersonal relationships, that is, relationships where the rewards exceed the costs for *both* blacks and whites. It is likely that in the case of work relationships (one of the m dimensions) this would be the case, while in the case of other relationships it may not be the case.

One of the research projects urgently needed is one that specifies how the n dimensions of difference are related to the m dimensions of successful contact. For example, a difference in trust in the American system of government might have strong implications for cooperation between a white and a black person in a business venture, while it may have little relevance for an intimate relationship; conversely, a difference in trust in the reliability of friends may have little significance in a relationship which is specified by a written contract but very large significance for an intimate relationship. We need to develop much greater understanding of how differences in subjective culture between blacks and whites have implications for some interpersonal relationships but not for others.

There is already enough research to indicate that acceptance in formal settings is more likely than acceptance in informal settings (Triandis and Davis, 1965; Goldstein and Davis, 1974; Pettigrew, 1969). We also know that when superordinate goals can be made salient, when contact receives institutional support, and when contact is associated with pleasurable events, it is more likely to lead to successful interpersonal relationships. In short, we already know some of the m dimensions. But there might be others that we still need to discover.

On the antecedent side of the coin we know that certain characteristics of the groups in contact help to predispose successful interpersonal relationships. When two groups have similar status and know each other's subjective cultures, there is a high probability of successful interpersonal relationships in those social situations which induce cooperation. This is not so when people are of different status or do not know each other's subjective culture.

It follows from this discussion that contact without the preconditions of similarity in status, knowledge of the other group's subjective culture, and similarity of goals may have undesirable consequences. Yet much of the current thinking on integration proposes exactly that kind of contact.

In addition we must learn a great deal more than we know now about successful intergroup contact. The aim should be to create in the shortest time the largest number of what we defined above as "successful interpersonal relationships." We must become an experimenting society (Campbell, 1969). As research on this topic gives usable answers, we might be able to create a new group of professionals—applied social psychologists—whose job it would be to counsel people on how to achieve successful interpersonal relationships in the shortest time. Such people might be called human relations catalysts. In situations where people with different subjective cultures must interact they would act as consultants to provide the kind of training and perspective needed to establish a successful interpersonal relationship. The human relations catalysts would know what skills, knowledge, and attitudes are needed to be successful in particular job settings, in schools, or in community activities. We already know much about this kind of problem (Brislin and Pedersen, 1976) but we still have too many research gaps to be able to train such professionals well today. However, after only a few years of successful research I am confident we could do a very good job.

A VISION OF THE FUTURE

What kind of society would emerge from such activities? As I see it, it would be one in which people would have more choices and their choices would be more acceptable to others. I see few situations that are more confining than unemployment. The unemployed person is forced to seek other avenues to gain status or income—crime is a common one. Yet that is often imposed by outside circumstances rather than a matter of free choice. Furthermore, a person with a steady job can seek better housing and better schools. This does not mean, in my view, that all blacks will want to live in white neighborhoods. Nor does it mean that all will want to send their children to integrated schools. But note the large difference between having to be segregated and deciding to be segregated. What I am advocating is increasing the number of times when people decide to adopt a particular life-style rather than have the life-style imposed on them via ideology, legal action, or economic pressure.

The situation I visualize is that some blacks will go to all black schools, some will work in all black companies, and some will live in all black neighborhoods, but they will do so as a matter of free choice. The catalysts, who will often be black, after careful examination of each case might conclude that integration of a particular individual is premature or unlikely to lead to successful interpersonal relationships. They would so advise a client, giving reasons for that advice. Then the client might voluntarily choose to go to an all-black school, or what not. Hopefully, over time, fewer and fewer persons would receive such advice. My emphasis is on dealing with individuals and recognizing that there are individual differences. I can see the law as giving everyone the right to integrate, but it may not be to everybody's advantage to exercise this right immediately. A child with low self-esteem who is placed in a school where failure is guaranteed is not served well.

One of the ways in which the catalysts might operate would be the analysis of the subjective culture of various groups of clients in relation to the known subjective cultures of various mainstream groups. Then, by identifying the smallest existing gaps in subjective culture they would advise their clients about the right move, and would train them to be successful in the new social setting in which they will have to work, live, or learn. Broadening the client's perspective concerning various subjective cultures seems to be an effective way to train for intercultural behavior (Triandis, 1976). It does increase cognitive complexity and makes a person more flexible in different kinds of social environments (Triandis, 1975). Thus, as I see it, the catalysts will keep constantly abreast of changes in the subjective culture, job requirements, specially needed skills, and so on of different job settings and will advise their clients to move into those situations in which their clients are likely to be most successful.

All of this discussion, however, does have a very strong overtone which I wish to dispel. All along I have been talking about contact across small gaps and what will happen over time. There are a few dimensions on which homogeneity is desirable. Total status is one of them. But in general I think homogeneity is undesirable. We need to learn to value different life-styles and assign equal status to them, in spite of the fact that they are different. Just as a Nobel-prizewinner in physics is different from a Nobel-prizewinner in literature yet one is not different in status from the other, so we must learn that different life-styles are perfectly viable. I suspect that we need cultural heterogeneity in order to have an interesting life, but also in order to invent the new life-styles needed in a fast-changing culture. What we do not need is the "different is inferior" viewpoints that so frequently have characterized humankind's interpersonal relations.

CONCLUSION

Pluralism, then, is the development of interdependence, appreciation, and the skills to interact intimately with persons from other cultures. It involves learning to enter social relationships where the rewards exceed the costs for both sides of the relationship. To achieve this state we need more understanding of social psychological principles and experimentation with new forms of social institutions, such as the catalysts.

My argument has been that our current attempts at integration, based on a legal framework, disregard individual differences and are attempts to eliminate cultural differences. I am advocating a shift from that perspective to one that provides for a marriage of the legal framework with our understanding of social psychological principles. Rather than integration, as conceived today, or assimilation, which involves the elimination of cultural differences, I am advocating *additive multiculturalism* where people learn to be effective and to appreciate others who are different in culture. Additive multiculturalism is by its very nature something that needs to be developed in the majority rather than the minority of the population. As more members of the minority learn to integrate in jobs and are given a chance to do so, the majority must learn to relate to the minorities with a perspective of additive multiculturalism. Within that framework and over a period of many years, we should develop a pluralism that gives self-respect to all, appreciation of cultural differences, and social skills leading to interpersonal relationships with more rewards than costs. Thus, when those who will celebrate our tricentennial look back they will be able to say: Those people 100 years ago had many difficulties making their society a good one but they tried many creative solutions, one or two of these solutions worked, and they finally succeeded in creating a truly good society.

REFERENCES

Brislin, R. W., and P. Pedersen. 1976. *Cross-cultural Orientation Programs.* New York: Gardner Press, 1976.

Campbell, D. T. 1969. Reforms as experiments. *American Psychologist* 24: 409–429.

Castañada, A., R. L. James, and W. Robbins. 1974. *The Educational Needs of Minority Groups.* Lincoln, Neb.: Professional Educators Publishers.

Epps. E. G. 1974. *Cultural Pluralism.* Berkeley, Calif.: McCatchan Press.

Feldman, J. 1974. Race, economic class and the intention to work: Some normative and attitudinal correlates. *Journal of Applied Psychology* 59: 179–186.

Goldstein, M., and E. E. Davis. 1973. "Race and belief: A further analysis of the social determinants of behavioral intentions." *Journal of Personality and Social Psychology,* 26: 16–22.

Landis, D., H. R. Day, P. L. McGrew, J. A. Thomas, and A. B. Miller. 1976. "Can a black 'culture assimilator' increase racial understanding?" *Journal of Social Issues* 32(2): 169–183.

Pettigrew, T. F. 1969. "Racially separate or together?" *Journal of Social Issues* 25(1): 43–69.

"Progress against poverty: 1964–74. 1976. *Focus on Poverty Research* 8–12.

Rothbart, M. 1976. Achieving racial equality: An analysis of resistance to social reform, in P. A. Katz (ed.), *Toward the Elimination of Racism.* New York: Pergamon.

Seelye, H. N. 1975. *Teaching Culture.* Skokie, Ill.: National Textbook Co.

Taylor, D. Q. 1974. "Should we integrate organizations?" in H. Fromkin and J. Sherwood (eds.), *Integrating the Organization*. New York: Free Press.

Triandis, H. C. 1975. "Culture training, cognitive complexity and interpersonal attitudes, in R. Brislin, S. Bochner, and W. Lonner (eds.), *Cross-cultural perspectives on learning*. New York: Halsted/Wiley.

_____ (ed.). 1976. *Variations in Black and White Perceptions of the Social Environment*. Urbana: University of Illinois Press.

_____, and E. E. Davis. 1965. "Race and belief as determinants of behavioral intentions." *Journal of Personality and Social Psychology* 2:715–725.

6

Ageism and Sexism

Ageism and sexism are relatively new social problems. Until recently it just seemed "natural" that women should be thought of as incapable and weak and that aging should be thought of as a disease that made people useless. These erroneous ideas are now understood to be part of our social structure's cultural rationalizations. Every society has such prejudices and discriminations based on age and sex. In some countries, the aged are seen as full of wisdom and are accorded special privileges. In ours, they are thrown away. Women are treated as inferiors in many societies. In fact, it is only recently that they are treated as "people"; they were traditionally thought of as men's property.

Karp and Yoels show us how age and sex discrimination are interrelated with society's interpersonal power structure. Aging has a more socially and emotionally devastating effect on women than on men throughout the life cycle.

The very new problem of elder abuse, or "gram-slamming," illustrates how our interest in age discrimination can lead to societal recognition of what has apparently been a vicious practice for many years.

Sexual harassment on the campus is described by Benson and Thomson as a basic element of college life. It does not just hurt the approximately 30 percent of females who are directly harassed. It also reinforces the male dominance of much of college life and creates many biases in academic social interactions.

If women are to achieve equality in society, they must have political power. But, even though they are the majority of voters, this is an arena in which very little progress has been made. Margolis helps us to understand this persistent sexism in politics by describing how the organization of grass-roots politics keeps women from achieving meaningful roles.

Reading 18
Power, Sex, and Aging
David A. Karp
William C. Yoels

You have probably seen that ubiquitous bundle of packaged glamour and allure
called Zsa Zsa Gabor on one of the television talk shows. Zsa Zsa, like many other
Hollywood creations, always refuses to reveal her "real" age, and we all laugh
when she says, "But, dahling, I'm just going on 29!" So what difference does it
make that Zsa Zsa lies about her age and why should we, as students of behavior, be
concerned with such trivia? Well, we suggest it makes a great deal of difference.
Why aren't George Burns and George Jessel, for example, both of whom are well
into their 80s, reluctant to admit their real ages on television? In fact, when they
announce their ages, the audience will usually clap with approval and admiration for
these "spry old guys." But, we understand Zsa Zsa's reluctance to tell her age.
And in that understanding lies the need for an examination of the way in which the
aging process differentially affects the lives of men and women in our society.

In the ensuing discussion we will see that the power differences between men
and women run through the entire life cycle, from birth to old age. Zsa Zsa's
reluctance to reveal her age and our good-humored response to it are testimony to an
awareness of the lot of women in the Western world and the social evaluations men
make of women. Such evaluations impose standards of acceptable social performance and physical appearance on women that women themselves must acknowledge if they are to achieve any value in a male-dominated society.

From the time of their childhoods, little girls are taught to place a great deal of
emphasis on and subjective involvement in their physical appearances. Even today
we are still bombarded by the mass media with portrayals of women as creatures
ruled by vanity and appearance. We think it perfectly "normal" for women to sit in
public places and apply their lipstick, rouge, and eye make-up. Indeed, the ware-
house of equipment that women carry to maintain their appearances is certainly
indicative of the significance accorded to the physical attractiveness of females in
our society. Men, by contrast, are expected to publicly minimize their concern with
appearance and must utilize more private settings if they wish to engage in more
extensive body work.

Since physical beauty is an important "resource" for women in Western
society, it is understandable that the accumulation of years makes it increasingly
more difficult for women to keep that resource in its most "marketable" condition.
As the passage of time takes its toll on the physical body, the housewife with no

outside career is confronted with a terrifying question of social worth. Her male counterpart, who, from his early years, is evaluated in terms of what he is and does, may also experience a sense of physical deterioration as time ravages his body. But the male's response to that "toll" is likely to be much less devastating than the female's since in Western society he traditionally has his place and standing in the occupational world to draw upon as a source of social worth and self-respect. In effect, the response that society makes to the body is not simply a result of biological functioning, but rather a product of cultural, historical, and sociological conditions. Susan Sontag (1972:34) makes the important observation that

> Women do not simply have faces, as men do; they are identified with their faces. . . . A man's face is defined as something he basically doesn't need to tamper with; all he has to do is keep it clean. He can avail himself of the options for ornament supplied by nature: a beard, a mustache, longer or shorter hair. But he is not supposed to disguise himself. What he is "really" like is supposed to show. A man lives through his face: it records the progressive stages of his life. . . . By contrast, a woman's face is potentially separate from her body. She does not treat it naturalistically. A woman's face is the canvas upon which she paints a revised, corrected portrait of herself. One of the rules of the creation is that the face *not* show what she doesn't want it to show. Her face is an emblem, an icon, a flag. How she arranges her hair, the type of make-up she uses, the quality of her complexion—all these are signs not of what she is "really" like, but of how she asks to be treated by others, especially men. They establish her status as an "object."

Sontag remarks that in growing up men are judged by two sets of physical standards—one appropriate to boys, and another for men. The beauty standards for boys are similar to those for girls: "In both sexes it is a fragile kind of beauty and flourishes only in the early part of the life-cycle." As boys are socially transformed into men, our society allows them to be judged by another set of beauty standards—those relating to "maturity," such as "character" lines around the eyes and the effects of daily shaving on the skin. Women, however, are judged throughout their lives by one standard of physical beauty—that appropriate to *young girls*. Thus, the loss of girlishness, and our society's response to it, pressures women into fighting the natural ravages of time by an even more frantic concern with appearance through nose jobs, breast enlargments, face lifts, bottom lifts, and any other conceivable "lifts." The response of women to this dilemma, as dramatized by Zsa Zsa's "act," is to disguise, conceal, or lie about their real age. Such behaviors are tragic testimony to the "double standard of aging" in our society.

As we noted earlier in this chapter, because of the significance still accorded ascribed status characteristics in our society, women have traditionally been confronted with a much more restricted range of life-chances than their male counterparts. If we look at what happens to the position of women vis-à-vis men over time, we can get a broader view of this issue.

Statistics indicate that at some time prior to the thirtieth birthday the over-whelming bulk of the adult population in the United States will have been married at least one time. Since it is women's typical and traditional place to be a housewife, let us for the sake of this discussion focus on the case of a woman who marries in her early twenties, has children shortly thereafter, and has no alternative career to return to if she chooses to enter or reenter the work world. Let us also assume that her husband does have a traditional occupational career. In making these assump-tions we should stress that we are certainly not endorsing the notion that women are naturally suited for the home and men for "real" work, as opposed to "house-work." We hope that our commitment to equal rights for all and our opposition to oppression in any form is evident throughout this book. While feminist writers and social scientists have raised many a consciousness, there are still millions of men and women who are in the situation we will be discussing.

Years ago the sociologist Willard Waller (1938), in his discussion of courtship and dating, coined the phrase "the principle of least interest." Waller was suggest-ing that whoever had the least interest in maintaining a relationship also had the most power in it since the other party (or parties) was thereby required to work harder and demonstrate more involvement in it to keep the relationship going. Many of you may recall situations in which you were apathetic or indifferent about seeing a person who, by contrast, was very intent upon seeing you. Didn't you feel a certain sense of power in that relationship? And, by the same token, you have surely been involved with persons who were less interested than you in keeping the social tie going. Was your response not one of frustration and powerlessness in that relationship? Clearly what is involved here is a question of who has access to certain kinds of highly prized "resources": attractiveness, status, money, family back-ground, friends. Much sought after men and women can afford to "hang loose" and "play it cool" in their relations with others since they have numerous pos-sibilities from which to choose. With Waller's principle in mind, let us examine the case of the middle-class married couple to whom we earlier referred.[1] As the wife's entrenchment within the house becomes more and more total during the early years of childrearing, the husband may be achieving some small or major successes in the work world. Coupled with the wife's confinement to the home and children is the fact that she faces increasing difficulty maintaining her physical appearance, partic-ularly in the wake of the fatigue engendered by housework and caring for children.

---

[1]While the literature in family sociology indicates that middle-class husbands are more likely than working-and lower-class husbands to express a belief in husbands and wives making decisions mutually

. . . marital power is a function of income to a large extent, and egalitarian philosophies have very little impact on the actual distribution of power in the family. It seems clear that the authority of the male is used as a justification of power where it is useful (working-class), and new justifications will arise as they are useful, as in the case of professional men who demand deference because of their work, thus enabling them to accept the doctrine of equality while at the same time undermining it for their own benefit as males. (Gillespie, 1971:451)

By the time the family's life cycle has entered the stage that family sociologists refer to as the "empty nest," the wife is confronted with a threefold problem, the elements of which all occur simultaneously: her physical appearance requires increasing efforts to maintain; she has little training for any work other than housework; and she may be faced with a deep crisis over the meaning of her life now that she no longer has the opportunity to play the mother role to her grown children. In this regard, Pauline Bart's (1977) cross-cultural study of female menopause and middle age in a number of different societies underscores the importance of looking at aging from a broad social-psychological perspective. Her study of these cultures, entitled "The Loneliness of the Long-Distance Mother," led her to state that

> . . . middle age was not usually considered an especially stressful period for women. Consequently, purely biological explanations for the stress felt at this time by Western women can be rejected. Middle age need not be fraught with difficulty. (p. 282)

It is no accident, as Bart has previously noted (1970), that in our society mental depression most often occurs among middle-class married women, after the children have been "launched." For men, mental depression appears to coincide with retirement. Though the ages at which such depressions occur are different for men and women, the underlying dynamic is generally the same. That is, mental depression results from persons being denied the opportunity to play socially valued and rewarding roles after having previously been involved in such activities. In the case of men, retirement deprives them of all the resources—prestige, money, power— associated with the world of work. And while the Protestant ethic may be undergoing a transformation in American society, for large numbers of Americans to be unemployed, for whatever the reason, is to be treated like a second-class citizen and a less than fully productive human being.

The woman who has played most fervently the traditional role of mother-wife, finds herself in an existential void when her children are grown. Her dilemma is often exacerbated by the fact that she now sees her children, for whom she "sacrificed," as unappreciative and resentful of her loving efforts in their behalf. This indeed is what Pauline Bart (1970) has poignantly called "Mother Portnoy's complaint." In effect, over time, the husband's position in the marriage becomes much more advantageous than his wife's because he has the least interest in it. As he gets older, he is evaluated less and less in terms of physical attractiveness and more and more in terms of occupational success. In addition, he usually does not experience the restriction of socially rewarding role-playing until sometime in his sixties. It is also significant that in Western society it is considered perfectly "natural" and "normal" for an older man to have an affair with or marry a much younger woman. As the marriage continues, therefore, the husband's options are often increasing while the wife's are being further restricted. If the couple have children and decide to divorce, the wife is often assumed by both the larger society and its legal representatives, the courts, to be the natural caretaker of the children. Unfortunately, the notion of "maternal instincts" has had a very long life in our society.

Our preceding discussion has been based on what should, by now, be a very familiar point. Age, like any of our other personal attributes, acquires its meaning through interaction. The aging process certainly involves regular, predictable biological changes. However, from the interactionist perspective, stressing such concepts as definition of the situation and role performance, what most matters are the meanings given to those biological changes. We place different values on and have different expectations of persons at different ages.

To fully understand the aging process, we need to know how persons tune in to, interpret, and respond to repeated social messages about the meaning of age. For the last several pages we have been describing the quite different messages that men and women hear about aging. At the root of the differing life-curves of men and women in our society lies a power differential that "ages" women considerably faster than their male counterparts. Just as Jessie Bernard (1972) suggests that there is a "His" and "Her" marriage, so also is there a "His" and "Her" aging.

REFERENCES

Bart, P. 1970. "Mother Portnoy's complaint." *Transaction* 8 (November–December):69–74.

———— 1977. "The loneliness of the long-distance mother," pp. 281–290 in P. J. Stein et al., eds., *The Family*. Reading, Mass.: Addison-Wesley.

Bernard, J. 1972. *The Future of Marriage*. New York: Basic Books.

Gillespie, D. I. 1971. "Who has the power: The marital struggle." *Journal of Marriage and the Family* 33 (August):445–458.

Sontag, S. 1972. "The double standard of aging." *Saturday Review* (September 23):29–38.

Waller, W. 1938. *The Family: A Dynamic Interpretation*. New York: Dryden Press.

Reading 19

Elders Under Siege

Peggy Eastman

She is 79 and frail, a widow living with her married daughter. She has bruises on her arms and legs and is fearful and uncommunicative. Most of the time she stays locked in her room, afraid her daughter will come in and kick her, call her names, empty out her bureau drawers and throw her possessions all over. She is a victim of elder abuse.

According to estimates from Senate and House committees on aging, the number of cases of abused, neglected or exploited elderly in the United States ranges from 600,000 up to 1 million, or 4 percent of the elderly population. And the number appears to be growing.

One explanation for the increase in elder abuse could be the increase in the number of people older than 65: from 16.6 million in 1960 to 25.6 million in 1980 and a predicted 35 million by 2000. And among these, the 75-plus age group, the most vulnerable to abuse and exploitation, is the fastest-growing segment of the population.

Who would abuse a vulnerable older person? According to the profile that emerged in 1981 from a year-long investigation by the House Select Committee on Aging, an elder abuser is usually a relative, such as a son or daughter. Some studies suggest that not only are abused children more likely than others to become child abusers when they grow up, they have a one-in-two chance of abusing their dependent parents.

Researchers have also found that elder abuse is a recurring problem, not a one-time offense, and that stress aggravates it. In a survey conducted in Massachusetts, for instance, 63 percent of abusers perceived their elders as a source of stress because they needed extra care and were a financial burden on the family. Other pressures—poverty, alcoholism, drug abuse or marital fights—can push a potential elder abuser into that role.

Elder abuse can be physical, exploitative (confiscating a parent's savings, say), neglectful (failing to give food or medication) or psychological (name-calling). Abusers also often threaten to put their parents out on the street or to commit them to a mental institution or a nursing home if they complain about the abuse.

Most victims don't complain. They simply endure. Most are women, physically disabled and dependent. They fear abandonment, placement in an institution or further punishment if they attempt to get help.

Experts say tough laws are needed, requiring people who suspect cases of elder abuse to report them to state protective services agencies—exactly the kind of law to protect children from abuse that Congress passed in January 1974.

Representative Mary Rose Oaker of Ohio recently introduced a bill in Congress that would create the National Center on Adult Abuse and provide money to states for prevention and treatment programs—if those states have "immunity statutes" to protect reporting individuals from lawsuits. Slightly more than half the states have adult-protective service laws, but there is little uniformity among them. And not all of the states with protective statutes require mandatory reporting of elder abuse.

Daughter Dearest

My husband died 10 years ago. The house where we lived became mine exclusively. My younger daughter, who had two unfortunate marriages, was welcomed by us with her children. This began more than 18 years ago. The past three years, things have gotten steadily worse. My daughter locked me in the garage and left me there for more than an hour. She always parked her car behind mine in the garage so I could not get my car out except by her permission.

Whenever I tried to cook a meal, she would appear and turn the gas off and remove the grills so the only way I could cook was to hold the pan over the flame. If she found me using the electric toaster oven, my food was thrown on the floor and the toaster oven was removed and hidden for several days.

My daughter's treatment of me kept getting worse. Always hurting me physically and mentally; kicking me, pushing me, grappling with me, telling me to get out, at one time throwing a drawer down the stairs at me, calling me names, telling me I belonged in a nursing home and why didn't I go to one.

I was warned many times to get out of the house by my doctor, my lawyer, my protective counselor and my adviser at the Mental Health Association. They all knew my life was in danger while staying under the same roof with this emotionally very sick 45-year-old person. She is a well-educated woman, having graduated from college, continued in graduate school and gotten a master's degree in no less than social service.

From testimony by Mrs. X, a 79-year old Massachusetts resident, before a joint hearing of the Senate Special Committee on Aging and the House Select Committee, June 1980.

Reading 20

The Invisible Hands: Sex Roles and the Division of Labor in Two Local Political Parties

Diane Rothbard Margolis

The University of Connecticut, Stamford Branch

Women make up a majority of the U.S. electorate, yet they hold few high-ranking positions in government. Classic studies of the American political system, if they

Reprinted with permission from *Social Problems* 26 (February 1979):314–324, abridged by The Society for the Study of Social Problems and by the author.

mention women at all, generally limit their analyses to a note on the insignificance of women's participation (e.g., Duverger, 1972; Key, 1948; Lazarsfeld et al., 1944; Lipset, 1960). Recently, the women's movement has turned attention to women's role in politics and several reports have been published (e.g., Chamberlin, 1974; Kirkpatric, 1974; Tolchin and Tolchin, 1974; Diamond, 1977; Githens and Prestage, 1977). Most of these, however, concentrate on the few women who do achieve political standing, overlooking the many who take the first step beyond the ballot box into their local political organization, but who seldom advance further. Yet it is at the base of the political system, in the local organization, that many political careers are spawned while others are aborted (Almond and Verba, 1963; Kornhauser, 1959). We know little about what happens to women there.

The objective of this paper is to begin to fill this gap. It is based on a study examining in detail the day-to-day workings of two local political organizations. It seeks to reveal the social patterns and interpersonal behaviors by which the process of equality at the base of the political system yields to increasing inequalities as political hierarchies are ascended.

BACKGROUND AND METHODS

The thirteen female and twenty-three male respondents were the members of the Republican and Democratic Town Committees of Fairtown, Connecticut.[1] There, as in most other New England states, affairs of both political parties are conducted at the grassroots level by Town Committees. These bodies serve as a kind of personnel department for their towns. They interview and recommend candidates for appointive offices and they endorse candidates for elective offices. In addition, they run local political campaigns, serve as links to the state party organizations and determine the local party's position on issues.

Fairtown is an affluent, almost entirely (98.9 percent) white community of about 18,000. In 1970 the median years of education for Fairtowners was thirteen; the median family income was close to $17,000; almost 60 percent of the employed men (only 1.6 percent of the men were unemployed) worked as professionals, technicians, managers or proprietors; and over half of them worked out of town. Of the 10,000 voters registered in 1973, more than half were registered Republicans, the rest splitting almost evenly between Democrats and unaffiliated voters. The actual political divisions, however, were most complicated. Both parties were split between conservative and liberal or moderate factions, the latter having gained a bare majority on both party's Town Committees shortly before the study began.

The group under study was small and not statistically representative of the American population, nor even of grassroots political organizations, and therefore generalizations must be made with caution. Nevertheless, because the focus was on

[1]All names of persons and places are fictitious.

those ordinary, taken-for-granted acts that are part of the everyday fabric of our culture, intensive and detailed data collection techniques, impossible to perform with large samples, were necessary.

Members of the two Town Committees were interviewed frequently and observed at meetings and other political gatherings from September through December, 1974. In addition, at the initial interview all respondents were given a form on which to record all of their daily political activities. Although each committee member was asked to record *all* conversations that had any political content, and *all* the work each subject had done for the party, there were variations in the completeness of the logs. In general, the men were slightly better log-keepers than the women. This may exaggerate the amount of activity of the males and minimize that of the females, a possible bias in a direction opposite from the findings. Thus differences between the men and women might have been obscured, but none was likely to be introduced by uneven log-keeping.

AMOUNT AND LOCATION OF ACTIVITY

Men outnumbered women on both Town Committees—thirteen to six on the Republican Town Committee and ten to seven on the Democratic—but the women were far more active than the men. Of the 1,832 interactions recorded, 1,185, or about two-thirds, were performed by women. The average number of interactions per man was thirty-one, while the average for the women was three times that, or one hundred. This was an unexpected finding because men had seemed to be as frequently present as women at meetings, fund-raisers and work sessions.

The location of their activities helps explain why women seemed less busy than they actually were. Whatever the men and women were doing politically could range from the highly noticeable to the invisible. Public speeches were probably the most noticeable activity, while work done alone was the least noticed. In between were attendance at meetings, fund-raisers or group work sessions at which one would be seen by several others, and phone conversations which would be noticed by only one other. Women's activities tended to take place in situations where they would not be widely observed; the reverse was true of men's activities. . . .

SOCIAL NETWORKS

Although women were more likely to work alone or with just one other person, the range of their associations was greater than men's. Women's communications were not as restricted to members of their Town Committees as were men's. Forty-nine percent of women's interactions were within their own Town Committees as opposed to 58 percent of men's. Moreover, the average woman interacted with a greater number of other persons (18) than the average man (10). On the other hand, especially when venturing beyond their own Town Committees, women were much more likely than men to restrict their interactions to persons of their own gender. Clearly, then, all members of the Town Committees were parochial, interacting almost exclusively with others of their own party, if not necessarily with their Town Committee colleagues, and predominantly with persons of their own gender. However, men showed a somewhat greater tendency to be ideocentric—restricting their interactions to persons of the same political *persuasion*; women showed a greater tendency towards sexocentrism—restricting their communications more to persons of the same *gender* (72.4 percent compared to 63.2 percent for men).

TOPICS OF TALK AND KINDS OF WORK

What were all those communications about? When we look at the subjects that men and women discussed and the tasks they worked on, patterns emerge which further explain the invisibility of women and also indicate differences in the roles assumed by men and women. . . .

Women's Talk

Women's talk most often involved an exchange of information. When an extra meeting was called or when the time or place of a regular meeting was changed, women would spread than information. If facts had to be gathered, such as the rulings on absentee ballots, a woman would call some authority to find out. Not infrequently, if a man needed some information he would ask a woman to get it for him. (For example, a sample woman's log showed that Joe, a candidate, asked her to get information about absentee ballots from Janet, the town clerk.)

Women also talked about arrangements for work tasks. Whether it was a mailing that had to be sent out, a fund-raiser that had to be arranged, or some other task, women were almost invariably the ones who took upon themselves the responsibility of organization and management. They usually did this in committees or teams, and sometimes men were included. Profuse communications were generated in the coordination of every task and it often took far more separate interactions, if not more time, to get any job set up than it took to actually do the work. (For instance, a sample female log showed that it took six communications to arrange for absentee ballots to be sent to voters.)

Third, women talked—mostly among themselves, but sometimes with men—about the campaign. When a candidate issued a statement, or a speech was made, or some decision was needed about how to run a campaign, women sought out each other's opinion; and they discussed and analyzed the virtues and shortcomings of candidates and their campaigns—frequently and at some length.

The fourth most common topic of women's talk was problems on their own Town Committees.

Finally, women more often than men ranged from one topic to another. For example, nine of the twenty-two items on a woman's sample log covered more than one subject.

Men's Talk

The most common item on the men's logs was an attempt to influence another person. Most male talk about specific issues took place just before a vote was scheduled. Women's talk about most topics, even those on which a vote was eventually held, was usually spread over a protracted period before the issue came to a decision.

In addition to conversations aimed at influencing others, men's logs included more mentions of large group functions at which attendance would be noticed by many others—parties, fund-raisers, rallies and openings of campaign headquarters. . . .

To summarize: The subjects women talked about tended to be general and far-ranging, and they often covered several topics in a single conversation. Commonly when women wished a change of some sort they casually initiated issues to test for support. Men's talk, on the other hand, covered just a single subject; normally it arose at the moment when some issue was about to be decided; and generally it had a specific goal—to garner support for some position. Where women's talk was specific, it had as its goal not so much the influencing of another as an exchange of information or the organization of a work task.

Women took care of what needed to be done for the day-to-day maintenance of the Town Committees. Tasks which normally must be done on a regular monthly or yearly basis were more likely to be undertaken by women, especially if those chores were not attached to an official role. In contrast, men did only that work which was assigned to them by virtue of the official positions they held, and whatever they then did beyond that was usually a special or nonrecurring job. Women worked behind the scene; men worked in public.

THE UNOFFICIAL ROLES WOMEN PLAY

Up until now items in the logs have been grouped by gender as if all the men and all the women contributed equally to the work and talk of their parties. They didn't. Some men and some women were hardly doing a thing while others were working and talking prodigiously. In fact, thirteen men, more than two-thirds of the men keeping logs,[2] recorded less than forty interactions; three recorded between forty and sixty; and another three between sixty and one hundred. No man recorded more than one hundred interactions. The balance shifts in the opposite direction on the

[2]Two of the men and one of the women who did not keep a log resigned from their Town Committees before the study was completed. In addition two men and one woman refused to keep a log.

distaff side. Four women recorded more than one hundred interactions; one logged between sixty and one hundred; three between forty and fifty-nine; and three others logged less than forty.

What accounts for these differences in activity? Without exception those who recorded more than forty interactions were playing a special role. There was, however, a strategic difference between the roles played by men and those played by women. Only men who had titular status recorded more than fifty interactions, while most of the roles women played were parts without title or acknowledgment.

Party chairpersons were the most active men. The Republican logged eighty-two interactions and the Democrat sixty-seven. The Republican treasurer, a man, logged precisely the same number, fifty-two, as his Democratic counterpart, a woman. Two other men logging more than forty interactions were the former chairpersons of the party clubs. They continued to lead their factions after they were elected to the Town Committee by assuming the unofficial role of "Advisor-to-the-Majority." The sixth man with more than forty interactions was a Republican who assisted his party's Advisor-to-the-Majority.

All other unofficial roles were played by women.[3] There was no regular position for a person who would spread news throughout the Town Committee and keep the Committee in touch with other groups in town, and yet both parties had such a woman, whom we shall call the "Communicator-in-Chief." As has already been noted, there was a great deal of routine work especially related to getting out the vote and raising money which by unwritten rule was to have been shared equally by all the Town Committee members. It wasn't. Each Town Committee had a woman, whom we shall call the "Drudge," who assumed much of that burden. Again, when a Town Committee vote was nearing, someone had to call members to make sure they attended the meeting and voted with their faction. Only the moderate Republicans and liberal Democrats seemed to have such a person, a woman, whom we shall call the "Majority Whip." But the Majority Whip did not decide how her faction should act; for that she turned to the man we call the "Advisor-to-the-Majority." Most notable was the fact that, different as the parties were, almost identical roles appeared in both, and the gender of the persons filling parallel roles was the same in both parties.

The Communicator-in-Chief

The role that called for the most interactions was that of Communicator-in-Chief. It was played on the Republican Town Committee by Sophie Morelli, and on the

---

[3]Three of the women who played unofficial roles also held a titular position. However, the unofficial role they played was not a part of their official role. Thus the Republican "Whip" was her party's secretary, while it was the Vice-chairperson of the Democratic party who played that role. The "Communicator-in-Chief" of the Republican party was also the Vice-chairperson, but the "Communicator-in-Chief" for the Democrats had no official role. No man holding an official position assumed an unofficial one as well.

Democratic Town Committee by Janie Brown. They acted as intermediaries between the factions in their parties; carried information and other communications between the Town Committee and other groups in town; and even on occasion linked the two Town Committees. Although her political activities were extensive, they were but a small part of the Communicator-in-Chief's community participation—she was active in several organizations and this brought her into acquaintanceships with persons all over town.

Sophie Morelli, an eighty-year-old woman who had been active in Fairtown's Republican party for close to a half-century, ambled through Town Hall each day having a word with her relatives (a daughter and a grandchild) and others who worked there, picking up and spreading bits and pieces of the news of the day. She often lunched at a local diner whose clientele was made up mostly of conservative Republicans. They interspersed gossip about weddings, births, children and divorces with discussion of candidates and political issues. When there was an important development, Morelli would call her party chairperson. Whatever there was to say, she talked with several members of her Town Committee daily.

Although Janie Brown was clearly a liberal Democrat she worked hard to maintain her ties in other groups. Her party chairperson, a conservative, spoke with her more than with anyone else in the liberal faction. Indeed, of all the members on both Town Committees, Janie Brown was the one with the broadest network of contacts. The average woman on a Town Committee talked with only twenty other persons; in Brown's log there was mention of almost twice that number, thirty-eight.

Majority Whips

To get out the faction's vote there was in each majority faction a Whip. The Majority Whip usually notified the Advisor-to-the-Majority when concerted action was needed and then, after she and the Advisor had decided what was to be done, called others in their faction. Before an important vote was taken, Barbara Weatherton conferred with her two Advisors-to-the-Majority and then canvassed the Republican moderates.

Several times during that autumn the liberal Democrats decided to caucus. When they did they usually met at Marjorie Hasting's house and it was she who called the others to the meeting. Many additional meetings were also held at her house; it was usually she who acted as the unofficial moderator. The Whip had two other functions. If a position was open and no one to the liking of the faction came forward, the Whip would try to find a candidate. (In the Democratic party Hastings shared this job with Brown.) She also filled in whenever a male failed to carry out his assignment. For instance, the Democratic campaign manager took a trip to Europe two weeks before the election: Hastings then ran the campaign.

The role of Whip involved a large number of communications. Hastings listed 121 interactions with thirty-two different persons, and she was listed in other persons' logs forty-nine times. Weatherton was somewhat less active; she listed eighty-two separate interactions with twenty-six different persons and was mentioned in the logs of others only seven times.

Drudges

Another unofficial role that involved many interactions and was performed exclusively by women was that of "Drudge." The Drudge made most of the arrangements for fund-raisers; prepared more than her share of the food; decorated the room in which the fund-raisers were held; cleaned up afterwards; made arrangements for mailings and addressed more envelopes than anyone else. Unlike others on the Town Committee, a large percentage of the Drudge's work was done alone. Edna Halsey, the Democratic Drudge, logged a modest forty-six items, but for thirty-six percent of those items she was working alone preparing food, ironing tablecloths for a fund-raiser square dance and addressing envelopes. The Republican Drudge was Mary Kelley. Her log does not show such a high percentage of work done alone because she was also an assistant Communicator-in-Chief for Morelli. Also, as the Republican treasury was ample, most of their fund-raisers were catered, requiring many arrangements but not much solitary preparation.

Mary Kelley and Edna Halsey handled the role of Drudge differently. Halsey was assigned tasks by other women who organized the affairs at which she worked. Kelley was self-directed. She organized the tasks and tried to get others to help out, but then did most of the work herself. Both women were appreciated for what they did, but only Kelley was respected for it. A number of Republican men lauded her with the same words: "What we need in this party is more women like Kelley." And Kelley, fully a year before nominations were in order, was being urged to run for Selectperson or even for "First."

Edna Halsey was strictly a Drudge. A feminist Democratic woman said of her:

> I don't know why she was ever put on that Town Committee. She's a sweet lady, she does all the cooking and baking and fussing at parties, but political philosophy is beyond her.

CONCLUSIONS

Women who enter politics tend to be motivated either by a service orientation or by what Elazar has called a "moralistic" political orientation—belief that politics is "one of the great activities of man in his search for the good society" (1972:96–98). The service orientation lends itself to the role of Drudge, and women who view politics as a locale for giving are welcome in any political party. The idealistic orientation is not so welcome. Women who view politics as an opportunity to help bring forth a better world are likely to find their way into politics only where the system is open. Politics in Fairtown was open, but not so open that individuals filled roles by virtue for their talents rather than their gender.

This is, of course, not the first time a study has uncovered unofficial divisions of labor by gender where the rules called for equality. Rosabeth Moss Kantor (1977), for example, found that women in business corporations played special roles not unlike those played by Fairtown's Town Committee women. There were few ranking women in the corporation she studied, and she attributed their seemingly sex-linked roles and behaviors to their token status. In this study, the women, though a minority, were not tokens. Numbers seemed to have little to do with the situation. The proportion of women on the two Town Committees differed—thirty-two percent of the Republicans and forty-one percent of the Democrats—yet the roles played on both committees were linked to gender. Ideology was apparently not relevant. Four of the Democratic women were outspoken feminists; none of the Republicans was. Yet women played the same unofficial roles in both parties; indeed, the Democratic Majority Whip was a staunch feminist.

In her study of state legislatures, Diamond found that the women there, like the women in Fairtown, were extraordinarily conscientious, and she asks:

> Is that conscientiousness . . . a response to the expectation that women are incompetent unless they prove otherwise? Is it their way of adapting to their "marginal man" status in the legislature? Or is it an outgrowth of sex-role training, a manifestation of the "tidy housewife" syndrome? . . . [Or could it be] that these women actually have fewer outside conflicts in the allocation of their time than male breadwinners? (1977:95)

She does not answer, noting that "the question needs further exploration."

I would like to suggest that the overriding reason men and women take on the roles they do is that these are the roles they play in our culture wherever men and women come together in any sort of social organization, the prototypical one being the family. With only minor transformations, the roles the Fairtown men and women were playing on their Town Committees were the same ones men and women play in households. Men are thought to be the "heads" of their families; and men were the chairpersons of the Town Committees. Men have specific and narrow functions in the family—primarily to provide its income and sometimes to act as its public spokesperson. So, too, on the Town Committees they did only what was specifically required of them. Women, on the other hand, handle the day-to-day maintenance of the household, performing a plethora of tasks, some precisely defined such as preparing food, but many amorphous, such as bonding the nuclear family to others through social contacts. Similarly, on the Town Committees all the regular, official maintenance-type functions and also all tasks which could not be specifically defined fell to women. Another role women played in both the family and on the Town Committees was that of standby. They were there to step in whenever a man failed to accomplish his appointed task.

Women, then, take care of the maintenance of institutions and fill in the gaps. They are also the ones to *spot* gaps, bringing to the attention of men situations that call for a decision, and monitoring the early stages in decision making—gathering the necessary information and garnering support. But when it is time to settle an issue, to make a final decision, men come to the fore. The analogy between the family and the political party is so close that even when it comes to the selection of persons to fill official positions on the Town Committees and in town government, patterns characteristic of the family are followed—i.e., men aggressively seek positions, but women wait to be wooed.

The tendency among women to work in seclusion (while men seek to capture center stage) also has antecedents in the family. The women in this study, as in Kantor's (1977) and Diamond's (1977), were of the middle class. It is a class that has, over the past half-century, suffered some ambivalence towards work—especially the work that women do.

The Protestant ethic places a high value on work, but as Thorstein Veblen (1953) noted: "To be leisured is a sign of success while manual work is *declassé.*" Before World War II, it was a point of honor with the middle class that men did not do menial labor and women did not labor at all. Housework was done by paid help. After the war, household help rose in cost beyond the reach of most families, so that women who are now past forty (an age most common among the women on the Town Committees and in state legislatures) had to take on the menial work their mothers had spurned. Their situation changed, but their values did not. So, with the help of tips from women's magazines, they learned to do their housework in secret. The mark of a well-run household was freshly vacuumed carpets, gourmet meals, shinyfaced children and a neatly dressed wife-mother who was never seen cooking, cleaning or washing, not even by her husband.

When there is political work to do, the same women who learned to work this magic at home take pains to repeat it in the political arena. They are task-oriented, measuring their political performance by completed projects. The men, on the other hand, garner their self-esteem, not from tasks accomplished but from being included in decision making. For them, to be seen in a place where decisions are being made is more important than accomplishing any task. Carrying this orientation over to the Town Committees the men did little alone. The significant part of their political involvement was to *appear* to be running things, to *appear* to be part of the process, to be seen.

These differences have implications for the political careers of men and women. When work needs to be done, the women who in the past have so reliably performed tasks for their party are called upon again. But when ranking positions are to be filled, it is the men—ever conspicuous and desirous of titles—who usually get the nod.

REFERENCES

Almond, Gabriel A., and Sidney Verba. 1963. *The Civic Culture.* Boston: Little, Brown.

Chamberlain, H. 1974. *A Minority of Members: Women in the U.S. Congress.* New York: Praeger.

Diamond, Irene. 1977. *Sex Roles in the State House.* New Haven, Conn.: Yale University Press.

Duverger, Maurice. 1972. *The Study of Politics.* New York: Thomas Y. Crowell.

Elazar, Daniel. 1972. *American Federalism.* 2nd ed. New York: Thomas Y. Crowell.

Githens, Marianne, and Jewel L. Prestage. 1977. *A Portrait of Marginality: The Political Behavior of the American Woman.* New York: David McKay.

Kantor, Rosabeth Moss. 1977. *Men and Women of the Corporation.* New York: Basic Books.

Key, V. O. 1948. *Politics, Parties and Pressure Groups.* New York: Thomas Y. Crowell.

Kirkpatric, Jean. 1974. *Political Woman.* New York: Basic Books.

Kornhauser, William. 1959. *The Politics of Mass Society.* Glencoe, Ill.: Free Press.

Lazarsfeld, Paul, Bernard Berelson, and Hazel Gaudet. 1944. *The People's Choice.* New York: Columbia University Press.

Lipset, Seymour Martin. 1960. *Political Man.* Garden City, N.Y.: Doubleday.

Tolchin, Susan, and Martin Tolchin. 1974. *Clout: Women in the Mainstream.* New York: Coward, McCann and Geoghegan.

Veblen, Thorstein. 1953. *The Theory of the Leisure Class.* New York: Mentor Books.

Reading 21

Sexual Harassment on a University Campus: The Confluence of Authority Relations, Sexual Interest and Gender Stratification

Donna J. Benson
Gregg E. Thomson
University of California, Berkeley

Female workers have always been vulnerable to sexual abuse by male employees.[1] It wasn't until *Redbook* published a survey in 1976, however, that sexual harassment began to be recognized as a social problem (Safran, 1976). Since then,

Reprinted with permission from *Social Problems*, 29 (3) (February 1982): 236–251, abridged by The Society for the Study of Social Problems and by the authors.

[1]For observations on indentured servants and private household workers, see, Morris (1946), Lerner (1972), and Katzman (1978). Sexual exploitation of working girls and women as they were drawn into the industrial labor force is described by Sanger (1858), Bularzik (1978), Hymowitz and Weissman (1978), Farley (1978), and Backhouse and Cohen (1979).

numerous newspapers and magazines have contained accounts of female workers subject to disruptive and coercive sexual harassment by male supervisors and co-workers. In non-random surveys (e.g., Silverman, 1976) as many as 70 percent of respondents report harassment on the job. In Gutek et al.'s (1980) random survey in Los Angeles, 11 percent of the women experienced such non-verbal sexual behaviors as looks, gestures, and touching. Women in various occupations and institutions have taken legal action in response to sexual harassment or the repercussions of failing to comply with the sexual demands of male superiors.

As with rape (Rose 1977a,b), feminists have been instrumental in promoting the awareness that sexual harassment on the job is a serious social problem, and have encouraged victims to seek legal redress for their grievances. Administrators, responding to public pressure, have begun to acknowledge the prevalence of the problem.

The key to this recognition has been the conceptualization and labelling of a broad class of behaviors as sexual harassment.[2] MacKinnon (1979:27) notes: "Until 1976, lacking a term to express it, sexual harassment was literally unspeakable, which made a generalized, shared and social definition of it inaccessible." What heretofore have often been viewed as largely unrelated and in many instances inconsequential behaviors are now viewed as part of a single pattern:

> Sexual harassment can be any or all of the following: verbal sexual suggestions or jokes, constant leering or ogling, "accidentally" brushing against your body, a "friendly" pat, squeeze, pinch or arm around you, catching you alone for a quick kiss, the explicit proposition backed by threat of losing your job, and forced sexual relations. (WWUI, 1978: 1)

Observable differences between the sexes, previously viewed as social differentiation, are now recognized as reflecting social inequality. Sexual behaviors once treated as part of this differentiation—and indeed as manipulative behavior on the part of women—can be seen as an aspect of this inequality. All of the above behaviors therefore represent the unwarranted intrusion of male sexual prerogative into the work setting.

MacKinnon (1979) provided a persuasive sociological and legal argument that sexual harassment constitutes illegal sex discrimination. In 1980, the Equal Employment Opportunity Commission (EEOC, 1980) issued guidelines which made explicit the liability for sexual harassment under Title VII of the Civil Rights Act of 1964 which prohibits discrimination on the basis of race, sex, religion and national origin. Moreover, the guidelines specified that sexual harassment occurs whenever sexual behaviors substantially interfere with an employee's work performance or

---

[2]The term apparently was first defined in May 1975 in a survey developed by the women's section of the Human Affairs Program, Cornell University.

create an intimidating, hostile or offensive work environment. Employers are required to "take all steps necessary" to prevent sexual harassment.[3]

Legally, then, harassment is not limited to direct sexual assault, bribery, or retaliation for refusing to comply with sexual demands. It can also be distinguished from flirting, come-ons, and office romances (Quinn, 1977), in that harassment is unwanted and potentially coercive or disruptive, though in practice even a supposedly friendly come-on by a male superior may have an element of implicit coercion.

It is easy to see why the concept of sexual harassment has been applied to instructor-student relationships as well as those of employer-employee. Male teachers have the authority to evaluate the performance of female students and, accordingly, the opportunity to affect that performance by initiating sexual demands or behaviors. The Association of American Colleges' Project on the Status and Education of Women (1978) identified sexual harassment as a serious and widespread "hidden issue" on campus.

Surveys and reports of harassment corroborate both the seriousness of the issue and its growing visibility (Benson, 1977; Munich, 1978; Nelson, 1978; Lesser, 1979). Pope, Levenson, and Shover (1979) found that one in four recently trained women psychologists reported having had sexual contact with their professors (see also Fields, 1979). Pope, Shover, and Levenson (1980) highlighted the *ethical* implications of such behavior while plaintiffs in university sexual harassment cases have stressed, as do their counterparts in the workplace, the *illegal sex discrimination* involved. Sexual harassment is now recognized as a violation of Title IX of the Education Amendments Act prohibiting sex discrimination in federally assisted programs.[4] The National Advisory Council on Women's Education (Till, 1980) released a survey showing reports of sexual harassment were increasing. The council recommended that sexual harassment be explicitly established as sex discrimination and urged all U.S. colleges and universities to reduce tolerance for sexual harassment on the campus. . . .

METHOD

In the spring of 1978, we placed an advertisement in the University of California student newspaper inviting students to discuss experiences of "unwanted sexual

---

[3]In August, 1981, U.S. Vice-President George Bush said the existing regulations on sexual harassment were unworkable and indicated the Reagan administration intended to reverse the Equal Employment Opportunity Guidelines.

[4]In 1977, several women at Yale University initiated the lawsuit (*Alexander* v. *Yale University,* 1977) which established this principle. In 1979, 29 students at the University of California, Berkeley, filed a complaint with the Department of Health, Education and Welfare on similar grounds. Women Organized Against Sexual Harassment (WOASH, 1979) has helped coordinate charges of sexual harassment against a University of California professor as well as publicize the issue generally. Field (1981) discusses more recent developments, including a case involving a countersuit by the alleged harasser.

attention'' received from an instructor while at Berkeley. Informal interviews with the 20 women who responded helped us construct the seven-page questionnaire used for the present study.

In June, 1978, we mailed the questionnaire to a random sample of 400 female students in their senior year at Berkeley. A week later the sample was reminded of the survey by both telephone and mail. Despite the concurrence of final examinations and graduation ceremonies, 269 women (67 percent) returned the questionnaire.

A letter accompanying the questionnaire explained the purpose of the study and presented an inclusive definition of sexual harassment formulated by the Working Women United Institute (WWUI, 1978): ''Any unwanted sexual leers, suggestions, comments or physical contact which you find objectionable in the context of a teacher-student relationship.'' Purposely broad, we used this definition so that we could assess the full range of unwanted sexual attention from the ostensibly trivial to the obviously extreme. . . .

RESULTS

Awareness of Sexual Harassment on Campus

Our respondents estimated how frequently women students are sexually harassed at Berkeley and how serious a problem it is for those who are harassed. A majority (59 percent) estimated that sexual harassment occurs ''ocassionally,'' 9 percent thought it occurred ''frequently,'' and less than 2 percent said it ''almost never'' happens. There was a high degree of consensus, therefore, that sexual harassment is not an isolated or rare phenomenon and indeed is likely to be at least an occasional occurrence. Our respondents were divided on whether the problem of harassment is ''very serious'' (37.9 percent), ''moderately serious'' (34.4 percent), and only ''mildly serious'' or less (27.7 percent). As the accounts of actual sexual harassment indicate there is a considerable range in the degree of difficulty which sexual harassment presents for individual women. Results for our entire sample, however, suggest an overall perception that sexual harassment is a problem.

Confirmation that an awareness of sexual harassment is at least relatively widespread among our sample can be found in the fact that 93 women—more than one in three of the respondents—said they knew personally at least one woman who had been harassed at Berkeley. Because transfer students (59 percent of the sample) were not asked about acquaintances at previous institutions and, one assumes, minor harassment episodes may not be shared even among friends, this figure may be conservative. It certainly suggests that consciousness of harassment is part of the female university experience, even as the issue remains ''hidden'' from official recognition by a predominantly male faculty and administration.

Self-reports of Sexual Harassment

Thirty-one of 111 non-transfer students (27.9 percent) reported that they had been sexually harassed by at least one male instructor at Berkeley. Twenty-four of 158 transfer students (15.2 percent) also reported that they had been harassed after transferring to Berkeley. An additional 25 of the transfer students (15.9 percent) indicated that harassment had occurred at their previous college or university but not at Berkeley. Thus, a total of 80 out of 269 respondents (29.7 percent), or precisely one of every five women in our original sample of 400, reported at least one incident of sexual harassment at some point during their college career. We can estimate, therefore, that between 20 and 30 percent of the women in the senior class we sampled had been harassed.

Each of the 55 women who reported sexual harassment at Berkeley indicated the number of different male instructors who had harassed them. Thirty reported harassment by a single instructor, 15 by two, six by three, and two each by four and five or more instructors, respectively. Most of the women who reported harassment adopted strategies to minimize opportunities for future harassment. Nonetheless, nearly one hundred instances of harassment from different instructors were reported.

We made no attempt to estimate the degree to which the numerous separate reports of harassment may have reflected the behavior of a smaller number of individual faculty. We note, however, that those who reported harassment represented a wide diversity in majors and that, typically, the incident occurred while the student was enrolled in a course in her major. Based on respondents' estimates, the male instructors involved came from all age groups. Eleven of the instructors were identified as teaching assistants, seven as lecturers and the remainder as regular faculty. On the basis of this profile and descriptions of individual experiences, male instructors whom our respondents identified as harassers appeared to be widely dispersed among the faculty.

Types of Harassment

Of the 55 students who reported sexual harassment, 50 provided sufficiently detailed descriptions of their experiences to be useful for analysis. Examples are also drawn from the experiences of those who responded to our newspaper advertisement. The 50 incidents varied in form and degree of severity. Most typical were intrusive expressions of sexual and personal interest which respondents found objectionable.

Sexual propositions ranged from vague to blatant; invitations ranged from a dinner date to a weekend at a mountain resort. Sometimes a sexual advance or invitation was made only once, especially when the woman avoided subsequent contact with the instructor. In many other cases, categorizing the harassment experi-

Table 1   Types of Unwanted Sexual Attention Initiated by Male Instructors at the University of California, Berkeley, as Reported by Fifty Senior Women

Behavior	Examples	No. of Students
Verbal advances	Explicit sexual propositions, expressions of sexual interest	17
Invitations	For dates, to one's apartment, for week-end at cabin	17
Physical advances	Touching, kissing, fondling breasts	10
Body language	Leering, standing too close	9
Emotional come-ons	Talking about personal problems; writing long letters	7
Undue attention	Obsequiously friendly; too helpful	5
Sexual bribery	Grade offered in exchange for affair; sexual pressure-*cum*-evaluation	3
Total		68[a]

[a]Total is greater than 50 because some reports specified more than one type of behavior.

ence as simply a sexual advance or invitation does not convey adequately the persistence of the instructor's objectionable behavior. A number of respondents reported that the instructor would "call and call" or "not take 'no' for an answer."

Ten of the 50 respondents reported direct physical advances. Instructors frequently touched and occasionally kissed students in an objectionable and sexually provocative manner. More severe harassment occurred only once among our sample, but was described by three of the women in other exploratory interviews. The following example from the interviews is typical of all three experiences:

> I needed help with an assignment so I went to the professor's office hours. He was staring at my breasts. . . . It made me uncomfortable and confused. . . . He reached over, unbuttoned my blouse and started fondling my breasts.

Not as physically aggressive, but nonetheless irritating and sometimes anxiety-arousing, were incidents of leering and suggestive body language. Seven respondents described "emotional come-ons" which, though not directly sexually aggressive, were experienced as intrusive and containing obvious implications for sexual involvement. Some instructors confided, in person or by letter, details of problems with their marriage of loneliness, and pressed for emotional involvement with the student.

In contrast to reports of sexual harassment at the workplace, *overt* sexual bribery was rarely reported by our sample of female students. There were a handful of examples, however, of explicit offers of academic reward for sexual favors.

Sometimes the possibility of punishment for refusing such "bargains" was also communicated:

> He would make verbal expressions of his desires and would often give me a choice of having an affair and doing well in his class without hardly any effort, or refusing him and suffering in the course. He often made excuses to detain me after class and graded my papers very hard to force me to come to his office. I was tense and uneasy in his presence.

At the workplace, where a single supervisor often has the power of evaluation, promotion and even firing, the terms of sexual exchange are likely to be explicit and obvious. Explicit demands can also happen on campus, as illustrated by the following anonymous account written by a woman at Berkeley in 1978 and given to Women Organized Against Sexual Harassment (WOASH). Having politely refused a direct sexual proposition on a previous encounter with the explanation that she was happily married and did not do that kind of thing, the student wrote:

> In response to my question about which of the two grades appearing on the midterm would be recorded, he asked me which one I wanted, the higher grade or the lower one. (He was towering over me, peering down my blouse.) I said I wanted the grade I deserved. It appeared that he was trying to barter for my "affections"; he acted as though he was giving me something out of the goodness of his heart and whether or not I deserved it didn't matter. Ovbiously he was trying to make me feel obligated to return the "favor." How are students supposed to get a fair assessment of their work when professors use their power to give grades to get sexual favors? (WOASH, 1978)

More typically, however, an instructor's inducements were more gradual and less overtly linked to either concrete rewards (e.g., a higher grade) or immediate sexual obligation. Friendliness, extra help, flexibility in grading and extended deadlines were seen by respondents as means by which instructors tried to accumulate credit for potential sexual exchange. Similarly, attention and friendliness obviously unwarranted by the particular teacher-student relationship were recognized as reflecting sexual and not academic interest.

Instances of selective help given by men to covertly "press their pursuits" of attractive female students (Goffman, 1977) need not be blatant, however. The bluntness of a direct proposition can be avoided through manipulation of the authority and latitude of the faculty role. Indeed, one male faculty member who volunteered his perception of sexual harassment in response to our newspaper advertisement described some of his colleagues as fundamentally "dishonest" in this regard: they falsely praised female students' work to render them more vulnerable to future sexual advances. Sexual propositions and invitations, therefore, do not necessarily "come out of the blue." Male instructors may have laid the groundwork for such overtures through patterns of selective attention and reward.

MANAGING THE TROUBLE

Once a male instructor tries to "come on" to a female student, he is perceived as "trouble" if the attention is unwanted (Emerson and Messinger, 1977). The student must then *manage the trouble* and renegotiate her status as a student. As our study indicates, managing the trouble for many women in our sample meant not expressing their true feelings when harassed. Once an instructor had begun obvious and even highly objectionable sexual advances, the "power-dependence" (Emerson, 1962) aspect of the teacher-student relationship severely inhibited the initial attempts of many women to remedy the situation:

> I tried to let him know I wasn't interested in a personal relationship with him. I couldn't be as rude as I would have liked to have been. At the time I felt I had to put up with it because I was trying to get into the honor's program.

> I ignored it; I didn't want to make a scene and possibly jeopardize my student standing.

> I didn't say anything because I thought being outspoken might affect my grade.

> I didn't say anything, but I wanted to tell him to fuck off. But I needed the recommendation and I'm too polite—I didn't want to be totally rude.

Students used several indirect tactics to forestall escalation of the sexual harassment. These included ignoring or "tuning out" sexual innuendoes and directing disclosures of personal matters (e.g., marital dissatisfaction, "my wife and I have an open marriage," loneliness) back to academic discussion. Physical actions, such as bringing a friend to the instructor's office, pointedly leaving the office door open upon entering, and sitting at a safe distance, were techniques which carried an implicit message that the instructor's behavior had been troublesome.

Students often mentioned their boyfriends or husbands to instructors, both in relatively ambiguous situations and those which had reached the point at which acknowledging an instructor's sexual interest could no longer be avoided. In both instances, apparently, students believed that calling attention to a boyfriend—whether explicitly or implicitly—was the one effective means to "keep him at a distance."

> I had my boyfriend pick me up after class to make it clear to the professor that I was involved with someone.

> I just told him I was living with a man and was not interested in seeing anyone else.

> I told him I had a boyfriend, which I did not.

It is easy to understand why this tactic was used so frequently. Direct complaint would make sexuality the focus of the instructor-student relationship and make the trouble a "fully interpersonal matter" (Emerson and Messinger, 1977:125). Mention of a boyfriend both legitimates, rather than contests or sanctions, the introduction of sexual interest and simultaneously isolates the instructor's sexuality, denying it any connection with the student's. The tactic remains one of compromise.

Student Status

Only occasionally did the students in our sample directly complain to an instructor about his behavior; the risks may have been too great. Thirty percent of the respondents did not even communicate their displeasure directly to the instructor. This did not prove to be an effective way of managing the harassment, for in 13 of these 15 instances the unwanted sexual attention persisted. Predictably, the 70 percent of the respondents who communicated in various ways to the instructor that his sexual attention was not acceptable were more successful in stopping it. That instructors did not always honor even fairly direct appeals to desist may be attributed to the combination of their superior power and the belief (or perhaps rationalization) that a woman's "no" really means "yes."

There is evidence in our study that this may have been the case. Using Emerson's (1962) definition of power as "implicit in the other's dependency," we examined the effects of three likely indicators of an instructor's power: (1) tenured status of the professor; (2) student and professor in the same field; and (3) student aspirations for graduate school. When less than all three of these conditions were present, sexual harassment ceased in 21 of 24 cases when the student expressed her displeasure. However, when all three conditions were present, the harassment stopped in only five of 11 cases.

Even when an instructor stopped harassing a student, the strategies adopted to manage the trouble still may not have been entirely effective. In a few cases, women successfully "talked out" the problem with their instructor and re-established a mutually satisfying student-teacher exchange. Much more often, however, respondents said that faculty members inflicted punishment for not reciprocating sexual attention. Perceived reprisals included withdrawing intellectual support and encouragement, sharp and often sarcastic criticism of work once praised, and low grades. One woman felt she had successfully managed a professor's sexual interest by making her boyfriend highly visible, only to be caught by surprise at the end of the term:

> He wasn't so nice to me after I didn't show interest. I didn't think anything of the incident until I got my grade, then I realized that the grade I got was due to my reaction to him. I knew another woman in the class who did terrible work but got a higher grade than I. Since then, I've heard notorious stories about him.

More severe repercussions occurred where students had more interaction with instructors. A student who was also employed part-time by her professor reported:

Up until the time of our conflict he repeatedly told me that the work I was doing for him was good and that he was pleased with it. During the conflict period I was told the complete opposite: that my work was lousy, that I was lazy. . . . He tried to make me feel inept and incompetent. He then proceeded to prevent me from obtaining another job in the department. When the sexual conflict arose, my position was suddenly terminated and no explanation was given. As an employee and a student in the department my credibility was completely ruined. For a while, I really worried about the quality of my work. I questioned whether it was good or not, even though I knew it was.

In summary, a student's ability to monitor her instructor's behavior and to renegotiate her student status varied with the degree of power dependence in the teacher-student relationship. Thus, students frequently refrained from direct complaints for fear of reprisal; when direct complaints were made, they were sometimes not heeded and occasionally punished, despite attempts to avoid a confrontation.

The Tactic of Selective Avoidance

Kirkpatrick and Kanin (1957) found that women whose male dates had attempted forced sexual relations avoided situations where the act might be repeated. We, too, found that women used this tactic. Twenty-two students said they had no contact whatsoever with the instructor after the incident of sexual harassment. Twenty-four of the descriptions of harassment contained examples of avoidance:

> I avoided situations where we would have to converse. In short, I tried to have as little interaction with the person as possible.

> When he didn't respond to my hints and continued to give me unwanted attention, I avoided him.

> I never went to his office hours.

> I no longer went to section because of the uncomfortable situation.

> I never spoke to him alone again. He was an ignorant, insensitive person and I just avoided having to say anything to him.

Both non-verbal harassment, including various forms of "checking out" a student, and more direct come-ons were experienced as irritating and annoying in themselves. Yet they were also indicators that there might be more to come. Hence, selective avoidance was often used as a means to preclude the possibility of escalated harassment:

> I believe it started through the eyes: staring at my breasts, looking me up and down. . . . He was being overly helpful. . . . [As a result] I didn't trust the man and, thus, discontinued seeing him as my advisor. . . . I had the opportunity to work with this

professor during the summer, but because of his reputation, not only regarding me, but others, I did not take advantage of the opportunity.

Anticipated sexual harassment, then, was also a factor in teacher-student relationships, and students sometimes adopted a "better safe then sorry" course of action. But as a woman in Benson's (1977) survey of the Berkeley campus recognized, this tactic may mean foregoing a potentially valuable *academic* relationship:

> My academic relationships with particular professors have been inhibited by a sexual factor. I have not gotten too friendly with one professor who could help me with my academic work, because I feared he would be interested in some kind of sexual relationship. So, I avoided him, missing out on his academic support. (Benson, 1977: 6)

THE DIRECT COSTS OF SEXUAL HARASSMENT

Students who had little prior involvement with an instructor who harassed them often simply tried to withdraw from future interaction, wherever possible. Missed opportunities was the most obvious price paid for this management behavior. When the teacher-student relationship was more established, however, the costs tended to be more direct. Unlike the typical employer-employee relationship, a young woman in college is in the process of intellectual development and identity formation. Successful completion of this process may depend, at least in part, on interaction with, and evaluation by, faculty members.

Loss of Self-confidence

The abrupt surfacing of intrusive sexual interest in a relationship where there had been considerable interaction caused confusion and uncertainty among our respondents. Standards of performance became cloudy as the professor's sexual intent became clear:

> It became difficult to know whether I was doing a good job.

> I worried that he had given me an "A" on the midterm to convince me to go to bed with him. I could not make a clear decision about the quality of my work in the class for this reason.

> I wondered what my real status in the class was—my real ability.

Eighteen students experienced self-doubt and loss of confidence in their academic ability after harassment. This occurred when students were unable to avoid their instructor. Typically, they had extensive previous interaction with him and likely did not find it easy to simply blame him for the trouble and withdraw from the situation (Emerson and Messinger, 1977):

> As this particular professor knew me and my work better than anyone else, I came away feeling very insecure about my academic work—[afraid] that his support of me was skewed by his sexual attraction.
>
> All of a sudden I had an anxiety attack about my intelligence. . . . I wondered if all these years I had only gotten good grades because of my looks.
>
> For sometime afterwards I felt I had no ability in my major field; I couldn't analyze effectively or write clearly.

Disillusionment with Male Faculty

With only a single exception, students who reported loss of academic self-confidence also became disillusioned and cautious about male faculty in general.

> I was so disillusioned with academia. . . . [The experience] lessened my confidence on whether I felt it was worth going through with it all.
>
> I had just entered college. . . . After dealing with him I never took an in-depth study again.

Even women whose self-confidence was not shaken reported that they became suspicious of male instructors. Behavior which previously had appeared natural and helpful was thereafter perceived as calculated and sexually motivated, and subsequent interactions became constrained by a sense of distrust:

> I became disillusioned and suspicious of people I'd otherwise responded naturally to. I'm more cautious of male faculty in general.
>
> [With male faculty, I am] more cautious about being open and friendly.

Two respondents volunteered comments about the composition of the faculty:

> I wish there were more female teachers and faculty members on campus so I wouldn't have to face a similar situation. I became doubtful and fearful of male faculty; I thought they must all be the same.
>
> I'm much more guarded in relating to my professors and male [teaching assistants]. I'm so relieved if I find out they're gay.

THE CUMULATIVE EFFECTS OF HARASSMENT ON CAMPUS

Theoretically, women now compete on the same terms as men for training and the credentials required for professional careers. But to the extent that male instructors perceive that female students are not, or should not be, as talented or committed as male students, they can act or fail to act in a number of ways—often minor or subtle in themselves, but nonetheless accumulating to produce a "discriminatory environment" (Bourne and Wikler, 1978; Coser and Rokoff, 1971; Rowe, 1977). The pattern of sexual harassment that we have documented is an integral part of this phenomenon.

Changes in sexual attitudes and practices have led to a greater acceptance of both casual and intimate relationships between faculty and students. At one time college officials, acknowledging the very real danger of improper sexual advances by male instructors, often required that office doors remain ajar during consultation with female students (Bernard, 1964). The seduction of a coed may have been sufficiently scandalous to threaten dismissal at some point in the past; but casual and comradely sexual interaction between faculty and students is now fully tolerated.[5]

It is important, therefore, to clarify that the issue of sexual harassment does not derive from a moralistic concern with sexual expression per se. Rather, the problem of sexual harassment on campus is significant because of the specific—and at times highly ambiguous—manner in which the formal teacher-student relationship overlaps with the pursuit of sexual interest. In a setting where an overwhelmingly male faculty determines to a considerable degree academic rewards (and punishments), intellectual self-esteem, and the possibility of a professional career, individual instructors also have the power to initiate or impose sexual relationships with female students.

A faculty member's power to force compliance with his sexual interest doubtlessly varies. It is frequently the case with graduate training that a single faculty member has as much influence over a student's career prospects as an employer does over an employee's. In such contexts, one readily imagines, the coercive effects of sexual intrusion can be quite consequential.

Individual professors and teaching assistants typically have less direct power over the lives of undergraduate women. But in a society where few women have received support for intellectual accomplishment, an instructor's ability to manipulate both academic validation and his own sexual self-interest is hardly innocuous. The unexpected intrusion of sexual harassment alone can threaten self-confidence and commitment to academic pursuits.

Similarly, the direct costs of actual reprisals (e.g., lower evaluations, with-

[5]Professor Elizabeth Scott, in a personal communication (March 1979), recalled that custodians at Berkeley were once instructed to enforce a university policy which forbade daybeds, cots and covered doors in faculty offices.

drawal of support, termination of employment) are obvious, though they apply to only some of those harassed. More subtle, and more common, are the effects inherent in the implicit threat when a student rejects her instructor's sexual overtures. And because sexual harassment continues to be a prevalent institutional practice, no actual reprisals are necessary to reinforce the belief that women should be sexually and personally accommodating to male authority. The male prerogative to define the terms of the relationship—to use sexual rather than official criteria to evaluate a woman's worth in academia—remains unchecked.

Women continually confronted with the possibility of sexual harassment are put in a double-bind situation. Responding to unwanted sexual attention, many women in our study adopted individual ad hoc management strategies which, ironically, further removed them from opportunities for professional advancement. Avoiding and mistrusting male faculty—the logical and practical reaction of many women in our study—hinders the formation of serious mentor relationships. Without comfortable access to the informal channels of professional socialization, women ultimately experience less control over their academic lives.

Telling an instructor that one has other emotional/sexual commitments ("I have a boyfriend") only confirms that a woman is defined in relation to a man rather than as an independent scholar or professional. Historically, sexual or gender-specific definitions have been used to disqualify women from positions of responsibility (Cott, 1978). And, as Bourne (1977) has suggested, pre-professional or professional women today who are categorized as "sexy" find their competence and authority devalued.

The experience of sexual harassment is, after all, only the most conclusive indicator that many male instructors continue to impose a sexual and gender-specific definition on their female students. Women learn that even simple friendliness and academic enthusiasm are often misinterpreted as an invitation for sexual advances and are forced to change their behavior accordingly. Men, on the other hand, interpret a wary stance adopted to forestall sexual harassment and stereotyping as an indication of coldness and a difficult emotional disposition (Wikler, 1976). Women who do not conform to the appropriate feminine stereotype may be perceived as technically competent but, lacking moral psychological "goodness," devoid of real authority (Bourne, 1977).

CONCLUSION

The practice of sexual harassment both reflects and reinforces the devaluation of women's competence and helps erode their commitment to competitive careers. Approached as the confluence of male formal authority and sexual interest, sexual harassment should not be seen as an isolated or deviant phenomenon. Rather, attention to harassment should be routine in any study of authority and gender in male-dominated institutions. For, as our research suggests, sexual harassment may be endemic to the university, and women must bear the costs of the latitude and ambiguity operating between a male-dominated system of formal authority and the sexual interests of numerous individual male instructors.

REFERENCES

Acker, Joan R. 1980. "Women and stratification: A review of recent literature." *Contemporary Sociology* 9 (January):25–35.

Backhouse, Constance, and Leh Cohen. 1979. *Secret Oppression: Sexual Harassment.* Toronto: Macmillan.

Benson, Donna J. 1977. "The sexualization of the teacher-student relationship." Unpublished paper, Department of Sociology, University of California, Berkeley.

Bernard, Jessie. 1964. *Academic Women.* University Park: Pennsylvania State University Press.

Blau, Peter. 1964. *Exchange and Power in Social Life.* New York: John Wiley.

———. 1973. *The Structure and Organization of Academic Work.* New York: Academic Press.

Bourne, Patricia. 1977. " 'You can't use it, but don't lose it': Sex in medical school." *Proceedings of the Conference on Women's Leadership and Authority in the Health Professions.* Washington, D.C.: Department of Health, Education and Welfare, Health Resources Administration, Office of Health Resources Opportunity.

———, and Norma Juliet Wikler. 1978. "Commitment and the cultural mandate: Women in medicine." *Social Problems* 25 (April):430–440.

Coser, Rose, and Gerald Rokoff. 1971. "Women in the occupational world: Social disruption and conflict." *Social Problems* 18 (Spring):535–554.

Cott, Nancy. 1978. "Passionlessness: An interpretation of Victorian sexual ideology, 1790–1850." *Signs* 4 (Winter):219–236.

EEOC (Equal Employment Opportunity Commission). 1980. "Discrimination because of sex under Title VII of the Civil Rights Act of 1964, as amended: Adoption of interim interpretive guidelines." *Federal Register* 29 (March 11):1604. Washington D.C.: U.S. Government Printing Office.

Emerson, Richard. 1962. "Power-dependence relations." *American Sociological Review* 27 (February):31–41.

———, and Sheldon Messinger. 1977. "The micro-politics of trouble." *Social Problems* 25 (December):121–134.

Fields, Cheryl M. 1979. "One-fourth of women psychologists in survey report sexual contacts with their professors." *Chronicle of Higher Education* 11 (September 17):1, 10.

Goffman, Erving. 1977. "The arrangements between the sexes." *Theory and Society* 4 (Fall):301–331.

Gutek, Barbara, Charles Y. Nakamura, Martin Gahart, Inger Handschumacher, and Dan Russell. 1980. "Sexuality and the workplace." *Basic and Applied Social Psychology* 1 (October): 255–265.

Kirkpatrick, Clifford, and Eugene Kanin. 1957. "Male sex aggression on a university campus." *American Sociological Review* 22 (February):52–58.

Lesser, Ellen. 1979. "Sexus et veritas: Yale sued for sexual harassment." *Seven Days* 3 (February):25–26.

MacKinnon, Catherine. 1979. *Sexual Harassment of Working Women: A Case of Sex Discrimination.* New Haven, Conn.: Yale University Press.

Munich, Adrienne. 1978. "Seduction in academe." *Psychology Today* 11 (February):82–84, 108.

Nelson, Anne. 1978. "Sexual harassment at Yale." *Nation 226* (January 7–14):7–10.

Pope, Kenneth S., Hanna Levenson, and Leslie R. Shover. 1979. "Sexual intimacy in psychology training: Results and implications of a national survey." *American Psychologist* 34 (August):682–689.

Quinn, Robert E. 1977. "Coping with Cupid: The formation, impact, and management of romantic relationships in organizations." *Administrative Science Quarterly* 22 (March):30–45.

Rose, Vicki McNicle. 1977a. "Rape as a social problem: A by-product of the feminist movement." *Social Problems* 25 (October):75–89.

————. 1977b. "The rise of the rape problem," pp. 167–195 in Armand L. Mauss and Julie C. Wolfe (eds.), *Our Land of Promises: The Rise and Fall of Social Problems in America.* Philadelphia: J. B. Lippincott.

Rowe, Mary P. 1977. The Saturn's rings phenomenon: Micro-inequities and unequal opportunity in the American economy." *Proceedings of the Conference on Women's Leadership and Authority in the Health Professions.* Washington, D.C.: Department of Health, Education and Welfare, Health Resources Administration, Office of Health Resources Opportunity.

Safran, Claire. 1976. "What men do to women on the job: A shocking look at sexual harassment." *Redbook* (November):148–149.

Silverman, Dierdre. 1976–77. "Sexual harassment: Working women's dilemma." *Quest: A Feminist Quarterly* 3 (Winter):15–24.

Till, Frank J. 1980. "Sexual harassment: A report on the sexual harassment of students." Report of the National Advisory Council on Women's Educational Programs. Washington, D.C.: U.S. Department of Education.

Wikler, Norma. 1976. "Sexism in the classroom." Paper presented at the annual meeting of the American Sociological Association, New York, September.

WOASH (Women Organized Against Sexual Harassment). 1978. Anonymous personal communication. Unpublished.

————. 1979. "Sexual harassment: What it is, what do do about it." Pamphlet available from WOASH, University of California, Berkeley.

WWUI (Working Women United Institute). 1978. *Sexual Harassment on the Job: Questions and Answers.* New York: WWUI.

Four

FAILURES OF SOCIAL INSTITUTIONS

7

Family and Educational Problems

Our society's divorce rate is very high. Couples begin their lives together hoping, but not at all sure, that their relationship will endure. Some critics say that marital instability is inevitable because we form a unit as societally important as the family on only nebulous feelings of "romantic love." Solomon points out that the figures of speech used by lovers tells us how they define love and think it should be expressed. Perhaps these definitions should be examined before a couple makes a commitment. If someone who is looking for a "fair exchange" is involved with someone who feels love must be "worked at," a successful relationship is unlikely.

Many children in our society grow up in households with only one parent. Often this situation is treated as being riddled with drawbacks. Weiss reports that even though such children regret that they did not have two parents, they also feel pride that they have successfully met more challenges than have children in two-parent households.

Next we have an example of the politics of social problem definition. When a woman stays with a man who abuses her, she is automatically defined by the experts as being in need of support services. No matter what her family situation, we expect the "natural" response to be to leave home. Loseke and Cahill show how the experts constructed this social problem to create a clientele to serve.

Social definitions are also important as they relate to how children perform in school. Students performances have been shown to be strongly related to how these youngsters are defined and treated by their teachers. We cannot realize our goals of equality in education until such biases are understood and corrected. Ryan points out that the self-esteem of many lower- and working-class children is being destroyed because of the low expectations for them shown by school personnel.

Reading 22
The Love Lost in Clichés

Robert C. Solomon

University of Texas at Austin

We'd known each other for years; and for months, we were—what?—"seeing each other" (to choose but one of so many silly euphemisms for playful but by no means impersonal sex). We reveled in our bodies, cooked and talked two or three times a week, enjoying ourselves immensely, but within careful bounds, surrounded by other "relationships" (another euphemism), cautiously sharing problems as well as pleasures, exorcising an occasional demon and delighting each other with occasional displays of affection, never saying too much or revealing too much or crossing these unspoken boundaries of intimacy and independence.

Then, we "fell in love." What happened?

There was no "fall," first of all. Why do we get so transfixed with that Alice-in-Wonderland metaphor, and not just that one but a maze of others, obscuring everything; what is a "deep" relationship, for example? And why is love "losing" yourself? Is "falling for" someone really "falling for"—that is, getting *duped*? Where do we get that imagery of tripping, tumbling, and other inadvertent means of getting *in*-volved, *im*mersed, and *sub*-merged in love, "taking the plunge" when it really gets serious? If anything, the appropriate image would seem to be openness rather than depth, flying rather than falling. One makes love (still another euphemism, this one with some significance), but our entire romantic mythology makes it seem as if it happens, as if it is something someone suffers (enjoying it as well), as if it's entirely natural, a need and something all but unavoidable.

We look at love, as we look at life, through a series of metaphors, each with its own language, its own implications, connotations, and biases. For example, if someone says that love is a game, we already know much of what is to follow: relationships will tend to be short-lived. Sincerity will be a strategy for winning and so will flattery and perhaps lying ("all's fair. . ."). The person played with is taken seriously only as an opponent, a challenge, valued in particular for his or her tactics and retorts, but quickly dispensable as soon as someone has won or lost. Playing hard to get is an optional strategy, and being "easy" is not immoral or foolish so much as playing badly, or not at all.

On the other hand, if someone sees love as God's gift to humanity, we should expect utter solemnity, mixed with a sense of gratitude, seriousness, and self-righteousness that is wholly lacking in the "love-is-a-game" metaphor. Relationships here will tend to be long-lasting, if not forever fraught with duties and obligations dictated by a gift that, in the usual interpretations, has both divine and secular strings attached.

The game metaphor is, perhaps, too frivolous to take seriously. The gift-of-

Adapted from *Love: Emotion, Myth & Metaphor* (New York: Doubleday, 1981). Reprinted with permission of the author.

God metaphor, on the other hand, is much too serious to dismiss frivolously. Not surprisingly, these love metaphors reflect our interests elsewhere in life—in business, health, communications, art, politics, and law, as well as fun and games and religion. But these are not mere figures of speech; they are the self-imposed structures that determine the way we experience love itself. For that reason, we should express reservations about some of them.

LOVE AS A FAIR EXCHANGE

One of the most common love metaphors, now particuarly popular in social psychology, is the economic metaphor. The idea is that love is an exchange, a sexual partnership, a trade-off of interests and concerns and, particularly, of *approval*. "I make you feel good about yourself and in return you make me feel good about myself." Of course exchange rates vary—some people need more than others—and there is a law of diminishing returns; that is, the same person's approval tends to become less and less valuable as it becomes more familiar. (This law of diminishing returns, which we experience as the gradual fading of romantic love, has been explored by the psychologist Elliot Aronson of the University of California at Santa Cruz. His theory has been aptly named by the students "Aronson's Law of Marital Infidelity.") In some relationships, the balance of payments may indeed seem extremely one-sided, but the assumption is, in the words of the Harvard sociologist George Homans, that both parties must believe they are getting something out of it or they simply wouldn't stick around.

The economic model has much to offer, not least the fact that it gives a fairly precise account of the concrete motivation for love, which is left out of more pious accounts that insist that love is simply good in itself and needs no motives. But the problem is that it too easily degenerates into a most unflattering model of mutual buying and selling, which in turn raises the specter that love may indeed be, as some cynics have been saying ever since Marx and Engels, a form of covert prostitution, though not necessarily—or even usually—for money. "I will sleep with you and think well of you or at least give you the benefit of the doubt if only you'll tell me good things about myself and pretend to approve of me."

It may be true that we do often evaluate our relationships in this way, in terms of mutual advantage and our own sense of fairness. The question "What am I getting out of this, anyway?" always makes sense even if certain traditional views of love and commitment try to pretend that such selfishness is the very antithesis of love. But the traditional views have a point to make as well, which is simply that such tit-for-tat thinking inevitably undermines a relationship based on love, not because love is essentially selfless, but because the bargaining table is not the place to understand mutual affection. Love is not the exchange of affection, any more than sex is merely the exchange of pleasure. What is left out of these accounts is the "we" of love, which is quite different from "I and thou." This is not to say that fairness cannot be an issue in love, nor is it true that all's fair in love. But while the economic exchange model explains rather clearly some of the motives for love, it tends to ignore the experience of love almost altogether, which is that such evaluations seem at the time beside the point and come to mind only when love is already breaking down. It is the suspicion, not the fact, that "I'm putting more into this than you are" that signals the end of many relationships, despite the fact that, as business goes, there may have been "a good arrangement."

LOVE AND ELECTRONICS

A powerful metaphor with disastrous consequences that was popular a few years ago was a communication metaphor, often used in conjunction with a relating metaphor, for obvious reasons. Both were involved with the then-hip language of media and information theory: "getting through" to each other and "we just can't communicate any more" gave lovers the unfortunate appearance of shipwrecked survivors trying to keep in touch over a slightly damaged shortwave radio. The information-processing jargon ("input," "feedback," "tuning in," and "turning off") was typically loaded with electronic-gadget imagery, and good relationships, appropriately, were described in terms of their "good vibrations." But, like all metaphors, this one revealed much more than it distorted, namely, an image of isolated transmitters looking for someone to get their messages. It was precisely this milieu that gave birth to Rollo May's *Love and Will* and his concern that people had rendered love impossible. Love was thought to be mainly a matter of self-expression—largely but not exclusively verbal expression. Talk became enormously important to love; problems were talked over, talked through, and talked out. The essential moment was the "heavy conversation," and talk about love often took the place of love itself. Confession and openness (telling all) became the linchpins of love, even when the messages were largely hostility and resentment.

Psychotherapist George Bach wrote a number of successful books, including *The Intimate Enemy* (with Peter Wyden), that made quite clear the fact that it was expression of feelings, not the feelings themselves, that made for a successful relationship. On the communications model, sex, too, was described as a mode of communication, but more often sex was not so much communicating as the desire to be communicated with. Sex became, in McLuhan's jargon, a cool medium. And, like most modern media, the model put its emphasis on the medium itself (encounter groups and the like), but there was precious little stress on the content of the programming. Not surprisingly, love became an obscure ideal, like television commercials full of promise of something fabulous yet to come, hinted at but never spoken of as such. The ultimate message was the idea of the medium itself.

LOVE AS WORK

A very different model is the work model of love. The Protestant ethic is very much at home in romance. (Rollo May calls love the Calvinist's proof of emotional salvation.) And so we find many people who talk about "working out a relationship," working at it," "working for it," and so on. The fun may once have been there but now the real job begins, tacking together and patching up, like fixing up an old house. This is, needless to say, a particularly self-righteous model, if for no other reason than that it begins on the defensive and requires considerable motivation just to move on. Personal desires, the other person's as well as one's own, may be placed behind "the relationship," which is conceived of as the primary project. Love, according to the work model, is evaluated above all on its industriousness, its seriousness, its success in the face of the most difficult obstacles. Devotees of the work model not infrequently choose the most inept or inappropriate partners, rather like buying a run-down shack—for the challenge. They will look with disdain at people who are merely happy together (something like buying a house from a tract builder). They will look with admiration and awe at a couple who have survived a dozen years of fights and emotional disfigurements because "they made it work. . . ."

THE BLAND LEADING THE BLAND

Blandness can be just as significant as excitement, and a metaphor may be intentionally noncommittal as well as precise. Thus we find the word "thing" substituted for everything from sexual organs (a young virgin gingerly refers to her first lover's "thing") to jobs, hangups, and hobbies (as in "doing your own thing"). Where love is concerned, the most banal of our metaphors is the word "relating," or "relationship" itself. There's not much to say about it, except to ponder in amazement the fact that we have not yet, in this age of "heavy relationships," come up with anything better. There is a sense, of course, in which any two people (or two things) stand in any number of relationships to one another (being taller than, heavier than, smarter than, more than 15 feet away from . . . and so forth). The word "relations" was once, only a few years ago, a polite and slightly clinical word for sex (still used, as most stilted archaisms tend to be, in law). People "relate" to each other as they "relate a story," perhaps on the idea that what couples do most together is to tell each other the events of the day, a less-than-exciting conception of love, to be sure. The fact that this metaphor dominates our thinking so much (albeit in the guise of a *meaningful* relationship) points once again to the poverty of not only our vocabulary but our thinking and feeling.

ESCAPE FROM ALONENESS

In our extremely individualistic society we have come to see isolation and loneliness as akin to the human condition, instead of as by-products of a certain kind of social arrangement that puts mobility and the formation of new interpersonal bonds at a premium. This individualistic metaphor, which I call the "ontology of loneliness," because it implies some kind of coherent law in the human organism's development, is stated succinctly by Rollo May: "Every person, experiencing as he [or she] does his [or her] own solitariness and aloneness, longs for union with another."

This viewpoint has been developed by the philosopher Ayn Rand into an argument for selfishness: "Each of us is born into the world alone, and therefore each of us is justified in pursuing our own selfish interests." But the premise is false, and the inference is insidious.

Not only in our infancy but also in adulthood we find ourselves essentially linked to other people, to a language that we call our own, to a culture and, at least legally, to a country as well. We do not have to find or "reach out" to others; they are, in a sense, already *in us*. Alone in the woods of British Columbia, I find myself still thinking of friends, describing what I see as if they were there—and in their language. The idea of the isolated self is an American invention—reinforced perhaps by the artificially isolated circumstances of the psychiatrist's office and our fantasies about gunfighters and mountain men—but it is not true of most of us. And this means that love is not a refuge or an escape, either. Our conception of ourselves is always as a social self (even if it is an antisocial or rebellious self).

Our language of love often reflects the idea of natural isolation, for example in the communication metaphor in which isolated selves try desperately to get through to each other. But this picture of life and love is unnecessarily tragic, and its result is to make love itself seem like something of a cure for a disease, rather than a positive experience that already presupposes a rather full social life. Indeed, it is revealing that, quite the contrary of social isolation, romantic love is usually experienced only *within* a rather extensive social nexus. "Sure, I have lots of friends and I like my colleagues at work but, still, I'm lonely and I want to fall in love." But that has nothing to do with loneliness. It rather reflects the tremendous importance we accord to romantic love in our lives, not as a cure for aloneness, but as a positive experience in its own right, which we have, curiously, turned into a need.

MADE FOR EACH OTHER?

Standing opposed to the "ontology of loneliness" is an ancient view which takes our unity, not our mutual isolation, as the natural state of humanity. Our own image of two people "being made for each other" is also an example of the metaphysical model, together with the idea that marriages are "made in heaven" and that someone else can be your "better half." The metaphysical model is based not on the idea that love is a refuge from isolated individualism but that love is the realization of bonds that are already formed, even before one meets one's "other half."

The ontology of loneliness treats individuals as atoms, bouncing around the universe alone looking for other atoms, occasionally forming more or less stable molecules. But if we were to pursue the same chemical metaphor into the metaphysical model, it would more nearly resemble what physicists today call "field theory.'' A magnetic field, for instance, retains all of its electromagnetic properties whether or not there is any material there to make them manifest. So, too, an individual is already a network of human relationships and expectations, and these exist whether or not one finds another individual whose radiated forces and properties are complementary. The old expression above love being a matter of ''chemical attraction'' is, scientifically, a century out of date; attraction is no longer a question of one atom affecting another but the product of two electromagnetic fields, each of which exists prior to and independent of any particular atoms within its range. So, too, we radiate charm, sexiness, inhibition, intelligence, and even repulsiveness, and find a lover who fits in. The problem with this view is that it leaves no room for the development of relationships, but makes it seem as if love has to be there in full, from the very beginning. . . .

THE ARTISTIC MODEL

Perhaps the oldest view of love, the pivot of Plato's *Symposium,* is an aesthetic model: love as the admiration and the contemplation of beauty. The emphasis here is on neither relating nor communicating (in fact, unrequited love and even voyeurism are perfectly in order). On this model, it is not particularly expected that the lover will actually do much of anything, except, perhaps, to get within view of the beloved at every possible opportunity. It is this model that has dominated many of our theories about love, though not, luckily, our practices.

It is this model about which women rightly complain when they accuse men of putting them up on a pedestal, a charge that too often confuses the idealization that accompanies it with the impersonal distancing that goes along with the pedestal. The objection is not to the fact that it is a pedestal so much as that it is usually a very tall pedestal; any real contact is out of the question. Or else it is a very small pedestal, ''and like any small place,'' writes Gloria Steinem, ''a prison.''

THE CONTRACT MODEL

What is crucial to the contract model is that emotion plays very little part in it. One accepts an obligation to obey the terms of the contract (implicit or explicit) whether or not one wants to. The current term for this ever-popular emasculation of emotion is commitment. In fact there seems to be an almost general agreement among most of the people I talk with that commitment constitutes love. (The contrast is almost always sexual promiscuity.) But commitment is precisely what love is not, though one can and often does make commitments on the basis of whether one loves someone. A commitment is an obligation sustained *even if the emotion that originally motivates it no longer exists.* And the sense of obligation isn't love.

THE BIOLOGICAL METAPHOR

The idea that science itself can be but a metaphor strikes us as odd, but much of what we believe about love, it seems, is based on wholly unliteral biological metaphors. For example, we believe that love is natural, even an instinct, and this is supported by a hundred fascinating but ultimately irrelevant arguments about "the facts of life": the fact that some spiders eat their mates, that some birds mate for life, that some sea gulls are lesbians, that some fish can't mate unless the male is clearly superior, that chimpanzees like to gang-bang and gorillas have weenies the size of a breakfast sausage, that bats tend to do it upside down, and porcupines do it "carefully." But romantic love is by no means natural; it is not an instinct but a very particular and peculiar attitude toward sex and pair-bonding that has been carefully cultivated by a small number of people in modern aristocratic and middle-class societies.

Even sex, which would seem to be natural if anything is, is no more mere biology than taking the holy wafer at high Mass is just eating. It, too, is defined by our metaphors and the symbolic significance we give to it. It is not a need, though we have certainly made it into one. Sex is not an instinct, except in that utterly minimal sense that bears virtually no resemblance at all to the extremely sophisticated and emotion-filled set of rituals that we call—with some good reason—making love. And where sex and love come together is not in the realm of nature either, but in the realm of expression, specific to a culture that specifies its meaning.

There is one particular version of the biological metaphor, however, that has enjoyed such spectacular scientific acceptance, ever since Freud at least, that we tend to take it as the literal truth instead of, again, as a metaphor. It is the idea that love begins in—or just out of—the womb, and that our prototype of love—if not our one true love—is our own mother.

Our models and prototypes of love include not only our parents but also brothers, sisters, teachers in junior high school, first dates, first loves, graduating-class heroes and heroines, hundreds of movie stars and magazine pictures, as well as a dozen considerations and pressures that have nothing to do with prototypes at all. Indeed, even Freud insisted that it is not a person's actual parent who forms the romantic prototype but rather a phantom, constructed from memory, which may bear little resemblance to any real person. But if this is so, perhaps one's imagined mother is, in fact, a variation on one's first girlfriend, or a revised version of Myrna Loy. Why do we take the most complex and at times most exquisite emotion in our lives and try to reduce it to the first and the simplest? . . .

LOVE AS A LESS-THAN-PERFECT FIT

So what, after all, is love? It is, in a phrase, an emotion through which we create for ourselves a little world—the love-world—in which we play the roles of lovers and create our selves as well. Thus love is not, as so many of the great poets and philosophers have taken it to be, any degree of admiration or worship, not appreciation or even desire for beauty, much less, as Erich Fromm was fond of arguing, an "orientation of character" whose object is a secondary consideration. Even so-called unrequited love is shared love and shared identity, if only from one side and thereby woefully incomplete.

In love we transform ourselves and one another, but the key is the understanding that the transformation of selves is not merely reciprocal, a swap of favors like "I'll cook you dinner if you'll wash the car." The self transformed in love is a shared self, and therefore by its very nature at odds with, even contradictory to, the individual autonomous selves that each of us had before. And yet at the same time, romantic love is based on the idea of individuality and freedom. This means, first of all, that the presupposition of love is a strong sense of individual identity and autonomy that exactly contradicts the ideal of "union" and "yearning to be one" that some of our literature has celebrated so one-sidedly. And second, the freedom that is built in includes not just the freedom to come together but the freedom to go as well. Thus love is always in a state of tension, always changing, dynamic, tenuous, and explosive.

Love is a dialectic, which means that the bond of love is not just shared identity—which is an impossible goal—but the taut line of opposed desires between the ideal of an eternal merger of souls and our cultivated urge to prove ourselves as free and autonomous individuals. No matter how much we're in love, there is always a large and nonnegligible part of ourselves that is not defined by the love-world, nor do we want it to be. To understand love is to understand this tension, this dialectic between individuality and the shared ideal. To think that love is to be found only at the ends of the spectrum—in that first enthusiastic discovery of a shared togetherness or at the end of the road, after a lifetime together—is to miss the love-world almost entirely, for it is neither an initial flush of feeling nor the retrospective congratulations of old age, but rather, a struggle for unity and identity. And it is this struggle—neither the ideal of togetherness nor the contrary demand for individual autonomy and identity—that defines the dynamics of romantic love.

Reading 23

Growing Up a Little Faster: The Experience of Growing Up in a Single-Parent Household

Robert S. Weiss

University of Massachusetts and Harvard Medical School

On the basis of interviews with single parents, and with adolescent children living with single parents, a theory of the structure and functioning of single-parent households is proposed. The premise of this theory is that the two-parent household maintains a hierarchy—an echelon structure—that the one-parent household can forgo. The absence of hierarchy permits the single parent who works full time to share managerial responsibility for the household with the children. The consequences for the children may be a fostering of an early maturity.

A recent review of research on the impact on children of parental divorce points out that most attention has been given to the consequences for the children of the absence from their homes of their fathers (Longfellow, 1979). Generally father-absence was thought important because it implied that the children's home was without a source of discipline and a model for the development of appropriate sex rules (Biller 1974). The impact on children of loss of a parent who was for them an attachment figure has also received attention (Bowlby, 1973; Wallerstein and Kelly, 1974). The effects on children of changed relationships with custodial parents have been noted primarily by investigators working in a psychiatric or clinical tradition (Wallerstein and Kelly, 1974; also Klebanow, 1976). The effect on children of their changed responsibilities in their new households, and of their participation in households that are now differently organized has been less often considered. Gardner, a child psychiatrist, does observe: ''When parents separate, the children are generally required to assume new responsibilities and obligations (1976:169). And George and Wilding in a discussion of motherless households say: ''The mother's absence inevitably resulted in the children having to take on more responsibility in looking after themselves and helping the father to run the house'' (1972:73). But these writers are exceptional in recognizing that the organization of a one-parent household differs from that of a two-parent household.

It is surprising that so little attention has thus far been given to the effects on children's development produced by the modification of their household roles.

Reprinted with permission from *Journal of Social Issues* 35(4) (1979):97–111, abridged.

Changes in the children's roles and responsibilities are among the aspects most often noted by single parents themselves when commenting on how the single parent situation is different. Parents sometimes say their children "have had to grow up a little bit faster." Single parents may also comment that as a result of their having had to grow up a little faster, their children appear to them to be more mature than children of the same age living in two-parent households.

This earlier maturity may display itself as an unusual ability to understand adults' perspectives and to relate to adults, or as a sense of self-reliance more appropriate to an older child, or as unusual responsibleness. To be sure, early maturity is not necessarily displayed throughout a child's functioning. The same child who is precociously capable of sympathy for the parent may also be more needful of approval, more dependent, or more diffident with peers than other children. Yet a general impression from talking with single parents and with children who live in single-parent households is that the children have developed capabilities for independent functioning and for the assumption of responsibility, as well as some specific skills, unusual among their peers from two-parent households. How this early maturity comes about, the forms it takes, and some of its possible consequences are the subject of this paper.

The paper is based on data collected in a series of studies conducted within the research program of The Laboratory of Community Psychiatry, Harvard Medical School. In the course of these studies, well over two hundred single parents from a wide range of educational and occupational backgrounds have been interviewed, many of them several times over intervals of six months to a year. For comparison purposes, extensive interviews have also been held with a small number of married couples. In addition, individual interviews have been held with children ranging in age from six to young adult, from about twenty families, and group interviews have been held with another twenty or more adolescent children.

THE SINGLE-PARENT FAMILY AND THE ABSENCE OF AN ECHELON STRUCTURE

In most well-functioning two-parent households, there is not much opportunity for children to enter into household decision-making. Young children and even adolescents generally have little influence on familial matters. The children may decide on the decorating scheme for their rooms, select their own clothes, choose their friends and their hobbies. But household issues, such as when mealtimes are scheduled and which household jobs are assigned to the children, and familial issues, such as where the family will go on the parents' vacation, tend to be decided by the parents, perhaps after limited consultation with the children. The maintenance and direction of the family unit is a parental responsibility.

Because the parents are jointly responsible, each parent feels pledged to support the other. Should there be no prior agreement on a particular issue, each parent is expected to respect the position assumed by the other, at least while the parents are in the presence of the children. In reality, one parent may countermand the other's directives or may collude with the children to frustrate the other's wishes, but behavior of this sort is understood as irresponsible and, perhaps, hostile in intent. In a well-functioning two-parent household, each parent can count on the other to support that parent's rulings.

Goffman (1961) has given the name "echelon structure" to an authority structure in which a partnership agreement, not necessarily explicit, exists among those on a superordinate level which has the effect of giving anyone on that level authority in relation to anyone on a subordinate level. The army maintains this sort of authority structure; so do hospitals; so do two-parent families. One-parent families do not. The parent in the one-parent family need not check with the second parent before acceding to the children's wishes in an area in which the second parent is known to have strong commitments. The parent in the one-parent family need not avoid alliances with the children which might prove embarrassing should it become necessary to back up the second parent. No longer is there a structure in which the parent is unable to make common cause with the children for fear of betraying a prior understanding with the other parent. Without a second parent in the household, the echelon structure of the two-parent family dissolves.

Although the collapse of the echelon structure does not require that a parent's relationship to the children undergo change, it makes certain types of change possible. In particular, it makes possible the development of a new relationship in which the children are defined as having responsibilities and rights in the household not very different from the parent's own. Children now can be asked not only to perform additional chores—this would have been possible within an echelon structure as well—but also to participate in deciding what is to be done.

If a single parent is working full-time, and, especially, if the parent has more than one child to care for, then the parent is likely to find that sharing responsibility with the children is very nearly necessary to maintain the functioning of the household. Some single parents report having called their children into a family council at which they announced to the children that now, with only one parent in the household, the family would have to be run in a new way, with every member of the family assuming a full share of responsibility. The following is from an interview with a mother of four children who ranged in age from about ten or eleven to about sixteen:

> As soon as I was on my own, I sat down with the children—I always had a good rapport with the children—and I told them, "Now things are different. Instead of, more or less, it being a family of mother and four children, we're all one family with all equal responsibility, and we all have a say, and we're all very important. And if it is going to work right, we all have to be able to cooperate with each other."

In this new definition of the household structure, the children are expected to do their share, just as is the parent. Children, though they may not at first be as reliable as they later become, usually prove equal to this expectation. Children of only three are able to keep their toys in order; children of four or five can make their own beds, although they may complain that the beds will only have to be unmade in the evening; eight-year-olds can vacuum floors and clean up a kitchen; ten-year-olds can cook; adolescents are capable of looking after themselves and younger children through much of a weekend. A man with three daughters aged four to nine described how they helped during their breakfast rush:

> It is a matter of survival. Each of the kids has a chore. Patsy makes her bed in the morning when she gets up. That is one less job that I have to do. Shirley gets the cereal down if we are having cereal. Lenore clears the table and puts the dishes in the dishwasher. While one is in the bathroom the other has something to do. By the time we leave the house in the morning, the beds are made, the table is cleared, and the dishes are put away in the dishwasher.

But the single-parent household is different from the two-parent household not simply because children are likely to be asked to do more household tasks. It is different because children are held responsible, not only for the chores themselves, but also for the continued functioning of the household. They are asked to accept that the functioning of the household is as much dependent on their contributions as on the contributions of the parent. They are asked, in a way, to assume some of the concerns of management, to move from the role of subordinate member of the household to that of junior partner.

The difference between the child's role in the one-parent and the two-parent household is made manifest when the child fails to perform an expected task. In the two-parent household, the parents may decide that the chore is beyond the child's capacity, or that getting the child to help is more trouble than it is worth, or that the child requires discipline or a lecture on household citizenship. In any event, a decision will usually be made on the parental level regarding how the issue is to be handled. In the one-parent household the child will be directly confronted by the parent. The child is failing to meet a *partnership* responsibility. One mother insisted that her children inspect her work-roughened hands so that they would realize that she was doing *her* part. Several single parents reported exploding, ''I can't do it all myself. I *must* have your help!'' In the two-parent family a chore undone may mean more work for the parents. In the one-parent family it means this and more: the same chore represents a threat to the partnership understandings the parent has attempted to establish with the children in order to keep the household going.

The definition of the children as junior partners in the management of the household permits the children new rights and authority as well as requiring new responsibilities of them. Given that the children are affected by the decisions and will be expected to cooperate in their realization, to consult them seems only sensible. One woman, mother of two girls aged seven and five said:

We all make decisions together as far as making plans on where we're going, what we're going to eat, or, if they go with me to the store, they help make decisions as far as things that I buy for the house. They make decisions on their own clothes, of course.

One way in which a single parent may share managerial responsibility with a child is by making the child responsible for younger children in the family. This delegation of parental responsibility may happen even though the older child is still quite young. Another way in which a single parent may share managerial responsibility is by asking a child to assume responsibilities that might, in a marriage, have been assumed by the spouse. Thus, a single father may rely on an elder daughter to act as hostess and housekeeper as well as to keep an eye on the other children; and a single mother may rely on an elder son to do the heavy work around the house. One mother said:

> I expect my seventeen-year-old son to understand that even if his friends don't explain to the plumber what happened, that in his particular situation he should do it, because a plumber will pay more attention to another male.

Parents are sometimes brought up short when others remark on the shift that has taken place in their relationships with one or more of the children. One woman found it entirely natural to consult her six-year-old son, her only child, about when they would have supper, until a friend remarked that few other six-year-olds were treated by their parents as though they were peers. Occasionally parents are forced by a sudden sense of incongruity to recognize the shift themselves. One woman described wondering, on being criticized by her fifteen-year-old son for being late with dinner, whether she had encouraged her son to assume the prerogatives of man of the house.

Single parents sometimes report that one of their children competes with them for the leadership role within the family. The child may intrude, challenging the parent's authority, when the parent is talking with one of the other children. Or a child may attempt to play the role of parent in a helpful fashion, just as might the second parent in a two-parent household. One mother said:

> My oldest son has taken on that role of being a parent, telling the others what they should do and what they shouldn't do and how he will send so-and-so to bed if so-and-so doesn't do this or that. And he'll take on all kinds of responsibilities. And I don't think it's good for him, because he's only eleven.

Parents react in quite different ways to these developments. Some are concerned; others are more complacent. Some assume that it is only to be expected that if there is a vacant parental role one or another of the children will want to fill it. One mother of four children spoke of her eldest son as being piqued because her second son, apparently a more attractive boy, had become the one the youngest two children looked to for direction. Sometimes the issue of the vacant parental role becomes a matter for family discussion. One mother reported that after she and her husband separated, her oldest son said that he was not about to become man of the family for her. She said she replied, "I just got rid of one. Why should I want another?"

If single parents work or have evening activities that take them out of the home, their children sooner or later are required to assume a great deal of responsibility for themselves in addition to their other familial responsibilities. The children are likely to be required to look after themselves, for intervals of varying lengths of time, beginning when the children are quite young. One woman said:

> I leave for work at seven-thirty and my son doesn't leave for school until eight-thirty. Five years ago if you had said, "What do you think about leaving an eight-year-old," I'd have looked at you in horror.

Many parents who work, like the parent above, must leave home before their children leave for school and then use the telephone to keep in touch with their children when the children have returned home. And so children may be required to make their own breakfasts and fix their own lunches, get themselves off to school, and then look after themselves on returning home from school, perhaps at that point remaining within their homes so their parents can be assured that they are staying out of trouble.

In a single-parent household, there may be no one other than the children for the parent to confide in or to turn to for advice or company, especially about household and family problems. In a well-functioning two-parent household, parents bring to each other their tensions and uncertainties. Even in a badly functioning two-parent household, the echelon structure of the household encourages parents to discuss central family-related issues with each other. Certainly it acts as a deterrent to either parent confiding in the children. In a one-parent household the children easily become friends and confidants. Thus there is often greater closeness between the single parent and the children than there was when the parent was married. (George and Wilding, 1972, also comment on this point.) In addition, the parent can justify sharing worries with the children because the children are understood as having some responsibility for the household. Said one parent: "You're hit with these bills and who can you talk to about it but the kids? It's the only other people that you can really talk to. You have to have someone to share it with and so you share it with the people that you're doing it for. And, every so often, if they're bugging me for something that costs too much money, that's out of proportion to what I can afford, I take the bills out and show them the bills, show them what we get in monthly and say, 'Now you make sense of it.'"

The ending of the echelon structure permits children to define themselves as peers of the parent—younger peers, but still peers—and the sharing of responsibility together with the development of companionship between parents and children encourages the children in this definition. But parents may go beyond simply being open and companionate with their children. Especially during the troubled months immediately following the ending of their marriages, single parents may rely on their children for comfort, reassurance, and the sort of nurturant caring that might be called parental. One mother of two boys, aged four and six at the time of her divorce, said:

> At the time of my emotional instability I stayed with the kids and I really did draw from them a lot of strength. I'm not sure that was good for them or for me, but that was what I did.

We might, in these instances, characterize the parent-child relationship as in a state of role reversal. Role reversals seem usually to be of brief duration. The inappropriateness of the reversed roles appears to be recognized by both parent and child, and to create discomfort for both. The parent's discomfort may be especially strong should a child assume the role of admonitory adult. The child in the following report was about ten:

> I called my house and Mark said, "When are you coming home?" And I said, "Pretty soon." And he said, "Ma, it's a quarter of eight. Now you had better get home here quick." And I said, "Okay, Mark. I'm just having drinks with a few friends." And he said, "Well, don't drink too much and be home soon." And I said, "All right, give me about an hour." And he said, "Are you sure?" And I said, "Yes, about an hour." And I got off the phone, and I said, "I did this with my mother when I was a kid! I'd call up and have to give these excuses! And I'm still doing it and I'm twenty-nine years old!"

THE EFFECTS OF THE CHILD OF CHANGED HOUSEHOLD ROLES

There are many reasons why children in single-parent households become more responsible, more independent, and more alert to adult values and concerns than other children of the same age. They are likely to be required to make greater contributions to the functioning of their families than are other children, to be more actively involved in family decision-making, to play the roles of junior partners to their parents in the management of their households and, often, to serve as quasi-parents to younger siblings. Also, they may be encouraged to develop relationships with their parents that are more like the relationship of friend and confidant than like that ordinarily understood as holding between child and parent. The changes in the child are functional for the parent and for the family unit. Are they of value to the child?

Those observers who have noted the changed roles of children in single-parent families have been cautious in assessing their meaning for the children. Gardner writes, "Some regress in response to the new demands and others rise to the occasion and attain a new salutary maturity. There are others, however, whose new maturity is spurious" (1976:169). And George and Wilding report that the single fathers in their study were divided about the value of the additional responsibility their children were required to assume: "Some felt it made children more independent and they thought it would stand the children in good stead one day. Others felt that their children suffered as they had less time to play, to do school work or other things they wanted to" (1972:73).

Our respondents generally saw the changes produced in their children by the children's new responsibilities to have been largely beneficial, although they sometimes regretted that their children had not had a more carefree childhood and adolescence. With the exception of a few parents who worried that they had lost control of their children, parents were pleased that their children had proven so capable of rising to the challenge of increased responsibility.

Adolescents living within single-parent families, although they tended to agree with their parents that they had been required to move toward early maturity in a number of ways, seemed to see the experience as of mixed value. It meant less security; they learned to share their parents' worries. Several adolescents whose parents were separated or divorced said that they were constantly aware that their parents were financially pressed. Their fathers complained to them of their mothers' financial demands, and their mothers complained of their fathers' unwillingness to help. Or their mothers asked them to tell their fathers that they needed clothes or school books or money for orthodonture, while the fathers told them to tell their mothers to be more reasonable. A few children had shifted their residence from mothers' homes to fathers' homes and had then been made aware of disputes between the parents over whether their fathers remained liable for support payments. One adolescent girl, reviewing her childhood, said:

> You don't have, not necessarily the childhood, but you don't have the freedom of not worrying about things, about money.

Some adolescents report having been made quite insecure by their parents' concern about money. One girl told of checking her downstairs food pantry to reassure herself that it was filled with canned goods.

Awareness of their parents' problems and uncertainties led adolescents to recognize that their parents were people like themselves, with frailties as well as strengths. Further impetus to seeing their parents as vulnerable came from adolescents' observations of the parents' attempts to establish new cross-sex relationships. They learned that their parents could be elated when things went well in the parents' dating life, and depressed when they went badly, just as was true for them. They may also have been led to recognize their parents' uncertainty in sexual matters, and to see their parents as beset by some of the same conflicts that troubled them. This more realistic view of their parents was strengthened when the parents turned to them, as junior partners in the household or as confidants, for understanding and support. Recognizing the parents' frailties reduced the adolescents' ability to rely unquestioningly on them and led to feelings of insecurity as well as to resolutions to be self-reliant: indeed, adolescents implied that they had become self-reliant just because there seemed no one else on whom they could rely. Here is a comment by a sixteen-year-old girl that expressed this feeling:

> I have become very independent. I am an independent person. I can probably get along by myself if I have to. Not completely. If my mother died, I'd be crying. But I'd get along. I think it's because I already do a lot of things by myself that, I suppose, if I had both parents, I wouldn't have to.

These children sometimes describe themselves as "loners": not isolated, but not deeply enmeshed in the peer culture either. Other children sometimes see them as unusually serious and mature. One girl spoke of being used as "Dear Abby" by her friends. But most prominent in the self-description of these children is their sense of unusual competence. In contrast to children in two-parent homes, these children may regularly cook or clean the house, be responsible for their clothes, be responsible for younger children. They are likely to take pride in being able to carry more responsibility than their friends from two-parent households who, in their view, have been pampered. Here is a comment by a sixteen-year-old girl:

> I get very angry at times, like when I hear this girl, she said, "My mother yelled at me this morning because I didn't make my bed, and I am so upset today." And, I just think, "You little twerp! I have to make my bed, my mother's bed, I have to clean the whole house, I have to cook the dinner, I have to take trash out!" And I was just so angry.

These children, on recognizing how much more capable they are in certain respects than other children, may feel enhanced esteem for themselves. But they may also feel some envy of children who have had fewer responsibilities. One girl said:

> If there were two parents, it might be better. It would be kind of like when my grandmother comes. You come home and there is Grandmother. You know she's going to be there, you know she's going to have the house cleaned up and the table set. I don't know, just silly little things, that you don't have to come home and worry about it and do it yourself or try to get your sisters help to do it, because Mother isn't there.

It would seem accurate to say that most children of single-parent families, though they may be pleased that they proved able to meet the challenges of new expectations, also regret having had to do so. . . .

REFERENCES

Biller, H. 1974. *Paternal Deprivation*. Lexington, Mass.: D. C. Heath.

Bowlby, J. 1973. *Attachment and Loss. II: Separation: Anxiety and Danger*. New York: Basic Books.

Gardner, R. A. 1976. *Psychotherapy with Children of Divorce*. New York: Aronson.

George, V. and P. Wilding, 1972. *Motherless Families*. London: Routledge & Kegan Paul.

Goffman, E. 1961. *Asylums*. Garden City, N.Y.: Doubleday.

Klebanow, S. 1976. Parenting in the single-parent family. *Journal of the American Academy of Psychoanalysis*. 4:37–48.

Longfellow, C. 1979. "Divorce in context: Its impact on children," in G. Levinger and O. Moles (eds.), *Divorce and Separation*. New York: Basic Books.

Wallerstein, J. S., and J. B. Kelley. 1974. "The effects on parental divorce: The adolescent experience," in E. J. Anthony and C. Koupernik (eds.), *The Child and His Family— Children at a Psychiatric Risk*, III. New York: John Wiley.

Reading 24

The Social Construction of Deviance: Experts on Battered Women

Donileen R. Loseke
Spencer E. Cahill

Skidmore College

SOCIOLOGICAL IMPLICATIONS OF THE QUESTION

The question "why do they stay?" implicitly defines the parameters of the social problem of battered women. By asking this question, the experts imply that assaulted wives are of two basic types: those who leave their mates and those who do not. Not only are possible distinctions among assaulted wives who remain with their mates implicitly ignored, but so too are the unknown number of assaulted wives who quickly terminate such relationships. By focusing attention on those who stay, the experts imply that assaulted wives who remain with their mates are more needy and deserving of public and expert concern than those who do not. In fact, some of the experts have explicitly defined battered women as women who *remain* in relationships containing violence (Ferraro and Johnson, 1983; Pizzey, 1979; Scott, 1974; Walker, 1979).

Moreover, the experts' common and overriding concern with the question of why assaulted wives stay reveals their shared definition of the normatively expected response to the experience of battering. To ask why assaulted wives remain with

Reprinted with permission from *Social Problems* 31(3) (February 1984):296–310, abridged by The Society for the Study of Social Problems and by the authors.

their mates is to imply that doing so requires explanation. In general, as Scott and Lyman (1968) have noted, normatively expected behavior does not require explanation. It is normatively unanticipated, untoward acts which require what Scott and Lyman term an "account." By asking why battered women stay, therefore, the experts implicitly define leaving one's mate as the normatively expected response to the experience of wife assault. Staying, on the other hand, is implicitly defined as deviant, an act "which is perceived (i.e., recognized) as violating expectations" (Hawkins and Tiedeman, 1975:59).

In other words, once the experts identify a woman as battered, normative expectations regarding marital stability are reversed. After all, separated and divorced persons are commonly called upon to explain why their relationships "didn't work out" (Weiss, 1975). It is typically marital stability, "staying," which is normatively expected and marital instability, "leaving," which requires an account. However, as far as the experts on battered women are concerned, once wife assault occurs, it is marital stability which requires explanation.

In view of the experts' typifications of relationships within which wife assault occurs, this reversal of normative expectations seems only logical. Although research indicates that the severity and frequency of wife assault varies considerably across couples (Straus et al., 1980), the experts stress that, *on the average,* wife assault is more dangerous for victims than is assault by a stranger (U.S. Department of Justice, 1980). Moreover, most experts maintain that once wife assault has occurred within a relationship it will become more frequent and severe over time (Dobash and Dobash, 1979), and few believe that this pattern of escalating violence can be broken without terminating the relationship.[1] It is hardly surprising, therefore, that the experts on battered women define "leaving" as the expected, reasonable, and desirable response to the experience of wife assault.[2] Staying, in contrast, is described as "maladaptive choice behavior" (Waites, 1977–78), "self-destruction through inactivity" (Rounsaville, 1978), or, most concisely, "deviant" (Ferraro and Johnson, 1983). For the experts, battered women who remain with their mates pose an intellectual puzzle: Why are they so unreasonable? Why do they stay?

To ask such a question is to request an account. Experts who provide answers to this question are, therefore, offering accounts on behalf of battered women who remain with their mates. According to Scott and Lyman (1968), two general types of accounts are possible: justifications and excuses. A justification is an account which acknowledges the actor's responsibility for the behavior in question but

[1]There has been little systematic study of the possibility of change in relationships. Walker (1979) reports that her pessimism is based on clinical experience. See Coleman (1980) for a more optimistic prognosis.

[2]Of course, this commonsense deduction is also based on the common, although often unspoken, assumption that humans are "rational actors." If the basis of human motivation is a desire to maximize rewards and minimize costs, then why would a battered woman remain in such an obviously "costly" relationship?

challenges the imputation of deviance (''I did it, but I didn't do anything wrong''). An excuse, on the other hand, acknowledges the deviance of the behavior in question but relieves the actor of responsibility for it (''I did something wrong, but it wasn't my fault'').

Clearly, these different types of accounts elicit different kinds of responses. If the behavior in question is socially justifiable, then the actor was behaving reasonably, as normatively expected. The actor's ability or competence to manage everyday affairs without interference is not called into question (Garfinkel, 1967:57). In contrast, excusing behavior implies that the actor cannot manage everyday affairs without interference. Although the behavior is due to circumstances beyond the actor's control, it is admittedly deviant. By implication, assistance from others may be required if the actor is to avoid behaving similarly in the future. In order to fully understand the experts' responses to battered women who remain with their mates it is necessary, therefore, to determine which type of account they typically offer on behalf of such women.

THE EXPERTS' ACCOUNTS

Experts on battered women are a diverse group. This diversity is reflected in the emphasis each expert places on various accounts, in the number of accounts offered, and in how series of accounts are combined to produce complex theoretical explanations. Despite such diversity, however, there is a sociologically important similarity among the experts' accounts. None of the experts argues that ''staying'' is justifiable. ''Staying'' is either explicitly or implicitly defined as unreasonable, normatively unexpected, and, therefore, deviant. By implication, the accounts offered by the experts are excuses for women's deviant behavior, and they offer two basic types.[3] Battered women are said to remain with their mates because of external constraints on their behavior or because of internal constraints. In either case, the accounts offered by the experts acknowledge the deviance of staying but relieve battered women of responsibility for doing so.

External Constraints

Almost all contemporary experts on battered women maintain that staying is excusable due to external constraints on women's behavior (Dobash and Dobash,

---

[3]A third type of explanation for why victims of wife assault remain with their mates is seldom found in the literature on battered women and, therefore, will not be reviewed here. This type of explanation is based on a systems theory analysis of family interactions. Straus (1974) suggests the empirical applicability of such an approach, and Denzin (1983) provides a phenomenological foundation. Erchak (1981) used this approach to explain the maintenance of child abuse, and Giles-Sims (1983) has used this to explain the behavior of battered women.

1979; Freeman, 1979; Langley and Levy, 1977; Martin, 1976; Pagelow, 1981a,b; Pizzey, 1979; Ridington, 1977–78; Roy, 1977; Shainess, 1977).

> Why does she not leave? The answer is simple. If she has children but no money and no money and no place to go, she has no choice. (Fleming, 1979:83)

Clearly, such accounts are based on the assumption that battered women who stay are economically dependent upon their mates. If a woman has no money and no place to go, she cannot be held responsible for the unreasonable act of staying. She has no choice.

Although this excuse is the most prevalent in the literature on battered women, further elaboration is necessary. In its simplest form, such an account can be easily challenged: What about friends, family, the welfare system, and other social service agencies? In response to such challenges, experts must offer accounts which will excuse women for not taking advantage of such assistance. Experts meet these challenges with at least two further accounts of external constraints. First, experts claim that most battered women are interpersonally isolated. Even if they are not, family and friends are said to typically blame women for their problems instead of providing assistance (Carlson, 1977; Dobash and Dobash, 1979; Fleming, 1979; Hilberman and Munson, 1977–78; Truninger, 1971). Second, experts claim that social service agencies typically provide little, if any, assistance. In fact, experts maintain that the organization of agencies (bureaucratic procedures and agency mandates to preserve family stability) and the behavior of agency personnel (sexism) discourage battered women who attempt to leave (Bass and Rice, 1979; Davidson, 1978; Dobash and Dobash, 1979; Higgins, 1978; Martin, 1976, 1978; McShane, 1979; Pizzey, 1979; Prescott and Letko, 1977; Truninger, 1971). In other words, the experts maintain that battered women can expect little assistance in overcoming their economic dependency. According to the experts, the excuse of economic dependency should be honored given the additional excuses of unresponsive friends, family, and social service agencies.

Although the external constraint type of excuse acknowledges that staying is unreasonable, it relieves battered women of the responsibility for doing so. Battered women who remain with their mates are portrayed as "more acted upon than acting" (Sykes and Matza, 1957:667). The implication, of course, is that women would leave (i.e., they would be reasonable) if external constraints could be overcome. The experts provide a warrant, therefore, for intervention in battered women's everyday affairs. In order to act reasonably and leave, battered women must overcome the external constraint of economic dependency which they cannot do without the assistance of specialized experts.

Despite the prevalence of external constraint accounts in the literature on battered women, most experts consider such excuses insufficient. Instead of, or in addition to, such accounts, the experts maintain that battered women face a second type of constraint on their behavior. Although few contemporary experts argue that women stay because they enjoy being the objects of abuse, that they are masochistic, the experts do maintain that battered women face various "internal constraints."[4]

Internal Constraints

Some experts have proposed that biographically accumulated experiences may lead women to define violence as "normal" and "natural" (Ball, 1977; Gelles, 1976; Langley and Levy, 1977; Lion, 1977). Likewise, according to some experts, women define violence as a problem only if it becomes severe and/or frequent "enough" (Carlson, 1977; Gelles, 1976; Moore, 1979; Rounsaville and Weissman, 1977–78).[5] If violence is not subjectively defined as a "problem," then women have no reason to consider leaving.

For the most part, experts have focused their attention on documenting internal constraints which are said to prevent women from leaving their mate *even when* violence is subjectively defined as a problem. Experts suggest two major sources of such internal constraints: femininity and the experience of victimization.

To many experts, the primary source of internal constraints is the femininity of battered women. Attributes commonly regarded as "feminine" are automatically attributed to battered women, especially when these characteristics can conceivably account for why such women might remain with their mates. For example, women who stay are said to be emotionally dependent upon their mates (Dobash and Dobash, 1979; Fleming, 1979; Freeman, 1979; Langley and Levy, 1977; Moore, 1979; Pizzey, 1979; Roy, 1977); to have a poor self-image or low self-esteem (Carlson, 1977; Freeman, 1979; Langley and Levy, 1977; Lieberknecht, 1978; Martin, 1976; Morgan, 1982; Ridington, 1977–78; Star et al., 1979; Truninger, 1971); and to have traditional ideas about women's "proper place."[6] In isolation or in combination, these so-called feminine characteristics are said to internally constrain women's behavior. According to the experts, women find it subjectively difficult to leave their mates even when violence is defined as a problem.

[4]Theories focusing on feminine masochism have been proposed by Snell et al (1964) and Gayford (1975). Waites (1977–78) suggested that the "appearance" of masochism results from "enforced restriction of choice." Most experts argue that the concept of masochism is not applicable to battered women (Breines and Gordon, 1983).

[5]Empirical testing of the association between leaving and childhood experiences has not confirmed this theory (Pagelow, 1981a; Star, 1978; Walker, 1977–78). Likewise, empirical testing of the association between leaving and "severity/frequency" has also not supported theory. See Pagelow (1981b) for a complete discussion.

[6]"Traditional ideology" includes such beliefs as: divorce is a stigma (Dobash and Dobash, 1979; Langley and Levy, 1977; Moore, 1979; Roy, 1977); the children need their father (Dobash and Dobash, 1979); the woman assumes responsibility for the actions of her mate (Fleming, 1979; Langley and Levy, 1977; Martin, 1976); or feels embarrassed about the family situation (Ball and Wyman, 1977–78; Fleming, 1979; Hendrix et al., 1978).

Internal constraints are also said to follow from the process of victimization itself. According to the experts, battered women not only display typically feminine characteristics, but they also develop unique characteristics due to the victimization process. For example, some experts have argued that once a woman is assaulted she will fear physical reprisal if she leaves (Lieberknecht, 1978; Martin, 1979; Melville, 1978). Other physical, emotional, and psychological after-effects of assault are also said to discourage battered women from leaving their mates (Moore, 1979; Roy, 1977). Indeed, battered women are sometimes said to develop complex psychological problems from their victimization. These include the ''stress-response syndrome'' (Hilberman, 1980), ''enforced restriction of choice'' (Waites, 1977–78), ''learned helplessness'' (Walker, 1979), or responses similar to those of the ''rape trauma syndrome'' (Hilberman and Munson, 1977–78). A symptom common to all such diagnostic categories is that sufferers find it subjectively difficult to leave their mates.

As with external constraint excuses, these internal constraint accounts also acknowledge the deviance of remaining in a relationship containing violence while, at the same time, relieving battered women of responsibility for doing so. They function in this way, as excuses, because the various internal constraints attributed to battered women are identified as beyond their personal control. Clearly, battered women are not responsible for their gender socialization or for the physical violence they have suffered. In other words, both external and internal constraint accounts portray battered women who stay with their mates as more acted upon than acting. What women require, ''for their own good,'' is assistance in overcoming the various barriers which prevent them from acting reasonably. Thus, both types of accounts offered by the experts on behalf of battered women who stay provide grounds for expert intervention in these women's everyday affairs.

As Scott and Lyman (1968) have pointed out, the criteria in terms of which accounts are evaluated vary in relation to the situation in which they are offered, the characteristics of the audience, and the identity of the account provider. In the present context, the identity of the account provider is of particular interest. When experts provide accounts which implicitly serve to promote their right to intervene in others' affairs, an important evaluative criterion is the quality of supportive evidence they offer. Experts who speak on behalf of others are expected to do so on the basis of uncommon knowledge. If, therefore, the evidence which the experts offer in support of their accounts for why battered women stay fails to confirm the expectation of uncommon knowledge, then their claim to be speaking and acting on such women's behalf is open to question.

THE EVIDENCE FOR EXPERTS' ACCOUNTS

How do experts obtain their knowledge about the experiences and behavior of battered women? In order to explore the experts' claim to uncommon knowledge, we address three questions: From whom is evidence obtained (the issue of generalizability)? By what means is evidence obtained (the issue of validity)? How consistently does the evidence support the accounts offered (the issue of reliability)?

Generalizability

Experts on battered women claim to have knowledge of the experiences and behavior of women who remain in relationships containing violence. Yet, while there is general agreement that many battered women suffer in silence, with few exceptions the experts have studied only those assaulted wives who have come to the attention of social service agencies, many of whom have already left their mates.[7] Women who contact social service agencies have decided that they require expert intervention in their private affairs, and there is good reason to believe that such women differ from women who have *not* sought assistance.

The decision to seek professional help is typically preceded by a complex process of problem definition, and this process is invariably more difficult and of longer duration when the problem involves the behavior of a family member (Goffman, 1969; Schwartz, 1957; Weiss, 1975; Yarrow et al., 1955). Regardless of the nature of the problem, this definitional process seems to follow a fairly predictable pattern. Only as a last resort are professional helpers contacted (Emerson and Messinger, 1977; Kadushin, 1969; Mechanic, 1975). Since it is primarily the experiences of women who have reached the end of this help-seeking process which provide evidence for experts' accounts, the generalizability of this evidence is questionable.

Validity

When not simply stating their own perceptions of battered women, experts obtain their evidence in one of two ways. They sometimes question other experts and they sometimes directly question women. Clearly, others' perceptions, whether expert or not, are of uncertain validity. However, even the evidence based on battered women's responses to the question "why do you stay?" is of doubtful validity.

To ask a battered woman to respond to this question is to request that she explain her apparently deviant behavior. This leaves her two alternatives. She can either justify her staying ("I love him;" "he's not all bad;" "the kids need him") or she can excuse her behavior. Since experts have predefined staying as undeniably deviant, it is unlikely that they will honor a justification. Indeed, some experts on battered women have explicitly characterized justifications for staying as "ra-

---

[7]Exceptions are Gelles (1976), Hofeller (1982), and Rosenbaum and O'Leary (1981), who included matched samples of persons not receiving services, and Prescott and Letko (1977) who used information from women who responded to an advertisement in *Ms.* magazine.

tionalizations,'' accounts which are self-serving and inaccurate (Ferraro and Johnson, 1983; Waites, 1977–78). Given the experts' presuppositions about the behavior of "staying" and the typical desire of persons to maintain "face" (Goffman, 1955), it is likely that the only accounts the experts will honor—excuses—are subtly elicited by the experts who question battered women. If this is so, then the experts, by asking women why they remain with their mates, have merely constructed an interactional situation which will produce evidence confirming the accounts they offer on women's behalf.[8]

It is hardly surprising, therefore, that the experts on battered women offer remarkably similar accounts of why women stay. This is particularly visible in the evidence which supports the external constraint accounts. By almost exclusively interviewing women who turn to inexpensive or free social service agencies and then constructing an interactional situation which is likely to elicit a particular type of account, experts practically ensure that their presuppositions about external constraints are confirmed.[9] In brief, the validity of the experts' evidence is doubtful.

Reliability

Relying primarily on evidence from interviewing and observation, the experts on battered women offer amazingly similar accounts of why women remain. There are, however, many ways to obtain evidence. The question at hand is whether evidence gained from interviewing and observation is similar to evidence obtained using other methods.

If the economic dependency (external constraint) excuse is to avoid challenge, it must be supplemented by the additional excuses of unresponsive friends, family members, and social service agencies. Yet, evidence to support these supplementary external constraint excuses is less than overwhelming. In fact, some evidence undermines the excuse that social service agencies and providers discourage battered women from leaving their mates. Pagelow (1981a) found little relationship between her measures of "agency response" and the amount of time battered women had remained with their mates. Hofeller (1982) found that many battered women self-reported being either "completely" or "somewhat" satisfied with the efforts of social service agencies on their behalf.[10]

As with the excuse of unresponsive social service agencies, available evidence

---

[8]The situation is more complicated when women who have left are asked why *did* you stay? Or, as Dobash and Dobash (1979:147) asked: "Why do you think you stayed with him as long as you did?" In such situations, the question asks women to retrospectively reconstruct their personal biographies based on their current circumstances and understandings.

[9]However, Rounsaville (1978) found that "lack of resources" did not distinguish between women who had left and women who had not left.

[10]The "satisfaction" of victims with social services varies considerably by the type of agency (Hofeller, 1982; Prescott and Letko, 1977).

conflicts with various internal constraint accounts offered by the experts. For example, available evidence does not support assertions that battered women hold traditional beliefs about "women's proper place," or that these beliefs internally constrain women from leaving their mates. Walker (1983) reports that battered women perceive themselves to be *less* traditional than "other women," and the results of experimental studies conducted by Hofeller (1982) and Rosenbaum and O'Leary (1981) indicate that women who have *not* been victims of wife assault hold more traditional attitudes than women who are victims. Moreover, Pagelow (1981a) reports that her measures of "traditional ideology" did not help explain the length of time battered women remained with their mates.

The experts have also maintained that the low self-esteem assumed to be common to women in general is exacerbated by the process of victimization, producing a powerful internal constraint on the behavior of battered women. Yet in their now classic review of research evidence regarding sex differences in self-esteem, Maccoby and Jacklin (1974:15) labelled as a popular myth the commonsense deduction that "women, knowing that they belong to a sex that is devalued . . . must have a poor opinion of themselves." Contrary to this commonsense deduction, sex differences in self-esteem have rarely been found in experimental studies, and when they have, women's self-esteem is often higher than men's. In addition, at least two studies contained in the literature on battered women refute the statement that battered women have lower self-esteem than women who have not experienced assault. Walker (1983) found that battered women reported their self-esteem has higher than that of "other women," and Star (1978) found that shelter residents who had *not* experienced wife assault scored lower on an "ego-strength" scale than residents who had been assaulted.

In short, the evidence provided to support expert claims about battered women is, by scientific standards, less than convincing. In fact, it appears as if the experts' accounts are presupposed and then implicitly guide both the gathering and interpretation of evidence. In constructing their accounts, the experts have employed the commonsense practice of automatically attributing to individual women (in this case, battered women) sets of traits based on their sex. As females, battered women are automatically assumed to be economically and emotionally dependent upon their mates, to have low self-esteem, and to hold traditional attitudes and beliefs. Methodologies which might yield conflicting evidence are seldom used, and when seemingly conflicting evidence is uncovered it is often explained away. For example, Walker (1983:40) implicitly argues that battered women have an inaccurate perception of themselves. She interprets the finding that battered women consider themselves to be in control of their own behavior as a "lack of acknowledgment that her batterer *really* is in control" (emphasis added). Likewise, Pagelow (1981a) discredits seemingly conflicting evidence by challenging her own measures; the presupposed accounts are not questioned. In other words, the interpretive force of the "master status" of sex "overpowers" evidence to the contrary (Hughes,

1945:357). What the experts on battered women offer in support of their accounts for why women remain is not uncommon knowledge, therefore, but professional "folklore" which, however sophisticated, remains folklore (Zimmerman and Pollner, 1970:44).

This does not mean that evidence which conflicts with the experts' accounts is itself above question. On the contrary, the generalizability, reliability, and validity of conflicting evidence is also problematic. For example, both Pagelow (1981a) and Star (1978) used paper and pencil tests, and both studies were primarily concerned with residents of shelters in urban southern California. Likewise, Walker's (1979, 1983) findings are based primarily on clinical records of an unrepresentative group of women, and evidence regarding self-esteem is primarily derived from experimental studies involving only college students.

The sociologically intriguing issue is not, however, the "truthfulness" of accounts. In a diverse society, a variety of different vocabularies of motive (Mills, 1940) are available for making sense out of the complex interrelationships between actor, biography, situation, and behavior. Under such circumstances, "what is reason for one man is mere rationalization for another" (Mills, 1940:910). Any attempt to ascertain battered women's "true" motives would therefore be an exercise in what Mills termed "motive-mongering." What is of sociological interest is that the experts' accounts are not based upon uncommon knowledge but upon commonsense deductions best described as folklore. Clearly, this should raise questions about both the experts' claim to be speaking on battered women's behalf and their claim to have the right to intervene in such women's private affairs.

Given the experts' claim to be speaking and acting in battered women's "best interests," the sociologically important issue is the relative plausibility of the particular vocabulary of motive used by the experts. According to the experts, their primary concerns are the condemnation and elimination of wife assault, tasks which are likely to require specialized expertise. The vocabulary of motive which supports this agenda is one of highlighting "constraints" on women's behavior which must be overcome in order for them to behave reasonably—that is, in order for them to leave. But such a vocabulary is not the only plausible way to make sense of women's behavior.

AN ALTERNATIVE VOCABULARY OF MOTIVE

Prior to the 1970s, the problems of battered women received little attention. In contrast, the contemporary experts have portrayed women as little more than victims. The tendency has been to define both battered women and their relationships with their mates almost exclusively in terms of the occurrence and effects of physical and emotional assault. Battered women are simply defined as assaulted wives who remain with assaultive mates (Ferraro and Johnson, 1983; Pizzey, 1979; Scott, 1974; Walker, 1979), and their relationships are portrayed as no more than victimizing processes. Such a focus leads to what Barry (1979) has termed "victimism," knowing a person only as a victim. One effect of the victimism practiced by the experts on battered women is that possible experiential and behavioral similarities between battered women and other persons are overlooked. It is simply assumed that the occurrence and experience of assault clearly distinguishes battered women and their relationships from individuals in cross-sex relationships which do not contain violence. However, even a cursory review of the sociological literature on marital stability and instability suggests that, at least in regard to their reluctance to leave their mates, battered women are quite similar to both other women and to men.

This literature consistently indicates that marital stability often outlives marital quality. Goode (1956) found that such stability was only sometimes due to the obvious, objective costs of terminating the relationship ("external constraints"). Contrary to predictions that relationships will terminate when apparent "costs" outweigh apparent "benefits," it is not at all unusual for relationships to be sustained even when outsiders perceive costs to be greater than benefits. Although experts on battered women have argued that leaving a relationship means that a woman's status will change from "wife" to "divorcee" (Dobash and Dobash, 1979; Truninger, 1971), a variety of family sociologists have noted that terminating a relationship is far more complex than is suggested by the concept of "status change." Over time, marital partners develop an "attachment" to one another (Weiss, 1975), a "crescive bond" (Turner, 1970), a "shared biography" (McLain and Weigert, 1979). As a result, each becomes uniquely irreplaceable in the eyes of the other. Such a personal commitment to a specific mate has been found to persist despite decreases in marital partners' liking, admiration, and/or respect for one another (Rosenblatt, 1977; Weiss, 1975). Battered women who remain in relationships which outsiders consider costly are not, therefore, particularly unusual or deviant.

Moreover, the sociological literature on marital stability and instability suggests that the process of separation and divorce, what Vaughan (1979) terms "uncoupling," is typically difficult. One indication of the difficulty of this process is the considerable time uncoupling often takes (Cherlin, 1981; Goode, 1956; Weiss, 1975). It is also typical for a series of temporary separations to precede a permanent separation (Lewis and Spanier, 1979; Weiss, 1975; Vaughan, 1979). In brief, the lengthy "leaving and returning" cycle said to be characteristic of battered women is a typical feature of the uncoupling process. Further, the guilt, concern, regret, bitterness, disappointment, depression, and lowered perception of self attributed to battered women are labels for emotions often reported by women and men in the process of uncoupling (Spanier and Castro, 1979; Weiss, 1975).

Although the experts attribute unusual characteristics and circumstances to battered women who remain with their mates, the reluctance of battered women to leave can be adequately and commonsensically expressed in the lyrics of a popular song: "Breaking up is hard to do." It can also be expressed in the more sophisticated vocabulary of sociological psychology: Individuals who are terminating intimate relationships "die one of the deaths that is possible" for them (Goffman, 1952). The sociological literature on marital stability and instability does suggest, therefore, an alternative to the vocabulary of battered women's motives provided by the experts on battered women. Because a large portion of an adult's self is typically invested in their relationship with their mate, persons become committed and attached to this mate as a uniquely irreplaceable individual. Despite problems, "internal constraints" are experienced when contemplating the possibility of terminating the relationship with the seemingly irreplaceable other. Again, if this is the case, then women who remain in relationships containing violence are not unusual or deviant; they are typical.

Some experts on battered women have reported evidence which supports this alternative characterization of the motives of women who remain. Gayford (1975) reports that half of his sample of battered women claimed to be satisfied with their relationships, and Dobash and Dobash (1979) note that, apart from the violence, battered women often express positive feelings toward their mates. Moreover, Ferraro and Johnson (1983) report that battered women typically believe that their mates are the only person they could love, and Walker (1979) reports that battered women often describe their mates as playful, attentive, exciting, sensitive, and affectionate. Yet, because of the victimism they practice, experts on battered women often fail to recognize that such findings demonstrate the multi-dimensionality of battered women's relationships with their mates. Indeed, some of these experts have explicitly advised that battered women's expressions of attachment and commitment to their mates not be believed:

> The statement that abused wives love their husbands need not be taken at face value. It may represent merely a denial of ambivalence or even unmitigated hatred. (Waites, 1977–78:542).

> The only reasons the woman does not end the marriage are dependence—emotional or practical—and fear of change and the unknown. These are often masked as love or so the woman deludes herself. (Shainess, 1977:118)

Such expressions of commitment and attachment are *justifications* for why a person might remain with [her] mate. To honor such a justification would be to acknowledge that staying in a relationship which contains violence is not necessarily deviant. In order to sustain their claim to expertise, therefore, the experts on battered women cannot acknowledge the possible validity of this alternative, "justifying" vocabulary of motive even when it is offered by battered women themselves. In other words, the experts discredit battered women's interpretations of their own experiences. The justifications offered by battered women are reinterpreted by the experts as merely "symptoms" of the Stockholm Syndrome (Ochberg, 1980), of an "addiction" which "must be overcome" (Waites, 1977–78), or as the "miracle glue" which "binds a battered woman to her batterer" (Walker, 1979:xvi). By reinterpreting the justifications of battered women in these ways, the experts sustain their claim that such women require the assistance of specialized experts.

CONCLUSIONS

This case study of the social construction of deviance by a group of experts illustrates how members of the knowledge class create a new clientele for their services. In effect, experts discredit the ability of a category of persons to manage their own affairs without interference. The actors in question are portrayed as incapable of either understanding or controlling the factors which govern their behavior. In order for them to understand their experiences and gain control over their behavior, by implication, they require the assistance of specialized experts. Because the category of actors which compose such a clientele are characterized as unreasonable and incompetent, any resistance they offer to the experts' definitions and intervention is easily discredited. For example, battered women's attempts to justify staying with their mates are often interpreted by the experts as further evidence of such women's unreasonableness and incompetence. Experts are able to sustain their claims to be speaking and acting on others' behalf, therefore, despite the protests of those on whose behalf they claim to be speaking and acting.

We do not mean to suggest that experts' potential clientele do not benefit from experts' efforts. For example, the experts on battered women have played a major role in focusing public attention on the plight of the victims of wife assault. In doing so, they have helped to dispel the popular myth that these women somehow deserved to be assaulted. In turn, this has undoubtedly encouraged the general public, the police, the courts, and various social service agencies to be more responsive and sensitive to the needs of such women. Yet, battered women may pay a high price for this assistance.

The experts on battered women define leaving one's mate as the normatively expected, reasonable response to the experience of wife assault. By implication, staying with one's mate after such an experience requires explanation. In order to explain this unreasonable response, the experts have provided accounts, that is, ascribed motives to battered women which excuse such deviance. As Blum and McHugh (1971:106) have noted, "observer's ascription of motive serves to formulate . . . persons." In offering accounts on behalf of battered women who stay, the experts propose a formulation of the type of persons such women are. For example, the experts characterize this type of person as "oversocialized into feminine identity" (Ball and Wyman, 1977–78), "bewildered and helpless" (Ball, 1977), "immature" and lacking clear self-identities (Star et al., 1979), "overwhelmingly passive" and unable to act on their own behalf (Hilberman and Munson, 1977–78), and cognitively, emotionally, and motivationally "deficient" (Walker, 1977–78).

Moreover, these women are described as suffering from either the ''battered wife syndrome'' (Morgan, 1982; Walker, 1983) or the ''adult maltreatment syndrome'' in Section 995.8 of the International Classification of Diseases. They are ''society's problem'' (Martin, 1978). Clearly, the categorical identity of battered women is a deeply discrediting one. As Hawkins and Tiedeman (1975) have noted, such typifications of persons by experts often have significant, practical consequences. The experts' descriptions of such ''types'' often serve as ''processing stereotypes'' which influence the perceptions and responses of social service providers. Indeed, Loseke (1982) documented how the experts' typifications of battered women served as a processing stereotype which influenced workers' perceptions and service provision at a shelter for battered women.

In summary, once a woman admits that she is a victim of wife assault, her competence is called into question if she does not leave. She is defined as a type of person who requires assistance, a person who is unable to manage her own affairs. As a result, the experts on battered women have constructed a situation where victims of wife assault may lose control over their self-definitions, interpretations of experience, and, in some cases, control over their private affairs. In a sense, battered women may now be victimized twice, first by their mates and then by the experts who claim to speak on their behalf.

REFERENCES

Ball, Patricia G., and Elizabeth Wyman. 1977–78. ''Battered wives and powerlessness: What can counselors do?'' *Victimology* 2(3, 4):545–552.

Barry, Kathleen. 1979. *Female Sexual Slavery*. New York: Avon.

Bass, David, and Janet Rice. 1979. ''Agency responses to the abused wife.'' *Social Casework* 60 (June):338–342.

Breines, Wini, and Linda Gordon. 1983. ''The new scholarship on family violence.'' *Signs* 8 (Spring):490–531.

Carlson, Bonnie E. 1977. ''Battered women and their assailants.'' *Social Work* 22 (November):455–460.

Cherlin, Andrew J. 1981. *Marriage, Divorce, Remarriage*. Cambridge, Mass.: Harvard University Press.

Coleman, Karen Howes. 1980. ''Conjugal violence: What 33 men report.'' *Journal of Marital and Family Therapy* 6 (April):207–214.

Davidson, Terry. 1978. *Conjugal Crime*. New York: Hawthorne.

Denzin, Norman K. 1983. ''Towards a phenomenology of family violence.'' Paper presented at the meetings of the American Sociological Association. Detroit, August.

Dobash, R. Emerson, and Russell Dobash. 1979. *Violence Against Wives: A Case Against the Patriarchy*. New York: Free Press.

Emerson, Robert M., and Sheldon L. Messinger. 1977. ''The micro-politics of trouble.'' *Social Problems* 25 (December):121–134.

Erchak, Gerald M. 1981. ''The escalation and maintenance of child abuse: A cybernetic model.'' *Child Abuse and Neglect* 5:153–157.

Ferraro, Kathleen J., and John M. Johnson. 1983. "How women experience battering: The process of victimization." *Social Problems* 30 (February):325–339.

Fleming, Jennifer Baker. 1979. *Stopping Wife Abuse*. New York: Garden City, N.Y.: Anchor.

Freeman, M. D. A. 1979. *Violence in the Home*. Westmead, England: Saxon House.

Garfinkel, Harold. 1967. *Studies in Ethnomethodology*. Englewood Cliffs, N.J.: Prentice-Hall.

Gaylord, J. J. 1975. "Wife battering: A preliminary survey of 100 cases." *British Medical Journal* 1:194–197.

Gelles, Richard J. 1976. "Abused wives: Why do they stay?" *Journal of Marriage and the Family* 38(4):659–668.

Giles-Sims, Jean. 1983. *Wife Battering: A Systems Approach*. New York: Guilford Press.

Goffman, Erving. 1952. "On cooling the mark out: Some aspects of adaptation to failure." *Psychiatry* 15 (November):451–463.

———. 1969. "Insanity of place." *Psychiatry* 32 (November):352–388.

Goode, William J. 1956. *After Divorce*. Glencoe, Ill.: Free Press.

Hawkins, Richard, and Gary Tiedeman. 1975. *The Creation of Deviance: Interpersonal and Organizational Determinants*. Columbus, Ohio: Charles E. Merrill.

Hendrix, Melva Jo, Gretchen E. LaGodna, and Cynthia A. Bohen. 1978. "The battered wife." *American Journal of Nursing* 78 (April):650–653.

Higgins, John G. 1978. "Social services for abused wives." *Social Casework* 59 (May):266–271.

Hilberman, Elaine. 1980. "Overview: The 'Wife-beater's wife' reconsidered." *American Journal of Psychiatry* 137 (November):1336–1346.

———, and Kit Munson. 1977–78. "Sixty battered women." *Victimology* 2(3, 4):460–470.

Hofeller, Kathleen H. 1982. *Social, Psychological, and Situational Factors in Wife Abuse*. Palo Alto, Calif.: R. and E. Associates.

Hughes, Everett. 1945. "Dilemmas and contradictions of status." *American Journal of Sociology* 50 (March):353–359.

Kadushin, Charles. 1969. *Why People Go to Psychiatrists*. New York: Atherton.

Langley, Roger, and Richard C. Levy. 1977. *Wife Beating: The Silent Crisis*. New York: Pocket Books.

Lewis, Robert A., and Graham B. Spanier. 1979. "Theorizing about the quality and stability of marriage," pp. 268–294 in Wesley R. Burr, Reuben Hill, F. Ivan Nye, and Ira L. Reiss (eds), *Contemporary Theories About the Family*, Vol. 1. New York: Free Press.

Lieberknecht, Kay. 1978. "Helping the battered wife." *American Journal of Nursing* 78 (April):654–656.

Lion, John R. 1977. "Clinical aspects of wifebattering," pp. 126–136 in Maria Roy (ed.), *Battered Women: A Psychosociological Study of Domestic Violence*. New York: Van Nostrand Reinhold.

Maccoby, Eleanor Emmons, and Carol Nagy Jacklin. 1974. *The Psychology of Sex Differences*. Stanford, Calif.: Stanford University Press.

McLain, Raymond, and Andrew Weigert. 1979. "Toward a phenomenological sociology of family: A programmatic essay," pp. 160–205 in Wesley R. Burr, Reuben Hill, F. Ivan

Nye, and Ira L. Reiss (eds.), *Contemporary Theories About the Family,* Vol. 2. New York: Free Press.

McShane, Claudette. 1979. "Community services for battered women." *Social Work* 24 (January):34–39.

Martin, Del. 1976. *Battered Wives.* San Francisco: Glide Publications.

———. 1978. "Battered women: Society's problem," pp. 111–142 in Jane Roberts Chapman and Margaret Gates (eds.), *The Victimization of Women.* Beverly Hills, Calif.: Sage Publications.

———. 1979. "What keeps a woman captive in a violent relationship? The social context of battering," pp. 33–58 in Donna M. Moore (eds.), *Battered Women.* Beverly Hills, Calif.: Sage Publications.

Mechanic, David. 1975. "Sociocultural and social-psychological factors affecting personal responses to psychological disorder." *Journal of Health and Social Behavior* 16(4):393–404.

Melville, Joy. 1978. "Women in refuges," pp. 293–310 in J. P. Martin (ed.), *Violence and the Family.* New York: John Wiley.

Mills, C. Wright. 1940. "Situated actions and vocabularies of motive." *American Sociological Review* 5 (December):904–913.

Moore, Donna M. 1979. "An overview of the problem," pp. 7–32 in Donna M. Moore (ed.), *Battered Women.* Beverly Hills, Calif.: Sage Publications.

Morgan, Patricia A. 1981. "From battered wife to program client; The state's shaping of social problems." *Kapitalistate* 9:17–40.

Morgan, Steven M. 1982. *Conjugal Terrorism: A Psychological and Community Treatment Model of Wife Abuse.* Palo Alto: Calif.: R. and E. Associations.

Ochberg, F. M. 1980. "Victims of terrorism." *Journal of Clinical Psychiatry* 41:73–74.

Pagelow, Mildred Dailey. 1981a. *Woman-Battering: Victims and Their Experiences.* Beverly, Hills, Calif.: Sage Publications.

———. 1981b. "Factors affecting women's decisions to leave violent relationships." *Journal of Family Issues* 2 (December):391–414.

Pizzey, Erin. 1979. "Victimology interview: A refuge for battered women." *Victimology* 4(1):100–112.

Prescott, Suzanne, and Carolyn Letko. 1977. "Battered women: A social psychological perspective," pp. 72–96 in Maria Roy (ed.), *Battered Women: A Psychosociological Study of Domestic Violence.* New York: Van Nostrand Reinhold.

Ridington, Jillian. 1977–78. "The transition process: A feminist environment as reconstructive milieu." *Victimology* 2(3, 4):563–575.

Rosenbaum, Alan, and K. Daniel O'Leary. 1981. "Marital violence: Characteristics of abusive couples." *Journal of Consulting and Clinical Psychology* 49(1):63–71.

Rosenblatt, Paul C. 1977. "Needed research on commitment in marriage," pp. 73–86 in George Levinger and Harold L. Raush (eds.), *Close Relationships: Perspectives on the Meaning of Intimacy.* Amherst: University of Massachusetts.

Rounsaville, Bruce J. 1978. "Theories in marital violence: Evidence from a study of battered women." *Victimology* 21(1, 2):11–31.

Rounsaville, Bruce, and Myrna M. Weissman. 1977–78. "Battered women: A medical problem requiring detection." *International Journal of Psychiatry in Medicine* 8(2):191–202.

Roy, Maria. 1977. "A current survey of 150 cases," pp. 25–44 in Maria Roy (ed.), *Battered Women: A Psychosociological Study of Domestic Violence*. New York: Van Nostrand Reinhold.

Schwartz, Charlotte Green. 1957. "Perspectives on deviance: Wives' definitions of their husbands' mental illness." *Psychiatry* 20(3):275–291.

Scott, Marvin B., and Stanford, M. Lyman. 1968. "Accounts." *American Sociological Review* 33 (December):46–62.

Scott, P. D. 1974. "Battered wives." *British Journal of Psychiatry* 125 (November):433–441.

Shainess, Natalie. 1977. "Psychological aspects of wifebattering," pp. 111–118 in Maria Roy (ed.), *Battered Women: A Psychosociological Study of Domestic Violence*. New York: Van Nostrand Reinhold.

Snell, John E., M. D. Richard, J. Rosenwald, and Ames Robey. 1964. "The wifebeater's wife." *Archives of General Psychiatry* 11 (August):107–112.

Spanier, Graham, and Robert F. Castro. 1979. "Adjustment to separation and divorce: An analysis of 50 case studies." *Journal of Divorce* 2 (Spring):241–253.

Star, Barbara. 1978. "Comparing battered and non-battered women." *Victimology* 3(1, 2):32–44.

———, Carol G. Clark, Karen M. Goetz, and Linda O'Malia. 1979. "Psychosocial aspects of wife battering." *Social Casework* 60 (October):479–487.

Stark, Evan, and Anne Flitcraft. 1983. "Social knowledge, social policy, and the abuse of women: The case against patriarchal benevolence," pp. 330–348 in David Finkelhor, Richard J. Gelles, Gerald T. Hotaling, and Murray A. Straus (eds.), *The Dark Side of Families*. Beverly Hills, Calif.: Sage Publications.

Straus, Murray A. 1974. "Forward," pp. 13–17 in Richard J. Gelles, *The Violent Home*. Beverly Hills, Calif.: Sage Publications.

———, Richard J. Gelles, and Suzanne Steinmetz. 1980. *Behind Closed Doors: Violence in the American Home*. Garden City, N.Y.: Anchor.

Sykes, Gresham, and David Matza. 1957. "Techniques of neutralization: A theory of delinquency." *American Sociological Review* 22 (December):664–669.

Truninger, Elizabeth. 1971. "Marital violence: The legal solutions." *Hastings Law Journal* 23 (November):259–276.

Turner, Ralph. 1970. *Family Interaction*. New York: John Wiley.

Vaughan, Diane. 1979. "Uncoupling: The process of moving from one lifestyle to another." *Alternative Lifestyles* 2 (November):415–442.

Waites, Elizabeth A. 1977–78. "Female masochism and the enforced restriction of choice." *Victimology* 2(3, 4):535–544.

Walker, Lenore E. 1977–78. "Battered women and learned helplessness." *Victimology* 2(3, 4):525–534.

———. 1979. *The Battered Woman*. New York: Harper & Row.

———. 1983. "The battered woman syndrome study," pp. 31–48 in David Finkelhor, Richard J. Gelles, Gerald T. Hotaling, and Murray A. Straus (eds.), *The Dark Side of Families*. Beverly Hills, Calif.: Sage Publications.

Wardell, Laurie, Dair L. Gillespie, and Ann Leffler. 1983. "Science and violence against wives," pp. 69–84 in David Finkelhor, Richard J. Gelles, Gerald T. Hotaling, and

Murray A. Straus (eds.), *The Dark Side of Families*. Beverly Hills, Calif.: Sage Publications.

Weiss, Robert. 1975. *Martial Separation.* New York: Basic Books.

Yarrow, Marian Radke, Charlotte Green Schwartz, Harriet S. Murphy, and Leila Calhoun Desy. 1955. "The psychological meaning of mental illness in the family." *Journal of Social Issues* 11(4):12–24.

Zimmerman, Don, and Melvin Pollner. 1970. "The everyday world as a phenomenon," pp. 80–104 in Jack Douglas (ed.), *Understanding Everyday Life*. Chicago: Aldine.

Reading 25

Expect and Ye Shall Receive

William Ryan

There is an apocryphal story about an energentic teacher who was quite convinced that she gave her very best to every member of her classes and, in turn, got the very best out of each one of them. She was satisfied that this was so because, every year when school began, she would diligently collect information about the aptitudes of all of her pupils and keep their IQs—individual by individual—under the glass top of her desk, until she had virtually memorized them. At the end of every year, when she compared the achievements and grades of the students with their IQs, she found an almost perfect match—those with high aptitudes, with high IQs, did best; those with low IQs did worst. Every single child was performing to his capacity.

When a new principal came to the school, the teacher explained her system to him and demonstrated it in the classroom. She called on a pupil with a high IQ and he gave the right answer, and then on one with a low IQ, who gave a wrong answer. The principal was very interested and asked to borrow her list of IQs. The next day he came back to give it to her and said, "You're certainly right about the kiddoes performing just about the way these numbers say they should. I must tell you one thing, though. Instead of copying down your pupil's IQs, you've copied down their *locker numbers.*"

This story illustrates the central mechanism in the classroom by which the miracles of sorting and labeling that I discussed in the preceding section are accomplished: human beings, and particularly children, act the way we *expect* them to act, because we unconsciously convey to them what those expectations are. The teacher in the story expected children with high locker numbers to perform well, and those with low numbers to perform poorly, and they did.

Reprinted with permission from *Equality* (New York: Vintage, 1981), pp. 130–135 by Random House, Inc.

This process has now been demonstrated rather thoroughly in real life. Kenneth Clark and his associates in the HARYOU project, for example, concluded that Harlem schools were doing a poor job of educating Harlem children because the teachers in those schools *expected* the children to learn very little, and, naturally, they got what they expected. A few years later, Rosenthal and Jacobson demonstrated this point in their dramatic "Pygmalion in the Classroom" experiment.

This study has become very well known over the past few years, but I will summarize it very briefly. The experimenters were looking for the effects of expectations on behavior, the so-called self-fulfilling prophecy, and they tested it in the classrooms of an elementary school in San Francisco. At the end of one year, they administered a newly developed intelligence test to all the children in the school, but they gave it a meaningless high-sounding name, the "Test of Inflected Acquisition," and described it to the teachers as a new kind of test that would pick out children who were likely to show sudden intellectual improvement—"spurters" who would abruptly start to do much better in their school work. The test was obviously nothing of the sort, and they didn't use it for that purpose; rather, they just randomly selected 20 percent of the children—about five from each class—and casually informed the teachers that these were the ones the test had selected as potential "spurters." There was no intervention beyond this. At the beginning of the next year, they gave this false information to teachers in the hope of setting up expectations in their minds, before they even had a chance to see the children or get to know anything about them. Then they sat back to see the effect, which they measured by retesting the children later in the year and by getting personality and behavior ratings of the children from the teachers.

The results were striking. Most of the children who had been randomly picked out and labeled as potential "spurters" did in fact "spurt," particularly the younger children in the early grades, who showed tremendous gains on their tests. In addition, these children were seen by the teachers much more favorably than were their classmates; they appeared more curious and better adjusted, among other things. Finally, and in some ways most interesting of all, children *not* labeled as "spurters" who spurted anyway—who went *against* the expectations that had been set up in the teachers' minds—were viewed much more negatively, as showing undesirable behavior, being poorly adjusted, and so on.

Ray Rist followed up the Pygmalion experiment with a study in which he tried to find out more about how expectations form in teachers' minds in the ordinary classroom situation without any experimental intervention. He focused his attention on a single class in a ghetto school, all black children, starting with them in kindergarten and following them into the second grade, stopping along the way for frequent formal and informal observations of the classroom goings-on and for interviews with teachers. Again, the results are rather startling.

On the eighth day of school, the kindergarten teacher was prepared to divide thirty children into three distinct ability groups. Two and one-half years later, in the second grade, ten of the thirty were still in the same building (others had moved, had not been promoted, or were in other second-grade classes in an annex). Of the ten, six had been in the top-ability group in kindergarten. All six were in the top group in second grade. The other four had been in the middle and low groups in kindergarten. All were in the middle group in second grade. (By the second grade, the lowest group was made up predominantly of children who were repeating the year.) What an incredible evaluating and prognosticating ability that kindergarten teacher had! Think of it: after eight days of school with thirty little five-year-olds she had never seen before—that is, after an acquaintance of not much more than thirty hours—this teacher was able to sort them out precisely in terms of their academic abilities in a manner that would hold up for at least two and one-half years (and, as we know from other studies, would hold up almost as well for the full twelve years of school).

Rist watched the teachers and the children very closely during that first year of kindergarten, and he found some interesting relationships. It was quite clear in the teacher's own mind how she went about dividing up the children: the nine children at table one, she explained, were her "fast learners," the other twenty-one, at tables two and three, "had no idea of what was going on in the classroom." How could she spot the "fast learners" so quickly? Rist did notice a number of objective characteristics and behavior that differentiated the "fast learners" from the others. First of all, the "fast learners," as she labeled them, were all neatly dressed in clean clothes; this was true of only one of the twenty-one other children. Second, the table-one elite all interacted readily with the teacher and each other. Third, they were more verbal and used standard middle-class English almost all the time; the others were much less responsive verbally and tended to use the phrases and syntax of so-called Black English. Finally, the children differed in a number of background characteristics that were known to the teacher from preschool registration: the parents of the table-one children had much better educations, jobs, and incomes than had the parents of the others. None of these families were on welfare, whereas six of the twenty-one others were. Only one-third of the table-one children did not have both parents living in the home, whereas the great majority of the others— sixteen out of the twenty-one—came from one-parent families. These and similar social-class characteristics sharply differentiated the three groups, even more than did relative cleanliness and verbal skills. Somehow, then, the teacher's estimation of a five-year-old's academic ability, whether or not he was a fast learner, coincided precisely with whether or not he was a neat, clean, verbal kid from a middle-class family.

At this point, we can consider three possible explanations of this uncanny course of events. The first is that the kindergarten teacher had an eerie, almost clairvoyant capacity to sense the abilities of five-year-olds and that the remarkable correlation between her judgments and the background of the children was purely coincidental.

The second explanation involves what might be termed the Coleman-Herrn-stein hypothesis—that, because of either genetic or cultural differences, middle-class children do indeed have greater verbal skill, greater learning potential, and that an accurate prediction of who the fast learners will be inevitably means picking out the middle-class children.

The third explanation is that the teacher has a preconceived idea of what "fast learners" look and act like (namely, like the teacher herself), that her expectations are based on these preconceived ideas, and that her teaching style is such that she treats children from different class groups differently, conveys to them her own evaluations and expectations, and thereby produces the anticipated results.

Rist's observations tend to support the last explanation. For example, although the three tables faced a blackboard that ran along the entire length of the wall, the teacher consistently tended to stand in front of table one and to write on the board directly in front of her "fast learners." She gave the overwhelming majority of her attention to the table-one children and usually called on them to respond to questions, to tell what they did on Halloween, to take attendance, and to act as monitors. In one classroom hour that Rist observed, the teacher communicated exclusively with the children at table one, except for two commands of "Sit down!" directed at children seated at the other tables. To sum up the year, it is quite clear that the teacher *taught* the children at table one, and either ignored, belittled, or disciplined the other children. At the end of the year, of course, the table-one children had finished all of their kindergarten work, and were ready for the first grade and the great adventure of learning to read. The teacher was still persuaded that these were the children who were most capable and interested in school and that the others were "off in another world" and basically "low achievers." The latter were, in fact, already behind, and when they went to the first grade, they were not *permitted* to start the first-grade reading lessons until they had finished up the kindergarten work that their teacher had neglected to teach them the previous year. The process continued into the second grade, the gap widened, and the differences among the children became more pronounced. As Rist put it, "The child's journey through the early grades of school at one reading level and in one social grouping appeared to be preordained from the eighth day of kindergarten."

In addition, he noted that the belittling of the lower-track children was imitated by the high-track children, who gradually began to verbalize their own sense of superiority over those in the lower tracks. The labeling process was made quite manifest in the second grade, where the three different tables—instead of being called one, two, and three, as in kindergarten, or A, B, and C, as in the first grade—received characterizing labels that left no doubt in anyone's mind: the top group were the "Tigers," the middle group the "Cardinals," and the lowest group the "Clowns."

Other recent studies have discovered, with much more reliability and precision, the specific details of what Rist had been able to see so clearly at a more general level. Brophy and Good, and others, have developed detailed procedures for observing and coding interactions in the classroom between teacher and pupils and have shown that, even when there is no substantial difference in the *quantity* of interaction between high-expectancy and low-expectancy groups, the *qualitative* differences are enormous. With students of whom they hold high expectations, teachers more often praise correct answers, or ''sustain'' the interaction if the answer is incorrect—that is, they repeat or rephrase the question, give a clue, and in general try to get the student to continue to work toward a correct response. With pupils of whom they expect little, teachers are more inclined to accept correct answers with minimal praise and to criticize incorrect answers. In addition, the teacher is much more likely to limit her interactions with these students to matters of class organization and discipline.

The summated data of all these recent studies appear to explain quite clearly how the tracking process works, mediated by teacher expectations. First of all, teachers always assume that some students will learn and that others will not. Second, they tend to take for granted that it is the children of middle-class background and characteristics who will be the fast learners, and that those of working-class background will do poorly. The teachers make their expectations come true—apparently not consciously—by their grossly different treatment of the children. Oversimplifying the vast array of available data, one might say that teachers instruct and praise the middle-class and upper-class children, making them feel superior, and that they discipline and criticize the working-class children, making them feel inferior. The result is that the former gain confidence, tend to like school, develop high educational aspirations, and act out the expectations conveyed to them; the latter also act out the expectations they perceive, by coming to believe in their own lack of aptitude, by disengaging from school, and by dropping out as soon as they decently can.

The saddest part of the whole process is the destruction visited upon the spirits and self-esteem of the poor and working-class children, many of whom are gradually convinced—by the behavior of the teachers and administrators, as well as by that of their peers who are labeled good students—that they are dumb, incompetent, unfit for intellectual activity, destined to be on the bottom of the heap in real life as they are in the classroom as little children. Sennett and Cobb, in *The Hidden Injuries of Class,* have documented this ravaging of the spirit, which is one of the major functions of the school system.

8

Power Concentrations and Health Care

The Disability Movement is gaining strength in our country. Its members are trying to make us see that defining a particular physical or mental condition as a "handicap" is not a medical fact, but a social and political decision. Those who are different in some way are still very similar to the majority of people in that they want the independence and freedom valued by all Americans. Roth discusses the importance of recognizing that, if the same proper supports are provided, "different" is not necessarily weak or inferior.

Surviving in a bureaucracy is not easy. Even though American bureaucratic communication appears to be informal and friendly, Vidich and Bensman show us that there are "messages" underneath the seemingly innocent and polite phrases being exchanged. If a superior says "You haven't reached your full potential in this job," you had better translate it to mean "You're not fired, but don't expect a raise or promotion." Or if you hear, "We can't stand in the way of your growth," you have actually been told, "You're fired."

The bureaucracies in modern society have become so large and complex that they can no longer perform the functions for which they were intended. Originally, a bureaucracy was thought to be the most efficient and "fair" form of organization. Elgin and Bushnell give us 16 reasons why this form of organization will soon be totally unable to function. The size, alone, of most modern organizations make them impossible for any one individual to understand. Since no one can comprehend the total system, no one can stop its growing deterioration.

Reading 26
Handicap as a Social Construct
William Roth

Although there is clearly a biological difference between the disabled and the able-bodied, this is not the decisive difference between the two groups. Handicap is a social construction. There is a biological substratum, but what it means to be handicapped to others and to oneself is overwhelmingly social and decisively political.

A black is biologically different from a white. The hair may be kinkier. There is likely to be more melanin in the skin. The nose may be flatter. Resistance to malaria may be enhanced, as may susceptibility to sickle-cell anemia. With the exception of greater susceptibility to sickle-cell anemia, none of these biological differences cause the black distress. But in a social context, biological difference is a flag signaling the likelihood of certain conduct by parts of white society. Such behavior, beliefs, and actions have been called racism. It is racism, a social and political artifact, rather than the biology of race, which causes the black distress, unhappiness, and a predisposition toward poverty and those maladies that attend poverty. For example, blacks pay more money into Social Security than they take out, an index of premature mortality that derives in large measure from the social and political construction of race.

A similar situation exists with sex. Obviously, men and women are biologically different. A woman can bear children, a man cannot. The shape of the genitals and later the secondary sex characteristics are different. But it is not such biological difference which distresses the woman. Here, too, sexual difference acts as a flag. Here, too, society makes of difference that social and political artifact labeled "sexism," which indeed causes women economic, psychological, even physical pain. That women, on the average, earn about 60 percent of what men do is one measure of this social and political difference.

The biological difference associated with a handicap, however, may itself occasion distress at times. Yet here, too, biology is important far beyond itself. Here, too, biological difference is a flag signaling the most distressing sorts of social and political artifact rendered all the more distressing because it is so easy to think them biologically necessary—as indeed, once upon a time, many thought that sexism reflected the natural biology of women and racism the natural biology of blacks. While sometimes hidden, what society does with the biological difference of handicap is far-ranging and deep, leading *inter alia* to poor education, training for failure, desexualization, unemployment or underemployment, loneliness, greater likelihood of psychological complication, a history of learned inferiority, the awkward glances of others, discrimination of all sorts—indeed, even a definition of being through negation: *not* able-bodied, *not* able to function in certain ways, *not* as agile, *not* as intelligent, *not* as flexible, *not* as firm, *not* with a future.

It seems hard for society to accept difference without somehow ranking it, thinking of it as inferior, deficient, dysfunctional. We seem to find it difficult to distinguish between difference and inequality. People are accepted as equal insofar as they are like the rest of us. It is to be lamented if blacks must act like whites in order to achieve equality, if women must emulate men, and if disabled people must aspire to able-bodied behavior and values. To expect sameness is unjust not only to the minority group from which sameness is expected, but to that society which has much to learn from the diversity that the members of these groups articulate.

Disabled people are talking, not only through words, but through gestures, legislation, litigation, political presence, and other modes of political and social communication. Having started to think of themselves as a politically and socially constructed and disenfranchised minority, the disabled, like other minority groups, are using the knowledge of their stigmatized identity to change themselves and the society in which they exist. To change society, to rewrite a social contract of oppression, is to emancipate oneself.

Changes in public policy are necessary. It is important that policy makers listen and understand before wasting dollars on non-optimal programs. What kinds of housing, transportation, education are appropriate for handicapped people? For the first time such issues have been brought to the agenda and consciousness of public policy. The issue of work is of central importance. If many disabled people can and want to work, then the current transfer system, which frequently makes work financially costly, must be recalibrated. And current policy which would increase the supply of disabled workers should be coupled with policy to increase the economy's demand for disabled workers.

A rethinking is in order. The reasons mandating such rethinking include the escalating costs of Social Security Disability Insurance and other transfer-payment programs, the recent waves of legislation to guarantee rights of handicapped people that many able-bodied people have taken for granted at least since the Declaration of Independence, the discussion of costs and benefits occurring among policy makers and social scientists, and an emerging political organization of disabled people which has learned many of the lessons of other minority groups and has begun to impress the needs and requirements of disabled people on both policy makers and the public.

STICKS AND STONES

The conjunction of the words *politics* and *disability* still perhaps seems strange, despite increasing legitimation by some assemblies. This strangeness is perhaps a reflection of an actual political disjunction in society. Such speech is sensible, and only a social error of the ear hears sensible messages as strange. An inversion dwells on the conjunction of *politics* and *disability* that suggests the possibility of its sensible articulation.

To undertake such an investigation is to embark on a voyage that many disabled people have already undertaken. It is to disengage certain political foci of disabled people and expose their potentiality and character. In so doing, it is, inevitably, to comment as well on certain political attributes of that society through which disability is refracted and constructed. It is to explore the interconnections that disabled people have with the political society that contains them, connections that, unlike the self-evident truths of the Declaration of Independence, are not self-evident but distorted, if not inaudible.

Although we all think we know what disability is, it is difficult to put it into words. The words opted for, if they articulate the current social-role structure, preclude the possibility of finding any sense in the conjunction of politics and disability. Should there be words that make it nonsense to speak of disability and politics together, and other words that make it sensible, then perhaps one of the characteristics of disability is its vulnerability to definition. And insofar as a disabled person *is* a disability, disabled people are vulnerable too. Indeed, the word *vulnerability* has a political quality that may be part of disability. Further, the claiming of other definitions of disability, particularly on the part of the disabled, may itself be a political act.

One language used in discussions of disability has it that the disabled person is permanently sick. By now enough has been written on the politics of medical speech immediately to raise the suspicion that its words are political. As R. D. Laing and Thomas Szasz have shown regarding those aberrations of the mind called mental illness, Seymour Sarason and John Doris regarding mental retardation, and Michel Foucault regarding physical malady, to speak of a person as "sick" is hardly apolitical.

Many labels appear to be a case of "Sticks and stones may break my bones, but names will never hurt me." But there are labels which help or hurt, and when they do so, help or hurt politically. Indeed, the language of medicine entails social actions. When the disabled person is called "sick," the fact of this definition and its consequences reveal more about social and political artifact than they do about the natural biological order of things. And when the disabled person is treated according to social convention and thought of according to social habit, such treatment and thought is altogether political. If society speaks of a disabled person in the language of medicine, it may do so with a purpose. To speak of social purpose is to enter headlong into the thick of the political. What might such social purpose be?

In part, it might be to separate and protect the able-bodied. In speaking of some as sick and others as healthy, sickness and health define boundaries. Further, to speak of people as sick is to locate the problem within the body of the sick person and encapsulate it by the medical system.

Alcoholism has had a political stake in its recognition as a disease rather than a moral attribute. To speak of it as a disease was to locate a problem that had grown alarmingly in scope and class distribution in a supposedly apolitical medical lexicon, absolving society of responsibility and depoliticizing its relationship to the alcoholic. What alcoholism has struggled for has come naturally to disability. Here, too, the scope was large and the class distribution wide. Here, too, there was now a need for social isolation and insulation, and, ultimately, for de-politicization. That disability falls so well within the medical lexicon demonstrates how far away it has been thrust from politics—and perhaps how close to politics it would be without a medical buffer.

Politics has been characterized as an arena of asymmetrical relationships. The disabled person is reckoned a (weaker) patient, thus obscuring political attributes to concentrate on his failings as refracted through an ideal of health. Activity is legitimated only insofar as it contributes to individual, apolitical recovery, usually adjustment or acquiescence, since cure is, by definition, impossible. The disabled person is de-politicized, spoken of in terms of deviance and subservience; he is rendered apolitical, spoken of simply as a "good patient."

Disabled people share their subservient place. The ability to demarcate a region in political space can be little solace to a victim, particularly when the political nature of that space is obscured. Many people throughout history have shared such a power of the weak. But seldom has the political quality of the weakness been so well disguised.

The major political goals of disabled people are achieving social recognition that their struggle is indeed political, achieving a political definition that unites them with other oppressed minorities, and acting not as victims but as equals. It is an awesome agenda, already begun.

In exploring what is and what can be, it is frequently useful to recollect what has been. In large measure the history of disabled people, like the history of so many ordinary people, is unwritten. But we do have some idea about the evolution of those structures which were fashioned to house and handle them. Of particular importance in the politicization of disability is the recent history of litigation and legislation.

In 1954, the Warren court issued its famous decision in *Brown* v. *Topeka Board of Education*. This decision did not come out of the blue, nor, as social scientists sometimes like to think, did it issue from the discoveries and evidence of social scientists. A long legal process—carefully orchestrated, well-planned, and consistently pressed—had started in the courts decades earlier. The *Brown* decision emerged through legal and political struggle.

In principle, it seemed the decision was applicable to groups other than blacks. The idea that separate was not equal provoked reconsideration of the relationship of retarded people, prisoners, patients, institutionalized people, and people in the armed forces to this polity's legal structure and to the polity itself.

The example of *Brown* inspired the plaintiffs and lawyers involved in the landmark decisions of the recent history of disability that eventually, in 1975, led to Public Law 94–142, the Education for All Handicapped Children Act. Another law, the Rehabilitation Act of 1973, contained the revolutionary sections 504, 503, and 501. These sections have been called a civil rights act for disabled people.

Changes in law and changes in implementation had some effect on the polity. Their effects on disabled people were profound. Sometimes political action by the disabled was the result of law; sometimes its origins were independent. Sometimes political action was individual rebellion; sometimes it was carefully planned in concert with others. Sometimes it was an insistence on rights that others had long taken for granted; sometimes it seemed to stake out new rights, opportunities, and obligations. It is instructive to catalogue a few of these diverse political actions.

A woman in a wheelchair who was qualified for a teaching job was refused it, fought back, and won; elsewhere, a governor signed a bill probibiting job discrimination against disabled people. One airline refused to carry a handicapped person, who fought back and won; another airline published a booklet on special services for disabled people. Handicapped people in Washington fought to force inclusion of elevators into the then-projected Metro subway system and lost; in another large city, special seats for elderly and handicapped people were marked out on public transporation. A disabled lawyer who could not appear at a legal process against him because there was no way for his wheelchair to enter the building fought back; a state senate approved bills designed to facilitate access to public buildings and other facilities by disabled people. The Justice Department charged the world's largest wheelchair manufacturer with collusion, monopolistic practices, price rigging, inordinately high salaries for executives, and nepotism; later, this wheelchair giant finally came out with an outdoor electric wheelchair, honoring a need met in the breach by small manufacturers, such as an outraged paraplegic who designed a particularly impressive wheelchair, christened "Advance," in a garage.

A computer was developed which transduces printed material into spoken words, a promising use of space-age technology for handicapped people. Private groups promote travel by disabled people, package tours, and in general open up leisure activities that others have long enjoyed. The federal government published a book of information for disabled people wanting to use the national park system.

In 1977, there were demonstrations at HEW regional offices, Washington headquarters, and the home of the Secretary of HEW demanding that the department issue the regulations for Section 504 of the Rehabilitation Act passed 4 years earlier and appropriately administered by the Office of Civil Rights. The regulations were issued.

Many disabled people met each other in an atmosphere of friendship and politics at the White House Conference on Handicapped Individuals. A mayor of a city estimated to have a million disabled people established an office of the handicapped to amplify the voices of its handicapped citizens.

With support of his parents and lawyers, a high-school freshman without an arm contested a decision excluding him from football training. A person in a wheelchair was kept from a marathon; with ACLU lawyers, he brought the case to the courts and won. A disabled Boy Scout was denied his eagle badge because of his age; he fought back and got his badge, making eight other handicapped Scouts eligible.

Such events signal handicapped people's responses to problems of access, organization, politics, and civil rights; at the same time, they tell something about the way society labels, brands, and stigmatizes handicapped people.

POLITICAL SELF-RELIANCE

A discussion of handicapped people as political beings raises points of comparison with other groups that, upon reflection, do not seem strange. In some ways, disabled people seem like other minority groups; in other ways, they are different, although still comparable.

Many of the political actions concerning disabled people were, to paraphrase Lincoln, for them, but not by and of them. For example, the court cases leading up to P.L. 94-142 were not pressed by disabled people themselves but by their parents, lawyers, and friendly professionals. There is strength in this. Disabled people have friends who are sufficiently potent politically to cause change. This is because disabled people are usually born to able-bodied parents; are distributed across income levels, prestige levels, races, and strata of power; and, like motherhood and apple pie (before that conjunction became too sexist), are something which few can be against (that disability has been de-politicized has meant that it has been free of overt political attack). And it is easier to leave political action to others, especially if one is disabled, with a sufficiently complicated life already. But there are drawbacks in leaving political action to others. Here Lincoln's desiderata of democracy are applicable. The disabled cannot depend upon others to make their cause primary; there are other agendas, and the most important of these are not even hidden. The medical system, the educational system, and various other interest groups have their own agendas. In the past such agendas have led to arrangements like institutionalization and structures of special education which, at least by today's standards, have harmed disabled people. Of course, some actions on behalf of the disabled are well directed as well as well intentioned; other well-intentioned efforts can be appropriately redirected by disabled people. Deciding which efforts are, in fact, well directed is a crucial part of disabled people's political agenda; it demands some ongoing presence of disabled people on the political stage.

The Bill of Rights provides for freedom of assembly, a right appropriately deemed necessary to citizenship. Changes in social organization and technology since the writing of those amendments have raised the possibility of substitutes for freedom of assembly. Thus, various communication devices like the telephone, radio, and television in some measure supplant freedom of assembly as techniques for politics, organization, and citizenship. Arguably, it is due to such technological innovation that the disabled movement started in the first place. Freedom of assembly, however, is still vital to disabled as well as able-bodied people. This right, which in so many ways precedes authentic citizenship, is a right which disabled people must pursue politically. Currently, much architecture incorporates barriers to disabled people. Transportation built around the able body may not serve the disabled body, and transportation is antecedent to freedom of assembly. Add to this the frequent poverty of many disabled people, and freedom of assembly becomes not a right guaranteed but a right to be sought.

In some measure, the right of free assembly is denied to any minority group. Minorities, particularly in preorganizational stages, have difficulty in identifying each other, securing access to the media, and formulating programs that will bring people together. Yet these difficulties are more extreme for disabled people. In addition to the social obstacles faced by other minority groups, the disabled are confronted with the barriers constructed by an able-bodied society as well as those less significant problems predicated on biological difference. Disabled people have simply found it hard to get together, a prerequisite to getting it together. It has not been easy for them even to talk, a prerequisite to organized action. Considering such obstacles, the current organization of people with disabilities is a noteworthy political achievement.

Disabled people are often fragmented according to disability group. People with particular disabilities have social interests in common, but social fragmentation often prohibits the articulation of uniform political interest. No one disability group has the power substantially to change public and private policy, although some have had occasional successes. To secure what is necessary to disabled people and to redeem the promise of a political movement, the politics of disability will have to involve all disabilities, all ages, parents, interested professionals, friends, etc. Such a coalition is difficult to put together and maintain.

Disabled people share with other minorities the danger of competition with other groups when resources become scarce, as they have been and as more they will be. One group may gain, but at the expense of another. Organizational problems seem overwhelming, and organizational success in their face is striking. The social structure creates subgroups whose interests are not necessarily consonant with the interests of other subgroups. The achievement of the general good for disabled people will require some sublimation of individual interest into group interest—an appropriate lesson for citizenship, but a difficult one when resources are scarce. But it is more than a lesson; it is a test of the ability of disabled people to define a general interest and act on it politically in such a way that all would be better with than without such action.

The political inexperience of disabled people—something to be expected from any politically oppressed group—is frequently distressing. By definition and construction, politically oppressed people are denied political skills and resources. Given that status, any political skill is remarkable—a marvel shared with other minority movements.

The question of political talent, charisma, and organizational expertise in a group of people systematically denied access to these qualities is a fascinating one. In the disabled community, this question seems to have been at least partly resolved in ways not readily open to other minority groups. Disabled children have able-bodied parents who may be in positions of power and frequently will not act as oppressed people. The disability movement has been assisted by those who became disabled after having formed a consciousness of themselves as potent, effective people. To such people the social construction of disability comes as a cruel and artificial barrier. From such people we can expect a rhetoric and a political skill and will that derives from a history, not of oppression, but of relative advantage cut short. Further, many disabled people, even if born disabled or rendered disabled as children, grow up in two worlds. One is the world of society at large, a world perhaps filled with oppression; the other is the world of the family, a world poten-tially filled with love. The effects of growing up in two worlds may be disastrous; or they may be benign or even beneficial, leading to the growth of active political citizens. Research in the political socialization of disabled people has yet to be done. It is a fertile topic. That it has not yet been pursued is a reflection of the view of disabled people as intrinsically apolitical.

Part of the disability movement, derived in some measure from the women's movement, is consciousness raising. It is political consciousness to realize that one's disability is a political situation rather than a medical condition. Such political realization is not psychological recognition. Many disabled people have been con-fused about the psychological meaning of disability, and coming to grips with it may involve some form of psychotherapy or simply growing up. But the political and social meaning of disability cannot usually be reached by individual therapy or aging; it requires group experience, organized action, and political direction. Con-sciousness raising is difficult, but it seems to be almost necessary for a politics of disability and for the sociological and even psychological well-being of the handi-capped person.

Implicit in consciousness raising is the difference between individual recovery, particularly individual medical recovery, and social and political recovery. This is not to be confused with adjustment, coping, rehabilitation, or any of the other euphemisms which have guided and coerced individual disabled people. These are not social recovery, but acquiescence to society. Social and political recovery requires learning that one is in the same boat with others and then learning how to sail.

Consciousness raising is made difficult by the problems disabled people have in getting together and communicating. Nonetheless, disabled people have much to learn from each other. The problems disabled people share because of their constriction by society and their biological differences are the ground on which to erect a social and political awareness leading to liberation.

Disabled people as "sick" are worthy of sympathy. They are almost universally counted among the deserving poor not only because they are disabled through no fault of their own, not only because "there but for the grace of God go I," not only out of self-interest which reckons the possibility that any person might become disabled. For whatever reasons, able-bodied society has traditionally had sympathy for the handicapped.

This raises a problem for political organization. Insofar as sympathy is predicated on the apolitical nature of handicapped people, their politicization destroys it. However handicapped people may feel about sympathy—and frequently they feel badly about it, and with good reason—much necessary good flows to many handicapped people from it; the apolitical vision of the handicapped accords even those who engage in political activity an assurance of gentle treatment (as in the sit-ins around the regulations for 504). Since the onset of the medical vision of that social situation, none have been lynched.

Many disabled people need the resources that now come through sympathy. To say they have a right to them jeopardizes them. The handicapped person has much more to lose than chains. If political organization means an end to sympathy, then political organization carries the risk of the loss of that good will and those resources that are diverted toward handicapped people from charity. This makes political organization difficult.

There are analogies with other minority groups. Women enjoy various privileges which arise out of a sexist society. Blacks need the good will of whites. Poor people need the resources of the well-off. For all of these groups, claiming a political identity is jeopardizing what they have. All of these groups have experienced organizational difficulties because of this jeopardy. But despite similarities, this problem is so quantitatively different for the handicapped than for other minority groups that it marks a virtual demarcation between them. Sympathy can be insulting, and resources gained through charity have a price. It is no easy problem; there are no easy solutions.

LIBERALISM AND AUSTERITY

The composition of the disability movement is noteworthy and in part accounts for its ideology and its issues. Special disability groups, parent groups, professional groups, and other organizations contribute in some measure to the disability movement. At its political core, however, it is composed largely of middle-class whites, a composition not so different from the women's movement. Some effects of this composition are shared with that movement. Thus the ideology of the disability movement arises in part from a constituency who may find little reason to question the dominant ideology of liberalism. This is the ideology into which they were socialized; it is simply how society works. And since a disabled person sees little hope in working without the system, he or she must work within it. The system is liberal. The ideology of the disability movement is overwhelmingly and classically liberal. The disability movement does not say that it wants something different, never mind special, but that it wants to be included in the social contract that has been part of this nation since its founding.

One of the words most important to American rhetoric and that of the disabled movement is *independence*. And the frequent use of the word *rights* indicates that the disabled want those same rights enjoyed by others. Disabled people speak of "access" to rights and of "barriers" to rights. In short, they want in where they have been kept out, just like everyone else.

This ideology, consonant with the dominant American ideology of liberalism, is politically modest in its consumerism and self-help. Rarely does it invoke the word *citizenship* over *consumerism,* and *self-help* is, on the face of it, similarly apolitical, in that self-help can be isolated from the broader issues of politics. Another liberal word is *individual.* Rarely is the collective thought of explicitly.

Much of the leadership in the disability movement comes from adults who were disabled in that time between late youth and early adulthood. They had had little cause to question liberalism. After having achieved that degree of political consciousness which revealed that most problems faced by the disabled are social and political problems, they interpreted these problems as excluding them from the system in which they had grown up. Further, many political changes related to disability are attributable to disabled veterans and public response to them. It is difficult to question the ideology on behalf of which the disability was incurred.

There are other reasons for the adoption of liberalism as an ideology. Not only does it come easiest, but there seems little reason to take on yet other problems than those with which the disabled person is already preoccupied. Further, disabled persons tend to think of themselves as marginal to rather than alienated from society; the remedy to this is entirely within the perimeter of liberal society. Liberalism regards certain rights held by disabled people as unalienable. And liberalism allows for certain distinctions in language which, at least theoretically, make it possible to speak of differentness without speaking of inequality. It is frequently useful to pretend that one is within the system rather than outside. But in general with the disability movement, it has not been pretense, it has been aspiration. The liberal ideology of the movement has led to certain problems, certain opportunities, certain advantages, certain disadvantages. It is an ideology that may be sorely tested in forthcoming years of fiscal austerity, since austerity itself falls under the classic liberal banner.

There are certain problems with liberalism as an ideology for the disability movement. Discrimination against blacks and women, for example, is less inherent in architecture, transportation, employment, and social organization generally than is discrimination against the disabled. When the disability movement speaks of equality of opportunity, each equality may involve some elaborate and at least initially expensive changes in society. Whether such changes are entirely conceivable within the status quo is a question.

They are conceivable within classic liberalism provided that the market, which has come to be its jewel, is suitably smoothed. Such smoothing may be partially achieved through cost-benefit calculation, which accounts for externalities in those many instances where the immediate conversion of social organizations is not in the individual interest. What happens when classic liberalism leaves the market, however, is messy. In large degree it is a mess that we have made our own in modern liberalism. The disability movement must be realistic about the market and willing to entertain mess. Nonmarket countries apparently find it easier to employ and educate disabled people. What can happen there as a matter of course can happen here only as a matter of conscious deliberation.

Conscious deliberation usually means government intervention. Insofar as the current administration promises less conscious intervention, it is not a promising one for the disability movement. Political presence in the arena of federal government must surely continue, despite what may seem to be less tangible rewards. But disabled people may also have to turn to sources of power other than government. It might be promising to face private industry directly, while asking government for more tax incentives to hire disabled people.

In the past this movement has, understandably, not concentrated on issues of employment. But these issues are of overarching importance. They justify public investments in education (soon to be cut back); they provide income to disabled people to buy goods and services necessary individually and for political organization. Employment is the skeleton for meaningful life in a market society.

Issues of architectural access and education were natural and appropriate ones for the beginning of the movement. That movement is now mature, and the political environment has changed. Given that maturation and that change, employment and its ramifications should become major issues of this decade.

The birth and growth of the disability movement have been remarkable. Immense resourcefulness and adaptability are necessary for its perseverance. What has happened and what has been learned in the last decade are encouraging omens of continued life. Whether, in fact, the politics of disability shall be survivor, victor, or casualty in this new world is a question whose answer remains to be recorded by the action of politics.

Reading 27

The Bureaucratic Ethos

Arthur Vidich

Joseph Bensman

One important aspect of the New Society is the ever-increasing growth of the administrative structure of bureaucracy and of the scale of large organizations. Government, industry, education, trade unions, and churches carry out the internal and external operations of the society by use of the bureaucratic mechanism. It is critical to note that the exact counterpart of the growth of the middle class is the growth of the administrative structure of bureaucracy which administers this enormous productive and service-oriented society.

In describing the characteristics of bureaucracies and especially European political bureaucracies, Max Weber provided the foundations for the technical description of large-scale business organization. The key theme in Weber's description of bureaucracy is the separation of the administrator from the means of administration, just as the soldier in an earlier epoch had been separated from the ownership of his weapons, and the worker from the means of production. Bureaucracies are characterized by relatively fixed hierarchies and spheres of competence (jurisdictions), and they depend on files and legalistic regulations for specifying their operations. The entire bureaucracy depends on technical experts who are engaged in a lifelong career and who are dependent on their jobs as their major means of support. Thus discipline, obedience, loyalty, and impersonal respect for authority tend to become psychological characteristics of the bureaucrat.

Even more important, however, is the bureaucrat's habit of making standardized categorical decisions which are rationally calculated—in form if not in content—to administer thousands of cases which become relevant because they fall into a category predescribed by administrative regulation and procedure. Weber describes bureaucracy as a giant machine in which all individuals, both administrators and subjects, are cogs. This Weberian nightmare is so awesome and horrifying in its portrayal of the dehumanization of men and the disenchantment of society that it has been hard to swallow in all its implications. It is only Weber's academic style that has prevented him from being treated as another George Orwell.

For Weber, bureaucracy did not arise out of a devilish plot. Rather it was a dominant institution emerging from the administrative efficiency that results from size, scope, and categorical application of cases. Bureaucracy is adaptive to large-scale enterprises in all areas of society, as governmental and private activities expand in response to the growth of societies from localistic (feudal) and small units to giant large-scale enterprises that are national and international in scope. In many respects, Weber saw bureaucracy as almost self-generating, with one important qualification: the desire of leaders of large-scale enterprises to extend their own freedom, autonomy, and opportunity for rational decision-making by limiting the assertiveness, the interference, the power, and the irrationality of others within their sphere of administration. Thus those who control large-scale institutions limit the freedom of others in order to maximize their own freedom. Seen from the point of view of leadership, bureaucracy must always be something more than a technical system of administration. It is also a system for the organization and distribution of power and the formulation of policy within institutions, between institutions, and within societies. From this perspective, bureaucracy, in its full form, is diametrically opposed to the Jeffersonian and Jacksonian image of a viable democracy.

American social and political scientists did not find it easy to accept Weber's discussion of bureaucracy. For the most part they reacted against the image of the officious, legalistic bureaucrat and criticized Weber for universalizing the image of the uniform-happy, tyrannical German bureaucrat, later overdrawn in the image of the Prussian Junker or the Nazi official. Americans contrasted the German stereotype to the oft-perceived style of the American official, who appeared to be easygoing, equalitarian, breezy, friendly, personal, and nonofficious, even though a bureaucratic official. What they failed to realize was that the American tradition, stemming as it does from the Jeffersonian and Jacksonian frontier style, causes the power holder to conceal his power in proportion to its growth. The Weberian bureaucrat does not look like the American manager because the *cultural* style surrounding bureaucracy is different in America. As a result of this mask, the subordinate in any organization has at subliminal levels the ability to make precise estimates of the actual power positions of each officeholder in the organization. With this as his framework, the formal, equalitarian, personal, and friendly responses of co-workers are based on these estimates. In the American system the official knows how to be informal and friendly without ever intruding into the office of the superior, and the superior knows how to be equalitarian without ever losing his authority. Thus bureaucracy functions in the classical Weberian way while retaining an air of American friendliness and informality.

This special bureaucratic by-product of Jeffersonian and Jacksonian democracy creates a bureaucratic style in which it becomes a major requirement to mask authority relations. As a result, very substantial changes have taken place in the ideology of the social worker, the human relations specialist, the psychological counselor, the personnel officer, and in interpersonal relations in almost all bureaucratic job situations. In the United States a whole range of bureaucratic subspecialties have been created in welfare, government, and business bureaucracies for the express purpose of concealing bureaucratic authority. In American bureaucracy it is possible to sustain a rhetoric of agreement, respect for the individual personality, and rewards for technical ability as the critical factors governing the relationship between boss and subordinate.

In actual bureaucratic practice the subordinate is expected to agree voluntarily with his superior and to suggest the conditions for his subordination without ever openly acknowledging the fact of his subordination. The rhetoric of democracy has become the sine qua non of bureaucratic authoritarianism.

So complex is this masking process that in a literal sense a linguistic revolution has taken place that allows us to conceal from ourselves the inequalitarianism of bureaucratic social relations. Bureaucracy, like any dominant institution, has developed a structure of linguistic euphemisms which allow the retention of an equalitarian, friendly, personal ideology while concealing the authoritarianism and at times the harshness of bureaucracy. The following expressions, placed opposite their euphemisms, are intended only to suggest some of the possibilities.

Euphemism	Real Meaning
Obedience	
We expect your cooperation.	Obey.
I'd like to have consensus on this issue.	I expect you to repress all differences.
Obligation and duty require this.	My job and responsibilities require your obedience.
Being reminded of one's place	
It's a wonderful idea, but at the present we don't have the time to give your idea the attention and consideration it needs.	Drop it.
You're kidding, aren't you.	You're out of line.
That's an interesting idea that needs further developing.	Let's not discuss it now.
We must respect the autonomy and individual rights of others.	You're overstepping your authority.
You can do that if you want to, but I'll take no responsibility for it if it gets out of hand.	You do it at your own risk, but I'll take the credit for it if it's successful.
With some development and elaboration, the germ of your idea could be useful.	I'm stealing your idea; forget it, the idea is no longer yours.
That was a good idea you had at our meeting yesterday.	I'm giving it back to you.
Ways to get fired	
You've been late three times in the past month.	Warning of forthcoming dismissal.

Your work is not up to your usual standards.	Warning of forthcoming dismissal.
You haven't reached your full potential in this job.	You're not fired, but don't expect a raise or promotion.
We feel that this organization can do no more to further your career.	You're fired.
We can't stand in the way of your growth.	You're fired.
You're too well trained for this job.	You're fired.
We'll give you excellent references.	Please leave without making a scene.
We'll give you an extra month's severance pay.	Please leave and forget you ever worked here.

At other levels

Free lunch	A small, somewhat ambiguous bribe setting the stage for bigger bribery.
Fringe benefits	Fairly serious bribery.
Hanky-panky	Serious bribery.
A preliminary meeting	Setting out to rig a forthcoming meeting.
A well-organized meeting	A rigged meeting.
An informal coffee meeting	An incipient plot.
A private meeting	A plot.

Although this whole area of linguistic usage is central to the functioning of society, few writers apart from George Orwell, Hannah Arendt, and Shepherd Mead have emphasized it. The bureaucratic aspects of the New Society could well be studied through the revolution in linguistics of which we have suggested only a few examples.

Reading 28

The Limits to Complexity: Are Bureaucracies Becoming Unmanageable?

Duane S. Elgin

Robert A. Bushnell

Social systems tend to decline in performance as they become bigger, more complex, and increasingly incomprehensible. They also become less amenable to democratic control, and more vulnerable to disruption at key points. There now appears to be evidence that we may be pressing against the relative limits of our ability to manage large bureaucracies.

Modern society must face up to the prospect that we may be reaching the limits of our capacity to manage exceedingly large and complex bureaucracies. Already there is considerable agreement regarding the details of bureaucratic malfunction, such as massive but ineffective urban governments and huge but wasteful governmental programs. Indeed, there is growing concern whether many of the largest bureaucracies can survive.

Consider a sampling of recent statements by opinion leaders:

Ten years ago government was widely viewed as an instrument to solve problems; today government itself is widely viewed as the problem.
Charles Schultze and Henry Owen,
Setting National Priorities. 1976

We're frantically trying to keep our noses above water, racing from one problem to the next.
U.S. Senator Adlai Stevenson,
U.S. News and World Report.
November 10, 1975

The demands on democratic government grow while the capacity of democratic government stagnates. This, it would appear, is the central dilemma of the governability of democracy which has manifested itself in Europe, North America, and Japan in the 1970s.
Report to the Trilateral Commission on the Governability of Democracies.
1975

These statements raise the possibility that, with an enormous increase in our technological capacity, we have rushed to create bureaucracies of such extreme levels of scale, complexity, and interdependence that they now begin to exceed our

Reprinted with permission from *The Futurist* (December 1977):337–349.

capacity to comprehend and manage them. We are discovering that the power to create large, complex social bureaucracies does not automatically confer the ability to control them.

Recognition of the growing complexity of social systems as a problem worthy of attention in its own right emerged during a recent study, conducted by the Center for the Study of Social Policy, a division of SRI, Inc., in Menlo Park, California, which was seeking to identify important future problems that now are receiving insufficient attention.

PROBLEMS OF LARGE, COMPLEX SYSTEMS

After an extensive review of literature pertaining to the problems of bureaucracies, 16 propositions were selected as a useful sample of the problems associated with the growth of social systems. (See list.)

Problems of Large, Complex Systems

Summary

It is hypothesized that if a social system grows to extreme levels of scale, complexity, and interdependence, the following characteristics will *tend* to become manifest:

1. Diminishing relative capacity of a given individual to comprehend the overall system.
2. Diminishing level of public participation in decision-making.
3. Declining public access to decision-makers.
4. Growing participation of experts in decision-making.
5. Disproportionate growth in costs of coordination and control.
6. Increasingly de-humanized interactions between people and the system.
7. Increasing levels of alienation.
8. Increasing challenges to basic value premises.
9. Increasing levels of unexpected and counterintuitive consequences of policy action.
10. Increasing system rigidity.
11. Increasing number and uncertainty of disturbing events.
12. Narrowing span of diversity of innovation.
13. Declining legitimacy of leadership.
14. Increasing system vulnerability.
15. Declining overall performance of the system.
16. Growing deterioration of the overall system unlikely to be perceived by most participants in that system.

These propositions are not necessarily problems per se, but they become problematical in accordance to the relative *speed* of systems growth, its relative *size* (the absolute number of elements grouped together), its *complexity* (the number and diversity of elements in the system), and *interdependence* (tightness of coupling among elements both within and between bureaucracies). Thus, although the size of a social system is not the exclusive consideration in formulating these propositions, it is the primary point of reference from which the patterns of growth of large, complex systems are explored.

This article focuses on problems of large social bureaucracies as exemplified by the welfare system, the Medicare-Medicaid programs, and major metropolitan governments. These bureaucracies are very large and complex, highly interdependent, and concerned primarily with the delivery and consumption of public services. They are further characterized by high levels of human interaction and by ambiguous and sometimes conflicting objectives.

Although this article is directed principally to the problems of bureaucracies in the public sector, it also has relevance for private sector bureaucracies (such as large corporations). Crucial differences between these two categories of bureaucracies, however, prevent the direct application of this discussion to private sector bureaucracies.

The 16 problems are as follows: (Note: Each problem should be read as if it began with "When a bureaucracy grows to extreme levels of scale, complexity, and interdependence, then. . . .)

1. The relative ability of any individual to comprehend the system will tend to diminish. This proposition applies both to the public that is served by the social system and to the decision-makers who run it. To manage a social system effectively, a decision-maker must acquire knowledge at a rate at least equal to the pace at which decisions become more numerous and complex.

As a system grows in scale, the parts of the system will increase generally in an arithmetic progression but the interrelationships between the parts will tend to increase in a geometric progression. Hence, the *knowledge required* to comprehend both the discrete parts and their interrelationships will tend to increase geometrically, but due to the decision-maker's biological, mechanical, and temporal limitations, the *knowledge available* is likely to grow relatively slowly.

The importance of this problem is stated succinctly by seasoned bureaucrat Elliot Richardson in his book, *The Creative Balance* (New York: Holt, Rinehart and Winston, 1976):

> For a free society, the ultimate challenge of the foreseeable future will consist not simply in managing complexity but in keeping it within the bounds of understanding by the society's citizens and their representatives in government.

Thus the size and complexity of social systems may jeopardize representative democracy itself. There is evidence to suggest that the relative levels of the public's comprehension of social systems may be declining significantly. For example, over a number of years, the Survey Research Center in the University of Michigan has asked people if they agreed or disagreed with the following statement: ''Sometimes politics and government seem so complicated that a person like me can't really understand what's going on.'' In 1960, 40 percent of those responding disagreed with this statement and in 1974 only 26 percent disagreed.

The fact is that the stuff of public life seems to elude the grasp of many people. Bureaucratic processes have become specialized and professionalized. Yet, many of the larger bureaucracies are plagued with the unspoken but undeniable feeling among management and staff that no one truly is in control, that the dynamics of the organization are beyond the comprehension of any one individual.

Nor does the mere aggregation of information necessarily contribute to the understanding of the system. Although the computer revolution has vastly increased the amount of information at our disposal, it has exacerbated the difficulty of decision-making by confronting the manager with a mountain of information that he has no hope of ever assimilating given the crisis management that prevails in many of the largest bureaucracies. Thus, the ability to collect massive amounts of information does not automatically assure that it will be used or be useful in the management of large systems. It is possible to be information-rich and knowledge-poor as a manager or consumer of public services.

2. The capacity and motivation of the public to participate in decision-making processes will tend to diminish. As discussed in Proposition 1, the relative capacity of all constituents of a social bureaucracy to participate knowledgeably in decision-making may diminish as the system grows. At larger scales, the perceived significance of an individual's participation in systems governance, especially through the act of voting, is impaired by the participation of large numbers of people in the process.

At smaller scales there is much greater opportunity for an individual citizen to have a discernible impact, but these small-scale decisions are likely to be relatively inconsequential. Robert Dahl, in an article on ''The City in the Future of Democracy,'' concludes:

> Thus for most citizens, participation in very large units becomes minimal and in very small units it becomes trivial.

To the extent that the cost (in time or money) of informing oneself for participation in the system is substantial and the perceived return from that information is trivial, then a rational response is to remain ignorant and passive. In his book, *Inside Bureaucracy,* urbanist Anthony Downs explains:

> Therefore, we reach the startling conclusion that it is irrational for most citizens to acquire political information for the purposes of voting. . . . Hence, ignorance of

The "Ratchet Effect": Reasons Why Bureaucracies Grow Too Large

Imprecise means of measurement. The "rule of profit" may be harsh, but for business firms it is a relatively certain yardstick against which to measure the efficiency of a given scale of activity. In contrast, governmental bureaucracies and other social systems must attempt to measure efficiency via a number of qualitative, multidimensional, often conflicting, and ambiguous measures and objectives. With virtually no measures of system health, bureaucracies can conceivably grow to excessive scales of social organization.

Responding to the needs of a given population. A business firm can choose its scale of operation so as to maximize efficiency. However, many government bureaucracies are obliged by law and/or by egalitarian principles to attempt to respond to the needs of an entire population or population segment (e.g., all old people, all school-age children, all poor people who are in ill health). There may be little choice as to the size of the bureaucracy if it is largely dictated by the size of system needed to respond to a given population segment.

Bureaucratic imperative. If the size of a system or subsystem is considered an important source of status and power to the managers of that system, then systems managers may attempt to foster the growth of a system in order to secure greater benefit for themselves—even at the cost of a decline in overall systems efficiency. This "tragedy of the commons" behavior within a bureaucracy may be prompted by the search for a larger staff, a larger budget, greater responsibility, and so on. If many bureaucrats pursue this behavior, the collective effect could be considerable in producing an inefficient scale of activity in social bureaucracies.

Technological imperative. Technology provides the possibility to vastly expand the scale of social systems, and this possibility often seems to be translated into a necessity. Social systems may be designed so as to reap the maximum benefits from potent technologies (ranging from computers to photocopying machines) only to find that the overall system (which includes the human element) now exceeds its most efficient scale. Thus, uncritical adoption of technologies may push a system to excessive scales of social organization.

Growth is good. A central value premise in the industrial world view has been that growth is good. This has created a climate in which a concern for the bigness of our social bureaucracies would be less likely to be questioned.

Something for everyone. Political bureaucracies employ the art of compromise in an attempt to provide "something for everyone" so that no important constituency will be alienated or angered. The bureaucracy defends its own interest group and draws support from the many persons who depend on its continued existence. Intrinsic to democratic political processes, then, is a pattern of expectations and demands which tends to inhibit the reduction of bureaucratic activity which, once instituted, becomes the norm.

politics is not a result of unpatriotic apathy; rather it is a highly rational response to the facts of political life in a large democracy.

An initially diminished capacity to participate as a result of mounting complexity is thus coupled with incentives that further reinforce the diminished capacity. As part of a self-fulfilling pattern, the power and willingness to make decisions are shifted from the public to the systems managers.

3. The public's access to decision-makers will tend to decline. Regardless of the size of his constituency, there is only one mayor, one governor, one Secretary of Health, Education and Welfare, and one President. As the number of persons under his jurisdiction grows, an inevitable consequence is a reduction in the amount of time that a manager can spend with any one person. Beyond some threshold size, general access to the leader will, for all practical purposes, be eliminated.

In his discussion of the effects of scale upon a political system, Robert Dahl states:

> The essential point is that nothing can overcome the dismal fact that as the number of citizens increases the proportion who can participate *directly* in discussions with their top leaders must necessarily grow smaller and smaller.

Certainly the actual degree of public access to its leaders has steadily declined as the scale of institutions has increased.

Despite this gradual erosion of access, the perception of this process by the public seems relatively recent. A 1975 Louis Harris survey reveals substantial changes in citizen perceptions of distance from their leadership during the period of 1966 to 1975. Although this period included the unusual events surrounding Watergate and the Viet Nam War (which exacerbated the feeling of distance between the American people and their leaders), the statistics, nonetheless, are striking.

> The feeling that "What I think doesn't really count much any more" has risen from 37% to 67% since 1966; the view of the "People with power are out to take advantage of me" has jumped from 33% to 58% over the same period; the notion that "People running the country really don't care what happens to me" has gone up from 33% to 63%.

As our bureaucracies burgeon, they recede from the comprehension, the familiarity, and the control of the public.

4. Participation of experts in decision-making will tend to grow disproportionately, but this expertise will only marginally counteract the effects of geometrically mounting knowledge requirements for effective management of the bureaucracy. It seems reasonable for a decision-maker faced with a large number of complex problems to seek expert advice in trying to grapple with those problems.

Yet, as Elliot Richardson has warned in *The Creative Balance,* this apparently rational response to complexity may reduce the ability of the public to participate in decision-making:

> Unless we in America can succeed in [managing complexity] . . . we shall lose our power to make intelligent—or at least deliberate—choices. We shall no longer be self-governing. We shall instead be forced to surrender more and more of our constitutional birthright—the office of citizenship—to an expert elite. We may hope it is a benevolent elite. But even if it is not, we shall be dependent on it anyway. Rather than participating in the process of choice, we shall be accepting the choices made for us.

Moreover, it is possible that exponentially growing needs for knowledge in decision-making will eventually overwhelm the expert as well as the decision-maker. The expert ultimately faces the same human limitations to his acquisition of knowledge as does the decision-maker and the general public.

Further, there appear to be intrinsic limits to the assistance that experts can render to decision-makers. Expert knowledge may be so fragmented, as a result of specialization, that it is below the necessary threshold of aggregation to be useful to the decision-maker. Also, the information may be exceedingly complex and difficult to transmit efficiently from expert to decision-maker. Accordingly, expert information may be ignored for very rational reasons.

5. The costs of coordinating and controlling the system will tend to grow disproportionately. Initial increases in scale allow greater efficiency by facilitating specialization and division of labor and by allowing the use of more advanced technologies (which may only become cost-effective for larger organizations). Yet, at some scale of activity, the number of units in the system will grow so large that the costs of coordinating and controlling those units will more than offset any increases in efficiency that accrue from the larger scale.

As the bureaucracy grows and top management becomes increasingly divorced from day-to-day functioning of the system, decision-making responsibility and authority must be delegated to successively lower levels within the system. This, however, requires increases in staff, paper work, travel budgets, and communication costs if the plans and decisions of a vast number of separate decision-making units are going to mesh. Beyond some critical threshold of size, then, the costs of coordination grow disproportionately.

6. An attempt may be made to improve efficency by depersonalizing the system. Since human diversity adds enormously to a system's complexity, a potential means of coping with complexity is to reduce the diversity of human interactions within the system. Rational management techniques may attempt to depersonalize the system by standardizing human responses within the organization.

To the extent that efficiency is valued over human diversity, the human interaction with the system must acquire attributes that increasingly conform to the systemic preference for uniformity and predictability. Employees, constituents, or clients will tend thus to become increasingly depersonalized in their interactions with the system.

7. The level of alienation will tend to increase. A 1975 Louis Harris survey reveals that in the period from 1966 to 1975, the number of people who say "I feel left-out of things going on around me" has risen from 9 percent to 41 percent. These and related data suggest that the level of public alienation may be reaching pathological proportions.

Nor is the sense of alienation limited to a particular segment of society. In a 1976 *Saturday Review* article, Leonard Silk and David Vogel examined the crisis of confidence in American business and concluded that it is a part of a larger pattern of alienation:

> The mood for business leadership is strikingly similar to that of other groups in one important respect: a feeling of impotence, a belief that its future is in the hands of outside forces. For business, as for other groups, frustration often turns to hostility. Feelings of alienation that began in the black community soon spread to the children of the middle class, moved into the white working class, and have affected the military and the police. This mood has now reached the business community. . . . It is a remarkable society in which so many groups, even the "Establishment," feel that "someone else" is in charge, "someone else" is to blame for whatever goes wrong.

Sociologist Melvin Seeman postulates five historical trends that may form the causal basis for the emergence of alienation. These are directly or indirectly tied to the emergence of very large social systems:

1. The expansion of scale of population and social institutions.
2. The decline of kinship and the consequential increase of anonymity and impersonality in social relations.
3. Increased physical and social mobility.
4. Social differentiation arising from specialization and division of labor.
5. Decline of traditional social forms and roles.

These observations suggest a rather direct linkage between alienation and the growth of large social systems.

8. The appropriateness of basic value premises underlying the social system will tend to be increasingly challenged. This proposition assumes that as a system grows, the sheer *quantitative* aggregation will ultimately result in the emergence of a *qualitatively* different system. Thus, the value premises upon which the system was initially established will become increasingly incompatible with the changing demands of a quantitatively enlarged and qualitatively altered system.

To the extent that large, complex social systems have been created by value premises that have become functionally obsolete, then either the system must change to reflect the original values, or the basic value premises themselves will have to change to reflect the character of the changed system. Social conflict will increase until either the value premises or the system itself is changed so as to reestablish congruence between them.

Contemporary challenges to the legitimacy of traditional value premises have assumed such forms as women's liberation, black power, third world ethics, the antiwar movement, the hippy counterculture, the flourishing of Eastern religions, and the conservation and ecology movement. These disparate trends do not individually signify the transformation of historic value premises. Yet, considered collectively, they suggest that major challenges to traditional values are occurring.

9. The number and significance of unexpected consequences of policy actions will increase. As a system grows, it may be subject to the "law of requisite variety" as stated by W. Ross Ashby in *An Introduction to Cybernetics*. This law asserts that the complexity of any policy solution must, in the long run, be equal to the complexity or variety of the problem. To the extent that diminished levels of systems comprehension (Proposition 1) force managers to apply relatively simple solutions to increasingly complex problems, then the law of requisite variety will not be satisfied and unexpected consequences of policy action may result.

Professor Jay Forrester of the Massachusetts Institute of Technology has suggested another reason why the behavior of large systems may result in outcomes that run counter to expectations. In social systems, political pressures often favor short-term policy measures, but when short-term actions, which previously produced favorable results, are redoubled without regard for their long-term consequences, changed circumstances within and without the system may produce both unexpected and even disastrous results.

With smaller and less interdependent bureaucracies, a wrong decision has only limited consequences because of the small scale and loose coupling between social systems. With very large and highly interdependent systems, however, a wrong decision can have far-reaching implications as its impact affects a pervasive and tightly interconnected web of socio-economic systems. Therefore, the number of unexpected outcomes of policy actions and the disruptive potential of these unexpected outcomes may be expected to expand as social systems grow in scale.

10. The system will tend to become more rigid since the form that it assumes inhibits the emergence of new forms. Economist Kenneth Boulding has written, "Growth creates form, but form limits growth." This principle suggests that as a system grows in size, complexity and interdependence, it will seek an enduring, predictable form that will, in turn, limit the ability of the sytem to generate new forms. Large bureaucracies seem to exhibit this characteristic. Richard Goodwin, writing in *The New Yorker,* describes the resistance of large social systems to fundamental structural changes:

> [T]he passion for size, reach, and growth is the soul of all bureaucracy. Within government, the fiercest battles are waged not over principles and ideas but over jurisdiction—control of old and new programs. Radically new pronouncements and policies are often

digested with equanimity, but at the slightest hint of a threat to the existing structure, . . . the entire bureaucratic mechanism mobilizes for defense. Almost invariably, the threat is defeated or simply dissolves in fatigue, confusion, and the inevitable diversion of executive energies.

As growing bureaucracies lock themselves into relatively static and inflexible forms, creative management becomes an exercise analogous to swimming through progressively hardening concrete and the flow of social and organizational evolution is impeded.

11. The number and intensity of perturbations to the system will tend to increase disproportionately. As a social system grows, the number of elements aggregated together also grows. As Donald Michael notes in his book, *The Unprepared Society,* if the same proportion of those elements malfunction, then the increase in absolute numbers aggregated together should yield a greater number of disturbing events within the system.

Further, as the number and diversity of activities within a system increase and relationships among the activities are established, the number of interconnections within the system will tend to increase geometrically. If a significant proportion of those connections are vulnerable to disruption, then the number of perturbations could increase more rapidly than increases in scale.

12. The diversity of innovation will tend to decline. As a system grows, the span of diversity of innovation will tend to constrict, because innovation is confined within the narrowing boundaries of what the system can assimilate without itself undergoing fundamental change. Further, as the system acts to ensure its own survival, diversity of innovation may become confused with disorder.

Moreover, it seems plausible that as social forms become increasingly concretized, greater reliance will be placed on technological rather than social innovation to cope with social problems. Consequently, both the breadth and the depth of innovation will tend to decline.

13. The legitimacy of leadership will tend to decline. To the extent that a system manager must draw his power to govern from the consent of the people, then, within limits, he must demonstrate to his constituency his ability to manage the system well. As the system grows in scale and complexity, relative levels of comprehension at all levels may decline, counterexpected and unexpected consequences may mount, system resilience may diminish, and, for other reasons, the performance of the system may decline. The public will hold the manager of the system responsible for the poor performance. Then, according to the rules of the game, other leaders who wish to be elected will endeavor to persuade the public that they have the "right" and "true" answers to solve the mounting problems of systems malfunction. Thus, a doubly dangerous situation is created: there is the appearance of understanding (in order to get elected or to retain power), but the reality of understanding may be diminishing. Public expectations for effective decision-making may be inordinately high at the same time that the relative capacity to make informed decisions declines. As the gap between expectation and reality grows more pronounced, the legitimacy of the decision-maker will diminish.

One of the most pervasive themes to be found in an examination of the state of health of our sociopolitical systems is the crisis of confidence in leadership and the withdrawal of legitimacy. Pollster Louis Harris described the situation this way in a 1975 talk:

> The toll on confidence in the leadership of institutions has been enormous, both in the public and private sectors. . . . But perhaps the most serious drops have taken place in the case of two of our most central points of power: American business and the federal government. High confidence in business has slipped from 55% in 1966 to 18% in 1975; in the White House it has fallen from 41% to 14%; Congress from 42% to 14%; the U.S. Supreme Court from 51% to 28%. . . . Basically, however, the startling news is that the two major institutions viewed as out of touch with the reality of what people think and want are American business, which for so long has prided itself as correctly anticipating public needs, and American political leadership, which so often has claimed to head up the most responsive democratic system in the world.

Nor is this an isolated finding. The University of Michigan Survey Research Center found that the proportion of people trusting the government in Washington to do what is right "just about always" or "most of the time" dropped from 81% in 1960 to 61% in 1970, and by 1974 the proportion had dropped to 38%. A 1975 report to the Trilateral Commission stated that "Leadership is in disrepute in democratic societies."

To the extent that the capacity to govern requires the consent of those governed, then the pervasive and sustained withdrawal of legitimacy could well cripple the capacity of democracies to manage their affairs.

14. The vulnerability of the system will tend to increase. If we assume that most of the problems of large systems move in concert or on parallel paths, then with rising scale the combined effects of the problems will render the system increasingly vulnerable to disruption. Eric Sevareid forcefully describes the vulnerability of our social systems:

> We now live in and by the web of an enormously complicated, intensely interrelated technology, the whole no greater than its parts and its strongest parts at the mercy of its weakest links. This is a way of life that depends absolutely on order and continuity and predictability. But it happens that we have simultaneously reached a point of discontinuity in the political and social relations of men, where little is predictable and disorder spreads.

One hijacker can capture a multimillion dollar airplane and catapult nations into political confrontation. One defective capacitor can prevent the communication of two presidential candidates with more than 100 million constituents. The shut-down of a single brake plant can stop production at major auto assembly plants throughout the country. A localized power grid failure can plunge the entire eastern seaboard of the U.S. into darkness. The consequences of otherwise isolated and relatively insignificant events, therefore, jeopardize the continued functioning of large systems sensitive to the slightest disruption.

15. The performance of the bureaucracy will tend to decline. If we assume that the previously stated propositions are valid, then as a social system grows to extremes of scale we would expect that the costs of coordination and control will escalate, the comprehensibility of the system will decline, the number and intensity of perturbations will increase, and so on. When these individual problems reach a critical threshold and thereby collectively and intensively reinforce each other, the decline of system performance will be accelerated.

There is no lack of opinion that the performance of many of our largest bureaucracies is rapidly deteriorating. This is graphically reflected in a statement by U. S. Representative James C. Cleveland:

> There is no question that the American people are coming to the conclusion that their Government couldn't run a two-car funeral without fouling up the arrangements.

16. The full extent of declining performance of the system is not likely to be perceived. In most large bureaucracies there are few reliable measures of sys-tems performance. This is partially attributable to the fact that the complexity of the system obscures the operation of the system. Also, the bureaucrat, in order to acquire or retain power, may minimize the significance of malfunctions and error, and maximize the public visibility of his own achievements. Further, there may be delayed, ambiguous and conflicting feedback concerning the effectiveness of vari-ous programs. These and other forces make it difficult to monitor the performance of a massive bureaucracy and thereby make it unlikely that most persons will be able to perceive the true extent to which performance is declining. . . .

COPING WITH INSTITUTIONAL "LIMITS TO GROWTH"

A number of different strategies could be applied in coping with the problems of large, complex bureaucracies.

- Develop alternative models of the behavior of bureaucracies as they evolve over time to ever greater levels of scale, complexity, and interdependence.
- Conduct surveys to ascertain the present status of key social bureaucracies whose continued vigor seems central to a healthy society. Such a survey could, for example, engage the politician and bureaucrat in the process of describing the behavioral properties and problems of large, complex social bureaucracies.

- Develop a spectrum of systems indicators—patterned after economic and social indicators—that may better inform us as to the state of "health" of our central social bureaucracies.
- Encourage the President to consider the state of the social bureaucracies when examining the state of the nation.
- Fund research on the least understood of the four hypothesized outcomes from a period of "systems crisis"—namely, what the nature and form of transformational change of major social bureaucracies could be.
- Explore new individual learning modes that could increase the rate and richness of our acquisition of knowledge (the internalization of information).
- Develop new group learning processes to enable more effective knowledge aggregation and patterning.
- Fund television programs (such as *Nova*) that are educational/informational at much higher levels and across a much broader range of topics and thereby attempt to inform the public of major issues of critical national importance—including the problem of the malfunctioning bureaucracies.
- Pursue governmental reorganization designed, where reasonable and possible, to reduce the scale, interdependence, and complexity of social systems.

The foregoing responses to the problems of bureaucracies are primarily restorative—they are intended to help ameliorate the severity of these problems and to help maintain the existing form of these bureaucracies. A different kind of response would be to search for innovative alternative systems whose "performance" surpasses existing bureaucracies.

Illustrative of these kinds of activities that may engender responses to surpass rather than merely maintain bureaucracies are the following:

- Fund small-scale social and technological experiments and provide "social space," relatively free of bureaucratic impingements, within which these innovations can be tested. This might take the form, for example, of a range of different types of small-scale intermediate new communities that employ different technological and social forms to cope with the new scarcity and other problems that beset our larger systems.
- Develop intermediate or appropriate technology that can increase systems resilience by increasing the self-sufficiency of local communities.
- Encourage national opinion leaders to become informed about the role that small-scale, social innovation could play in coping with larger systems problems and begin the process of building greater social legitimacy for action of this kind.

Among these various responses, perhaps the most powerful but most neglected is that of small-scale social innovation. Consequently, it seems useful to explore briefly the present status of small-scale social innovation in our society.

We are blanketed with large-scale social innovations (e.g., social security, food stamps, Medicare) and with large-scale technological innovations (e.g., mass transit, space shuttle). There are many fewer attempts at small-scale technological innovations (e.g., new agricultural technologies), and there are extremely few small-scale, diversely conceived, social innovations.

The source of creative social innovations has traditionally been the local government. However, the federal government seems to have preempted many major areas of innovation from the state and local government. Perhaps more significantly, the federal government has sapped the vitality from innovation at the local level. Richard Thompson in his book *Revenue Sharing* (Revenue Sharing Advisory Service, Washington, D.C., 1973), examined the impact of federal funding policies and observed that "the federal government has stepped in and many localities have become administrative mechanisms for implementation of national policies rather than dynamic centers of authority and creative problem solving." In a vicious circle of abdication of responsibility for local vitality, small-scale social innovation is seldom tolerated, let alone encouraged.

There seem to exist two substantial stumbling blocks to small-scale social innovation. First, our cultural "opinion leaders" (in business, government, education, and so on) perhaps do not themselves recognize the crucial role that small-scale social innovation can possibly play in responding to increasingly severe, large-scale systems problems. Consequently, small-scale social experimentation may be seen as an activity of only peripheral significance. Yet, support of the larger society appears important since truly creative innovation requires a willingness to risk the possibility of failure.

Few people at the grass roots level seem willing to engage in such risk taking without the tolerance and support of the larger community—particularly when the payoff is not windfall profits to an individual but greater resiliency of our social structures. Even if contemporary opinion leaders did no more than publicly acknowledge and affirm the importance of small-scale social experimentation, it could still result in an outpouring of creative talent.

A second barrier to innovation is that such experimentation can be viewed as a threat to existing institutions (whose participants may not perceive the larger, longer-term threat of a systems crisis). Existing institutions may act in self-defense and attempt to prevent social innovation by engulfing the process in so much "red tape" that it never gathers the momentum or the social space necessary as a precondition to success. Thus, there needs to be sufficient "institutional relaxation"—providing social space relatively free from bureaucratic impingement—to allow these small-scale, social experiments to emerge of their own accord. The advice given by Donald Michael in his book *The Unprepared Society* a decade ago seems even more relevant today in suggesting that the right place to initiate the process of social learning

> . . . may very well be in a "societal interstice" where there may develop or be preserved a different standard and lifestyle. Thereby, at some later, more propitious

time, this enclave or subculture could serve as a model for many other people as our larger society struggles to find its confused and dangerous way.

Evolution is not stasis. Everything alive is impermanent. If our bureaucracies are alive, they will assuredly prove to be impermanent as well. One direct way to recognize the life and vitality of our social systems is by fostering diverse social experimentation so that, in due course, existing social forms may gradually yield to the new forms they have helped to create.

PART Five

CHALLENGES TO THE QUALITY OF LIFE

9

Urban Life and Working

Once socioeconomic springboards to millions of impoverished immigrants, cities no longer offer such economic opportunities. In the first selection, sociologist John D. Kasarda analyzes the consequences of the mismatch between urban employment opportunities and the qualifications of many urban residents. Advances in transportation and communication have intensified the plight of America's economically distressed cities, creating chronic high unemployment.

The deterioration of an urban neighborhood into abandoned apartment houses and rubble-strewn vacant lots, with arson and violence a common occurrence, is an ugly reality in many cities. In their case study of "Woodlawn: The Zone of Destruction," Winston Moore, Charles P. Livermore, and George F. Galland, Jr., illustrate the processes by which such communities self-destruct. They point out those inhabitants are not the only victims and that we all have a stake in restoring economic viability to inner-city neighborhoods.

Using Cleveland as an example, Norman Krumholz, in "The Aging Central City: Some Modest Proposals," suggests neither massive infusion of federal funds to reconstruct central cities nor regional government uniting cities and suburbs is the solution to ending the decline of central cities. Instead, a philosophy of "growing old gracefully" through "constructive shrinkage" and recycling of urban neighborhoods are his alternatives for a return to urban stability.

As technological advances continue to revolutionize occupational fields, creating new jobs and making others obsolete, the problem of career choice is a very real one for today's college students. Marvin Cetron and Thomas O'Toole identify the trends and job growth opportunities ahead in "Careers with a Future," the final selection in this chapter.

Reading 29
Caught in the Web of Change

John D. Kasarda

Two fundamental, yet conflicting, transformations mark the recent history and near-term prospects of our older, larger cities. First is a *functional* change: these cities are becoming administration, information, and higher-order service centers, rather than centers for producing and distributing material goods. Secondly, there is *demographic* change: the residents are no longer predominantly whites of European heritage, but are predominantly blacks, Hispanics, and members of other minority groups.

Concomitant with the functional transformation of these cities have been changes both in the composition and the size of their overall employment bases. During the past two decades, most older, larger cities have experienced substantial job growth in occupations associated with knowledge-intensive service industries. However, selective job growth in these high-skill, predominantly white-collar industries has not nearly compensated for post–World War II employment declines in manufacturing, wholesale trade, and other predominantly blue-collar industries, which once constituted the urban economic backbone. As a result, the total number of jobs available in most of these cities has shrunk considerably over the past three decades.

Analogously, concomitant with the ethnic and racial transformations, there have been substantial changes in the socioeconomic composition and total size of the cities' residential populations. As predominantly white, middle-income groups have dispersed (initially to the suburbs and now increasingly to nonmetropolitan areas), they have been only partially replaced by predominantly lower-income minority groups. The result has been dramatic declines both in the aggregate sizes and the aggregate personal-income levels of the cities' resident populations, while concentrations of the economically disadvantaged continue to expand.

The simultaneous transformation and selective decline of the employment and residential bases of the cities have contributed to a number of serious problems, including a widening gap between urban job-opportunity structures and the skill levels of disadvantaged residents (with correspondingly high rates of structural unemployment), spatial isolation of low-income minorities, and intractably high levels of urban poverty. Accompanying these problems have been a plethora of social and institutional ills further aggravating the predicament of people and places in distress: rising crime, poor public schools, and the decay of once-vibrant residential and commercial subareas.

Responsive to the hardships confronting cities and their inhabitants, the federal government has introduced a variety of urban programs over the past fifteen years. Unfortunately, these programs have had little effect in stemming urban decline or improving long-term employment prospects for the underprivileged. Indeed, mounting evidence suggests that the plight of economically distressed cities and their underprivileged residents is worse than before America's urban programs began.

The poor track record of these federal urban programs is attributable primarily to the failure of our policymakers to appreciate fully the technological and economic dynamics underlying industry's locational choices, on the one hand, and an inadequate consideration of the changing roles of older cities in an advanced service economy, on the other. I will focus on these dynamics and transformations, especially as they have altered the capacity of America's older cities to offer employment opportunities and social mobility for disadvantaged resident groups.

SOCIOECONOMIC SPRINGBOARDS

Cities always have and always will perform valuable social and economic functions, but changing technological and industrial conditions (both national and international) alter such functions over time. Apropos of the assimilation and socioeconomic upgrading of masses of disadvantaged persons historically, it must be remembered that cities performed these functions most effectively during an industrial and transportation age now gone.

During the late nineteenth and early twentieth centuries, America's industrial revolution fostered dramatic national economic development, creating millions of low-skill jobs. Most of this economic development and employment growth occurred in the cities, which possessed comparative advantages over other locations. For firms concentrating in the cities, costs were substantially reduced and efficiency was increased. Among the advantages were superior long-distance transportation and "break in bulk" terminal facilities; abundant and ambitious immigrant labor, willing to work for extremely low wages; essential complementary businesses; and private and public municipal services, such as police and fire protection, sewage systems, and running water.

Territorially restricting transportation technologies and the burgeoning manpower needs of a labor-intensive manufacturing economy generated unprecedentedly high urban concentration. Because the transit and terminal costs of coal were high, manufacturers sought to minimize expenses by clustering together around rail or water terminal sites and sharing bulk carriage costs. Since the main terminal was also where most other raw materials used in the production process were received, and where finished products were shipped, additional cost advantages accrued to factories concentrating near terminal points.

The lack of efficient short-distance transportation technology likewise acted to confine the sites of complementary businesses as well as the residences of the urban labor force. Wholesale establishments, warehouses handling finished goods, and ancillary businesses that serviced the factories or used their by-products reduced costs by locating close to the factories. Similarly, most workers employed by the factories and related business establishments, unable to afford commuting, were clustered within walking distance of their place of employment. Indeed, as late as 1899, the average commuting distance of workers in New York City was approximately two blocks.

Our industrial cities thus evolved in the late nineteenth century as compact agglomerations of production and distribution facilities and as places where millions of unskilled or semiskilled migrants both lived and worked. Spatially circumscribed by prevailing transportation technologies, industrial development and concentrative migration occurred together, generating explosive urban growth. Chicago, for example, which was incorporated in 1833 with a population of 4,100 grew to be a city of more than 2 million residents by 1910, the vast majority of whom lived and worked within a three-mile radius of the city's center.

Spurring the dramatic growth of our industrial cities were a rapidly advancing western resource frontier and burgeoning commercial markets. A powerful entrepreneurial spirit held that individualism, competition, the pursuit of profit, and economic growth were uniformly positive and beneficial. In this political-economic climate, urban industrial development surged, catapulting the entire country into a period of enormous economic expansion. By the dawn of the twentieth century, the output of America's industrial cities had surpassed the *combined* total industrial output of Britain, France, and Germany, the world's leaders in 1860.

It cannot be overemphasized that the employment bases of our early industrial cities were characterized by entry-level job surpluses; today, entry-level job deficits characterize urban employment bases. It was these job surpluses, with few requisites for entry, that attracted the waves of migrants and offered them a foothold in the urban economy. In turn, the rapidly expanding job base that accompanied national economic growth provided ladders of opportunity and social mobility for the migrants, most of whom were escaping areas of economic distress.

Access to opportunity and social mobility was obtained at significant human cost, however. Prejudice, discrimination, hostility, and (frequently) physical violence greeted the new arrivals. Lacking financial resources, unaccustomed to city ways, and often without English language skills, immigrants were given the lowest status and were segregated in overcrowded dwellings in the least desirable areas. A polluted, unsanitary physical environment contributed to high morbidity and mortality, as did the hazardous working conditions found in the factories. Political corruption and exploitation were common, working hours were long, and there was no such thing as a minimum wage. Virtually all immigrants held so-called dead-end jobs.

Nonetheless, there was an abundance of jobs for which the only requisites were a person's desire and physical ability to work. Overall economic growth and this surplus of low-skill jobs gave our older industrial cities a unique historical role as developers of manpower and springboards for social mobility.

During the first half of the twentieth century, numerous advances occurred in transportation, communication, and production-distribution technologies. These served to reduce markedly the previous locational advantages that our older, compactly structured cities had held for manufacturing and warehousing and made uncongested suburban sites more cost-effective. Among these advances were the shift from rail and barge transport to trucking, the spread of peripheral highways and public utilities, and automated assembly-line techniques. By 1960, further advances in transportation and communication technologies, together with growing industrial competition from nonmetropolitan areas and abroad, made our larger, older cities all but obsolete with respect to manufacturing and warehousing. A massive exodus of blue-collar jobs began—an exodus that accelerated during the past decade.

Exacerbating blue-collar job losses in the cities has been the post–World War II flight of retail trade and consumer services, which followed their traditional middle- and upper-income patrons to the suburbs and exurbs. Between 1954 and 1978, more than 15,000 shopping centers and malls were constructed to serve expanding suburban and exurban populations. By 1975, these shopping centers and malls produced more than one-half of the United States' annual retail sales. As a consequence, central cities have suffered marked job losses in standard retail and consumer-service industries.

Significant countertrends, however, are under way in certain retail and service sectors, as businesses and institutions offering highly specialized goods and services continue to be attracted to downtown areas. The specialized nature of these establishments often makes it advantageous to locate at centralized nodes that maximize accessibility to people and firms in the metropolitan area. Advertising agencies; brokerage houses; consulting firms; financial institutions; luxury goods shops; legal, accounting, and professional complexes—these have been accumulating in the central business districts. Traditional department stores and other establishments—unable to compete effectively or unable to afford the skyrocketing rents— are being replaced.

The past two decades have also witnessed a remarkable growth of high-rise administrative offices in the central business districts of our largest cities. Even with major advances in telecommunications technology, many administrative headquarters still rely on a complement of legal, financial, public relations, and other specialized services that are most readily available in the central business districts. Unlike manufacturing, wholesale trade, and retail trade—which typically have large space-per-employee requirements—most managerial, clerical, professional, and business-service functions are space-intensive. In addition, persons performing these service functions can be "stacked" vertically, layer after layer, in downtown high-rises without losing any productivity. Indeed, office proximity often enhances the productivity of those whose activities entail extensive, nonroutinized, face-to-face interaction. The result has been an office-building boom in the central business districts.

EMPLOYMENT-DEMOGRAPHIC DISARTICULATIONS

The growth of administrative, financial, professional, and similar "knowledge class" jobs in the central business districts of our large cities, together with substantial losses of blue-collar jobs, has altered the important role the cities once played as opportunity ladders for the disadvantaged. Aggravating the problems engendered by the deterioration of historical blue-collar job bases has been the flight of middle-income population and traditional retail-trade and consumer-service establishments elsewhere in the city. Further, these movements have combined to erode city tax bases, damage secondary labor markets, and isolate many disadvantaged persons in economically distressed subareas where the opportunities for employment are minimal.

Particularly hard hit by post–World War II declines of middle-income population and blue-collar jobs are our larger, older cities in the northern industrial belt. Unfortunately, it is many of these same cities that have experienced the largest postwar migration inflows of persons whose educational backgrounds and skills are ill-suited for the information-processing jobs which have partially replaced the lost blue-collar jobs. Consequently, inner-city unemployment rates are well above the national average and are inordinately high among educationally disadvantaged minorities, whose numbers continue to grow in our urban centers.

Data presented in Table 1 for our four largest northern cities illustrate the scope of urban employment decline in the postwar period. New York City and Chicago, for example, have each lost more than 300,000 manufacturing jobs since 1947, with the most pronounced employment losses occurring after 1967. Also ravaged have been Philadelphia and Detroit.

Table 1   Employment Changes in Major Northern Cities

	Manufacturing	Wholesale	Retail	Selected Services	Total
New York					
1948–77	−330,535	−122,071	−208,595	153,250	−507,951
1967–77	−285,600	−82,925	−94,053	30,992	−431,586
Chicago					
1948–77	−301,407	−51,827	−100,803	57,874	−396,163
1967–77	−180,900	−41,023	−49,829	45,246	−226,506
Philadelphia					
1948–77	−171,130	−26,573	−63,263	15,263	−245,703
1967–77	−106,400	−19,328	−23,743	2,242	−147,229
Detroit					
1948–77	−185,073	−21,980	−78,804	−4,484	−290,341
1967–77	−56,400	−20,617	−32,632	−10,706	−120,355

Source: Censuses of Manufacturing and Censuses of Business.

Wholesale and retail trade employment in all these cities likewise deteriorated considerably. However, there are temporal differences. Whereas most retail-employment losses occurred before 1967, wholesale-employment declines (like those in manufacturing) accelerated after 1967, during which more than two-thirds of the total 1974–77 job declines occurred. The accelerating pace of central-city job losses in the manufacturing and wholesale sectors reflects the technological forces discussed above as well as the growing diseconomies of central-city locations for production and warehousing activities.

The selective nature of job declines in the twelve large cities noted above is indicated by employment-change data for their service industries. Only Detroit showed a net loss in service-industry jobs between 1947 and 1977, and this loss is entirely accountable by service-industry job losses since 1967. Chicago and New York City, on the other hand, have shown substantial vitality in their service industries since World War II. Even in these cities, though, service-industry job growth was overwhelmed by employment declines in manufacturing, wholesale trade, and retail trade. Overall, Chicago lost nearly 400,000 jobs between 1947 and 1977; during the same time period, New York City lost more than 500,000 jobs. In each case, the vast majority of overall job losses are attributable to blue-collar employment declines. Moreover, detailed analysis of sectoral employment change demonstrates that all of the net increase in service employment in New York City, Chicago, and Philadelphia has been in knowledge-intensive industries (e.g., finance, health and legal services, colleges and universities, engineering firms, and such business services as accounting, advertising, data processing, management consulting, and R&D). Conversely, service-sector employment opportunities with lower educational requirements (e.g., in hotels, personal services, and a full range of such consumer services as auto repair) have declined markedly.

Thus, a rather clear picture emerges. Central-city employment in those industries which traditionally sustained large numbers of less-skilled persons has declined precipitously. These employment losses have been partially replaced by newer service industries, which typically have high educational requisites for entry. The dissonant expansion in large northern cities of population groups whose educational backgrounds place them at a serious disadvantage deserves attention.

Obtaining an accurate account of each city's changing demographic composition (by race and ethnicity) is not without its complications. Because Hispanics (most of whom are classified as whites in the census) are typically considered a racial-ethnic minority, one cannot determine actual minority compositional changes in the cities without separating this group from whites, blacks, and others. Published census data do not permit one to do this. However, the 1970 fourth-count summary computer tapes and the 1980 system's File-1A computer tapes both contain information on how the Hispanic/Spanish-origin population was allocated for each city across "white," "black," and "other." With this information, it is possible to reconstruct each city's 1970 and 1980 non-Hispanic white population, non-Hispanic black population, and non-Hispanic "other" (primarily Asian) population in addition to its Hispanic population. These adjustments permit refined analysis of each city's racial-ethnic residential compositional changes and their actual minority demographic transformation. (See Table 2.)

New York City, which experienced an overall population decline of 823,212 during the 1970–80 decade, lost 1,392,718 non-Hispanic whites. Thus, in just ten years, New York's non-Hispanic white population (i.e., its nonminority population) dropped by an amount larger than the *total* population of any other U.S. city with the exception of Los Angeles, Chicago, Philadelphia, and Houston. Approximately 25 percent of the loss of non-Hispanic whites in New York City was replaced by an infusion of more than 200,000 Hispanics during the 1970s and, to a somewhat lesser extent, by the growth of non-Hispanic "others" and non-Hispanic blacks. The transition to minority residential dominance of our nation's largest city seems all but assured.

Chicago's demographic experience during the 1970s was similar to New York City's, but at about one-half the scale. Registering a net population drop of 357,753

Table 2   Demographic Changes in Major Northern Cities

	Total Population	Non-Hispanic			Hispanic Population[a]	Percent Minority
		Whites	Blacks	Other[a]		
New York						
1980	7,071,639	3,668,945	1,694,127	302,543	1,406,024	48%
1970	7,894,851	5,061,663	1,517,967	112,940	1,202,281	36
Change	−823,212	−1,393,718	176,160	189,603	203,743	
Chicago						
1980	3,005,072	1,299,557	1,187,905	95,547	422,063	57
1970	3,362,825	1,998,914	1,076,483	39,571	247,857	41
Change	−357,753	−699,357	111,422	55,976	174,206	
Philadelphia						
1980	1,688,210	963,469	633,485	27,686	63,570	43
1970	1,948,609	1,246,940	646,015	10,975	44,679	36
Change	−260,399	−283,471	−12,530	16,711	18,891	
Detroit						
1980	1,203,339	402,077	754,274	18,018	28,970	67
1970	1,511,336	820,181	651,847	9,254	30,054	46
Change	−307,997	−418,104	102,427	8,764	−1,084	
Total Change						
1970–80	−1,749,361	−2,793,650	377,479	271,054	395,756	

[a]The term "Hispanic" is used for all those classified as Hispanic or Spanish origin. "Non-Hispanic Other" is used for those classified as Asians, American Indians, and Pacific Islanders.

residents between 1970 and 1980, Chicago's non-Hispnaic white population declined by 699,357, whereas the city's minority population (non-Hispanic blacks,
non-Hispanic "others," plus Hispanics) grew by 341,604. More than 50 percent of
Chicago's minority population increase during the decade consisted of Hispanics
(174,206). By 1980, 57 percent of Chicago's resident population was composed of
minorities.

Among the four largest northern cities in the United States (New York, Chicago, Philadelphia, and Detroit), the City of Brotherly Love had the smallest
aggregate population decline, losing slightly over a quarter of a million residents
during the 1970s. Both the number of non-Hispanic whites and non-Hispanic blacks
declined in Philadelphia between 1970 and 1980, while other, non-Hispanic minorities and Hispanics increased. Philadelphia's substantial decline in non-Hispanic
whites (283,471) together with its net increase of 23,072 minority residents during
the 1970s raised its minority proportion to 43 percent in 1980.

Detroit experienced the highest rate of non-Hispanic white residential decline
of any major city in the country. Between 1970 and 1980, Detroit lost more than
one-half of its non-Hispanic white residents (from 820,181 to 402,077). Concurrently, Detroit had the fourth-largest absolute increase of non-Hispanic blacks of
any city in the country (102,427), falling just behind Chicago in black population
increase. Combined with modest increases in Hispanics and other minorities, Detroit's large increase in black residents and precipitous drop in non-Hispanic white
residents transformed the city's residential base from 46 percent minority in 1970 to
67 percent minority in 1980.

Between 1970 and 1980, our four largest northern cities suffered an aggregate
loss of 2,793,650 non-Hispanic whites, while their Hispanic residential bases increased by nearly 400,000. Added to the Hispanic increase during the 1970s were
substantial cumulative increases of non-Hispanic blacks (377,479) and other non-
Hispanic minorities (271,054), resulting in a total increase of more than 1,040,000
minority residents in the four cities. These compositional changes have further
implications.

CONSEQUENCES OF MISMATCH

It has been noted that job opportunities matching the educational backgrounds and
skills of many minorities have disappeared from major northern cities. Concurrently, as higher-income white-collar workers moved to the suburbs and exurbs,
white-collar jobs increased substantially in the central city. One consequence of the
residence–job opportunity mismatch is increased commuting in both directions
between central cities and outlying nodes. This mismatch manifests itself each
weekday morning on the radial urban expressways, where one observes heavy
streams of white-collar workers commuting into the central business districts from
their suburban residences; simultaneously, in the opposite lanes, streams of inner-
city residents are commuting to their blue-collar jobs in outlying areas.

The job opportunity–residential composition mismatch has had especially deleterious consequences for minorities and blue-collar ethnic whites left behind in the inner city. As blue-collar industries have deconcentrated, they have become scattered among suburban, exurban, and nonmetropolitan sites. Their dispersed nature makes public transportation from central-city neighborhoods to most outlying locations impractical, requiring virtually all city residents who work outside the central city to commute by private automobile. The high and increasing costs of inner-city automobile ownership, insurance, and maintainance imposes a heavy financial burden on these people. Moreover, a large portion of inner-city residents, particularly low-income minorities, can afford neither the luxury nor the employment necessity of owning an automobile. In Chicago, for example, four out of five inner-city blacks do not own automobiles. The result is rising rates of urban structural unemployment, especially among disadvantaged minorities who traditionally had found employment in those industries which have relocated in the suburbs, nonmetropolitan areas, and abroad.

In our four largest northern cities, unemployment rates among minorities have risen dramatically. (See Table 3.) With the exception of industrially crippled Detroit, the rise in unemployment rates among whites in these cities between 1971 and 1980 corresponded very closely with the rise in the national unemployment rate. The moderate rise in youth unemployment among whites also echoed national trends. Black and other minority unemployment rates, however, soared. Worst hit was Detroit, where adult male minority unemployment rates rose to nearly 30 percent in 1980. Recall that Detroit also experienced a major increase in black residents between 1970 and 1980. Youth minority unemployment rates for Detroit, already high in 1971 (44.4 percent), rose to 52.1 percent in 1980.

Table 3   Changing Unemployment Rates in Major Northern Cities

	New York (%)		Chicago (%)		Philadelphia (%)		Detroit (%)	
Race, Sex, and Age	1971	1980	1971	1980	1971	1980	1971	1980
White								
Men, 20+	5.8	6.6	4.0	8.6	3.4	7.0	6.5	18.2
Women, 20+	5.5	7.1	3.7	6.9	4.4	6.3	5.3	11.8
Both sexes, 16–19	20.4	23.8	14.2	21.0	14.2	19.4	17.4	22.2
Black and other								
Men, 20+	6.2	11.0	6.4	14.3	7.7	19.4	10.4	29.3
Women, 20+	7.4	7.7	7.1	11.5	3.5	15.7	13.6	19.8
Both sexes, 16–19	26.3	40.0	36.3	55.0	22.7	46.4	44.4	52.1

Source: Current Population Surveys and Geographic Profiles of Employment and Unemployment, 1971 and 1980.

New York City, with its huge white outmigration, experienced negligible growth in adult white male unemployment between 1971 and 1980. But unemployment rates for adult black males nearly doubled during the decade, and rates for black youth unemployment rose from 26.3 percent to 40 percent. Chicago lost a much larger proportion of its jobs than New York City during the 1970s and registered significant increases both in its white and black resident-unemployment rates. By 1980, adult black male unemployment reached 14.3 percent, and black youth unemployment had climbed to 55 percent—nearly triple the unemployment rate for white youths.

The picture in Philadelphia is no brighter, with adult male minority-unemployment rates reaching nearly 20 percent and minority youth unemployment rates exceeding 46 percent in 1980. Diverging from the pattern in other major northern cities, unemployment rates for adult minority women increased *fourfold* in Philadelphia between 1971 and 1980.

The extent of unemployment in these four cities is not fully captured by the rates just cited, for they refer only to those jobless persons actively seeking employment during the month before the survey was taken. Thus these figures exclude workers who have given up searching and others who have dropped out of the labor force but who would work if presented with an opportunity. If such persons were included in the unemployment statistics, central-city jobless rates would, no doubt, be much higher.

WHAT NEXT?

It is certain that chronically high unemployment will plague large portions of the urban underclass so long as the demographic and job-opportunity structures of the cities move in conflicting directions. Despite a variety of public policy efforts to slow the departure of blue-collar jobs from our cities, the exodus continues apace. Government subsidies, tax incentives, and regulatory relief contained in existing and proposed urban programs are not nearly sufficient to overcome the technological and market-driven forces that are redistributing jobs and shaping the economies of our major cities.

Cities that can exploit their emerging service-sector roles may well experience renewed economic vitality and net job increases in the years ahead. However, it is doubtful that those on the bottom rungs of the socioeconomic ladder will benefit, since they lack the appropriate skills for advanced service-sector jobs. Indeed, their employment prospects could further deteriorate. New York City, for instance, capitalizing on its strength as an international financial and administrative center, experienced a net increase of 167,000 jobs between 1977 and 1981. Yet, while the city's overall employment base was expanding, its minority unemployment rates continued to climb. This is because virtually all of New York's employment expansion during the four-year period was concentrated in white-collar service industries, whereas manufacturing employment dropped by 55,000 jobs and wholesale and retail-trade employment declined by an additional 9,000 jobs. These figures, together with the other data for New York City presented above, provide dramatic testimony that the urban residence–job opportunity mismatch and corresponding minority unemployment rates can worsen even under conditions of overall central-city employment gains.

The seemingly dysfunctional growth of underprivileged populations in our urban centers at a time when these centers are experiencing serious contractions in lower-skill jobs raises a number of interrelated questions: What is it that continues to attract and hold underprivileged persons in inner-city areas of distress? How are the underprivileged able to stay economically afloat? What, in short, has replaced traditional urban jobs as a means of economic subsistence for the underclass?

Answers to these questions may be found in the dramatic rise since 1960 of two alternative economies that increasingly dominate the livelihood of the urban underclass: the *welfare economy* (public housing, food stamps, aid to families with dependent children, etc.) and the *underground economy* (illegal activities and unreported cash and barter transactions). These alternative economies have mushroomed in our cities, functioning as institutionalized surrogates for the declining production economies that once attracted and sustained large numbers of disadvantaged residents.

Yet, while the burgeoning production economies of our urban past provided substantial numbers of the disadvantaged with a means of entry into the mainstream economy as well as with opportunities for mobility, today's urban welfare and underground economies often have the opposite effects—limiting options and reinforcing the urban concentration of those without access to the economic mainstream. Most urban welfare programs, for example, have been specifically targeted to inner-city areas of greatest distress, thereby providing the subsistence infrastructure that keeps disadvantaged people there. Dependent on place-oriented public housing, nutritional assistance, health care, income maintenance and other such programs, large segments of the urban underclass have become anchored in areas of severe employment decline. Racial discrimination and insufficient low-cost housing in areas of employment growth further obstruct mobility and job acquisition by the underclass, as do deficiencies in the technical and interpersonal skills so necessary to obtain and hold jobs. The upshot is that increasing numbers of potentially productive persons find themselves socially, economically, and spatially isolated in segregated inner-city wastelands, where they subsist on a combination of government handouts and their own informal economies. Such isolation, dependency, and blocked mobility breed hopelessness, despair, and alienation which, in turn, foster drug abuse, family dissolution, and other social malaise disproportionately afflicting the urban underclass.

My comments here should not be interpreted as implying that government aid to people and places in distress is unnecessary or without merit. Most urban welfare programs have had important palliative effects, temporarily relieving some very painful symptoms associated with the departure of blue-collar jobs—poor housing, inadequate nutritional and health care, and so on. Still, while some success has been achieved in relieving these pains, underlying structural disarticulations are growing worse. These disarticulations, to reiterate, are rooted in conflicting demographic and functional transformations in our cities, resulting in a widening gap between their residents' skill levels and new job-opportunity structures.

Reading 30

Woodlawn: The Zone of Destruction

Winston Moore

Charles P. Livermore

George F. Galland, Jr.

America has always had slums. But for the most part they have been "good" slums, as slums go: They stayed put for a while, they had a certain stability, sometimes they endured, and if they changed, they did so slowly. Woodlawn, by contrast, was a terrible slum: *It did not last.* Large parts of it simply disappeared, and towards the end it disintegrated with extraordinary speed. In other neighborhoods in other cities across the nation, other slums are increasingly doing just what Woodlawn did—disappearing. The problem with this process is that it creates human pain and tragedy on an immense scale. That much is understood by practically everybody now, thanks to the attention paid to Woodlawn by the media. It isn't pretty to watch whole communities self-destruct in the heart of the cities of the world's richest country, nor is it good for America's self-respect to feel that it has a case of incurable cancer. But just to feel bad about it, or deplore it, is not quite enough. We also need to take a serious unsentimental look at the reasons for the collapse of neighborhoods like Woodlawn, for until we understand this process, we are not going to be able to abate the suffering and other problems it entails—and we may in fact unwittingly exacerbate them.

THE CYCLE OF ABANDONMENT

Some of the larger reasons for what happened in Woodlawn are clear enough. First, we are at the end of an historic cycle of displacement. The huge European migrations of the 19th and early 20th centuries are now over, and the 20th-century

Reprinted with permission of the authors from *The Public Interest* 30 (1973):41–59, abridged. Copyright © 1984 by National Affairs, Inc.

migrations of blacks from the rural South to the urban North have slowed down. The succession of newly arrived population groups which caused neighborhoods to shift from older to newer immigrants is at an end, and in older neighborhoods like Woodlawn there is no new group on the horizon to succeed the blacks. These older black communities are therefore losing population and have housing surpluses. They are largely populated by a destructive residual underclass. This underclass is not something brought into the city by rural-to-urban migration or an indigenous black culture; it is instead largely the product of urban welfare policies, which institutionalize poverty, stifle upward mobility, and discourage stable family formation for large numbers of blacks. As a result, the environment of these older neighborhoods becomes so dangerous and the management of housing so risky that no new population will move into them, and no one will invest in them except as part of a large-scale development which has the capacity to *exclude* the underclass.

Second, there is the arithmetic of housing. Real estate is a business. You can make money on used housing if you can sell it or rent it for a profit. If you can't do either, there is no reason to hold it. As long as middle-class and working-class families lived in neighborhoods like Woodlawn, it was possible to charge rents sufficient to make a profit on rental housing. But along with their white counterparts, black middle-class families have been leaving Woodlawn for newer communities where they can own their own homes. Those who couldn't afford to become homeowners have had to move out as the growth of lower-class crime has made the neighborhood unsafe to live in. That has left only the very poor, who cannot move. There is money to be made by developers and builders of new subsidized housing. But there is no money to be made from used private housing for the black lower class, and neither the black or white middle class will reclaim it. So it is abandoned. . . .

Third, much of the housing occupied by the black families who came in the big migrations during and after the World Wars was already old and worn out when they arrived. Old housing may last forever in rural New England towns and in stable communities, but it wears out rapidly when subjected to abuse or even hard use by poor people with large families.

Fourth, personal security in neighborhoods like Woodlawn has broken down so completely that few families with any choice want to live there. Traditional police techniques for maintaining order depend on assistance from ordinary community and family institutions which most neighborhoods can take for granted. When a neighborhood like Woodlawn reaches the end of its historical line of succession, these institutions no longer function. Being the only enforcer of neighborhood security is a new role for local government, one which it has not yet learned to perform effectively. We haven't yet found ways to deal with the problems of kids in these neighborhoods who get into trouble, or to get adequate school supervision over kids who get none at home, or to provide proper law enforcement when all fear to testify.

As conditions get worse, everybody runs who can. All that is left is a population no landlord wants, a dangerous underclass spawned by poverty, joblessness, misguided welfare policies, and ineffectual corrections and educational programs. In the final stage, the kids and young adults of this underclass cannibalize their own neighborhoods, stripping vacant apartments of anything of value, doing $30,000 worth of damage to a house to get a few pounds of brass fittings and copper wiring to sell to junk dealers for a few pennies.

These, as we said, are the general outlines of the abandonment process, which are well known. But why it happens in any particular neighborhood, and what precisely goes on there, is not so well understood. Woodlawn provides a vivid illustration of one particularly grave case of the general phenomenon. As we shall see, it does not happen altogether automatically, and both government and private institutions play a significant role.

A PORTRAIT OF AN OLD NEIGHBORHOOD

Woodlawn is a neighborhood of less than two square miles near Lake Michigan, immediately south of the University of Chicago and eight miles south of Chicago's Loop. Population began to accumulate in the Woodlawn area after 1880. Never notably fashionable, the neighborhood developed a large white transient population in boarding houses and apartment hotels built during the first decades of this century. Its major foreign groups were Irish, German, and English, but apparently it never developed the pronounced "ethnicity" characteristic of some other Chicago neighborhoods. Its racial transition covered 40 years. Blacks in Woodlawn, according to the U.S. Census, increased from 13 percent of the total population in 1930 to 39 percent in 1950. During the 1950s the transition accelerated, and by 1960 only 8,450 whites were left, most of them living on the southern fringe of the University of Chicago.

As Woodlawn went black, its total population rose—from about 66,000 in 1930 to some 81,000 in 1960. The age composition also changed: in 1930 only 4.8 percent of Woodlawn's inhabitants were under five, and only 21.7 percent were under 20, but by 1960, 13.6 percent were under five and 34.2 percent were under 20. As Woodlawn's housing grew older, it grew more crowded. The total number of dwelling units rose from 27,624 in 1950 to 29,616 in 1960, an increase due to subdivision (mostly illegal) of existing structures, since new construction came to a halt in Woodlawn during this period. Of the total number of dwelling units, only 8.8 percent were owner-occupied in 1960 (the city-wide figure was 32.7 percent). Particularly significant was the high concentration of large apartment houses: 14,359 of the 29,616 total dwelling units were in structures with 10 or more dwelling units apiece. This concentration of large, generally absentee-owned rental buildings was matched elsewhere in Chicago only by the wealthy new lakefront areas. This is a critical fact in understanding neighborhood decay, since abandonment is usually a problem of rental housing, not privately owned homes.

In 1960, at the beginning of Woodlawn's disastrous decade, the community was a crowded, largely rental-occupied black neighborhood, most of whose housing was at least 40 years old. An awesome collapse followed. During the 1960s Woodlawn's population declined from 81,000 to 52,000, a drop of 36 percent, and it is still dropping; the core of Woodlawn, between Cottage Grove Avenue and Jackson Park, lost 41 percent of its population. These losses exceeded those suffered by any other Chicago community. Between 1965 and 1971, the city demolished over 400 Woodlawn buildings. Lately the city has been demolishing at a rate of 500 dwelling units a year in Woodlawn and currently has a demolition backlog there of over 1500.

HOW THE HOUSING MARKET COLLAPSED

Numbers like these are evidence of a complete collapse in the housing market. The dismal arithmetic of Woodlawn real estate can be looked at from either the supply side or the demand side. Ironically, what originally began to deflate demand for Woodlawn's rental housing was the expansion in housing opportunities for black families in other areas of Chicago. During the 1950s and 1960s, large numbers of white families left the central city and bought homes in the suburbs. The same pattern has been taking place, on a smaller scale, within the black community. In 1940 the black population of Chicago was 282,244, three quarters of whom lived in just three neighborhoods on the Near South Side—Douglas, Grand Boulevard, and Washington Park—which were Chicago's only black-majority neighborhoods. By 1960 Chicago's black population had grown threefold, to 812,637, and 15 community areas were now predominantly black. In 1940, only about 5 percent of black-occupied dwelling units were owner-occupied; by 1960, however, the proportion had risen dramatically to almost 15 percent. The growing black population was moving into white neighborhoods where single-family houses predominated, and for the first time developers were putting up new housing to sell to blacks, especially on the far South Side.

The blacks are thus following the pattern set by many white immigrant groups, who first established themselves in older rental housing and then gradually moved outward toward homeownership as they moved up the economic ladder—a process described by the "trickle-down" theory of the housing market. But the difference between such previous groups and the blacks is that no one is replacing the blacks as they move out of older rental neighborhoods like Woodlawn. There is no group left for the housing to trickle down to, and middle-class blacks do not have to continue living in it. Today a middle-class black family is not forced to rent housing in older "renter" neighborhoods such as Woodlawn. It can generally buy a house in one of the changing neighborhoods, or in one of the new developments aimed at blacks.

. . . The result of all this is that demand for the kind of housing that predominates in Woodlawn—large, rental, walk-up apartment buildings—is increasingly concentrated at the low-income end of the spectrum. Except in a few special situations, this particular kind of housing seems to have lost favor with prevailing American tastes. Areas with large concentrations of single people or newly formed families still seem able to support large concentrations of older rental walk-up housing, but by and large this kind of housing is for people who have the least choice. The "core" of demand in the Woodlawn housing market—demand by middle-class families—has disappeared. Thus even in the absence of criminal behavior and the other disincentives of a deteriorating community, Woodlawn's housing would have held decreasing attraction for the middle class, black or white.

Woodlawn's rental housing could probably have continued to serve the many working families who had enough income to pay rents required to make the housing profitable, but who were unable to become homeowners. Such families form the nucleus of many of Chicago's white working-class communities, and rental housing in these areas still seems viable. But when the explosion of lower-class crime in Woodlawn forced out even those who could not afford to improve their housing situation, the bottom dropped out of the demand for Woodlawn's housing. In short, changing tastes and opportunities caused those to leave who could afford to move up the housing ladder; criminal terror pushed out the rest. . . .

Perhaps the most concise description of this cycle comes from a group of predominantly black-run banks and savings and loan associations. They hold mortgages on properties in Woodlawn and similar neighborhoods. In a brief document pleading for government assistance to housing they wrote:

> The mortgage usually starts with an average mortgage of 70 per cent of the appraised value of the building, for an average term of 15 years. When the mortgage is made the building is basically sound and in good condition.
>
> However, because these buildings are old they deteriorate at a very rapid rate. Added to this is the problem of rising expenses such as taxes, fuel, insurance and maintenance. The only expense that remains constant is the mortgage note. These expenses rise at a greater rate than the landlord can raise rents. The result is that, on the average, in five years a building that made a profit at the beginning of the mortgage term no longer makes a profit.
>
> The owner in order to make ends meet cuts back on the only expenses that he has some control over—maintenance. This reduction in maintenance is at a period in the building's economic life when more and not less maintenance is required just to retard normal deterioration—old things deteriorate at a faster rate than new things. The value of the building is, of course, diminishing during this time.
>
> The mortgage balance during this five-year period has not been reduced by a third, because a mortgage balance reduces more slowly at the beginning of the mortgage term. With the value of the building diminishing faster than the mortgage balance is reducing, what began as a 70 per cent mortgage becomes a 90–100 per cent mortgage.
>
> The regulations governing the mortgagee would not allow further advances or increases of the loan when these conditions occur, along with the fact that it would not be good

business to send good money after bad. Needless to say, generally other avenues of financing repairs and rehabilitation are not available. With no repairs and rehabilitation, demolition is the ultimate result.

. . . Woodlawn is a perfect inner-city case study not only for the collapse of its housing market, but also for the cycle of crime that combined with the arithmetic of real estate to wipe almost the entire community off the map. Woodlawn's crime problem became nationally famous. For years its street gangs were surrounded by an aura of romanticism and ideological controversy that made it difficult for many well-meaning people to see what they really represented. But now that the drama is drawing to a close in a heap of rubble, it is possible to pick out the stages that crime in Woodlawn went through.

The cycle began with a rapid build-up of poor blacks—many of them part of large families headed by dependent mothers—in Woodlawn's dense apartment clusters. Disorganized families who cannot get into public housing have few choices. Homeowners in the black community avoid renting to them because of their destructiveness. They must seek out large, absentee-owned apartment buildings that are increasingly shunned by more prosperous families. Because of its abundance of such buildings. Woodlawn was practically guaranteed a denser concentration of disorganized families than any other black area of Chicago. While many Chicago neighborhoods were "going black" during this period, it was the older, heavily built-up neighborhoods like Woodlawn that received most of the underclass. Gangs formed, as they always have in poor neighborhoods. But until about 1963 or 1964, they were small and they seemed little different from the traditional street gangs fighting over their turf.

. . . The gangs fascinated people concerned with social problems. Senator Jacob Javits made a trip to Chicago and invited them to dine with him. They accepted—and kept their hats on during the meal in the hotel dining room. During this same period, Martin Luther King, launching the Southern Christian Leadership Conference's (SCLC) open housing campaign in Chicago, was encouraged to enlist the Woodlawn gangs in his cause. Already having found a sympathetic ear in some of the socially conscious newspaper reporters, [gangs such as] the Blackstone Rangers now had the mantle of racial heroes thrust upon them.

Such flattery was fuel to the gang leaders' fire. If intimidation through violence on a small scale produced a trickle of affluence, on a larger scale it could produce a flood. Their power depended on their numbers; their numbers depended on vigorous recruitment; recruitment depended on terror; and so terror became the name of the game. It was simple—join the Rangers or be shot.

THE TERROR

"Stones run it" was their claim—and as far as the streets were concerned, they did. To prevent shooting in the local high school, gang members were made hall monitors. Over one thousand students fled Hyde Park High School in a single year, many of whom apparently went to live with relatives in the South. There was hardly a doorway in any rented building in Woodlawn that was not painted with the initials of the gang. Due to the recent marketing of a spray-paint can, scores of buildings could be decorated in a very short time. The walls of schools, churches, houses, and even police stations helped carry the message. Those who couldn't read were beaten up. Murder and arson eliminated resistance.

. . . This expansionary phase of gang activity and underclass crime carried the death blow to a community already beset by problems and whose increasingly unprofitable rental housing was on the verge of abandonment. Even without underclass gang terror the working and middle classes had a tendency to leave Woodlawn's older rental housing for newer neighborhoods. But the terror of the gangs finally put to flight even those who couldn't afford anything better. That destroyed whatever economic viability was left in Woodlawn's rental housing. Not everybody left, of course; to this day there remain in Woodlawn many families that survived the chaos, homeowners who couldn't sell their houses or who refused to flee. . . .

THE DEVASTATION OF WOODLAWN

A wave of arson and vandalism completed the community's criminal cycle. Vandalism is profitable to various people for various reasons. It has been speculated, although not proved, that owners sometime hire arsonists to gut their buildings. Destruction by fire is the clearest way under the income tax law to claim a tax loss. One unidentified real estate manager told a Chicago *Daily News* reporter, "It is known that if you want a fire to occur, you can arrange to have it done. And if you can't make money on a building, you sure as hell can collect insurance on it by burning it down. I know that if I wanted a fire, all I'd have to do is make a phone call—let it out—saying I wanted a fire. The word circulates and I would be contacted. The going price is $600."

But owner-sponsored arson probably accounts for only a small part of the fires. In abandoned or semi-abandoned buildings, thieves strip the fixtures, beginning with major items like water heaters and continuing down to the plumbing and wiring. Setting fires makes it easier for vandals to get at fixtures buried in the building structure and to push out the remaining tenants so that the whole building can be stripped down. And many fires probably represent arson just for the hell of it.

The theory that a real estate developers' conspiracy is responsible for the final collapse of Woodlawn has such an attraction that even experts who don't believe it sometimes espouse it, apparently just to see whether they can get away with it. . . .

The trouble with the conspiracy theory is not that it is implausible, but that the forces dismantling Woodlawn need no help from conspirators. Conceivably a few could be found, but the Woodlawn process does not depend on them. This is becoming evident as neighborhoods in less desirable locations have begun to go through the same process. No one has thought of the west side of Chicago as a real estate developer's dream; yet when fires and abandonment began there, the Northwest Community Organization passed a resolution charging that "a conspiracy of city officials, real estate speculators, mortgage houses, and others is responsible for the fires in order to scare us so they can tear down our neighborhood to build a high-rise for people in the suburbs." Building abandonment and fires are beginning to plague other black neighborhoods far inland, which hold no self-evident charms for speculators. One such neighborhood, Lawndale, has probably suffered more heavily than Woodlawn, according to a recent federally sponsored study of abandoned buildings in Chicago and elsewhere.

SHOULD SOMETHING BE DONE?

What can be done to prevent what happened in Woodlawn from happening elsewhere? That question raises another question: *Should* anything be done? There are obvious advantages to letting the Woodlawn process go on. After all, as long as there is any housing left in the city, there will always be somewhere for the poor to live. As the more affluent classes, black and white, flee from the advancing underclass, the black poor will take over the housing they leave behind—and this, in turn, may well mean that the supply of housing for the black poor will get better. They have finally worn out much of the oldest housing; the neighborhoods they will inherit from here on will be newer.

Furthermore, while there are losses involved, they are borne largely by private investors, often other blacks, who lose their equity and by lenders who hold mortgages. This doesn't show up as a direct loss to the average taxpayer. And losses in the city may be compensated by gains elsewhere. The pressure on the white and black middle-class population to get out of reach by moving to the suburbs lays the foundation for a building boom there. There is even room in such a boom for a little suburban integration.

Moreover, the abandonment process clears land and relocates families "free." That will make it easier and cheaper to rebuild on a large scale. A few of the areas being abandoned are prime locations, such as Woodlawn, which lies between Lake Michigan, a huge park, the University of Chicago, and a large cemetery. And perhaps the problem of the underclass will wear itself out. In the next 15 or 20 years we may see declining birth rates among lower-class blacks as well as the violent death or incarceration of their more destructive underclass. In 20 years the inner-city may be ready for rebuilding on a scale that will dwarf the reconstruction after the Chicago fire. And there is reason to believe that such reconstructed areas could be integrated both racially and economically.

There is another side to this, however. It is a profligate society that is willing to squander the resources generations have created. In the path of advancing decay lie not only homes but job-providing factories, schools, churches, shopping centers, universities, and other institutions. The Woodlawn process may be "accomplish-ing" what it took a war to "accomplish" for European cities. . . .

People get chewed up in the Woodlawn process. Violence is already a prin-cipal cause of death among black youths under 25. Many of the victims have been good students who had the makings of community leaders, the kind of people we were expecting to depend on in the future. And the zone of destruction is a pitiful environment for people to live in, existing day and night with the threat of violence and fire, surrounded by collapse. Can a society be indifferent to such a process? Can letting such a process continue any longer be considered a defensible public policy? Can the hostilities such a process breeds ever be healed?

WHO ARE THE VICTIMS?

Look closely at who the victims of the process are. There is a tendency to focus on the poor black families who are left in the neighborhood when it finally comes crashing down. Their plight is obvious and grave. But at least in material terms they have relatively little to lose. The most threatened groups are the black and white working people, who can't afford to run away when the decay process presses against their communities: the "respectable" poor, the working poor, the elderly, the abandoned, traditional poor, the residue of hard-working ethnic communities that have yet to make it into the professional and white-collar classes. It is as if the economy has played a huge trick on them. It gave them the opportunity to become modest homeowners; then it turned around and produced a process of decay that threatens to wipe out their gains, the hard-won achievements of their lives. When applied to these people, the policy of letting-what-has-been-happening-continue not only is an affront to simple justice but also produces conflict that will increase the instability of the city and harden racial prejudice. The prospect of the poor and the near-poor fighting over a diminishing supply of cheap housing in the city is not a pretty one. . . .

Even those members of the middle and upper classes, black and white, who can *afford* to keep running away from the problem even if it means changing cities, may not be as secure from the decay process as they think. But, more important, no family of modest means—and this applies particularly to the black middle class, struggling to establish respectable and stable communities, mostly within the limits of the central city—can feel immune from a process which could wipe out all its gains. This destroys the basic condition for a long-term resolution of America's race problem—the ability of the black middle class to develop the community, financial, commercial, and other institutions it needs so badly. Nothing is more inimical to the formation of such stable institutions than the fear that one's own neighborhood is only a few years removed from what happened in Woodlawn.

THE "CONTRIBUTION" OF GOVERNMENT

Ironically, what happened in Woodlawn is partly traceable to public policies that were inspired by noble national ideals. For instance, the discovery in the 1930s that a third of the nation's families were ill-housed brought to light an intolerable national condition, and on the theory that every problem would yield to a program, massive public housing projects were built to replace slums. However, these provided housing for the "worthy" poor, not the families of the underclass, who were screened out or evicted. Until very recently, the majority of families in public housing were headed by working people. The areas around the public housing projects housed many of the families who had been rejected by the housing authorities as being too disorganized. An uneasy balance developed between the two groups, confined to the ghetto as they were by the wall of segregation. In the 1950s the wall cracked. Many of the working-class and middle-class black families got out—not to integrate into white neighborhoods, but to establish black middle-class communities within a still generally segregated area.

As this process accelerated, public policy focused next on the neighborhoods to which the underclass was relegated and found them unacceptably shabby. Strict code-enforcement programs were implemented to oblige the slum owner to bring apartments up to safe and sanitary standards. Housing that could not economically be brought up to such standards was to be torn down. The result, for a time, was a significant shrinkage of the housing supply. In Chicago, the pressure of code enforcement seems to have played a critical role in almost one third of all demolitions in the city between 1948 and 1970, even during a period of extensive demolition as a result of expressway and public housing construction. Some of the code-enforcement programs were coupled with urban renewal projects, which focused primarily on middle-class areas threatened by the underclass.

In retrospect, it is apparent that public policy toward housing has been unwilling to make the class distinctions that have governed the behavior of families, white and black, who have had to live with the threat of the nearby underclass. As long as the neighborhoods to which that underclass was relegated lasted, it was possible to sustain the illusion that things were getting better. Urban renewal *did* transform Southwest Washington from slum to shiny new upper-class district. Code-enforcement programs *did* succeed in forcing many landlords to improve their buildings. Census statistics *did* reassure us that the total percentage of deteriorated or dilapidated dwelling units was getting smaller. It took Woodlawn and its counterparts in other cities to point out the catch: After 40 years of programs which ignored the existence of the underclass, the neighborhoods on which we implicitly depended to provide this class with housing were suddenly collapsing on a massive scale. Of course, we can continue to ignore or deny this issue—but it is no longer painless to do so.

THE CASE FOR STABILIZATION

We submit that the issue now is not how to end slums, but how to stabilize and upgrade them. This has a crass ring to it, to be sure. Years of rhetoric about making war on poverty have taken for granted the inspirational notion that, given the will and the proper means, everyone can be assured an "adequate income" and a "decent home." The idea of government policy consciously promoting the "stability" of slums goes against the grain; it lacks the sense of uncompromising high-mindedness which we have come to expect of national social policy. Yet it is precisely such "high-minded" and "inspirational" policies which have helped to create the plight of the Woodlawns of America. And in any event, what these devastated or about-to-be-devastated neighborhoods need isn't eradication, but rather assistance in stabilizing themselves. If the case of Woodlawn proves anything, it proves the urgency of finding ways to keep the communities that house black lower-class families from falling apart.

One reason for redesigning public policy so that its aim is to stabilize slums lies in the interests of the black underclass itself. The dissolution of this class, to quote Moynihan, is going to be "the work of a generation." After the early hopes of the war on poverty, the great difficulties of working with this class have become widely known. Any effort to convert the underclass into responsible, self-sufficient persons—whether through job training, school programs, welfare experiments, social work, "black capitalism," or whatnot—is undermined by their incessant drifting. Urban underclass families don't stay put very easily. This is a difficult problem even under the best of circumstances, but when neighborhoods collapse around them as Woodlawn did, they have no choice but to pack up and move on. The process of dissolving lower-class behavior depends on building up community institutions and the sense of responsibility that are the hallmark of the middle and working classes. The obvious prerequisite for this, of course, is a "community," one that lasts. Today this prerequisite does not exist.

The problem goes far beyond the suffering of people trapped in the last stages of a neighborhood like Woodlawn. The collapse of housing economics in the inner city is turning the underclass into nomads. They are the kiss of death to each successive community that they occupy. This is not to blame them in a personal sense. It is simply to state the plain fact that the economics of lower-class housing no longer work. And there is no advantage at all to the lower class in this process. If antipoverty programs must chase these people from one neighborhood to another, they will never have any meaningful impact on them.

The second part of the case for stabilizing lower-class neighborhoods stems from the interests of those who are in the path of destruction, particularly the black working and middle classes. In a city like Chicago, there are a lot of blacks who have made it. They have jobs, good incomes, homes which they own, solid neighborhoods. Some of them are becoming successful businessmen. A black investment community is beginning to form. Communities are beginning to show the capacity to respond on their own to their problems. Political power is heading their way, slowly but surely. All these gains are real, but they are recent and they are still on a very shaky basis. In general, the institutional strength of the black community is substantially less than that of otherwise comparable white communities, and this fact makes the recent gains of the blacks more vulnerable to pressure from the underclass.

The extent of this vulnerability is illustrated by the fate of a community south of Woodlawn called Chatham. Ten years ago it was the showcase of the successful Chicago black community. Today Chatham is becoming uneasy. Refugees from Woodlawn are beginning to filter into Chatham's big, solid apartment houses. Ten years ago a property owner in Chatham could sell ''up''; today, it is said, he may have to sell ''down.'' This short life of black middle-class communities should be of concern to everyone. The path to racial equality in this country depends on blacks achieving the same middle-class stability and power that the whites have. This takes time, concentration, and a modicum of security. The successive dissolving of communities under the pressure of the underclass deprives them of all three.

The third branch of the case for stabilizing our low-income neighborhoods is the question of justice for those of the poor, black and white, who take the brunt of the loss when a community falls apart. The rampage of the underclass has introduced a new factor into urban land economics. The prospect of a community's ''going black,'' and now the prospect of its subsequent mutilation, has paralyzed the market for whole sections of inner-city land. The general tendency in the American economy over the past 30 years has been for land values to rise. Even in older sections of the inner-city land might easily be redeveloped (and in many places is redeveloped) for commercial or industrial or residential uses—were it not for a generalized fear of underclass ''invasion.'' This hits blacks as well as whites, as the Chatham example shows. In practical terms, it freezes the urban land market and leaves the present group of owners holding the bag.

The present group of owners, of course, is usually the lower-middle class and working class. They own neighborhood after neighborhood of good, modest, cheap houses, decent if unglamorous apartment buildings, small business establishments, and the like. Without the threat of underclass violence it is hard to say what the market for this property would be. Possibly there would still be little demand for it; this is the belief of a number of authorities, such as George Sternlieb, who see an irreversible trend from urban to suburban living. But this view may be incorrect, and in any case has not been proved. Still, the paralysis of the market hurts whatever prospects present owners have both to maintain their communities and to recoup their investment when they want to sell.

To restore the economic viability of housing and to establish an acceptable level of personal security must be the two goals of any stabilization policy. We are not proposing that this be the full extent of national policy toward the central city. It is clear that most lower-class crime is the product of joblessness, bad education, and weak communal structures. But programs aimed at these fundamental problems are impossible to implement without a reasonably stable community—however shoddy from the liberal, suburban point of view—within which to develop them. Archimedes knew how to move the world, but even he acknowledged that he needed a place to stand.

The most important lesson to be drawn from the Woodlawn process, then, is that its victims are not just the inhabitants of Woodlawn. The principal victims will be the black and white working class, the lower-middle class, the traditional poor—those whom the accelerating process of decay threatens most directly. Furthermore, the Woodlawn process has become a major menace to the consolidation and growth of the black middle class itself.

The immense gains of the black population over the last 40 years—gains which the Woodlawn process menaces—were fashioned in the midst of poverty-stricken communties. The process of social advance has to start somewhere. The challenge is to assure it of a place to start. To do so will require the establishment of basic security for people and property, and more clearly focused efforts to maintain community stability in inner-city neighborhoods.

Reading 31

The Aging Central City: Some Modest Proposals

Norman Krumholz

Those familiar with the city planning profession are aware that its latest fad is "growth management." This year's annual conference of the American Society of Planning Officials even had "growth management" as its theme. From time to time I receive requests from Phoenix or San Diego asking what sophisticated techniques Cleveland is using to control growth and development. My response is wistful; I usually tell them I wish we had some growth to control. The absence of growth and the reality of stasis or decline call for new directions in the work of city planners and other public officials who labor in our older cities. Before considering what those new directions might be, I will first briefly outline what I see as the problems, based upon Cleveland data and generalizing where appropriate.

The population of the city of Cleveland has dropped significantly from its peak

Reprinted with permission from Edward W. Hanten, Mark J. Kasoff, F. Stevens Redburn (eds.), *New Directions for the Mature Metropolis* (Cambridge, Mass.: Schenkman Publishing Co., Inc., 1980), pp. 74–85.

in 1950 when it was 914,000. It is now down to only . . . [574,000, declining 37 percent] since 1950. From 1970 to 1976, Cleveland's population loss represented one of the sharpest declines of any city in the country, a loss of 125,263 people or 16.7 percent.

Along with the decline in numbers of people has come a substantial change in the composition of the remaining population. Cleveland's white population has fallen about 50 percent since 1950 and its percentage of blacks has risen above 40 percent. Considering the fact that blacks have appreciably lower incomes than whites on the average, the relative income level of city residents has been falling when compared to the level of incomes in the metropolitan area as a whole. In the 1960s Cleveland lost 25 percent of its families with incomes over the median for our SMSA. Today, about 20 percent of all Cleveland families receive Aid to Dependent Children and one-sixth of our families earns less than $2,000 a year.

The employment base for the entire Cleveland metropolitan area has been growing more slowly than for the nation as a whole. The city lost 71,000 jobs, about 15 percent of its total employment, in the 1960s and that loss has continued in the 70s.

Population loss, relative poverty and inflation have had a destructive impact on the housing market in some Cleveland neighborhoods. Because of rising costs of operation and ownership to private landlords and the declining ability to pay among lower-income tenants, there is an economic squeeze on rental property owners. To cope with this squeeze, some owners are first resorting to tax delinquency and then to abandonment. In some neighborhoods up to one-third of all property is tax delinquent, abandonment is increasing significantly and the city spends close to $2 million a year on the demolition of abandoned property. . . .

Let us examine more closely the structure of this decline so we can better understand the nature of the term "declining metropolitan areas." While the Cleveland SMSA lost 89,000 residents, Cleveland's suburbs still gained 24,000. This pattern appears to be characteristic of all declining metropolitan areas. In the central city, population and employment are declining, while in the suburbs they are rising. Suburbs are growing at a slower rate, but they are still growing, and central cities are losing population faster than ever. The term "metropolitan decline" tends to obscure this very important central city-suburban dichotomy. Thus, metropolitan decline is not metropolitan-wide in its impact. Central cities are absorbing the brunt of slow growth, statis, and no growth.

These problems are not unique to Cleveland. Nearly all SMSAs east of the Mississippi and north of the Mason-Dixon Line exhibit, to some degree, the same trends. Most of these cities are oriented toward manufacturing, which is no longer a rapidly growing sector of the national economy. Northeastern cities also tend to be highly unionized and have higher wage rates and more cumbersome work rules than cities in the South and West. This encourages companies to open new plants in Dallas, Phoenix and Houston instead of Cleveland, Buffalo and Detroit. Moreover, our increasingly hedonistic society seems to be placing an increasing value on sunshine and warm weather; and most other parts of the country have larger quantities of both. We can't do much about the weather, and it appears that labor and management are not likely to work out any agreements which will make older urban areas more competitive in attracting new industry. Therefore, it seems probable that, in the short run at least, the shift of economic activity and population to the South and West will continue.

Unfortunately, most of the reaction has been to the numbers involved in these trends and far too little attention has been given to their process and underlying structure. In the 1930s, Cleveland was the sixth largest city in the United States; by 1970 it ranked tenth, and [by 1980] it fell to eighteenth. This constituted a blow to the civic pride of many Clevelanders and prompted city council to pass a resolution urging the preparation of a plan calling for a central city population of one million by 1985. A population of this size may be living in the city by that year (although the probability seems slim), but it would be fair to venture that the future scale of development in Cleveland will not be determined by political desires, no matter how well meaning. In any case, the numbers mean little by themselves. Reconstruction and repopulation cannot proceed any faster than private markets can be found for cleared land, and at present the demand side appears quite weak.

The most negative aspect of metropolitan decline is rooted in declining job opportunities. The alleviation of this urban problem will require some redistribution of resources to the poor. While we have made some progress in this area, we have not done enough; and a declining local economy will make redistribution much more difficult to achieve. It is difficult to get middle and upper income groups to accept a smaller piece of a "larger pie," and I suspect it will be nearly impossible to get them to accept a smaller piece of a "smaller pie."

I perceive a very real danger of creating, perhaps perpetuating would be a better word, a permanent underclass without access to the comforts of middle class America. While there is much to criticize in the consumer life style of middle-class Americans; the sterile suburbs, the big car syndrome, ugly shopping centers, etc., few people would choose poverty over modest affluence. The problems of the urban poor are much more stark and elemental: paying the rent, feeding the kids, getting to the corner store without being mugged. Without a steady expansion of employment opportunities, many youths who are currently unemployed may never have the chance to hold a decent job. Their only alternatives will be crime and "the hustle," which will be destructive both to them and to those who live around them.

In all the discussions of our cities and their problems, we frequently overlook one very important fact—most people living in metropolitan areas, even declining ones, are not affected much by the urban crisis. The problems that constitute the heart of the urban crisis bear very heavily on some people, largely low and moderate income people living in certain neighborhoods, but never touch affluent suburbanites. If those who live outside the areas affected by the urban crisis are even dimly aware of the crisis, they generally mistake the symptoms for the real problems. They see the vacant land and abandoned buildings but ignore the social and economic realities that led to the present situation. This has led to some of the popular solutions to the urban crisis.

The first and most popular is the complete reconstruction of the central city through the massive infusion of federal funds. Nearly all the schemes presented have one thing in common; they imply that we can solve our problems by building something, a mall, a special purpose center, an arch, an automated downtown distribution system, or some other civic monument. The most recent variant of this theme is the so-called "Marshall Plan" for cities. Under this plan the federal government would initiate a massive program to rebuild the central cities in an effort to attract the fleeing middle class back into them. The keystone of this program is physical redevelopment to restore the central city in much the same manner as the "Marshall Plan" restored the countries of war-ravaged Western Europe. But, as Norton Long has pointed out, this analogy simply does not hold. An alien enemy force destroyed Western Europe in pitched battle, thus making a "Marshall Plan" necessary. The decay of our central cities was not visited upon them by some invading army, but rather was the result of social and economic forces deeply rooted in American society. They cannot be driven out like a foreign army. The much discussed "Marshall Plan" for cities differs little from the federal government's urban renewal program begun in 1949. Urban renewal did not save our cities in the 1950s, and a "Marshall Plan" won't save them in the 1970s. Such a program will not create a growing economic base, job opportunities, income, and a vigorous demand for the facilities the "Marshall Plan" would supposedly supply.

Why, then, does this idea have such staying power? There are a number of reasons. First, because massive development efforts benefit groups that have a lot of political influence; developers, builders, construction workers, landowners, etc. Building is their business and, naturally, they favor programs that stimulate building just as most of us tend to value what we produce. The second and most important reason is that this kind of proposal really does not ask us to do things any differently. It requires no changes in our values and mores, our ideology, if you will, and it ignores the really hard questions of:

- Why do children graduate from high school without learning how to read?
- Why can't our criminal justice system ensure a reasonable level of personal security?
- Why can't a sizable proportion of our work force find productive employment?

Meaningful programs which would resolve the issues raised by the above questions would do far more than any "Marshall Plan" to revitalize central cities. Unfortunately, solutions would require changes in our institutional arrangements and so are probably not likely to be forthcoming in the near future.

Another reasonably popular solution for the decline of central cities is regional government. This would supposedly unite central cities and suburbs into one over-arching government and would resolve problems created by the flight of taxable resources outside the boundaries of a single municipal boundary. The metropolitan approach may be fiscally desirable from the point of view of solving many major problems cited earlier, but it is politically rejected by central city blacks who are reluctant to give up their growing influence in city government, by the city and suburban office holders who do not want to lose their jobs, and by the suburban whites who see no pay-off to assuming a share of the tax burden of the central city. So who is left to support this "logical" future? Almost no one.

It would appear that both of the solutions mentioned above have a relatively poor chance of being implemented. Pervading each is a lack of political power or a challenge to well accepted and powerful personal or institutional arrangements. Instead, it seems much more likely that most urban areas will accept a future, at least for the near term, which is an extrapolation of present trends.

1. Central cities will probably continue to lose population, although perhaps at a slower rate.
2. The population residing in the central city will probably be less affluent than the rest of the metropolitan area.
3. Development will be largely concentrated in the suburbs.
4. Today's central city problems will spread slowly to the suburbs, but they will continue to be most pronounced in the central city.

Given this probability, there are two basic public policy alternatives open. The first is "to try to recapture lost youth." Advocates of this philosophy maintain central cities can regain the preeminence they enjoyed before 1950. That middle-class white and black families can be lured back to the central city in large numbers and that this should be the focus of public policy. The urban "Marshall Plans" and regional government plans are variants on this theme.

The second alternative is "to grow old gracefully." Proponents of this philos-ophy argue that while returning to the 1940s might be nice, it is extraordinarily unlikely to occur. Moreover, trying to become young again will divert us from opportunities to minimize the negative consequences of present trends, thus making the aging process more painful. We should be clear about the opportunity costs of spending our increasingly limited resources in frivolous, non-productive ways. It seems much more useful to accept our situation and manage our realistic options well.

While many arguments can be put forth as to why the philosophy of "recaptur-ing lost youth" will not work, suffice it to say that the "Marshall Plans" and energy crises will not send affluent suburbanites flocking back into central cities that have lost thirty percent of their population in the last two decades. Certain neighborhoods may experience growth, such as New York's Upper West Side,

Cleveland's Ohio City area, and Lincoln Park in Chicago for examples; but they will not come close to offsetting out-migration from other parts of the central city. The middle class may return in larger numbers sometime in the future when many of the problems of central cities have manifested themselves much more intensely in the suburbs, but the prospect of this happening in the next ten years is relatively small.

What can be done to help central cities who opt for the philosophy of "growing old gracefully?" One thing central cities clearly need is some means of balancing their budgets while maintaining an adequate level of public services. Voters are increasingly reluctant to tax themselves more heavily, so cities cannot rely on increased tax rates to balance budgets. Federal transfers, except for health and job development, are likely to stabilize or decline. The alternative is clearly better management so as to realize more effective use of the resources at hand. Of course, every administration pays lip service to the goal of more and better services without more taxes. Unfortunately, few achieve it; but it need not be as elusive as it has been in the past. For example, members of the Cleveland City Planning staff worked with the city's Division of Waste Collection and Disposal for over three years in order to improve its management capacity. By reorganizing collection procedures, reassigning manpower, and spending the Division's capital resources on cost-saving equipment, the city is now realizing a savings of several million dollars a year. When this project first started, the staff of the Division posessessed few planning or analytical capabilities. Now the Division head talks about picking up garbage heuristically! So approaches to improved management have some potential for success.

Perhaps the key element of any declining city's management strategy should be a program of "constructive shrinkage." As population declines, so should the need for new schools, recreation centers, and other expensive public facilities. Declining cities should be following a conscious policy of not adding to their capital stock. Most cities cannot even afford to operate and maintain the facilities they presently have. Building new ones merely increases the burden and hastens the deterioration of existing ones. The first principle of constructive shrinkage, then, should be a policy of devoting existing resources to the maintenance and improvement of present facilities rather than to the construction of new ones.

Beyond cutting back on new additions to its physical plant, cities may have to consider divesting themselves of certain responsibilities. Most cities have facilities which serve a regional population and constitute a heavy drain on the municipal treasury. Some of these can be transferred to a higher level of government with a broader financial base. In recent years the city of Cleveland has transferred its zoo, port, sewer and transit systems to regional authorities, thus relieving the city's residents of the sole responsibility for subsidizing these operations. By divesting these assets, the city has freed up millions of dollars a year that can be devoted to other purposes. There is a danger in this approach; however, for regional agencies often have little interest in central city problems. Affluent suburbanites comprise a much more potent political force than the urban working class and poor, and regional entities may choose to respond first to the suburbanites' requests regardless of the actual incidence of need. The recent history of regional transit authorities across the country is instructive in this regard. In spite of the fact that the need for increased mobility is greatest among the transit-dependent and the resources to operate transit systems are drawn from broad-based, often regressive taxes, the expenditures and programs of regional transit agencies tend to serve best the suburban commuter making a trip to work. Mass transit has become an instrument to serve the affluent at the expense of the working class and poor, many of whom don't have the option of driving since they cannot afford an automobile. As Mel Webber has written in reference to San Francisco's BART System, "the poor pay, the rich ride."

Negotiations over the transfer of the Cleveland Transit System to the Regional Transit Authority provide an excellent example. The negotiations took almost five months, but they could have been completed in a much shorter time had there not been a difference of opinion between the Cleveland City Planning staff on the one hand and the other parties to the negotiations, namely the business community, the local transit bureaucracy and the representatives of the suburbs on the other. It was the position of the Planning staff the city should obtain firm guarantees of reduced fares and improved service—especially to the transit-dependent population—before agreeing to the transfer. The other members to the negotiation took the position that Cleveland would benefit merely by "unloading" its seventy million dollar system without prior service and fare guarantees. After prolonged conflict the city obtained its guarantees. Granted they were somewhat less than had been hoped for, but they were infinitely greater than would have been realized had the city not been prepared with a well-defined position and a willingness to fight for it.

Naturally, the transit management complained that this would reduce their flexibility which, of course, was precisely our intent. But there appeared to be no other way of ensuring an adequate level of service for the people who need mass transit the most. Cities, in the course of divesting themselves of certain functional responsibilities, must make sure that as many safeguards as possible are maintained to protect the interests of the most dependent of their residents.

At the same time older cities are learning to manage declining resources better, they must also learn to target carefully their public subsidies so as to realize maximum benefits for subsidies expended. This is vital, for central city governments are under increasing pressure to provide public subsidies and other supports for private business ventures. Since the advent of urban renewal, government officials have accepted the notion that the city stands to benefit axiomatically from private development and that the use of city money to encourage it is appropriate. While cooperation with the private sector is desirable, even necessary, cities should not invest their scarce resources in private projects unless the benefits are actually there. This means careful cost-benefit analysis on a project-by-project basis to assure these projects are consistent with city objectives. Development should never be viewed as an end in itself; it should only be viewed as a means to accomplish other goals such as reducing unemployment among city residents and increasing city tax revenues.

During the past few years the Cleveland City Planning staff has reviewed dozens of subsidy proposals. It has routinely asked one overriding question: "who gets and who pays?" In those cases where the analysis has indicated that the public costs would likely outweigh the public benefits, or where the benefits were likely to accrue to those least in need of public support, the commitment of public funds to the projects has been opposed.

It is well understood that public officials are under substantial pressure to accept promises of progress at face value. When the headlines say "$350 Million Project Proposed to Save City," public officials find skepticism an uncomfortable role. The Cleveland City Planning Commission's opposition to such projects, then, has frequently embroiled it in heated political debate. Needless to say, it has often failed to halt the expenditure of public funds on such projects; but what it has done is to gain some public acceptance for the notion that the city and its residents should expect something in return for granting subsidies—a startling concept to those who view public funds primarily as a way to take all the private risk out of what used to be called private enterprise.

Cities should also begin planning for the recycling of inner city areas. Cleveland, for example, has several neighborhoods where the population is now one-third or less its 1960 level. From 25 to 35 percent of the properties in these areas is tax delinquent and presumably on the road to abandonment. Areas like these pose special problems for local government, for prospects for redevelopment in the short run are non-existent. In the meantime, the city incurs the costs of demolishing abandoned buildings and cleaning vacant lots while receiving little or nothing from property taxes. It appears that the only sensible strategy for dealing with these areas is a program of municipal land banking.

The Cleveland City Planning Commission assisted in developing legislation in Ohio that allows municipalities to take title to all tax-delinquent property that cannot be sold at a tax sale for the sum of all public liens against it. The city will be able to land bank this property and dispose of it when development opportunities arise in the future. This strategy has several strong points. First, it will serve as a way to recoup, at least partially, back taxes and demolition costs by making it possible to hold the land until the market value increases. Second, having a large number of parcels under one ownership will facilitate redevelopment and considerably reduce the need for eminent domain. Third, ownership is a much more effective way of controlling the future reuse of this land than any kind of zoning, for if the city owns the property it can decide how it should be redeveloped.

Land banking is primarily a means of dealing with areas that cannot be saved using conventional rehabilitation methods. If such areas are to be preserved, cities will have to make some hard choices as to how a city's resources will be spent.

These choices will be difficult, at best, considering the conflict between downtown interests and neighborhood interests. Property owners in the central business district are demanding more public investment in the downtown area while the neighborhood groups are demanding better municipal services and improved public facilities in their areas. This conflict grows more strident as a city's resources become more limited.

It would seem appropriate for cities to give much more attention to residential neighborhoods than to downtown investments. The rationale for this position is partly ethical and partly practical. Ethically, it seems proper to devote public resources to helping neighborhood residents because they have fewer resources of their own than do downtown investors. As a practical matter, helping central city neighborhoods is important because they represent the sole remaining source of decent, inexpensive housing still remaining in the entire metropolitan area. The price of new housing has risen to the point where only families in the top 25 percent of the income ladder can afford it. Even existing housing in the suburbs is beyond the reach of most central city residents. If we cannot preserve the housing stock in older neighborhoods, we may have to replace it at a much greater expense, or experience a significant decline in general housing standards. Moreover, a stable residential population is essential if the central city's tax base and commerical areas, downtown included, are to survive.

The foregoing concept of "growing old gracefully" may strike you as very modest in approach, not the kind of visionary proposals, the gleaming new towers in the parklike setting, that you are accustomed to hearing from city planners. In fact, the whole idea of "growing old gracefully" strikes some people as an admission of defeat. This is to be expected in a society that is as preoccupied with newness and youth as modern American society. However, it is important to remember that the aging analogy cannot be carried to its ultimate conclusion. No city is going to disappear from the map. Cleveland may be smaller in the future, it may look somewhat different; but it will still be a place where hundreds of thousands of people will work and live. The question, then, is how can Cleveland make the best of its situation?

It simply does not follow that older declining cities of the Northeast and Midwest need be less desirable places to live than the rapidly growing cities of the South and West. If growth were an unqualified blessing there would not be so many people opposing it in other parts of the country. And, of course, if we are successful in the modest tasks previously outlined, neighborhoods will become more desirable residential locations and will be well able to compete with other locations in the region.

We must not fall into the trap of hopelessness, giving up because the city seems to be declining in so many ways, for despair is the one unforgiveable sin, not only in theology, but in city planning as well, because it creates its own fulfillment. By the same token, we must not fall into the trap of pretending there are easy solutions. We cannot go back to the past. We cannot expect the federal government to bail us out. There are no grand and simple solutions, and pretending there are no serious problems is one sure way of never improving anything.

We must face the future much as a realistic person faces the whole of life itself, with all its mysterious blend of evils and potentialities. We must focus on the positive opportunities that are there with the resolution that we will persist in our efforts to take advantage of those opportunities, even though we know it will take years, even decades, to pursue them successfully. If our goal is to leave things better than we found them and we pursue this goal with verve, imagination, courage and, above all, persistence, we will succeed. After all, that is what life is all about.

Reading 32

Careers with a Future: Where the Jobs Will Be in the 1990s

Marvin Cetron

Thomas O'Toole

There will always be lawyers, but there won't be as many lawyers in the year 2000 as there are today because the demand won't be as great. There won't be as many doctors 20 years hence either, in part because there won't be the demand for doctors in 2000 that there is today. In fact, to turn a phrase on an old nursery rhyme, there won't be as many rich men, poor men, beggarmen, and thieves as there are today because the world's job markets will change dramatically in the next 20 years.

Well, maybe there will be just as many thieves in 2000 as there are today. But there won't be as many textile workers, automotive workers, or steel workers. The robotizing of the assembly line will see to that. There won't be as many clerical workers either—or as many sales people and stock clerks. The computer will see to that. Only one thing is sure about tomorrow's job markets: There will be major shifts in employment patterns—though it doesn't mean there will be major changes in the numbers of people employed anywhere inside the job market. . . .

The key question facing us in the 20 years ahead is, can the six billion people who will be alive in the year 2000 find work when so many of today's four billion are unemployed? Put it another way: Where will the new jobs come from in the next 20 years if we start to lose the old jobs to robots and computers? There's little question many of the old jobs will disappear, and not just because of robots and computers. Take textiles, an industry that has had wanderlust since the spinning

Reprinted with permission from *The Futurist* (June 1982):11–19, abridged.

wheel that started it all in the north of England. Pity the poor Hong Kong shirt-maker. The business he stole from the United States and Western Europe is already migrating to Mexico and Thailand, where the labor is cheaper than it is in Hong Kong. It won't be long before the Thais and the Mexicans lose their shirts to Egypt and Bangladesh. The same kind of thing is happening in steelmaking and shipbuild-ing. The business migrated out of the U.S. and Western Europe to Japan, where labor was cheaper. Now, it's moving to Korea and Taiwan, where labor comes cheaper than it does in Japan.

Concerns and worries about unemployment are hardly new to our society. After all, nineteenth-century steel barons thought their businesses would die when all the railroads were built. The railroad barons thought their businesses would die when cars and trucks and airplanes came along. One of their contemporaries talked about the "growing armies of the unemployed." Who was that? His name was Karl Marx. Well, the 1930s justified many of his fears, but the fifties and sixties should have buried them. Now, it's time to rejustify the fears of Karl Marx. At a rough guess, there are now 300 million unemployed people in the world. Almost 10 million of this army of the unemployed are in the United States, with another nine million in the industrialized countries of Western Europe.

ONE OF 30 WORKS THE LAND

There's little question that employment patterns are shifting and will continue to shift throughout the world. Take agriculture. When Ronald Reagan was born, almost one-third of America worked down on the farm. Now, barely one of 30 works the land in the U.S. The same trend is true in Europe and Japan, where one out of 20 works on a farm. The mechanization of the American farm led the American worker to heavy industry in World War II, then to the service industry after the postwar period. Nowadays, one-third of America's blue-collar workers are in services, meaning they don't manufacture anything. They simply service the machines and people who do the manufacturing in the blue-collar industry and the machines and people who grind out the paperwork in the white-collar industry. This shifting trend will continue as robots—the so-called "steel-collar" workers—take more of the jobs in manufacturing and computers take more of the jobs in the office.

We think one of the major jobs of the future will be the robot technician, whose numbers could run to more than two million by 2000. We say that because the robotizing of America (and all other industrial countries) will be the only way to raise industrial productivity. General Motors has already said it will spend $1 billion installing 14,000 robots on its assembly lines by 1990. Chrysler and Ford plan to follow suit. In fact, Chrysler put robots into its welding operation at its Jefferson plant outside Detroit and increased productivity 20 percent with 200 fewer workers. But robots aren't perfect. They have to be cared for. They have to be programmed before they go to work, maintained so they don't break down, and fixed when they do break down. If they break down, they have to be replaced by other robots ready to go to work. Who's going to see that the backup robots are ready? The robot technicians, that's who.

ROBOT TECHNICIANS

The next generation of robots will be able to see, touch, hear, smell, and even speak. They'll need extra loving care, which means lots of service jobs for the robot technicians. We predict there will be as many as 1.5 million robot technicians on the job in the U.S. alone by 1990, making a starting salary of $15,000 a year and a midrange salary of $24,000 a year. Unless you are the kind of pessimist who thinks robots will build robots to repair robots, you can count on a robot technician's job to be a ticket into the twenty-first century. Of course, if there are robot technicians, there will have to be robot engineers. We think you can count on a robot engineer's degree to be a first-class ticket into the twenty-first century, to a job that pays $28,000 a year to start. The robot engineers of the next century will design a third generation of robots.

COMPUTER PROGRAMMERS

The robots of the future will only be as smart and dexterous as the computer software that programs them, which spotlights another major job of the future. Nobody will be in demand in the next 20 years like computer programmers. Harvard University now insists that all of its undergraduates be able to write a simple, two-step computer program before graduating. That is a sign of the times to come. Another sign of the times to come is the microprocessing chip, which has inspired new electronic products like pocket computers and talking toys. The chip has also transformed old products into new ones, like washing machines programmed to use cooler water for gentler washing and telephone switchboards that will take and store messages. Some estimates suggest that in the U.S. alone, the demand for computer programmers already outstrips the supply by anywhere from 50,000 to 100,000. We think those estimates are conservative. We think that by 2000 there will be almost one million new jobs generated for computer programmers in the U.S., with starting salaries of $13,000 and midrange salaries of $25,000 a year.

LASER TECHNICIANS

It is often difficult to predict what new jobs will be created by new technologies. Often, we identify new technologies with job elimination instead of job creation. But when the invention of the transistor was announced in 1948, few technologists predicted the mushroom cloud that would follow it. Few people realized that this tiny electronic gate was the foundation of what soon will be the world's biggest business. Why should they have? After all, the transistor was conceived to be a replacement for the vacuum tube and no more. Even a few years after it was invented, one transistor still cost $15 and its use was restricted to things like hearing aids. The developments had not come along that cut its cost to a fraction of a cent and increased its use to thousands of new products. So it is with the laser, which came along 15 years after the transistor and which promises so many new uses that we predict it will be the transistor of the next 20 years. The laser will replace machine and foundry tools in every tool- and die-making shop in the world. The tool- and die-makers of the future will be laser technicians, whose numbers will mount so rapidly in the next 10 years that they will reach 2.5 million by 1990 and whose salaries will match those of the robot technicians.

ENERGY TECHNICIANS

Two industries that will spawn numerous new jobs are energy and hazardous wastes. The snags with energy jobs are the numerous energy projects, cyclical and almost always influenced by politics and forecasts of energy demand and prices. Typical of the uncertainty of the energy future is synthetic fuels. Will the Reagan administration pursue Carter's goal of producing two million barrels of synfuels a day by 1992? If Reagan decides on even half that goal, there will be a synfuels jobs bonanza that will create as many as 100,000 jobs for synfuels engineers alone by 1990, with midrange salaries of $30,000 a year. But if oil prices stay the same or even rise just a little, the jobs bonanza could just as quickly disappear because synfuels development will no longer be so urgent. We predict one energy jobs bonanza will not be influenced by politics. We predict that by 1990 there will be as many as 1.5 million new jobs for energy engineers and technicians. We think demand for energy technicians, making midcareer salaries of $26,000 a year, will exceed the supply for years to come in nuclear power plants, in coal, shale oil, and tar sands extraction plants, even in solar engineering plants. Why? Reaganomics dictates a move to supply-side energy production that can only result in thousands of new jobs. . . .

WASTE TECHNICIANS

We're not as certain about the hazardous wastes industry, but we'll go out on what we think is a short limb and predict 1.5 million new jobs for hazardous waste technicians, whose most experienced practitioners will earn $28,000 a year by the year 2000. While it's true that robots will be used to clean up the worst of our industrial wastes, there won't be enough robots in the world to clean it all up. Environmentalists estimate that decades, and billions of dollars, will be needed to clean up the nation's industrial mess. When the requirements for collection, transportation, disposal, and monitoring of radiological, biological, and chemical wastes are included, the number of workers needed will exceed 1.5 million. The cleanup of Three Mile Island alone will take an estimated 10,000 workers 10 more years to complete. It doesn't seem futuristic to us to predict that they'll be joined by an army of more than one million to clean up the rest of America.

THE GENE MACHINE

No new industry will make more of an impact on America and the industrial world in the next 20 years than the gene-splicing business, whose ranks of high-technology firms staffed by Ph.D. biologists and chemists will explode far beyond the turn of the century. Who can predict what the world of genetic engineering will bring? Already, gene splicing has been hailed as one of man's most awesome accomplishments, like splitting the atom was half a century ago. The "Gene Machine" is with us, whether we like it or not. Behind us are the laboratory syngrowth hormone, new antibiotics to treat bacterial infections, and new anticoagulants to break up blood clots in the arteries. Ahead of us are things like genetically altered corn and wheat that will suck nitrogen right out of the air and eliminate the need for ammonia fertilizers. Genetic engineering will produce fuels from wastes, plastics from sugar, and sweeteners from cheese. It will even leach metals from ores and clean up oil spills. Says Britain's *Economist* magazine: "It is one of the biggest industrial opportunities of the next 20 years." Our prediction? It's a modest one. We predict there will be at least 150,000 new jobs by 1990 for genetic engineering technicians alone, whose salaries will top $30,000 a year.

PARAMEDICS

There will be major new job breakthroughs in the delivery of health care in the next 20 years. If the demand for doctors goes down as we expect it will, the demand for paramedics to do the jobs once done by nurses and doctors will explode. One reason is the tools that medicine will have to diagnose what's wrong with people. These tools will eliminate the jobs of doctors at the same time they create jobs for paramedics. The increase in population and in the numbers of elderly people can only accelerate the demand for paramedics, whose numbers we think will increase by 1.3 million by 1990 and whose salaries will reach $29,000 a year by midcareer. Another explosive medical field will be that of the geriatric social technician, who will be essential to the mental and social care of the nation's aging. We forecast a need for one million workers, starting out at $16,000 a year, by 1990. Finally, we think that a distinctive job of the future will be a job we'll call bionic technician. These people won't be bionic themselves; they'll range from mechanics who make the bionic arms, legs, hands, and feet of the future to those who are involved in letting the blind see and the deaf hear with new bionic instruments. We think there will be at least 200,000 new jobs for bionic technicians in the next 10 years. They'll be paid well—$32,000 a year after a few years experience.

It's coming, all of it. Robots are coming that will eliminate jobs and create jobs in the factories, and computers are coming that will do the same things in the office. The U.S. Department of Labor now identifies 28,000 job titles in the American economy, many of them either obsolete or on their way to obsolescence (e.g., tea taster, linotype operator). By the time the Labor Department gets around to revising its list (it changes it every 10 years), most of the jobs on the list will have changed. That is one of the prices we pay to keep up with technological change. [Since this was written, in 1981, the Dictionary of Occupational Titles (DOT) published by the Department of Labor has been abolished.]

Artists who can create something original will be more richly rewarded than they are today. So will entertainers and professional athletes, who will be made America's richest people by cable television in the years ahead. Imagine the way cable television will bid to broadcast professional baseball's playoff and World Series games. The cable will offer baseball at $1 per seat for each first-round playoff game, $2.50 for each second-round game, and $5.00 for each World Series game. Assuming 35 million cable television sets and seven World Series games, that comes to a potential gross for the World Series alone of more than $1 billion. Now, imagine what the players will ask for as their rightful share of those receipts. If you want to grow up to be rich, be a baseball player. . . .

BAD NEWS FOR UNIONS

. . . What labor must watch most in the years ahead is technology, which in the past has often been one of labor's benefactors in the ways technology has improved working conditions. We think this is a condition that is changing. Take the celebrated strike in 1981 of the Professional Air Traffic Controllers Organization. When PATCO rejected a tentative contract in July of 1981, the union threatened to strike unless its demands for higher pay and more time off were met. The Reagan administration refused and the union went on to strike. Everybody remembers what happened. More than 12,000 union members were fired. Interestingly enough, the American public supported the Reagan administration against the union. What lies ahead for air traffic controllers? Technological obsolescence. The Reagan administraction had an ace in the hole during its eleventh-hour negotiations with the controllers. It was called AWACS, which everybody knows stands for Airborne Warning and Control System. Forget the *warning* part and concentrate on the *control*. One airborne AWACS can control the departures and arrivals of more than 150 airplanes around a major metropolitan airport. Look for a different kind of AWACS taking over for the air traffic controllers in the 1990s. It will be a satellite hovering over the United States—watching, tracking, and controlling airline flights in every major city of the country.

Just as technology can take jobs away from people, it can also give people jobs. In the long run, we think technology will give us more jobs than it takes away. While the Reagan administration was making it harder for air traffic controllers, it was making it easier for nuclear power plant operators by easing the regulations for the licensing of nuclear power plants. We believe that more nuclear power plants will be started up in the mid and late eighties, which will result in thousands of new jobs for nuclear power plant operators in the 1990s. There is another new technology aborning that will create new jobs. It's called synthetic materials. Synthetics are not new. We've had synthetic rubber since World War II, when the Japanese cut off our natural rubber supply from Indonesia and Malaysia and forced us to invent a substitute. A similar problem faces us in the years ahead, when metals like chromium, titanium, manganese, cobalt, and nickel will grow increasingly scarce. Technology is already at work inventing the synthetic ceramics, fibers, composites, polymers, and glasses that will take their place. Production of these synthetics will be done by thousands of new technicians working in laboratorylike plants bearing little resemblance to the steel mills and open-hearth furnaces of today. As worrisome as it might seem, new technology should not be viewed as a threat to labor. General Motors forecasts that by the year 2000 more than half its work force will be skilled tradesmen trained for their jobs by new technology. . . .

SOLAR TECHNICIANS IN THE SUN BELT

Some well-known trades and some brand new trades will flourish in the coming years. Among the old trades whose futures are bright are opportunities for what we might call operating engineers: people who can run cranes and bulldozers; automobile mechanics; heating, cooling, and refrigeration mechanics; and appliance servicemen. The most promising new trades are in the energy fields. Solar technicians in the Sun Belt, for instance. Energy conservation technicians in the Northeast. Reagan's deregulation of oil and natural gas will surely be followed by stepped-up drilling for both, so it's not hard to predict that there will be a rising demand for oil-field technicians of every stripe. These jobs involve long hours and hard work but the compensations are enormous. Oil-field workers often earn as much as $60,000 a year. Drilling for oil and gas at sea will trigger a new demand for an unusual job, that of professional diver. The risks of jobs like divers have come way down in the past 10 years. There is little risk at all to the divers staffing professional diving companies, most of which are located in Houston and New Orleans. Remember, jobs are concentrated in locations. You can't expect to graduate from a technical school in your hometown and right away find work as an aircraft mechanic if your hometown is in Maine and you don't live near an airport. For example, jobs in the electronics industry are mostly in California, Arizona, Massachusetts, Texas, and New York. If you want to work in electronics, move to those states and you'll have a better chance.

We'll forecast three new jobs for the future that the Bureau of Labor Statistics leaves out. One of these jobs we'll call housing rehabilitation technician, a catchall word for somebody who's expert at making a new house out of an old house or making a new house out of brand new materials. World population will double in the next 35 years, and that will intensify demand for housing so strongly that we think as many as 1.75 million new housing technicians will be needed by 1990. Our second new job is holographic specialist, a cousin of the robot technician, who will work in the robotized factory of the future specializing in servicing the optical computers that compare the inputs they're getting from the factory floors to the three-dimensional holographic data stored in other computers. We forecast a demand for 200,000 holographic specialists by 1990. Finally, there is the battery technician, the person who will service the next generation of fuel cells and batteries that will be used to power the cars and homes of the future. We think the demand for battery technicians will be 250,000 by 1990. In short, we do not believe there will be a shortage of jobs in the next 20 years. Only a shortage of creative, imaginative people to fill them.

All the future jobs we've mentioned so far are jobs we are predicting for the next 20 years. Are there other occupations that might take off out to the end of the century? Let's speculate for just a moment. Restaurant chefs could be in enormous demand, due to the increase in leisure time and the dual careers of husbands and wives. The rapid increase in the quality and quantity of frozen foods will cause a demand for more chefs and nutritionists by food packaging companies. There may be more city managers because there will be more satellite cities in need of them. The boom in leisure time will create vast numbers of new jobs for hotel managers and for public relations and advertising specialists, whose job it will be to promote new uses for leisure time. Rental assistants will proliferate because people will want help in finding vacation spots and summer rentals as well as homes. The same will hold true with dieticians, who will be consulted frequently as people become more conscious of their appearances. Geriatric food consultants will also be in demand, as well as licensed practical nurses for the elderly. The number of pharmacists will double in the next 20 years. After all, if the people of the future are going to live longer, they will need their corner druggists more than ever.

Does this article sound futuristic? Maybe, but 10 years ago, did we have any idea what a solar engineer did for a living? The impact of new discoveries and new technology is here now and much more is on the horizon. Accelerated change in these and other technologies will open up whole new arrays of occupations and careers. Indeed, Clyde Helms, president of Occupational Forecasting (Arlington, Virginia), has a whole firm that does nothing but forecast and train individuals for new occupations. These forecast occupations aren't limited to our children. If you have found yourself thinking of a career change, interesting possibilities are already here! Extensive updating of our current training and educational programs will be required to meet the demands of these new occupations, and educators of the future had better start making plans for what's coming next.

10

Population and Ecological Problems

Because we live in a technologically advanced country in which population growth has recently slowed, it is sometimes difficult for us to focus on the destructive impacts of overpopulation. Starvation, disease, and extremely high rates of infant mortality still affect a major portion of our planet. There is also the possibility that we Americans are not as safe as we think we are. We now recognize that ecologically, as well as politically, we are in a world system . . . a spaceship earth . . . and that major disruptions in our lives could be caused by continued rapid growth in less developed areas.

Paul Ehrlich, the author of *The Population Bomb,* and J. P. Holdren, define four unexpected ways in which our ignorance of ecological interconnections could lead to disaster. They prove that we do not sufficiently understand the consequences of the overconsumption of resources and technological modifications of nature that are caused by population increase.

We tend to feel erroneously that all our resources are endlessly renewable. Since most of the earth's surface is covered by water, and since droughts seem to be temporary, we feel that there will always be enough water. Bruce Ferguson explains that, on the contrary, we are rapidly using up our aquifers' groundwater and that drastic measures may soon be needed in some parts of the country to preserve existing water supplies.

Aurelio Peccei places our population and ecological problems in a global perspective. He warns that basic changes in our attitudes and political structures are the only solutions that will allow world survival. Unless we stop our war with nature, and again learn to become part of nature, the system could collapse.

Reading 33

Hidden Effects of Overpopulation

Paul R. Ehrlich

John P. Holdren

Several subtle aspects of the relationship between population growth and environmental degradation operate to make man's predicament even more perilous than superficial analyses indicate. Four to be considered here are *synergisms, threshold effects, trigger effects,* and *timelag effects.*

A *synergism* is the interaction (constructive or destructive) of two or more factors that yield a total effect greater than would occur if the factors operated independently. In colloquial terms, it is a situation in which the whole exceeds the sum of its parts. An illustrative synergism in environmental health is the interaction of sulphur dioxide (from coal-burning power plants) and asbestos particles (from automobile brake linings) in inducing lung cancer. The sulphur dioxide interferes with the process by which foreign particles are expelled from the lungs; that, in turn, increases the residence time of the carcinogenic asbestos and hence the chances of contracting the disease. Many other destructive synergisms are known, and one can speculate about even more ominous ones yet to be identified—perhaps an interaction between low-dose radiation and persistent pesticides, which could affect vital components of the ecosystem or man directly.

The connection of such effects to population growth is clear. As populations grow and the associated technologies increase in power and variety, a broadening array of biologically active wastes is distributed in ever more overlapping spheres of influence. Substances that previously rarely came in contact with each other now commonly occur together. Fertilizer residues and oil spills now pollute coastal waters once devoid of either, and pesticides, toxic lead compounds, and man-made radionuclides move simultaneously through important food chains.

A second aspect of the response of environmental systems to the wastes generated by human populations involves *threshold effects.* At levels or rates below a threshold, many sorts of impact are buffered by the environment without adverse effects. Manure is naturally processed into humus by microorganisms in the soil, and organic matter introduced into rivers is decomposed in a similar way. Increases in atmospheric carbon dioxide are partly self-correcting because they stimulate an increase in the rate of carbon dioxide-consuming photosynthesis (and part of any excess is absorbed by the oceans). Unfortunately, such systems are all too easily overloaded—the thresholds can be exceeded—with consequences ranging from nuisance odors to potential climatological disaster.

Reprinted with permission from *The Saturday Review*, August 1, 1970, p. 52.

Perhaps the classic example is the plight of many of the rivers of the developed world, whose capacity to absorb sewage and industrial wastes has long since been exceeded. Although a thousand people may dump their raw sewage into a stream with impunity, ten thousand may hopelessly pollute it; activities that appear entirely innocuous when carried on by a small population may be disastrous for a larger one. We understand only a few natural systems well enough to identify their thresholds quantitatively, but we continue to play the game of growth, a procedure guaranteed to find them all by experiment. The demise of so many of our rivers does not seem to have taught us the lesson; perhaps that of the oceans will.

A related third possibility, usually overlooked by those who insist that the population/environment crisis has been exaggerated, is the *trigger effect,* in which an environmental balance is upset by a relatively small man-made input. A little-known example is the triggering of earthquakes as a result of filling the reservoirs behind large dams—dams that are built to supply the water and power needs of growing populations. The stress associated with the weight of the water impounded by the dam may lead to fault slippage, which releases far more energy than man put in. Hundreds of seismic events, with magnitudes up to 5.0 on the Richter scale, resulted from the filling of Lake Mead in the years 1935–39, and an earthquake of magnitude 6.4, caused by the filling of the Kogna Dam, killed 200 people in India in 1967. Less bizarre and perhaps much more serious trigger effects may intrude wherever the environmental status quo is maintained by opposing forces in balance: in predator-prey relationships that affect the human food supply, in the soil and water conditions that encourage or inhibit the growth of certain viruses and other agents of disease, in the chemical reactions of the upper atmosphere that maintain the Earth's protective screen against ultraviolet radiation.

The difficulties in predicting, identifying, and alleviating any of the phenomena discussed above—synergisms, threshold effects, and trigger effects—are compounded because they may operate in conjunction with a fourth factor: *time delay.* Time delay refers to situations in which causes may precede their effects by years or even decades. This can come about in a number of ways. With many persistent pesticides, the process of concentration consumes time as the substances move from level to level up the food chains. This results in a substantial lag between the original application at low concentration and the appearance of pathological effects high in the food web. For reasons not entirely understood, induction of various forms of cancer by exposure to radiation is characterized by "latency periods" ranging up to thirty years. Particulate pollution, more than 50 per cent of it dust from agricultural activities, is cooling the Earth and bringing on climatic changes. The full consequences of this trend may not be apparent for decades or longer.

Many other conditions associated with man's environmental meddling are also characterized by dormant stages preceding the appearance of identifiable symptoms (e.g., certain parasitic diseases and genetic effects associated with various chemical pollutants). Usually such a time lag means that when the symptoms finally appear, corrective action is ineffective or impossible. If *all* use of persistent pesticides were stopped tomorrow, the concentrations of these substances in many critical organisms—and the associated damage—would continue to increase for some years to come.

Consideration of the four classes of phenomena discussed here—synergisms, threshold effects, trigger effects, and time-delay effects—suggests that population growth today is committing us to a degree of environmental degradation not yet fully apparent.

Reading 34

Whither Water? The Fragile Future of the World's Most Important Resource

Bruce K. Ferguson

Although water appears to be a vast renewable resource, its future is troubled by the same problem that plagues so many other natural resources—a growing population making demands on a finite supply.

The flow of water is not increasing in proportion to population growth. Nature's rate of cycling water through the ecosystem sets a fixed limit on the amount of water that can be diverted from natural flows for human use. In many regions that limit is rapidly being approached.

Yet water is perhaps man's most important resource. It is the major agent for such necessary tasks as cooling, cleaning, cooking, firefighting, and transporting urban wastes. Heavy industries such as steel mills and power plants account for about 85 percent of the nonagricultural water consumption in the United States. Manufacturing just one ton of nitrate fertilizer requires 600 tons of water.

But even after industrial use is subtracted, the consumption of water in U.S. cities is still in the astounding range of 150 to 200 gallons per person per day. For a city of one million persons, this amounts to 625,000 tons per day—54 times the daily urban input of food and fuel combined.

The human body itself is, by weight, 70 percent water. It can be visualized as a giant plastic bag of warm water, holding about 15 gallons in addition to a few pounds of chemicals and structural materials. Every day, a person consumes another five pounds of water—more than any other substance.

Feeding the human body requires prodigious amounts of water. The irrigation

Reprinted with permission from *The Futurist*, (April 1983):29–36.

systems on the 30 million irrigated acres in the United States require 110 billion gallons a day. A ton of sugar or corn, grown under irrigated conditions, requires 1,000 tons of water, and a ton of rice requires 4,000 tons of water.

But in the United States, the irrigated acreage is only a small percentage of all the land used for farming, grazing, and forestry. Growth on unirrigated lands accounts for a total of water usage many times that of the irrigated areas. For example, one acre of a typical unirrigated Pennsylvania forest uses 400 tons of water each month during the growing season. Water accounts for about 50 percent of the weight of each tree in the forest.

THE WATER CYCLE

The flow of water starts with rain and snow falling from the air to earth. Most of the water soaks into the soil, and eventually as much as half gradually goes back into the atmosphere through transpiration from the leaves of plants.

The rest of the water flows into the drainage system. Some of it becomes the flow of major rivers; some of it is stored in lakes, glaciers, and polar ice caps; and some of it soaks further down into the earth, becoming part of vast underground reservoirs in the pores and fractures of bedrock. Eventually all the water ends up in the sea, where it can evaporate into the air to start the cycle again.

When man uses water, he diverts one of these natural flows by dipping into rivers, lakes, or groundwater aquifers. Pumps and aqueducts carry this water to cities, industries, and irrigated farms. The amount of water available depends ultimately on the amount of precipitation in the watershed, which will remain fixed by nature until man achieves some sort of radical control over global weather patterns—and that control seems to be only a remote possibility.

In many areas, man's withdrawals from the watersheds now exceed nature's deposits. The problem is clearly illustrated by the depletion of the Ogallala Aquifer, which stretches from Nebraska to Texas in the U.S. High Plains. The 225,000 square miles of land overlying the aquifer comprise one of the nation's richest agricultural regions, supplying 25 percent of the nation's cotton, 38 percent of the grain sorghum, 16 percent of the wheat, and 13 percent of the corn. Forty percent of the nation's grain-fed beef is fattened there.

The irrigation water for all these crops comes from wells that draw water up from the aquifer, with water use increasing as farmers exploit their land more intensively. Sophisticated center-pivot irrigation devices are being installed in increasing numbers, each one spraying nearly 1.2 million gallons per day.

Although precipitation replaces some of the groundwater withdrawals, the rate of pumping exceeds the rate of replacement. Most of the water in the aquifer was deposited in a previous geologic era by the melting of receding Ice Age glaciers. Today's withdrawals therefore amount to ''mining'' a nonrenewable resource. So much water is being drawn from the Ogallala that the water level is falling three feet a year in some places. The farmers, who have begun to dig wells deeper into the aquifer and use more powerful pumps, are competing with each other for a limited amount of water, and are draining the water level down faster and faster in the process.

The whole region is headed for the day when the wells will run dry; researchers say that at the current rate of withdrawal the entire supply will be gone in 40 years. Before that time comes, however, many farmers may stop irrigating because of the high cost of energy to pump water from a declining water table.

Excessive withdrawals also deplete the flow of rivers, such as the Monongahela in Pittsburgh. The Monongahela is lined with the nation's greatest complex of steel mills, which use huge volumes of water. The river, crowded with barges carrying crucial supplies of coal, coke, and slag among mines and mills, conveys a greater annual tonnage than the Panama Canal. The steel companies want to divert more river water to expand their operations, but the barge navigation system requires a minimum depth of nine feet. In the early part of this century, the U.S. Army Corps of Engineers built a system of dams and locks to assure that depth. If the mills withdraw more of the water, the level will go down and the mills will lose their source of raw materials.

Meanwhile, the public is counting on a certain flow of river water to dilute industrial pollution. The steel companies are in a quandary. The economic growth of the whole region is being held back by the finite flow of river water. It may be that the capacity of the Monongahela watershed to support the development of heavy industry has already been reached.

The competition for water is aggravated in fast-growing regions such as the Sunbelt and the Rocky Mountain states, particularly in areas with low rainfall. Los Angeles, located in a desert region, has extended great aqueducts up to 444 miles, diverting water from every watershed between the Sacramento River in California and the Colorado River in Arizona. The competition for water among numerous cities and irrigated-farming interests in the arid Southwest will require acts of Congress to resolve.

Even in water-rich Pennsylvania, the state legislature is considering a law to establish governmental allocation of water among competing users. New York City long ago completed a huge system of aqueducts that brings water from reservoirs in the mountains of the Delaware River Basin; because the city is fortunate in being located in a relatively humid region, its aqueducts extend to a radius of only 120 miles.

RECAPTURING THE RAIN

Ironically, while cities import water from distant reservoirs, they deliberately shunt away *all* of the rain that falls directly on them. Roofs, roads, parking lots, and sidewalks are all made of impermeable asphalt and concrete. When rain falls on them, over 90 percent is concentrated in gutters and drains and carried away quickly into lakes and streams.

If you could stand next to a river in a typical urbanizing area for several years, watching the changes as the surrounding area develops, here is what you would see: Each year the flooding of the river is higher and more frequent, because rainwater that used to soak gradually into the soil now runs directly into streams. Land and buildings near the river are damaged. The increased flooding causes shore erosion, and the resulting sediment gradually turns the water a muddy brown. Fish in the river lose their habitat and die. The groundwater table goes down because it is not replenished by natural infiltration. And since groundwater is the only source of river flow between storms, the river is actually lower during the periods of "base flow" between floods. Both groundwater and river water become less suitable as potential water supplies.

Necessity is forcing some areas to find ways to recapture their rainwater. Long Island is one such region. Separated from the Connecticut mainland by Long Island Sound, it cannot count on inland mountain reservoirs for its water, as does nearby New York City. Even if a supply pipe were laid across the Sound, Long Island would find no water to carry: all the available mainland water is already being used up by the heavily populated mainland communities. With a rapidly growing population, Long Island is stuck with just one source of fresh water—the groundwater below its surface.

Geologically, Long Island can be visualized as a bathtub full of sand, with the pores between the grains of sand filled with fresh water. The pores remain filled with water, available for pumping, only as long as the rain that falls on the island soaks down through the soil into the groundwater aquifer.

To prevent sprawling urban development from shunting the rainwater off into the sea, Long Island's county governments now require developers to build "recharge basins"—depressions in the earth where storm water from streets, driveways, and downspouts is directed. The water then soaks down into the soil, "recharging" the water in the sand aquifer.

If you were to stand next to one of Long Island's streams for several years, you would not witness the impacts suffered by a typical urbanizing area. Instead, Long Island's rainwater completes a natural cycle by perpetually replacing the water drawn out of the underlying sand. The island's water supply is assured as long as the population doesn't outgrow the replacement rate of the rainfall and as long as sewage and toxic wastes do not contaminate the groundwater.

A solution to a more acute problem of rainwater loss is found on another island, Bermuda, where the water supply is even more scarce than on Long Island. In Bermuda, every community has two completely separate water supply systems. One is a salt water system, taken directly from the ocean, which is used for flushing toilets and other purposes where the salinity is unimportant. The other system supplies fresh water, used for drinking and cooking. The fresh water is collected into cisterns from rainfall on roofs and is purified before use. Each house has its own cistern and fresh water supply. During droughts, a community water tank truck periodically refills everyone's cistern. Systems as miserly as Bermuda's are rare so far, but as populations grow and the amount of rain does not, they are likely to become more common.

Even in regions where the water supply is not such a critical issue, storm water control techniques can provide substantial benefits. Land-use planners are encouraging developers to let storm water flow into grassy roadside swales rather than channel it into gutters and drains. This method allows the water to spread out, slow down, and soak into the soil. For example, at The Woodlands, a community near Houston, developer John Mitchell and land planner Ian McHarg have created a whole 25,000-acre system of swales and ponds where water flows gradually across the land, soaking into the soil and supporting the moisture-starved oak and pine forests.

SALVAGING SEWAGE

An even greater irony than their shunting off rainfall is that cities deliberately pump *away* almost as much water, in the form of waste water and sewage, as they pump *in* each day. The major output of an American city's metabolism is water and water-borne wastes. In a city of a million persons, the daily 625,000 tons of water input becomes 500,000 tons of sewage, the residual 125,000 tons having been permanently consumed or lost. Public sewerage systems serve 150 million Americans and collect a total of 750,000 tons of waste water each day.

Major sewage pollution arises where, due to floods, poor maintenance, or lack of funding for adequate construction, sewage collected by one of those public systems is discharged into a lake or river without complete treatment. In the smaller towns and suburbs, the essentially untreated wastes of 70 million Americans are being piped into private backyard cesspools and septic tanks where they may contaminate groundwater supplies.

Recycling treated sewage by land application could alleviate some of this problem. At University Park, Pennsylvania, treated sewage is piped to an area of fields and woods that overlies the major limestone aquifer for the region. The liquid sewage is sprayed out over the soil. As the water seeps down, the soil filters out the potential groundwater pollutants. These same potential pollutants then act as fertilizers for feed and timber crops. The water soaks on down into the aquifer, maintaining the water level in the region's major source of water.

Fully implemented, waste-water recycling may lead to a whole new kind of American community. A community that recycles its waste water will incorporate an open area of farms and forests in addition to the conventional residential, commercial, and industrial areas. Treated waste water will be recycled on the open land.

Unlike conventional contemporary land developments, the new type of community will be a hybrid of urban and rural components. If the community is properly planned, it can preserve prime agricultural land from urban development. The water and nutrients from the community's recycled waste would then help to support the growth of crops while the excess water would seep into the soil, replacing groundwater withdrawals.

The water shortage problem can only be met by creating a linkage among water supply, sewage disposal, and storm-water control. At present, these basic components of water management are typically handled separately, as if water were an unlimited resource whose use did not require much foresight.

But man's biological need for water will never go away—and nature's rate of supply of water in each region is not likely to expand. As the population grows, the need for sophisticated water conservation and recycling systems will increase. Someday we will become used to water shortages, just as we are already used to energy shortages. Just as we have had to wait in line for gas, someday we could turn on the water faucet and wait in vain for a drop to appear.

We need to conceive of water as a complex resource, with all of its parts interconnected, so that we will build our homes and our cities with foresight for the natural resources that sustain us.

Reading 35

Mankind at the Crossroads

Aurelio Peccei

At this advanced stage of human evolution, our destiny seems to be governed by the interplay of two quite recent and extraordinarily dynamic macrophenomena. One is the scientific and technological revolution which gives us undreamt-of knowledge and power, if not wisdom, and the other is the unexpected complexification of our world, which confronts us with enormous tangles of problems.

Ever since the time of its formation in 1968, the Club of Rome has stressed that the cross-impact of these dominant factors would lead to a period of extreme alternatives. Unprecedented human fulfillment and ultimate catastrophe are both possible. What the outcome will actually be, though, depends on a third major—and decisive—factor: our understanding and behavior on the global plane.

Ten years ago, the mood was still one of great expectations. Now, after an eventful decade, it appears not only that the world situations have substantially deteriorated but also that adverse trends are steadily gaining ground. True, the techno-scientific enterprise has continued to progress on many fronts; but its con-

Reprinted with permission from *The Futurist* (December 1978):374–378, abridged.

quests are neither systematic nor coordinated, and all too often originate new problems; meanwhile, still other problems of a political, social, and psychological character keep emerging; and all of them intertwine, so that the overall human condition becomes ever more difficult.

The perception that the current general crisis is going to get worse before it can eventually be turned around is, however, blunted by our reluctance to face up squarely to unpleasant realities. We prefer to trust in the miracles of science and technology, and even believe in the promises of politicians, the art of diplomacy and the beneficial effects of international declarations and resolutions, rather than make the effort of assessing the situation thoroughly and comprehensively. Whatever evaluation or forecasts we undertake, they are just sectoral, fragmented or short-term. Never is our vast assortment of resources mobilized across disciplines and boundaries with a view to pursuing common, global goals.

As a consequence, we are all pitifully unprepared to cope with the formidable challenges and threats looming ahead. Although such a bitter reality is seldom recognized, it is high time to understand at least two essential things.

One is that mankind as a whole is striding rapidly towards a momentous crossroads where there can be no place for mistakes; yet, its values, institutions and bearing are still a reflection of the past and certainly cannot carry it safely into the future. That something fundamental is wrong with its entire system is quite evident—for even now it is unable to assure the minima of life to all its members, to be at peace with itself, or to be at peace with Nature.

The second is mankind's desperate need to break this vicious circle, while it can still get free and mold its future.

MANY DANGERS LIE JUST AHEAD

Consideration of a few facts and trends suffices to warn us that many danger points lie just ahead.

The major single problem is global overpopulation—due to modern man's incapacity or unwillingness to control his own runaway numbers. According to the population clock of the Environmental Fund in Washington, the world's population [reached] 4.4 billion at noon on 28 November 1978, and every year sees 87.3 million more people, concentrated especially in poor countries. Even if fertility is somewhat checked, the world population gains between now and the year 2000 will be equal to the total population at the time of World War I.

This demographic pressure is subjecting the human system to new, unbearable burdens when its condition is already critical. More than one-third of the world's people are living beneath the poverty line and there can be no doubt that at least an equal proportion of its future children will be condemned to share the same fate even before they are born. There is much charitable talk about basic human needs but no earnest drive at the very roots of this knot of problems, no concrete commitment to eradicate hunger, deprivation and ignorance from the world, once and for all.

For instance, there are no long-term plans to settle the new waves of population decently; yet, merely to build the physical infrastructure of the human habitat required before the end of the century—houses, schools, hospitals, whole cities, roads, harbors, factories, etc.—entails a construction job similar to the one mankind has taken from the Middle Ages to complete. In itself this would be a colossal enterprise, tantamount to founding a ''second world'' in a couple of decades, but lack of foresight will make it well-nigh impossible, while producing untold new problems and suffering.

Neither are there reliable plans or even ideas on how to find work for the 300 million able-bodied men and women currently unemployed, or how to create the 1,000 million more jobs which will be needed during the 1980s and the 1990s. Unemployment, which is always a human tragedy—particularly for young people—and a shameful blot on society, at this macroscopic scale evidences the shaky foundations of the world order—and will eventually bring it to its knees.

Not even the proud industrial nations of the West know how to absorb their 16 million jobless and at the same time check inflation. The task is urgent because of the lengthening shadows of stagflation, protectionism and social unrest. The usual recipe is given: expand productive investment and raise annual growth to 5 percent. It should, however, be clear by now that, for all their endeavors, most nations are up against so many constraints that they find it impossible to apply such simplistic prescriptions. The obstinacy with which old, ineffectual, if not counterproductive, schemes are nevertheless upheld confirms that the entire thought process, rather than just the economic system alone, needs a good overhaul even in the developed countries. . . .

HUMANITY AT WAR WITH NATURE

Humans are not even at peace with Nature—in this, they are destined to lose disastrously in terms of habitat, health, and quality of life, if not the very capacity for survival.

The major problem is not, as generally thought, the depletion of the non-renewable resources. Although overexploited, these can still be found in respectable quantities in the earth's crust and oceans. Moreover, technology is at its best when the question is that of saving or substituting materials. Nevertheless, some resources are becoming either physically scarce or more expensive to extract or process, and hence more energy-consuming.

On the borderline lie energy and soil—matters of great concern. For energy, the situation is expected to stiffen greatly due to oil shortfalls sometime during the 1980s, before safe, acceptable alternative energy sources are sufficiently developed to take over. Once wars were waged in quest of salt; now energy is the salt of the economy; and the economic, political and military consequences of an energy crunch are unfathomable. Here we have the Achilles' heel of contemporary society.

Soil—just a minor part of the land mass which occupies about one-third of the world's surface—is essential inasmuch as it combines the physical and biological elements required by life. But good soils, too, are becoming scarcer.

The best ones are already being exploited, and precious croplands are degraded or eroded away almost as a routine by agricultural and water mismanagement, while pastures are destroyed by overgrazing. It is estimated that in the United States—the world's largest granary—topsoils are being lost eight times faster than they are being formed, and that at this pace by the year 2000 increased domestic consumption may well absorb all food produced in the country.

The new settlements needed to accommodate a swelling population will inevitably gravitate around cultivated areas, swallowing up yet more of them. Moreover, mostly due to human activities, deserts are advancing. They are already threatening one-tenth of South America, one-fifth of Asia and Africa and one-fourth of Australia.

The gravest dangers, however, concern the so-called renewable resources; and in the front line stands the progressive degradation of the world's biomass, on which human life itself depends.

One example is the reckless destruction of the tropical rain forests, which evolved in a stable state for tens of millions of years to constitute the most complex congregation of plant and animal life in existence. Forty percent of them have already been razed, while the remainder are being burned or cut down at the rate of 20 hectares a minute—equalling the combined territorial area of Denmark, Holland and Belgium every year. Unless this orgy of destruction is slackened, they will practically disappear in three or four decades—paralleling the practical drying up of oil fields, but with far more severe consequences for mankind.

Yet another example is the accelerated extinction of animal and plant wildlife. Species after species is being ruthlessly eliminated by man. This massacre is coupled with the final liquidation of the remaining pockets of wilderness—the very heart of Nature.

Whether moved by greed or caprice, negligence or ignorance, modern man employs his science and might to kill and corrupt everything that life took billions of years to create and perfect. Even if this wanton and stupid behavior had no consequences on his own existence, it would remain an insult to his vaunted humanity and will inflict an irreparable cultural loss on the generations to come.

MANKIND IS AT FATEFUL THRESHOLD

This is the chain of cold facts and actual trends we are witnessing at this fateful threshold to the future. They are of such a magnitude and nature and their interactions so critical that everything human is upset and made immensely more complex and hazardous. But not only can the difficulties become overwhelming; they are also part of a situation totally new in human experience.

Since *Homo sapiens* emerged, upwards of 10,000 centuries ago, time and again he has had to face supreme tests and trials. Scores of empires, civilizations, lineages and even races have disappeared from one part of the earth or another. But man, as a species, continued his ascent. Now that he has risen to absolute stardom on the planet, the dangers too are global, and can result in the total eclipse of his kind. On the other hand, though, and for the first time, man has the means of becoming almost absolute master of his own destiny.

Three basic questions are thus forced upon us.

- How much time has humanity got to come to its senses and set itself on a safer course?
- Who has the capacity to propose and initiate this new course?
- What in essence must be done to make it materialize?

If the analysis of the downtrend of human fortunes just made is substantially correct, then the time available to change the system and choose another course is decidedly short. A reasonable guess is that, at the present tempo of events, there are probably less than 10 years left before certain options which we still may have today will be irremediably lost.

For Americans, this means that the time during which mankind should take the road of renewal hardly goes beyond the next presidential term. For the Soviets, this time frame coincides with the 10th and 11th Five-Year Plans (1976–1985). For Western Europe, it is less than half of the period the European Community let go by since the Treaty of Rome without reaching economic or political unity. For the United Nations, it is the Special Assembly of 1980 on the Third Development Decade which should set the pace.

Altogether, there is no period of grace for mankind. It would be most imprudent—and possibly even fatal—for it to bank on a longer respite. . . .

GLOBAL COMMUNITY MUST BE OVERRIDING GOAL

The overriding goal is to produce a mature, responsible, self-governing and well-managed global community which—while preserving cultural identities and social dynamics—should give the conscience of the species precedence over national and class conscience. The process will no doubt be long, tortuous and painful, but it is certainly within the realm of the possible—if we all accept a few basic guidelines.

To start with, we must recognize that it is a vital necessity to reestablish satisfactory and sustainable equilibria, both within the human system and in its relations with Nature. There is in this an overarching nexus of shared interests uniting all nations, whatever their economic condition or political regime—for they all need, ultimately, to abide by global imperatives of social justice and good earthkeeping. The developed countries should do this by adopting much more realistic and austere modes of life, and the developing ones by bringing into practice the spirit of self-reliance not as an individual virtue, but as their joint effort, at least regionally.

We must further admit that it will be nevertheless impossible to move to a higher level of human organization without a modicum of global planning. Having become the major agent of change on earth, man can no longer count on the automatisms upon which he used to rely in the past, such as the regenerative capacity of Nature, the market's "invisible hand," and the checks and balances inherent in simpler democratic systems. Yet, since global coherence is ever more necessary, he must provide for it himself—by concerted forward planning.

The solution certainly cannot be sought in any form of centralized planning, which would soon engender a monstrous world-girdling and no doubt inefficient bureaucracy. A new kind of planning—of a global scope, yet adaptable to a variety of local conditions—is one of those major social inventions and innovations which have become indispensable in our age—much more so than any further techno-scientific progress.

A Club of Rome–sponsored project has proposed a set of ingenious and flexible planning and decision-making instruments which are now being tested in many countries—and which may be a first step in the right direction.

But even all this is not enough. The shocking discovery we have yet to make is that, for all his science and might and all his plans, structures, systems and tools, modern man cannot change his fate if he himself does not change.

Man's greatest problems and possible salvation lie in fact within himself. He has created his own, man-made world, where everything interacts with everything else at ever higher levels of complexity, thereby radically altering the natural flows of life on the planet, including his own life. But culturally and behaviorally he is lagging behind. A "human gap" is thus created, which endangers his existence— no less than mutations in the environment endanger the existence of every species that is unable to adjust to them.

Our condition is of course different; but only in that the human brain—a unique resource—has still a great latent potential to be harnessed. Here is the new frontier, the deciding factor of our collective destiny. Our survival will depend essentially on whether or not we are able to learn fast enough how to develop this untapped human potential—for it alone can move humanity to make a quality jump comparable to the technological one it engineered in its universe.

The great step is then for all of us, and especially for those who command knowledge and power, to realize that—if we will it—ahead lies not catastrophe but the best part of the human venture. The keystone is the full development of the human being—the human revolution which can guide and crown all other revolutions of our time.